NEW ILLUSTRATED
STARS &
PLANETS

This is a Starfire Book
First published in 2002

02 04 05 03

1 3 5 7 9 10 8 6 4 2

Starfire is part of
The Foundry Creative Media Company Limited
Crabtree Hall, Crabtree Lane, Fulham, London, SW6 6TY

Visit the Foundry website: www.foundry.co.uk

Copyright © 2002 The Foundry

ISBN 1 903817 96 X

A copy of the CIP data for this book is available from the British Library

Printed in China

SPECIAL THANKS TO EVERYONE INVOLVED WITH THIS PROJECT:
Lisa Balkwill, Jennifer Bishop, Penny Brown, Antony Cohen, Duncan Copp, Chris Herbert,
Ann Kay, Sonya Newland, Colin Rudderham, Graham Stride, Nick Wells, Polly Willis.

NEW ILLUSTRATED

STARS &
PLANETS

Chris Cooper, Pam Spence, Carole Stott

GENERAL EDITOR: IAIN NICOLSON

STAR
FIRE

CONTENTS

THEMES

Each A–Z entry is tagged by themes which can be followed as threads throughout the book

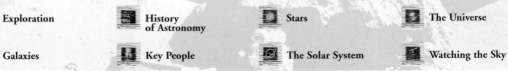

| Exploration | History of Astronomy | Stars | The Universe |
| Galaxies | Key People | The Solar System | Watching the Sky |

CONTENTS

INTRODUCTION

Thanks to the efforts of astronomers over the ages, we now have a comprehensive understanding of the Universe in which we live. We know that the Earth is one of nine planets that revolve around the Sun and that the Sun itself is an ordinary star. As such, it is an incandescent globe of high-temperature gas, powered by nuclear reactions taking place deep within its core. Each of the member planets of our Solar System (the system of bodies that revolves around the Sun) is a fascinating world in its own right. Some, such as Venus or Mars, share some common characteristics with the Earth, others, such as Jupiter and Saturn, are of a wholly different nature.

The stars are themselves suns, powered by nuclear furnaces. Some are thousands, even millions of times more luminous than our Sun, whereas others are cosmic glow-worms, thousands, or tens of thousands of times less brilliant than our neighbourhood star. Stars appear as mere points of light simply because they are so much further away from us than the Sun, so far, indeed, that light – travelling at 300,000 kilometres (186,000 miles) per second – takes more than four years to reach us from the nearest of them.

Astronomers have mapped out the life cycles of stars from birth to death and have come to realise that the very elements of which we, and planet Earth alike, are composed have been synthesised in, and spewed forth from, the interiors of stars. They have discovered a host of intriguing objects such as white dwarfs, neutron stars and, most enigmatic of all, black holes. During the past few years, they have begun to detect planets around other stars (exoplanets). By studying planetary systems beyond our own, we will gain a better understanding of how our own Solar System came into being and should get closer to answering that most tantalising of questions, 'Are we alone?'

The Sun is one of more than a hundred billion stars which, together with clouds of gas and dust, comprise the immense star system that is our Galaxy. Our Galaxy, vast though it is, is merely one of the hundreds of billions of galaxies that populate the observable Universe. Galaxies themselves are clumped together into groups or clusters which

themselves are gathered into loose, straggly structures called superclusters. Each galaxy, or cluster of galaxies, is receding from every other one; the entire Universe is expanding. Current data suggests that the Universe originated 12–15 billion years ago by erupting forth from an initial state of inconceivably high density and temperature – an event that has come to be known as the Big Bang.

By studying distant galaxies – some so remote that their light has taken ten billion years or more to reach us – and by analyzing the faint background of primordial radiation that permeates all of space, astronomers can investigate the processes that gave birth to galaxies and the first generation of stars, determine the overall 'shape' of space and chart the future evolution of the Universe. They have discovered that the Universe contains far more dark matter than luminous matter and that it may be dominated by a mysterious form of 'dark energy' that is causing its expansion to accelerate rather than decelerate.

In addition to sophisticated ground-based telescopes, astronomers have access to instruments borne aloft on high-altitude balloons and transported above the obscuring effects of our atmosphere aboard orbiting satellites. As a result, distant stars and galaxies can now be studied across virtually the entire electromagnetic spectrum, from gamma- and X-rays to radio waves. Closer to home, robot spacecraft have transformed our understanding of Earth's planetary siblings. Astronauts have visited the Moon and have begun to live and work in orbit around the Earth.

This book contains a wealth of information that has been arranged in a convenient A–Z format. The reader-friendly text, which is supported by some 300 illustrations, covers a wide range of topics relating to stars and planets and places them in the wider context of the Universe as a whole. Entries dealing with the exploration of space, the history of astronomy and some of the key people who have contributed to the advance of astronomical knowledge, reveal how we have arrived at our present-day view of the Universe.

Aimed at the general reader, who can dip into the text at random, this book has sufficient depth and detail to act as an authoritative reference source. With the aid of icons that identify entries which share common themes, the reader can establish links between related topics and build up a broader and deeper understanding of the subject. The reference aspect is reinforced by tables of planetary, stellar and galaxy data, information about human spaceflight missions and an extensive list of relevant web sites.

New developments are taking place all the time in this rapidly-advancing field. In the future, our best contemporary theories will seem simplistic and inadequate. But, for the moment, this book provides a comprehensive guide to our present-day knowledge of stars, planets, and the Universe which, hopefully, will inspire at least some of its readers to delve deeper into this most fascinating and dynamic of subjects.

IAIN NICOLSON

ABSOLUTE MAGNITUDE

The apparent magnitude (brightness) which an astronomical object would have if it were at a distance of 10 parsecs (about 33 light years). The absolute magnitude M can be found from the object's apparent magnitude m and its parallax π in arcseconds using $M = m + 5 + 5\log\pi$. Absolute magnitudes provide a means of comparing the luminosity of one object with that of another.

ABSORPTION LINE

A dark line or band observed in a spectrum caused by the absorption of electromagnetic radiation with a particular wavelength. If a light source with a continuous spectrum is viewed through a cool gas then dark absorption lines appear in the spectrum. The wavelengths of the lines are identical to the wavelengths of emission lines from the same gas when heated. Absorption lines are seen in the spectra of the Sun and other stars. Most of them are Fraunhofer lines but some of them arise in the cold interstellar gas along the line of sight and give clues to the physics and chemistry of the interstellar medium within our Galaxy. Absorption lines in the spectra of remote quasars carry information about intergalactic space.

ABSORPTION SPECTRUM

A spectrum produced when electromagnetic radiation is absorbed. If radiation from a hot source passes through cooler matter, then radiation at certain wavelengths is absorbed, producing dark absorption lines and bands.

)))➤ *Fraunhofer Lines, Spectrum*

ACCRETION DISK

Accretion – the increase in mass of a celestial body by the addition of matter or smaller objects – often

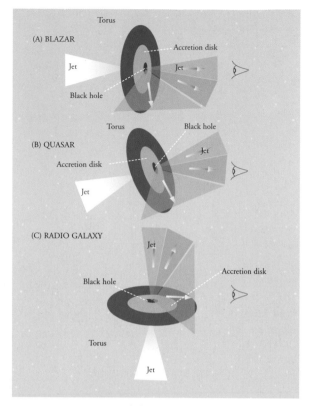

occurs via an accretion disk: a disk of material surrounding the accreting object. Accretion disks occur in close binary star systems in which gas is flowing from one star to the other, and at the centre of galaxies. They play a prominent part in active galactic nuclei.

ABOVE: Types of Active Galactic Nuclei. Where the high-energy radiation jet points towards the line of sight (A), the observer sees a blazar. Toward the central black hole over the edge of the torus (B), a quasar is seen, and where the central black hole is obscured by the torus (C), a radio galaxy.
BELOW: Where a cool, thin gas lies between the star and the observer, it absorbs light from the star, forming an absorption line spectrum.

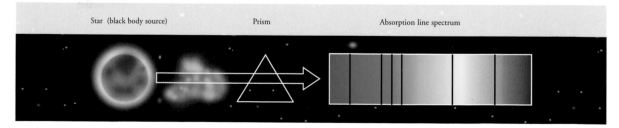

Star (black body source)   Prism   Absorption line spectrum

ACTIVE GALACTIC NUCLEUS (AGN)

The region at the centre of certain galaxies from which an enormous amount of energy is released. The energy is thought to come from matter accreting via an accretion disk on to a supermassive black hole of greater than 100 million solar masses. All the various forms of AGN may stem from a single type of source whose appearance depends on its orientation to the observer. In this model, a compact source is surrounded by a torus (a ring doughnut) of gas and dust; narrow jets of gas are emitted at velocities approaching the speed of light along the axis of rotation, which is at right angles to the ring. If the line of sight were through the torus, the central source would be obscured and the AGN would be seen as a radio galaxy. If the torus were tilted to our line of sight, the central source would be visible, corresponding to viewing a quasar. Blazars would be seen when the observer was looking directly along, or close to, the jet.

)))➤ *Accretion Disk, Black Holes, Seyfert Galaxy*

ACTIVE GALAXY

A galaxy emitting a large amount of energy from a central compact source. The observed activity is similar to that of quasars. It is not known whether active galaxies are truly different from the majority or whether all galaxies undergo this behaviour for a few per cent of the time. Active galaxies can be conveniently grouped into a few main types. Radio galaxies, as their name implies, are unusually strong sources of radio emission. At radio wavelengths they show a similar structure to that of quasars, with symmetric lobes and often a jet, but their centres are not as bright optically. Seyfert galaxies (named after the US astronomer Carl Seyfert, 1911–60, who identified the first ones in 1943) have optically bright centres, but are much less energetic than quasars and much more numerous. The great majority of Seyfert galaxies are spirals or barred spirals. Another type of active galaxy is the blazar, named after the source BL Lacertae. This object was once thought to be a variable star in our Galaxy, but is now recognized as an unusual form of galaxy. Blazars are both more luminous and more variable than standard quasars.

)))➤ *Active Galactic Nucleus, Blazars, Radio Galaxies*

ABOVE: Centaurus A, known as NGC 5128, the brightest radio galaxy and possibly the result of a merger between an elliptical galaxy and a spiral galaxy.

ADAMS, JOHN COUCH (1819–92)

English mathematician. By 1845, from his analysis of the motion of Uranus, Adams had worked out an approximate position for an unseen more distant planet. French astronomer Urbain LeVerrier (1811–77) arrived at a similar conclusion in 1846. Using LeVerrier's calculations, German astronomers Johann Galle (1812–1910) and Heinrich D'Arrest (1822–75) found Neptune on 23 September 1846. Today both LeVerrier and Adams are credited with the discovery of Neptune.

AGE OF AQUARIUS

The point where the Sun crosses from south to north of the celestial equator each year is the spring equinox. This crossover point gradually moves against the stars, owing to precession, Earth's slow wobble in space. Over 2,000 years ago, the crossover point lay in Aries. Subsequently it moved into Pisces, where it still lies. It will eventually reach Aquarius, nearly 600 years from now – which is when the much-heralded Age of Aquarius will start.

ALBEDO

A measure of the proportion of incident radiation that is reflected by a non-self-illuminating body. The scale runs from 0 for a perfectly absorbing black object to 1 for a perfectly reflecting white object. Spherical albedo assumes the object is a perfect sphere, with a diffuse surface reflecting incoming parallel light in all directions. Geometrical albedo is the ratio of the reflectance of the object to that which would be produced by a flat white surface of the same surface area at the same distance. Bond albedo is the fraction of the total incident energy reflected in all directions and calculated over all wavelengths.

ALCHEMY

In Arabic science, astronomy was closely related to alchemy, the forerunner of scientific chemistry. Jabir ibn Hayyan, who died *c.* AD 803, devised distillation techniques, which led to the discovery of new substances such as nitric acid and alcohol (in Arabic, *al-kohol),* derived from grape juice. Medieval European alchemy was built upon Arabic foundations, as was metal-lurgical chemistry. It was believed that the Sun, Moon and planets formed gold, silver and other metals in the Earth; alchemists believed they could speed up this process in their laboratories.

ALDRIN, EDWIN 'BUZZ' (b.1930)

American astronaut. The second man on the moon after Neil Armstrong on 20 July 1969 on Apollo 11. Aldrin followed 15 minutes after Armstrong and the pair busied themselves setting up seismic, solar wind and laser-ranging experiments, collecting more samples and taking pictures. They conducted a brief telephone conversation with President Nixon and unveiled a plaque on one of the legs of the Lunar Module (LM) celebrating the achievement of Apollo 'for all mankind'.

ALGOL

Some close double stars periodically pass in front of each other as they move along their orbits, temporarily blocking light from the other star. The prototype of these eclipsing binaries is Algol in the constellation Perseus, also known as Beta [β] Persei. Every 2 days 21 hours this 2nd-magnitude star dips to one-third of its usual brightness, remaining there for 10 hours before returning to normal, as its dimmer companion star partially eclipses it, blocking some of its light.

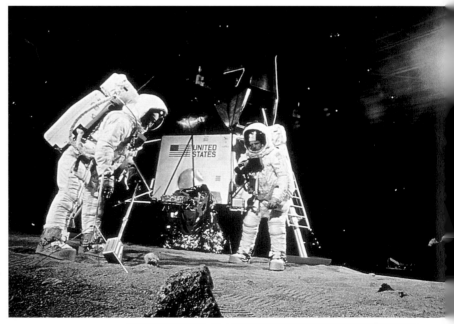

ABOVE: Edwin 'Buzz' Aldrin and Neil Armstrong on a training exercise for the lunar landing in Apollo 11 — the mission that finally won the Space Race for the USA.

ALHAZEN (c. AD 965–1039)

Arabic scientist. Alhazen, building on Aristotle's *Meteorologia*, did fundamental work in optics. Dissecting the eyes of cattle to reveal their optical structures, he went on to project images with a camera obscura, make simple lenses and study the colours into which white light broke down when refracted. Despite this, it appears that Alhazen never questioned Aristotle's premise that light coming from astronomical bodies was pure and white, and decomposed into six colours only when contaminated by a passage through air, water or glass – an idea later overthrown by Isaac Newton (1642–1727). Alhazen calculated that atmospheric refraction causes sunlight to scatter in the air when the Sun is 19° below the horizon. This led him to question the density of the atmosphere and the altitudes of clouds that reflected sunlight while the Earth's surface was still dark.

ALPHA CENTAURI

Alpha [α] Centauri is the third-brightest star in the sky, but even the smallest telescopes divide it into a glittering double. The brighter of these is almost identical in size and temperature to the Sun while the other, which orbits it every 80 years, is smaller and more yellow. Lying 4.4 light years away, Alpha Centauri is said to be the closest star to the Sun, but that honour strictly belongs to a third member of this multiple system: Proxima Centauri, an 11th-magnitude red dwarf, 4.2 light years away.

))))➤ *Double Stars*

ALTITUDE

The angular distance above an observer's horizon. Measured in degrees with 0° being at the horizon and 90° being the observer's zenith, altitude is one co-ordinate in the horizontal co-ordinate system. The other co-ordinate is azimuth. If an object is below the observer's horizon, its altitude has a negative value.

))))➤ *Azimuth*

Am STARS

Stars which show an excess of most heavy elements but are strangely deficient in some, notably calcium and scandium, are known as Am stars. Such stars must rotate slowly to avoid stirring up the atmosphere, and most seem to have achieved this through the braking effect of tidal forces supplied by a companion star.

))))➤ *Ap Stars*

ANDROMEDA

Andromeda contains M31, the Andromeda Galaxy, the most distant object you can glimpse with the naked eye. A telescope is needed to spot its small, elliptical companion galaxies M32 and M110. Andromeda also contains Gamma [γ] Andromedae, a binary of contrasting colours.

BELOW: The Andromeda Galaxy is only just visible to the naked eye.

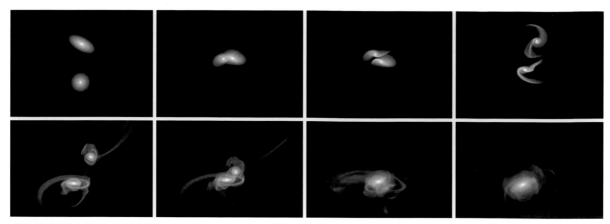

ANDROMEDA GALAXY

A spiral galaxy in the constellation of Andromeda (M31 in the Messier catalogue) – the first galaxy shown to lie definitely outside the Milky Way. In 1924, using the 2.5-m (100-in) telescope at Mount Wilson in California, Edwin Hubble took photographs of Cepheid variable stars in M31. These were much fainter than Cepheids observed within the Milky Way, indicating that the Cepheids in M31 lay much farther away. Hubble's images indicated that its distance was 10 times greater than the diameter of our Galaxy – M31 must be extra-galactic. Subsequent observations showed that Hubble had underestimated its distance. Taking into account its distance – currently estimated to be 2,400,000 light years – measurements of M31's apparent size and brightness imply it must be a stellar system larger than the Milky Way Galaxy.

))))➤ *Hubble, Edwin Powell*

ANGULAR MOMENTUM

A measure of the quantity of rotational motion contained in a body or a system of masses. Conservation of angular momentum means that if a collapsing cloud is rotating, it will spin faster and faster as it shrinks. Most stars, particularly lower-mass ones like the Sun, spin rather slowly, having lost most of their angular momentum. For these cooler stars, magnetic fields connect the body of the star to material spun off the surface, enabling the material to carry off the star's angular momentum. More massive stars do not have such magnetic assistance and most continue to spin rapidly.

ANIMALS IN SPACE

Before the Soviet Union or the United States could put a human into space they needed to establish the effect of spaceflight on life. During the 1940s the US Army launched two monkeys on a ballistic trajectory in the nose cones of captured German V-2 rockets; they did not survive. On 20 September 1951 a monkey and 11 mice reached the edge of space and returned safely to Earth on an Aerobee rocket. The first living creature to make an orbit of Earth was launched by the Soviet Union in November 1957. Laika, a dog, was housed in a pressurized compartment and showed no discomfort. More dogs followed between 1957 and 1966. Animal tests of NASA's Mercury capsule began

ABOVE: A computer simulation showing a future encounter between our own galaxy, the Milky Way, and our nearest neighbour, the Andromeda Galaxy (M31).

RIGHT: Ham the chimpanzee accepts an apple after returning safely from the third Mercury suborbital flight in 1961.

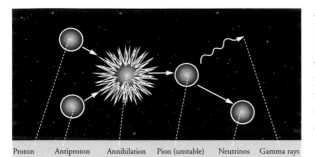

| Proton | Antiproton | Annihilation | Pion (unstable) | Neutrinos | Gamma rays |

in December 1959, when a monkey called Sam flew a suborbital flight. A second primate, Miss Sam, flew in January 1960. A chimp, Ham, made a suborbital flight in January 1961. A fourth chimp 'Enos' flew a two-orbit flight in November 1961.

ANNIHILATION

The annihilation process is the reverse of the creation process, which brought the matter of the Universe into existence and is subject to the same conservation laws. This means that a particle can annihilate only with its own antiparticle. When an electron and antielectron (otherwise known as a positron) annihilate, their masses are converted into gamma rays. When a proton annihilates with an antiproton their mass is converted into pions, which rapidly decay into gamma rays and neutrinos. Annihilation of matter and antimatter would therefore create large fluxes of gamma rays.

))» *Gamma Rays*

ABOVE: The annihilation of a proton and antiproton produces an unstable pion which decays into gamma rays and neutrinos.
BELOW: Small-scale annihilation of matter and antimatter occurs in our Galaxy between electrons and positrons, producing a faint glow of gamma rays mapped here by the Compton Gamma Ray Observatory.

ANTARES

Ruddy-coloured Antares pinpoints the heart of the constellation of Scorpius. Its name, of Greek origin, refers to its similarity in colour with Mars, the red planet. Antares is a colossal supergiant, around 400 times the diameter of the Sun and varies in brightness by a few tenths of a magnitude. Orbiting Antares every 900 years or so is a much smaller and hotter companion.

ANTHROPIC PRINCIPLE

The anthropic principle attempts to explain the values of the fundamental constants by arguing that they are the only ones consistent with the evolution of intelligent life in the Universe. It also provides an explanation of several coincidences which are found in Nature such as the 'resonance' occurring in the nuclear reactions in which the element carbon is synthesized in stars. The anthropic principle also provides answers to fundamental questions which might normally be considered outside the realm of physics. For example, planetary orbits would not be stable if space had anything but three dimensions.

Not all physicists are happy with the use of the anthropic principle to answer such questions. Although the principle does not argue that the Universe was made for the benefit of mankind, it does give human beings, the observers, a special role in the Universe and, to some physicists, this is counter to the objectivity of physics.

ANTIMATTER

Conservation laws dictate that antiparticles are produced every time a fundamental particle is created. Antiparticles have exactly the same characteristics as their particles except they have the opposite electric charge. Which we call 'matter' and which 'antimatter' is arbitrary. The creation of antiparticles would have created a Universe consisting of half matter and half antimatter. If antimatter does exist in the Universe then it must be very well separated from matter or the two would annihilate. However, current theories mostly assume that there was a slight excess of matter over antimatter in the very early Universe and that the mutual annihilation of particles and antiparticles resulted in the Universe being dominated by the surviving residue of matter.

Ap STARS

 A group of stars known as peculiar A stars (or Ap stars) have magnetic fields thousands of times stronger than the Sun's. As a result, certain elements such as silicon, chromium and europium are concentrated in spots on their surfaces, so that the stars' spectral features vary as the star rotates.

APHELION

The point in the orbit of a planet, comet or other celestial body that is farthest from the Sun.

))))➡ *Perihelion*

APOGEE

The point in the orbit of the Moon or of a spacecraft that is farthest from Earth.

))))➡ *Perigee*

APOLLO 11

On 20 July 1969 the first manned Moon landing was poised to touch down on the Sea of Tranquility. On board were Neil Armstrong and Edwin 'Buzz' Aldrin. Listening in the command module above was Michael Collins. At 20:17 UT, with just 20 seconds of fuel left, Armstrong touched down 19 km (12 miles) south-south-west of crater Sabine D. Over six hours later, a TV audience of a billion watched as Armstrong placed his left foot gingerly on the lunar surface and declared 'that's one small step for man, one giant leap for mankind'.

Aldrin followed him 15 minutes later and the pair busied themselves setting up seismic, solar wind and laser-

ABOVE: Astronaut 'Buzz' Aldrin steps out on to the Sea of Tranquility from the lunar module Eagle, during the historic Apollo 11 mission to the Moon.

TOO STEEP If the capsule entered at an angle above 7.2°, it would plummet through the upper atmosphere and burn up.

TOO SHALLOW The capsule attempting to enter at an angle below 5.2° would 'bounce off' the atmosphere and head back into space.

CORRECT ANGLE The capsule entering at between 5.2° and 7.2° will be capable of manoeuvring in the atmosphere, altering its trajectory and reducing its speed to allow it to splash down in the ocean with the aid of parachutes.

ranging experiments, collecting lunar samples and taking pictures. They also spoke by telephone with President Nixon and unveiled a plaque celebrating the achievement of Apollo 'for all mankind'. After two hours and 31 minutes on the surface they returned to their craft. The single rocket motor blasted the upper stage of the lunar module back into lunar orbit to rejoin Collins. Carrying their cargo of 22 kg (49 lb) of lunar samples, they splashed down 21 km (13 miles) from the aircraft carrier Hornet 1,529 km (950 miles) south-west of Hawaii on 24 July.

)))➤ *Aldrin, Edwin 'Buzz'; Armstrong, Neil*

APOLLO 13

When James Lovell (b.1928), Jack Swigert (1931–82) and Fred Haise (b. 1933) embarked on the third intended Apollo landing mission on 11 April 1970, the world was not paying much attention. But almost 56 hours into the flight of Apollo 13 a routine operation resulted in an explosion which shut down two fuel cells and began to leak oxygen into space. Using the Lunar Module (LM) engines to fire them around the Moon and back towards Earth, they shut down the damaged command module and retreated into the LM. The next nerve-wracking 86 hours were survived by switching everything off except the environmental control and communications systems. Temperatures dropped to

ABOVE LEFT: The Earth, taken from Apollo 11.
ABOVE: The angle 'window' through which a space capsule can successfully re-enter Earth's atmosphere is extremely small. Apollo 11, for example, had to enter at between 5.2° and 7.2° to the horizontal to ensure the survival of the crew and the recovery of the craft.

freezing and ice formed inside the spacecraft, making life dangerous and miserable. When exhaled gases threatened to poison them, mission control helped improvise a carbon dioxide scrubber. On reaching Earth they returned to the command module and splashed down after almost six days in space, surviving the disaster against the odds.

APOLLO SPACE PROGRAM

With less than three years before President Kennedy's deadline to reach the Moon ran out, the US's manned space programs were in trouble. A fire during a routine training exercise on the launch pad had killed the three-man crew of Apollo 1 in January 1967. Public and political support for the program was at an all-time low and the Moon seemed farther away than ever. Spurred on by their competitors, the Soviet Union, and a desire to honour a dead president's words, Apollo finally delivered the first humans to the Moon.

On the afternoon of 27 January 1967, the primary crew for Apollo 1 were simulating a countdown on internal power when a spark from the wires set fire to the interior of their capsule. The capsule quickly erupted into an inferno and the inward-opening door prevented the unfortunate crew from making their escape. Within only a matter of minutes they had all perished and seemingly with them had their opportunity of reaching the Moon. To prevent a repeat of the disaster, the command module was equipped with more fire-resistant materials and the escape hatch was redesigned to allow it to be opened from the inside. The pure oxygen was replaced with a mix of

BELOW: Apollo 17 was the last manned lunar mission. Here, geologist Harrison Schmitt stands before an electrically powered lunar car.

nitrogen and oxygen, effectively limiting the chances of a fast-spreading fire.

Test Flights

The equipment for reaching the Moon was tested in the unmanned flights of Apollos 4, 5 and 6. The next manned Apollo flight came in October 1968, when a crew of three spent 10 days in Earth orbit. Apollo 7 was the only manned test flight before astronauts were sent around the Moon. On 21 December 1968, Frank Borman, William Anders and James Lovell set off to the Moon on board Apollo 8. They became the first humans to leave Earth orbit and to travel to the far side of the Moon. Their trajectory placed them in lunar orbit on Christmas Eve. During their 20 hours and 10 lunar orbits, the three astronauts beamed back TV pictures of the views and read a Bible passage from Genesis, to a live audience of over a billion on Earth. The three heroes returned on 27 December 1968. The route to the Moon was open, but there was one ingredient left to be tested.

At the beginning of 1969, the Lunar Module (LM) which would descend to the Moon's surface and serve as a temporary lunar base had still not flown in space. Nor had the new Apollo space suits. Jim McDivitt (b. 1929), Rusty Schweickart (b. 1935) and Dave Scott (b. 1932) put that right in their Apollo 9 mission. In Earth orbit, on 3

March that year, Scott and Schweickart flew a LM called Spider, later completing a spacewalk in the new suits. Two months later Apollo 10's LM Snoopy, carrying Stafford and Cernan, descended to only 15 km (9 miles) from the lunar surface while the third crew member John Young orbited the Moon. Apollo 10 had completed the full and final dress rehearsal for the lunar landing.

Blast Off for the Moon

On 16 July 1969 the Apollo 11 crew of Neil Armstrong, Edwin 'Buzz' Aldrin and Michael Collins blasted off for the Moon. Once in lunar orbit Armstrong and Aldrin moved into the lunar module, Eagle, ready for their descent. Eagle landed in the Sea of Tranquility on Sunday 20 July. The time at mission control, Houston, USA was 3.17 pm. Over six hours later, Armstrong pulled a lever that deployed an instrument platform on which a TV

BELOW: This diagram shows the nominal descent trajectory of an Apollo lunar module. The thrust of its engines is used to reduce speed, to alter its angle with respect to the lunar surface and manoeuvre it onto a nearly vertical attitude to make a controlled landing.

camera would film his step on to another world. Nine rungs down, at the foot of Eagle's ladder, and now standing on the pad, he described the texture of the surface as 'very fine and powdery'. Then he took the first historic step on to the Moon. President Nixon called it 'the greatest week since the Creation...'.

Just four months later Apollo 12 returned to the Moon, making a precise landing in the Ocean of Storms, close to the unmanned Surveyor 3 spacecraft. Their colour TV camera was damaged and without pictures public interest waned. Curiosity was briefly rekindled when an explosion on Apollo 13 put the lives of the crew at risk in April 1970. A mixture of luck, the ingenuity of the mission controllers and the resilience of the crew eventually returned them safely to Earth. The spacecraft was redesigned before Apollo 14, commanded by America's first astronaut, Alan Shepard, touched down in the Fra Mauro highlands 10 months later.

Budget cutbacks led to the cancellation of Apollos 18-20, leaving only three more chances of visiting the Moon. These missions flew an improved LM which could carry more equipment and remain on the surface for up to three days. A battery-powered lunar rover vehicle also allowed crews to travel a lot further and be more productive. On the final mission geologist Harrison Schmitt was sent – the only scientist to visit the Moon. Crewmate Eugene Cernan became the last human to date to set foot on the surface. Apollo 17 blasted off from the Taurus Littrow Valley at 5.55 EST (10.55 UT) on 14 December 1972.

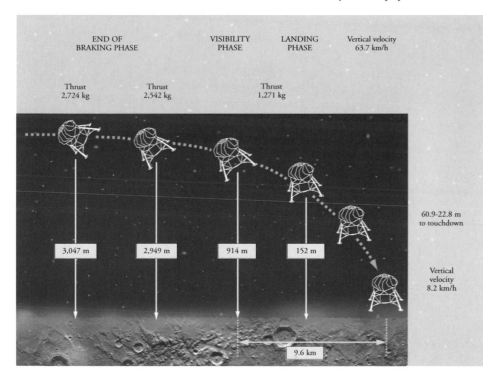

END OF BRAKING PHASE VISIBILITY PHASE LANDING PHASE Vertical velocity 63.7 km/h

Thrust 2,724 kg   Thrust 2,542 kg   Thrust 1,271 kg

3,047 m   2,949 m   914 m   152 m

60.9-22.8 m to touchdown

Vertical velocity 8.2 km/h

9.6 km

APOLLO–SOYUZ MISSION

At a Superpower summit in May 1972, an agreement was signed to launch a joint US-Soviet mission in 1975. Soyuz 19 lifted off at 12:08 UT on 15 July 1975, and was followed seven hours and 22 minutes later by an Apollo spacecraft. After over 50 hours of manoeuvres, both spacecraft were in the same orbit and visual contact was established. Once together, the actual docking was completed four minutes ahead of schedule. Astronauts Stafford and Slayton sealed themselves into the docking module. Once the remaining hatch separating the two crews was opened Soyuz commander Leonov's arm stretched through and clasped Slayton's. Millions of TV viewers around the world witnessed the embrace. The historic mission symbolized the extension of détente to space and the potential of international efforts in space exploration. Yet it would be 20 years before the next joint US-Russian docking flight, in 1995.

⫸ *Leonov, Alexei; Soyuz Space Program*

APPARENT MAGNITUDE

A star's brightness to the eye is known as its apparent visual magnitude. Ancient astronomers divided stars into six brightness classes, the faintest being sixth magnitude and the brightest first-magnitude. Modern astronomers have refined this scale so that a star of magnitude one is exactly 100 times brighter t han a star of magnitude six. Objects that are brighter still are assigned negative magnitudes, whereas fainter objects (below naked-eye visibility) have progressively larger positive magnitudes.

⫸ *Absolute Magnitude*

AQUARIUS

The zodiacal constellation of Aquarius the Water-bearer is the home of two famous planetary nebulae: the Helix and the Saturn. It also contains a group of four stars arranged in a Y shape, forming an attractive sight through binoculars. These stars mark the water jar held by Aquarius, from which water flows southwards towards Piscis Austrinus. Zeta [ζ] Aquarii, the central member of the Water Jar group, is an outstanding binary, divisible with small telescopes into twin white stars that orbit each other every 760 years.

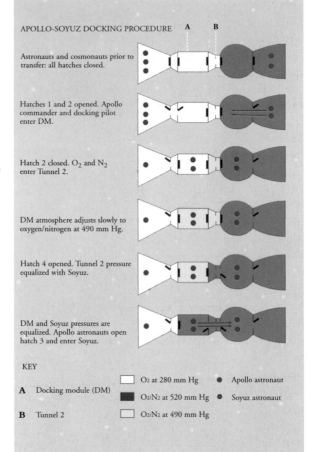

APOLLO-SOYUZ DOCKING PROCEDURE   A   B

Astronauts and cosmonauts prior to transfer: all hatches closed.

Hatches 1 and 2 opened. Apollo commander and docking pilot enter DM.

Hatch 2 closed. O_2 and N_2 enter Tunnel 2.

DM atmosphere adjusts slowly to oxygen/nitrogen at 490 mm Hg.

Hatch 4 opened. Tunnel 2 pressure equalized with Soyuz.

DM and Soyuz pressures are equalized. Apollo astronauts open hatch 3 and enter Soyuz.

KEY

A   Docking module (DM)

B   Tunnel 2

☐ O_2 at 280 mm Hg   ● Apollo astronaut

■ O_2/N_2 at 520 mm Hg   ● Soyuz astronaut

☐ O_2/N_2 at 490 mm Hg

ABOVE: For the Apollo and Soyuz crews to meet, the different atmospheric pressures and compositions used by the two craft had to be equalized. Apollo had an atmosphere of pure oxygen at a pressure of 280 mm Hg; Soyuz had oxygen/nitrogen at 520 mm Hg. (The hatches are counted left to right).

AQUILA

The constellation of Aquila the Eagle spans the Milky Way and contains a prominent dark dust cloud north of Gamma [γ] Aquilae, just visible to the naked eye. It has one open cluster, NGC 6709 of note and a small globular cluster, NGC 6760, but is rich in planetary nebulae. Its brightest star, Altair (α Aquilae), has an apparent magnitude of 0.8 and is the twelfth-brightest star in the sky.

⫸ *Globular Clusters, Open Clusters, Planetary Nebula*

ARABIC ASTRONOMY

Islam was founded in AD 622. After the building of a new Muslim capital at Baghdad in AD 762, the Abbasid Caliphs established the House of Wisdom in the new city. Here, Greek and Hindu works on astronomy, medicine and other sciences were translated into Arabic. Astronomy was vital to Muslims: the Qur'an encouraged the study of God's creation; astronomy was necessary to establish prayer times and to find the direction of Mecca, which Muslims must face while praying; and Islam needed a reliable calendar.

One of the greatest of Muslim scientists, Alhazen (c. AD 965–1039), built on Aristotle's *Meteorologia* to do fundamental work in optics, with relevance to astronomy. One of his most influential studies concerned the refraction of light by the atmosphere. Why, for example, do the Sun and Moon look distorted on the horizon, and why is there twilight before sunrise and after sunset?

Arabic astronomy was closely related to the other sciences, such as medicine. Human health was believed to be sensitive to the planets and their movements, and Arabic physicians therefore made use of astrology. At the same time Arabic astronomy developed a strong observational tradition. Al-Sufi produced the first major Islamic star chart c. 964 in Baghdad. Notable observatories included those at Maraghah in Iran, and at Samarkand, in Uzbekistan.

▶ Babylonian Astronomy, Chinese Astronomy

ARCSECOND (ARCSEC OR SECOND OF ARC)

A unit of angular measure, symbol ′, used to measure apparent distances between celestial objects, apparent diameters, or the resolving power of telescopes. There are 60 arcseconds in one arcminute (symbol ″) and 60 arcminutes in one degree.

ARCTURUS

Arcturus, the brightest star north of the celestial equator, lies in the constellation of Boötes. It is classified as a red giant, although to the eye it seems a warm orange colour. Its appearance in the evening sky is a welcome sign to residents of the northern hemisphere that spring is on its way.

ARISTOTLE (384–22 BC)

Greek philosopher. Aristotle's systematic and wide-ranging study of science formed the basis of Western thought for centuries. He considered the laws of physics in the heavens to be quite different from those on Earth. The 'natural' motion of the heavenly bodies was in circles (his universe was a construction of some 55 concentric spheres). The 'natural' motion of objects in the terrestrial realm was either towards the centre of the Earth (for objects consisting predominantly of the elements of 'earth' and 'water') or away from the centre of the Earth (for objects consisting mainly of 'air' and 'fire').

Aristotle also maintained that a force was needed to keep a body in motion. An arrow flying through the air, for example, was propelled by air displaced from the front rushing to the back and pushing the arrow along. Because such motion depended on the presence of the air, Aristotle concluded that a vacuum was impossible, or else the planets would not be moving at all. Aristotle's highly systematic approach to science, flawed though it was, survived for 2,000 years. But today very little of Aristotle's 'natural philosophy' has survived the rise of physics that began with Galileo Galilei (1564–1642) and Isaac Newton (1642–1727).

ARMILLARY SPHERE

Model of the Earth and celestial sphere, first used by Greek astronomers in the second century BC or earlier. A ball representing Earth was circled by rings representing the celestial equator, ecliptic and other reference circles, and the paths of the Sun, Moon and planets.

)))⏩ **Astrolabe, Celestial Sphere**

ARMSTRONG, NEIL (b. 1930)

American astronaut. The first man to walk on the surface of the Moon, Armstrong began flying at the age of 14. He had a pilot's licence by the age of 16, before he could drive, and colleagues commented that his love of flight bordered on religious devotion. Armstrong apparently even carried a piece of the original Wright Brothers' flier on board his Gemini 8 mission and treated it like a religious relic. Armstrong joined the Navy as a fighter pilot in 1949, flying 78 combat missions in Korea. On one mission he had to bail out when a wire stretched across a valley took the wing off his F9F-2 jet plane. Back in the US he studied for an aeronautical engineering degree and then joined Edwards Air Force Base as a test pilot in 1955, eventually flying the X-15 rocket plane to a height of 69 km (43 miles) at a speed of Mach 4. NASA selected him in 1962 and he flew on Gemini 8 and Apollo 11. Armstrong stayed with NASA after his pioneering Moon walk, but he never flew into space again and left in 1971 to pursue business and academic interests.

)))⏩ **Apollo 11**

ASTERISMS

Asterisms are unofficial patterns that can consist of stars from one or more constellation. The Square of Pegasus is an example of an asterism composed of stars from two constellations (Pegasus and Andromeda). The Plough, the Sickle of Leo, and the Teapot of Sagittarius are all asterisms within a given constellation.

)))⏩ **Constellations**

ASTEROID BELT

The region of the Solar System between about 2 and 3.3 times the distance of Earth from the Sun in which the majority of known asteroids move. Asteroids in the belt are known as main-belt asteroids. Within the belt exist gaps (the Kirkwood gaps) resulting from the gravitational pull of the Sun and Jupiter.

ASTEROIDS

Through a telescope, asteroids appear starlike, which gave rise to the name, which means 'little star'. They are in fact irregularly shaped and cratered chunks of rock and metal. Over 10,000 are currently known, and countless more remain to be observed. Most

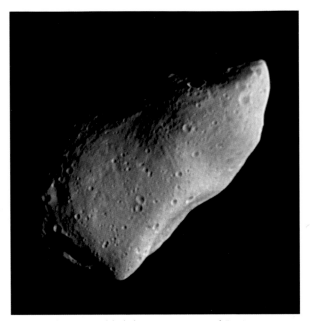

orbit in the asteroid belt between Mars and Jupiter. Jupiter's gravitational pull is thought to have prevented the material of the asteroids from accreting into a planet. Early in the Solar System's history there were probably fewer asteroids than today but of larger size. Collisions have since fragmented them and many of the fragments have been swept up by the planets. The largest main-belt asteroid is Ceres, 930 km (578 miles) across. Next in order of size are Vesta, 580 km (360 miles) and Pallas, 540 km (335 miles). Numbers increase rapidly as the size decreases.

Astronomers learn what asteroids are made of by analysing the spectrum of sunlight reflected from their

ABOVE: The asteroid Gaspa, photographed by the Galileo space probe, is just one of a myriad of asteroids which orbit the sun.

RIGHT: The peoples of the Middle East began to formulate ideas about astrology during medieval times.
BELOW: The astrolabe was perfected by the medieval Arabs. Its star map and astronomical scales enabled it to be used in navigation and time-finding.

surfaces. Their compositions turn out to be diverse, but there are several families that show certain similarities. For example, the C-type asteroids contain carbon; S-type asteroids are mixtures of rock and metal; while M-type asteroids consist largely or wholly of metal (iron and nickel). Our most detailed information about asteroid compositions comes from pieces that have been knocked off in collisions and have fallen to Earth as meteorites.

Outside the main belt, a group of asteroids called the Trojans orbits at the same distance as Jupiter but 60° ahead of or behind it in its orbit. Among the outer planets beyond Jupiter orbits a small group of icy asteroids called the Centaurs, which may have more in common with cometary nuclei than with the solid inner asteroids. The first of these to be discovered was Chiron, in 1977, which has shown signs of comet-like activity.

)))➤ *Edgeworth–Kuiper Belt*

ASTROLABE

The astrolabe was an observing and computing instrument that was used in the Middle Ages to determine the time, find direction and make calculations in spherical trigonometry. Its earliest form was described by Ptolemy in AD 125, but it was the Arabs who developed and popularized the instrument. In its mature form it consisted of a star map in brass filigree, called a rete (network), that rotated above a zonal or 'climate' plate. The plate was engraved with circles representing astronomical coordinate lines appropriate for a particular latitude. Turning the rete simulated the rotation of the stars.

ASTROLOGY

Astrology is the art and science of relating Earthly events and human traits to the movements of the Sun, Moon and planets. It had appeared in Mesopotamia by 2000 BC and passed from there to India, China and Greece. As astronomical tables were compiled over increasing lengths of time, and knowledge of celestial motions grew more accurate, astrology became more ambitious. Claudius Ptolemy, the greatest astronomer in the Greek tradition, wrote the *Tetrabiblos,* a major work which influenced Western astrology. 'Judicial' astronomy used the horoscope, or star chart, relating to a person's moment of birth to discover that person's character and the course of their life, or at least their life chances. And the 'aspects' of the heavenly bodies, their relative positions, at the moment of undertaking some enterprise were held to influence its chances of success. Judicial astrology was condemned by two fathers of the Christian Church, St Augustine (354–430) and St Thomas Aquinas (c. 1225–1274), but taken seriously by many European scientists until the triumph of Newtonian thought in the late seventeenth century.

)))➤ *Newtonian Cosmology*

ASTRONOMY, SEEING FOR YOURSELF

Astronomy is a fascinating hobby which can be enjoyed on many levels. The first step in observing is learning your way around the sky. Just as you become familiar with a new part of town by taking note of prominent landmarks, so you can start to explore the night sky by looking for the more prominent patterns in the constellations, and making a note of the brighter stars. You do not need special equipment to enjoy the sky – just your eyes, a star chart and a dark sky. Star charts provide a positional layout of constellations in the same way that a map of the earth shows roads. Yet even more celestial delights are revealed with a pair of ordinary binoculars. Progressing to a telescope is a bigger step, but many local astronomical societies possess a telescope through which they are always pleased to show people some of the jewels of the night sky.

If you are lucky enough to live away from city lights, the more stars and objects you will be able to see in the night sky. In very dark areas you can see thousands of stars, including the faint, misty trail of the Milky Way meandering across the sky.

ABOVE: A wide range of equipment is available for the amateur astronomer, from small, portable telescopes such as this simple refractor to larger instruments that may need a permanent housing. For many purposes, such as learning the constellations, a pair of binoculars will be adequate.

Observing the Stars

Your view of the night sky is also affected by your latitude and the time of year. If you live in the northern hemisphere, for example, (see pages 206–7) then you will not be able to see stars that lie near the South Celestial Pole, and the farther north you live, the fewer stars you will be able to see south of the celestial equator. Also, as the Earth orbits the Sun, the night side looks out at different parts of the Universe. This is why different constellations are on view at different times of the year.

To observe, choose a site as dark as possible and as far from trees and buildings as you can get. This gives you a better all-round view. Make sure you are warm; it is surprising how cold you can get, especially during winter evenings, and you need to stay out long enough for your eyes to become dark-adapted. Your eyes can take up to half an hour to achieve maximum sensitivity in the dark, and this dark adaption is quickly lost if a light is switched on. Instead of using an ordinary torch to read your star chart, use one with a red bulb as this helps you retain your dark adaption.

Try to gain an idea of where north is, as this will help you orientate yourself on star charts. Choose a prominent constellation or asterism on the chart and try and recognize it in the sky. You may be surprised to find how far apart stars are from each other in the sky; some patterns which appear obvious on the star chart can be very spread out and not quite so obvious when you are looking at them in reality. You may also find that some of the fainter stars are not visible, if for example you live in a very light-polluted area, and this changes some of the stellar patterns. Conversely, if you have a very dark sky, you may be overwhelmed by the number of stars which can confuse the stellar patterns.

Following Patterns

Starting from an obvious pattern – and there are many – follow the chart and try and lead yourself to another obvious pattern. This is the first step in star-hopping, a technique used by amateurs at all levels. You can star-hop with the naked eye, with binoculars,

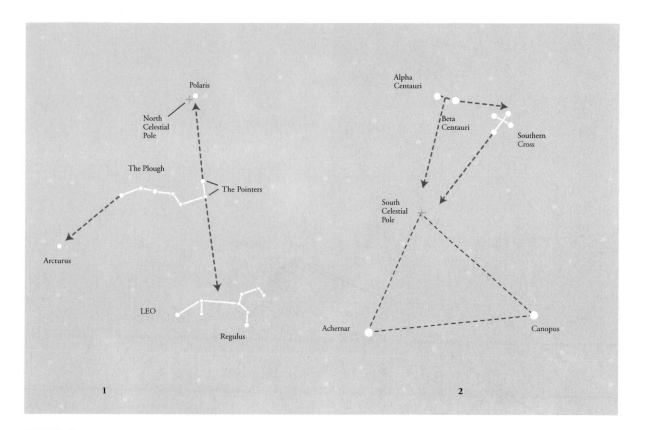

ABOVE: Use this diagram as a signpost to the sky.
1. Two stars in the bowl of the Plough act as pointers to the north pole star,
Polaris. Extending the pointers in the opposite direction brings you to Leo the
Lion. The Plough's curving handle points to the bright star Arcturus.
2. The bright stars Alpha and Beta Centauri act as pointers to Crux, the
Southern Cross. The long axis of Crux, and a line at right angles to Alpha and
Beta Centauri, points to the South Celestial Pole. The bright stars Canopus
and Achernar form a large triangle with the pole.

and through the eyepiece of a powerful telescope, although with increasing magnification the distances you star-hop become smaller, and your star charts become more detailed, showing objects of fainter and fainter magnitude.

Identifying Planets

Planets do not appear on star charts because they are constantly on the move. However some simple rules will help you identify a planet: a brilliant 'star' in the evening or morning twilight will be Jupiter; a fainter, yellowish star will be Saturn; while a bright reddish star will be Mars. Another way to distinguish between a planet and a star is that planets hardly ever twinkle – unlike stars they are not point sources of light and so are less affected by the air currents in the Earth's atmosphere that cause twinkling.

Many fine sights can be seen with just the naked eye, but do not expect to see the detail and colour of images produced by powerful telescopes. Even with a large amateur telescope, you will not see the colours revealed in long-exposure photographs, but there is colour in the night sky, and just looking with the naked eye will reveal that stars are not all the same.

When you actually stand under the dome of the celestial sphere and look at the faint fuzzy white patch of the Andromeda Galaxy, or the faint glow of the Orion Nebula, remember that the photons reaching the back of your retina have actually travelled light years through space from the object itself, a wonderful thought.

ATOMIC NUCLEUS

The central part of an atom consisting of positively charged protons and uncharged neutrons, thus having an overall positive charge. The nucleus contains most of the mass of an atom.

AURIGA

The constellation Auriga, the Charioteer, contains Capella, the sixth-brightest star in the sky. South of Capella lie two exceptional eclipsing binaries: Zeta [ζ] and Epsilon [ε] Aurigae. Zeta is an orange giant orbited by a blue star giving eclipses every two years eight months. Epsilon is a luminous supergiant with the longest known period of any eclipsing binary of 27 years. The nature of the orbiting companion remains in doubt. Auriga also contains a chain of three open clusters.

AURORA

The solar wind is a stream of charged particles that flow away from the Sun. Those particles that encounter Earth become trapped within two

ASTROPHYSICS

Physics applied to astronomy becomes astrophysics, the science concerned with the physical conditions in the Universe beyond the Earth. Newton created the first successful astrophysical theory when he discovered that the same force of gravity causing apples to fall from trees also guided the planets around the Sun. By extending terrestrial science to the cosmos, he showed that the whole Universe might be understood in terms of the same physical laws. But astrophysics really took off in the mid-nineteenth century with the rise of spectroscopy. Forming a spectrum of the light received from the stars made it possible to determine their composition, temperature, motions and other properties.

Astrophysicists ask questions such as how stars are born and die, how energy is generated inside them, how radiation is produced and absorbed, the nature of the gas and dust lying between the stars, how stars move within galaxies, and the source of the mysterious cosmic rays.

)))➤ *Newton, Isaac; Spectroscopy*

regions beyond the atmosphere called the Van Allen radiation belts. Sometimes the Sun releases an intense outburst of charged particles and the Van Allen belts 'overflow'. Particles cascade down into Earth's upper atmosphere, exciting molecules of atmospheric gases and causing them to emit visible radiation. This radiation is an auroral display. Most activity appears in the skies near the poles. In the north, the display is called the Aurora Borealis, and in the south, the Aurora Australis.

)))➤ *Magnetosphere, Van Allen Belts*

AZIMUTH

Azimuth is one of the co-ordinates in the horizontal system which identifies the position of a celestial object in the sky. It is the angular distance measured parallel to the horizon, eastwards from north. Azimuth is measured in degrees, from 0 to 360. The other co-ordinate in this system is altitude.

)))➤ *Altitude*

BL LAC OBJECTS (BL LACERTAE OBJECTS)

A class of active galactic nuclei (AGN) named after the first to be identified, BL Lacertae, typified by the lack of emission and absorption lines in their spectra. In the unified AGN model, a BL Lac object is thought to be produced when the central engine of an AGN is observed end-on, looking directly along, or close to, the jet.

BAADE, WALTER (1893–1960)

German-born US astronomer responsible for the idea of stellar populations, which led to the solution of a major riddle regarding the age of the Universe. Before the 1950s, geologists argued (correctly) that Earth was about 4.5 billion years old, whereas astronomers argued (incorrectly) that the age of the Universe was about 2 billion years. The astronomers' argument was based on the distances to other galaxies, from which the Hubble constant and age of the Universe could be calculated. Baade realized that there were two classes of pulsating variable star on which the distance scale was based, each of which had a different relationship between their period of pulsation and

luminosity. Use of the incorrect relationship had led astronomers to underestimate the distances of galaxies. Baade's revision of the astronomical distance scale doubled the known size (and hence age) of the Universe, and subsequent observations have increased these figures still further.

BABYLONIAN ASTRONOMY

The Babylonians were the first people to make regular records of celestial phenomena. The basic constellation figures probably date from before 3000 BC, and Mesopotamian tablets from 1100 BC depicting the Sun, Moon and zodiac figures still exist. Dated observations of eclipses, and of the positions of Venus and other planets in relation to the Sun, were recorded on clay tablets. These documents have proved invaluable to modern astronomers. Indeed, the Babylonians of around 1000 BC were the founders of systematic astronomy. They mistakenly believed that there were 360 days in the year, and it may have been in connection with this that they divided the circle into 360 degrees. Their astronomical records were built up for the purposes of political and religious astrology; in ancient times, no one looked at the sky for what we would now call scientific purposes – they saw it instead as a tool for prophecy. While war, famine

and disease made human life precarious, the heavens possessed a regularity which seemed to influence the Earth, through the solar seasons or lunar phases. But Babylonian astrology resulted in the basic concepts of scientific astronomy: observational data, mathematical analysis and verifiable predictions.

ABOVE: A shepherd contemplates the vast expanse of space with stars and planets in ancient times.

BAILY'S BEADS

The phenomenon seen at a solar eclipse when the Sun's disc is almost covered by the Moon and sunlight shines through the valleys at the Moon's edge, briefly producing 'beads' of light. If only one bead is visible, it is called the diamond ring. The effect was first described by Francis Baily (1774–1844).

BARIUM STARS

Barium stars are giant stars that had the misfortune to be too closely partnered to a star that completed its evolution and shot out the products of its nuclear burning all over its companion, especially barium. They therefore show enhancements of elements such as barium and strontium in their spectra.

BARNARD'S STAR

Barnard's Star, a red dwarf only six light years away, has the largest proper motion of any star, covering the apparent width of the Moon in 180 years. It was discovered in 1916 by E.E. Barnard.

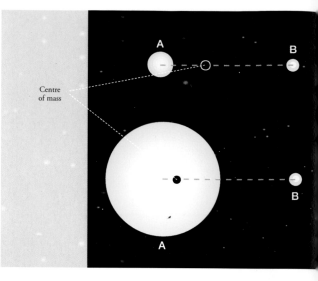

ABOVE: Centre of Mass (barycentre). In the upper pair of orbiting stars, the mass of star A is double that of star B. They orbit around a centre of mass one-third of the distance between the centres of the stars. In the lower pair, star A is 10 times more massive than star B. In this case, the centre of mass is much closer to the middle of star A, whose orbital motion is slight compared to star B. BELOW LEFT: The barred spiral galaxy NCG 1365. The long structure, the bar, across the centre of the galaxy defines this type of galaxy.

BARRED SPIRAL GALAXIES

Almost half of all spiral galaxies have a cigar-shaped structure across their centres known as a bar, consisting of stars, gas and dust, like a straight inner extension of the spiral arms. Bars can be up to five times as long as they are broad; sometimes, several bar-like structures of different sizes and with different orientations are found in a single galaxy. The bar can act like a giant mixer within the host galaxy, stirring together stars with different properties from different radii. Dust is often concentrated in tight lanes along the leading edges of the bar, while regions of star formation and gas clouds are often found near the ends of bars. Spiral arms originate from the ends of bars, not from the central bulge, and rings sometimes surround bars – a ring can be thought of as a tightly wrapped spiral arm. Our own Galaxy has a bar. The overall dimensions and masses of barred spirals are the same as those of ordinary spirals.

)))➤ *Spiral Galaxies*

BARYCENTRE

The centre of mass of two or more bodies revolving under the influence of gravity. It is the point about which they revolve. The barycentre of the Earth–Moon system lies within Earth, as Earth is so much more massive than the Moon.

BARYON

A class of elementary particles that have a mass greater than or equal to that of a proton (1.6726×10^{-27} kg), participate in strong interactions and have a spin of one half.

BEG, ULUGH (1394–1449)

Arabic astronomer. In 1420 he built a great three-storey, drum-shaped observatory, 30 m (100 ft) high, housing a 40-m (130-ft) radius masonry sextant set in the plane of the meridian. Alongside the graduated edge of this sextant, each brass degree spanned 68 cm (27 in). Astronomers observed the Sun, Moon or stars through a small hole at the geometrical centre of the instrument by attaching a finely graduated sliding pinhole eyepiece and scale between each degree. With this colossal sextent Beg determined the length of the solar year to within a minute of time. He also composed a Zij table which gave the precise positions of 1,018 stars.

BELL, JOCELYN (b. 1943)

English astronomer. As a student working on her doctoral thesis at the Mullard Radio Astronomy Observatory, Cambridge, England in 1967, Bell studied interstellar scintillation, the 'twinkling' of radio waves from distant sources by intervening interstellar material, as a method of searching for quasars. Bell noticed some strange squiggles on the chart depicting readings from a particular part of the sky, which, when examined in more detail, turned out to be pulses of radio energy repeating precisely every 1.3373 seconds. Soon other sources were found. Bell and her supervisor, Professor Antony Hewish (b. 1924), announced the discovery of these sources, called pulsars, in 1968. Other astronomers soon established that they were rapidly rotating neutron stars.

BESSEL, FRIEDRICH (1784–1846)

German astronomer. In 1838 Bessel announced that the star 61 Cygni had a parallax that placed it 10.3 light years away, only one light year closer than the currently accepted distance. As the precision of telescopes improved, so had hopes of measuring the microscopic parallax shifts that stars would show if they were at distances comparable to those Newton had estimated for Sirius, hence Bessel's successful result.

BETA PEGASI

Beta [β] Pegasi is a red giant that pulsates irregularly. It lies in the Square of Pegasus and can be found at any brightness between magnitudes 2.3 and 2.7.

)))) ➤ *Red Giant*

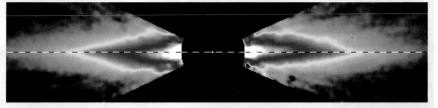

BETA PICTORIS

In the 1980s, a disk of dust and gas from which a planetary system may currently be forming was discovered around 4th magnitude Beta [β] Pictoris. This disk, which is presented edge-on to us, can only be seen with specialized equipment.

BETELGEUSE

A red supergiant lying at the top left of the constellation of Orion, marking his shoulder. It is the most obviously variable of all 1st-magnitude stars, ranging by about a magnitude in brightness with no firm period.

)))) ➤ *Supergiant*

ABOVE: A disk of dust and gas surrounding Beta Pictoris, photographed by the Hubble Space Telescope. The inner section of the disk is slightly tilted, suggesting the existence of a large planet in a clear zone closer to the central star. The colours in the disk have been added by computer to enhance detail.

BIG BANG

Measurements of the motions of distant galaxies have led cosmologists to the view that the Universe was formed from a single event which has become known as the Big Bang. From the Big Bang emerged not only the matter which forms all that we see now in the Universe, but time and space as well. Since time started at the Big Bang it is therefore meaningless, in science, to ask what happened before.

We live in a Universe dominated by matter. But that has not always been the case, for the relative importance of matter and radiation has changed as the Universe has expanded. Because of the equivalence of mass and energy expressed in Einstein's equation, $E = mc^2$, both matter and radiation contribute to the mass density of the Universe. As the Universe expands, the number of particles of matter per unit volume falls. The same is true for radiation, the number of photons per unit volume falling in the same way, but another effect also comes into play. Since the energy of a photon depends on its wavelength, the higher the energy the shorter the wavelength. As the Universe expands the wavelength increases (by the cosmological redshift) and so the photon energy falls. The

BELOW: The evolutionary stages of the cosmos from the earliest formation of matter just after the Big Bang to the Universe of present-day galaxies.

contribution to the mass density from radiation therefore falls more rapidly than that from matter leading to an increasingly matter-dominated Universe.

Radiation Energy

The energy density of radiation, most of which resides in the cosmic background radiation, is now quite feeble in comparison to the energy density of matter, but when the Universe was less than 10,000 years old most of its energy was in the form of radiation. The early Universe behaved as a black body and so it is possible to define a temperature from the spectrum of the cosmic background radiation. As the Universe expands, the wavelength of this radiation lengthens and so the temperature of the Universe decreases. As the Universe evolved, it passed through a series of critical times (known as epochs) each identified by a temperature.

It is known from experiments that when an electron inside an atom is given an energy of just a few electron volts it can escape from the atom. The energy can come from collisions between atoms, and at temperatures of about 3,000 K or more the collisions are energetic enough for electrons to escape. It follows that atoms could not exist in the Universe until its temperature had fallen below 3,000 K, since any atom that did form would be broken up again by collisions. Before this time the Universe was a sea of atomic nuclei and electrons – a

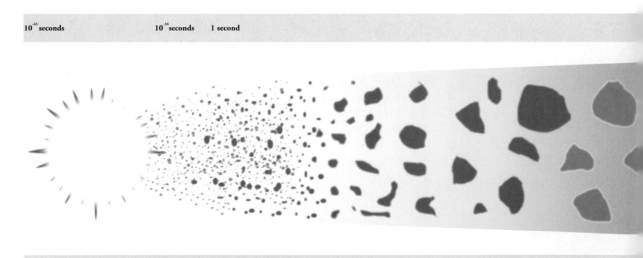

10^{-43} seconds	10^{-34} seconds	1 second
PLANCK ERA	INFLATIONARY ERA	HELIUM PRODUCTION

plasma rather than a gas. This plasma was opaque, radiation being continually emitted and re-absorbed so that matter and radiation were at the same temperature. When the Universe cooled below this critical temperature, stable atoms could form and so the link between matter and radiation was broken – they were 'decoupled' – and the two evolved independently of each other. Space became transparent for the first time and radiation could pass moreorless freely through the Universe. For this reason the period during which atoms formed is sometimes known as the decoupling era, although it is more often referred to as the recombination era (a slightly inappropriate name since nuclei and electrons were combining to form atoms for the first time rather than recombining).

interacting with matter. Before recombination the Universe was opaque, so the background radiation provides us with our earliest view of it. The temperature of the radiation is now 3 K, and since it was 3,000 K at recombination we know the Universe has expanded by a factor of 1,000 since then. With current cosmological models this places the start of recombination at a Universe age of about 300,000 years. The most distant galaxies that can be detected with present-day telescopes are seen at a time when the Universe was about 1,000 million years old. We have no observations of the Universe when its age lay between one million years and 1,000 million years, and the evolution of the Universe in this period, including the era of galaxy formation, remains very uncertain.

))))▶ *Hubble Time, Hubble's Constant, Hubble's Law, Inflationary Era, Steady State Theory*

Beyond Recombination

Since the recombination era, the cosmic background radiation has passed through the Universe without

ABOVE: German-born Physicist Albert Einstein (1879–1955) was responsible for the famous equation E = mc².

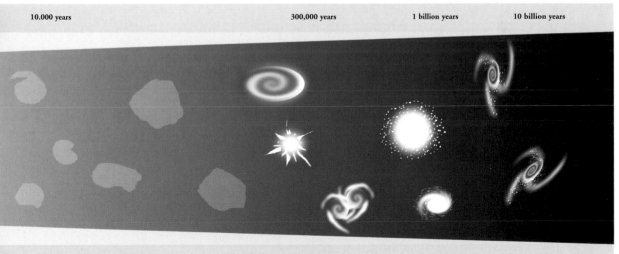

| 10.000 years | 300,000 years | 1 billion years | 10 billion years |

| END OF RADIATION DOMINANCE | RECOMBINATION ERA | GALAXY FORMATION | THE UNIVERSE TODAY |

BIG CRUNCH

The future of the Universe depends upon its total density. If it has a density greater than a so-called 'critical density', then some time in the future it will stop expanding and start to contract. Such a Universe will return to a very hot, dense state which is usually called the Big Crunch. If the density of the Universe is less than the critical density, it will continue to expand forever. With a density equal to the critical density, the Universe will continue to expand but its expansion rate will gradually slow.

))))➤ *Universe*

BINARY PULSARS

In 1974 two US astronomers discovered a pulsar in orbit around a neutron star. By making careful measurements of the pulse times, they could calculate the orbits of the stars with great precision. General relativity predicts that the two stars, orbiting each other in less than eight hours, will be radiating energy in the form of gravitational waves, and this should be revealed by the orbits slowly contracting as the stars spiral in towards each other with increasing speed. Within a few years, the orbits were found to be shrinking at precisely the rate predicted by general relativity. So compelling was this evidence for gravitational waves that the two astronomers, Joseph Taylor (b. 1941) and Russell Hulse (b. 1950), were deservedly awarded the Nobel Prize for physics in 1993.

))))➤ *Gravitational Waves, Pulsars, Neutron Stars*

BINARY STARS

Roughly half of all the stars in the sky are found to be in binary systems, in which two companion stars orbit their common centre of mass with periods ranging from hours to many thousands of years. In keeping with Kepler's laws, the wider the separation between the stars, the longer their orbital period. Binary stars may be born together from a rapidly rotating protostar that split, or one may capture the other in a close encounter after birth. Some may eclipse each other, causing variability in their observed brightness.

Binary stars are generally classified according to the means by which their binary nature is observed: in astrometric binaries only one component is observed, but the companion is inferred by perturbations in its proper motion; spectroscopic binaries are revealed by the Doppler shift of lines in their spectrum; in visual binaries both components can be resolved through a telescope. Binary stars are important for determining information about stellar masses. Some binary stars are so close that transfer of material can occur between the components affecting their evolution and producing variations in their light output.

))))➤ *Doppler Effect, Double Stars, Kepler, Johannes*

BLACK BODY

A black body is an object that completely absorbs all radiation that falls upon it, and is therefore 'black' at all wavelengths. An ideal absorber is also an ideal emitter, and a black body is thus an ideal thermal radiator. Black-body radiation is characteristic of the interior of an object in thermal equilibrium and has a characteristic, continuous spectrum that rises from low-intensity levels at short wavelengths, reaches a broad peak, and then falls away towards longer wavelengths. A black-body spectrum has the same shape no matter what the object is made of – there are no emission or absorption lines – and the position of the peak and the brightness of the radiation depend only on the temperature.

))))➤ *Absorption Line, Emission Line*

BLACK BODY RADIATION

The radiation emitted by a black body. The radiation is emitted (with differing intensities) across a continuous range of wavelengths, with the output peaking at a wavelength determined by the temperature of the black body. In the case of the Sun (which approximates a black body with a temperature of 5,800 K), the peak occurs at a wavelength of about 500 nm and corresponds to yellow light.

))))➤ *Black Body*

RIGHT: Black-body radiation at different temperatures. These graphs show the relative intensity of each colour in the light emitted by a black body at three different temperatures. Note that as the temperature of a black body rises, its peak emission moves towards shorter wavelengths.

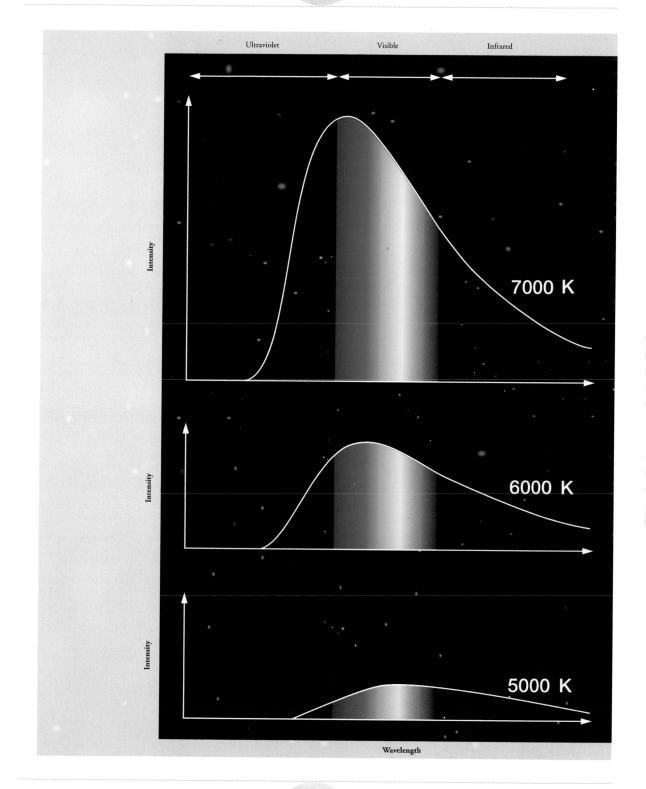

BLACK HOLES

Of all the objects that make up the Universe probably the most astounding are black holes. Stars reveal themselves by the radiation they generate, but black holes are different: they may be unseen by telescopes, yet are capable of swallowing whole stars. They are the science-fiction writer's dream – to those writers, black holes offer doorways to parallel universes and the possibility of time travel. There are three types of black hole: primordial, stellar and galactic.

Using Newton's theory of gravity, the French mathematician Laplace introduced the concept of a black hole around 200 years ago, although he did not use the name or suggest the more bizarre effects later attributed to them. At that time scientists thought light was a stream of particles and Laplace's view was that the pull of gravity would slow down light that was escaping from a star. If the light's speed was less than the escape velocity for the star the light would be unable to escape and would fall back into the star.

Newton versus Einstein

Einstein's theory of general relativity explains gravity in a quite different way from Newton's – not as a force of attraction between two objects but as a distortion of space–time. From this new approach followed two predictions: light follows the curvature of space–time, and gravitational fields affect the rate of clocks. If the body's gravity is sufficiently strong, space–time becomes so highly curved around the body that light is unable to escape from it. This occurs at the Schwarzschild radius, while the sphere around a black hole at the Schwarzschild radius is termed the event horizon. It is called a horizon because no information from within it can reach the outside world. Imagine, for example, trying to signal to the outside world with light rays (or radio waves, which would behave in the same way). The rays follow the curvature of space–time around the black hole, but within

the event horizon the curvature is so great that all light rays return to the black hole.

However, there is nothing to stop things, for example an unfortunate astronaut, from falling inside the event horizon – they may not even notice until it is too late and escape is impossible.

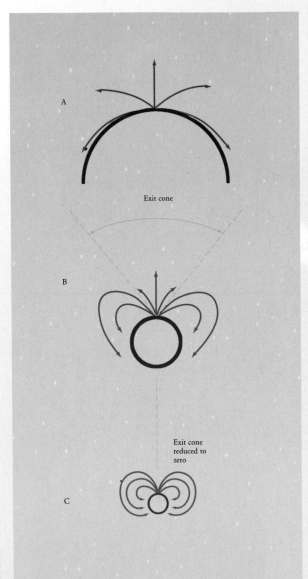

RIGHT: Light rays around a black hole. In a weak gravitational field (A), the light rays follow curved paths, but they all escape from the source. In a stronger gravitational field (B), only light rays within a region called the 'exit cone' can escape. When a black hole is at the Schwarzschild radius (C), its gravitational field is so strong that the exit cone has shrunk to zero and light cannot escape.

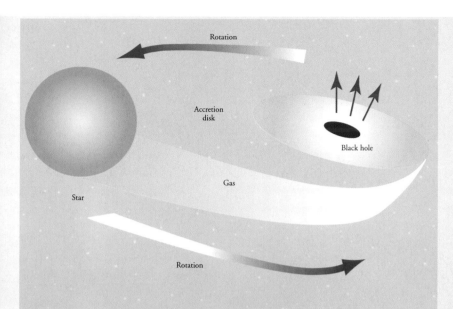

Rotation

Accretion
disk

Black hole

Gas

Star

Rotation

What happens to matter that falls into a black hole, through the event horizon? In the Schwarzschild model (which assumes the black hole is non-rotating), at the centre of a black hole is a singularity, a point of infinite density and zero radius where the laws of physics break down.

Energy Release

Matter falling towards a black hole can provide the energy for a powerful radiation source, but the gravitational energy released must be converted into heat outside the Schwarzschild radius. If matter fell directly into the hole, all its kinetic energy would be lost within the event horizon. But, like water disappearing down the plughole of a bath, matter approaching a black hole usually has angular momentum and so does not fall straight in – instead it creates a disk swirling around the black hole, known as an accretion disk. As in any orbiting system, the matter in the accretion disk moves faster the closer it approaches the event horizon, heating up through friction to temperatures as high as a billion degrees in its fastest-moving inner part. This heat is converted into high-energy radiation in the form of X-rays and gamma rays. As much as 30 per cent of the kinetic energy of the infalling matter can be converted into radiation in this way, about 10 times better than the efficiency of the nuclear processes which power the Sun. Also, the difference in speed between various parts of the accretion disk generates huge magnetic fields which are thought to power the jets often associated with black holes.

))))➤ *Hawking Radiation, Space-Time*

ABOVE: Where a black hole and a star are in a close binary system, the tremendous tidal pull of the black hole drags gas from its companion star into the black hole's rotating accretion disk, causing X-ray radiation to be emitted. LEFT: From the accretion disk around a black hole at the core of the elliptical galaxy M87, a jet of atomic particles emerges at nearly the speed of light.

BLAZARS

A class of active galactic nucleus (AGN) sharing some of the extreme characteristics of BL Lac objects having variations in their visible light by factors as large as 100, strong radio emission and strong optical polarization. In the unified AGN model, a blazar is thought to be produced when an AGN is observed end-on to the emitted jets.

)))⯈ *Active galaxy, Seyfert galaxy, Quasars*

BOHR, NIELS (1885–1962)

Danish physicist. The father of quantum mechanics, in 1911 Bohr developed a model of the atom based on electron orbits that obeyed the rules of the then-new quantum theory. He was awarded the Nobel Prize for this work in 1922.

During the 1920s Bohr headed a new institute in Copenhagen which became the centre for work on quantum mechanics. Bohr famously entered into a long-running debate with Einstein over the meaning of the new theory, developing what has become known as the Copenhagen interpretation.

BOLIDE

A bright meteor that produces a sonic boom during its passage through Earth's atmosphere. Bolides probably originate from asteroids rather than comets and often reach the Earth's surface as meteorites.

ABOVE: Niels Bohr, considered by many to be the father of quantum mechanics. He won the Nobel Prize in 1922 for his model of the atom based on electron orbits.
ABOVE RIGHT: The BOOMERanG detector which obtained measurements of the scale size of the variations in the cosmic background radiation in 1998.

BOOMERanG

BOOMERanG is a balloon-borne detector, flown from Antarctica, which measured the scale size of the variations in the cosmic background radiation. These measurements showed that the geometry of space is flat, which is what we would expect if the very early Universe had an inflationary phase. Similar results were obtained by another balloon-borne experiment called MAXIMA, which flew high above Texas.

Flat space implies the density of the Universe is equal to the critical density, but measurements show that the density falls far short of this, even when dark matter is included. This discrepancy would be removed if a cosmological constant or some other form of 'dark energy' exists.

)))⯈ *Cosmological Constant, Dark Matter, Inflationary Era*

BOÖTES

The constellation of Boötes the Herdsman contains four double stars of note. Epsilon [ε] Boötis is an orange star with a companion of a beautiful contrasting blue. Mu [μ] Boötes is a wide double with the fainter companion a close binary. In the north of the constellation lie Kappa [κ] and Iota [ι] Boötes, two easy doubles for small telescopes. Its brightest star is Arcturus.

)))⯈ *Arcturus*

BRAHE, TYCHO (1546–1601)

Danish astronomer. One of the leading astronomers of the Renaissance, as a youth he studied law at Leipzig, Wittenberg and several other European universities, but even by the age of 16, a

RIGHT: Although similar to the American Space Shuttle, the Russian Shuttle Buran was also able to fly remotely without being manned by a human crew.

passion for astronomy was uppermost in his mind. On 24 August 1563 Brahe made his first recorded observation of Jupiter and Saturn in conjunction. He also collaborated with Paul Hainzel of Augsburg in the construction of a quadrant for accurately observing the planets. Tycho's eccentric brilliance was recognized by King Frederick II of Denmark, who presented him with the Island of Hven on which he built his famous 'Castle of the Heavens', Uraniborg. Tycho lived and worked at Uraniborg between 1576 and 1598, amidst the research assistants and technicians of Europe's first scientific research academy. His aim was to prove astronomical theory by practice and mathematical analysis. Court politics caused him to leave Denmark, however, and he died in Prague in 1601.

))))▶ *Tychonic System*

BROWN DWARFS

If the mass of a protostar is less than about 8 per cent that of the Sun (80 times the mass of Jupiter), the gas at its centre will never get hot or dense enough to trigger hydrogen-burning nuclear reactions. Such failed stars are called brown dwarfs. Although not burning hydrogen, brown dwarfs are still quite warm, with surface temperatures of 1,000–2,000°C (1,800–3,600°F) from their collapse and perhaps from their failed attempts to ignite as stars. Hence they can be readily detected at infrared wavelengths. Brown dwarfs can be recognized by the presence of the light element lithium in their optical spectra: in any 'real' low-mass stars, convection would carry lithium into the interior where it would be destroyed by nuclear reactions, but this does not happen in brown dwarfs. If the gas ball were even smaller, below a mass of about 10 Jupiters, it would be classified as a planet.

))))▶ *Low-Mass Stars*

BURAN

The Russian Shuttle named Buran ('Snowstorm') was similar in appearance to the American Shuttle, but it differed in being able to fly remotely without a

crew. Buran was launched only once, from Baikonur on 15 November 1988. It completed two orbits of Earth before gliding back to Baikonur three hours and 25 minutes later. Substantial heat damage had occurred during re-entry with an area along the wings' leading edge melted by plasma. Further flights were planned to visit Mir, but severe economic decline in the Soviet Union and cheaper alternatives for flying to Mir meant the Buran project was abandoned.

))))▶ *Mir Space Station*

CALENDARS

The calendar established by the Roman emperor Julius Caesar in 45 BC continued in use in Christian Europe until 1582. Yet its 365¼ day year was too long by 10.53 minutes, and as a result, astronomical events fell earlier and earlier in each year as the centuries passed. This posed a serious problem for Christians, who, like Jews and Muslims, needed reliable calendars to regulate religious worship. The date of Easter, central to Christianity, was calculated in relation to the full Moon on or following the spring equinox. But when was the true equinox: 21 March, as in the calendar, or 11 March, the date on which the astronomical equinox was falling by 1574? A definitive solution was not found until Pope Gregory's 'Gregorian Calendar' of 1582, the calendar used in the West today.

))))▶ *Equinox, Solstice*

CALLISTO

Callisto is the farthest from Jupiter of the planet's four large satellites. It therefore experiences the least tidal action and hence has the lowest internal heating. It has a dark, cratered surface, indicating that little geological activity has occurred there for billions of years. Its diameter is approximately 4,800 km (2,986 miles); its mean distance from Jupiter is 1.88 million km (1.17 million miles).

))➤ *Galilean Satellites*

CALORIS BASIN

Mercury's largest geological formation is a circular lowland 1,300 km (800 miles) wide, fully one-quarter of the planet's diameter. It is named the Caloris Basin (from the Latin *calor*, meaning 'heat') because it faces the Sun when Mercury is closest to the Sun. The basin was excavated by an immense impact.

CARINA

The constellation of Carina, the keel, is dominated by Canopus (α Carinae), the second-brightest star in the sky. As well as its famous luminous blue variable, Eta [η] Carinae, Carina the Keel contains a rich open cluster, IC 2602, known as the Southern Pleiades. Surrounding Eta itself is NGC 3372, the Eta Carinae Nebula. A V-shaped lane of dust divides the nebula into two main parts.

CASSINI DIVISION

The rings surrounding the planet Saturn consist of three main subrings, called the A, B and C rings. Earth-based observations show a number of gaps within the rings, notably the Cassini division between rings A and B. It was discovered in 1675 by G. D. Cassini (1625–1712).

LEFT: The dark, cratered surface of Callisto, one of Jupiter's four largest moons, also known as the Galilean moons.

CASSINI-HUYGENS

Cassini-Huygens was launched on 15 October 1997. With sling-shots from Venus, Earth and Jupiter, it will reach the Saturnian system in 2004, firing its main rocket engine for over two hours to brake into orbit. The mission will later jettison ESA's Huygens probe, which will parachute into the orange cloud tops of Titan, descending to an unknown landing site where it might splash down into an ethane-methane ocean, or touch down on a rocky, icy shore. Instruments will photograph Titan's surface and sample its atmosphere. The orbiter will continue its charting of Saturn's rings and moons for over four years.

CASSIOPEIA

Cassiopeia lies in the Milky Way, its five brightest stars forming a distinctive W- (or M-) shaped pattern. It contains several star clusters. Prime among them is M52, a large open cluster that can be found with binoculars as a misty, somewhat elongated patch of light. Another open cluster easily located with binoculars is NGC 457, which includes the 5th-magnitude supergiant Phi [φ] Cassiopeia.

))➤ *Milky Way, Open Clusters*

CASTOR AND POLLUX

Castor and Pollux sit side by side in the sky like the mythological twins after whom they are named, but the stars themselves are not truly related. Pollux, slightly the brighter of the two despite being labelled Beta [β], is an orange giant 34 light years distant. Binoculars emphasize its colour-contrast with blue-white Castor to the north, 52 light years from us. Telescopes of only 60-mm (2.4-in) aperture can split Castor into a dazzling binary, the components of which orbit each other every 470 years or so. Castor was one of the first binary stars in which orbital motion was detected. Castor also has a faint red dwarf companion. All three of these visible stars are themselves spectroscopic binaries.

))➤ *Binary Stars, Spectroscopic Binaries*

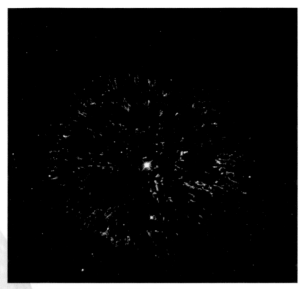

CATACLYSMIC BINARIES

Cataclysmic binaries (or variables) are binary stars in which the components are very close to each other. In such systems, a cool red dwarf star is partnered by a white dwarf. The two are less than one million km (600,000 miles) apart and orbit with periods less than half a day. Gas is drawn off the red dwarf by the gravitational strength of the white dwarf and it spirals on to an accretion disk around the compact star creating a bright hot spot at the point where the infalling stream of gas hits the disk. Every few days or weeks, instabilities in the disk cause surges in brightness of as much as 250 times (six magnitudes). The result is termed a dwarf nova.

Gas eventually spirals down through the accretion disk on to the surface of the white dwarf. When sufficient gas has built up, a 'hydrogen flash' can occur, a nuclear explosion which blows off a thin outer layer, and the star's brightness flares up 25,000 times (11 magnitudes) or so in a nova explosion. Nova eruptions may repeat after hundreds or thousands of years, and several such recurrent novae are known. In extreme cases, where the composition of the white dwarf is just right, the nuclear

ABOVE: Ejected gas surrounding Nova Persei, which exploded in 1901. At maximum the nova was around 200,000 times as luminous as the Sun. A nova is a type of cataclysmic binary.

RIGHT: Henry Cavendish was the first to measure the gravitational constant.

detonation may be so severe as to trigger a supernova of Type Ia.

)))**▶ *Accretion Disk, Binary Stars, Type I Supernova***

CAUSALITY

Causality is the principle that an effect can follow a cause, but cannot precede it. As a scientific concept it has far-reaching consequences, not least because ideas which violate causality are always rejected by scientists. The theory of special relativity predicts that the time interval between two events will be different for two observers if they are in relative motion, the difference they perceive depending upon their relative speeds – the faster they are travelling relative to each other the greater the difference. But there will be no change in the order of the events. If there were such a change then causality would be violated for one of the observers.

)))**▶ *Relativity, Special Theory of***

CAVENDISH, HENRY (1731–1810)

English physicist. The aristocratic Cavendish was a skilled experimenter who made the first experimental measurement of the gravitational constant, known as G, in 1798. He achieved this by mounting a small lead sphere at each end of a metal bar suspended at its centre by a wire. He placed two larger lead spheres nearby so that the smaller masses would be attracted towards them. By measuring the tiny angle through which the bar turned, Cavendish was able to calculate the force on the spheres and so work out the value of G. With G known, he could then calculate the mass and density of the Earth for the first time.

CELESTIAL EQUATOR

The great circle which is the projection of the Earth's equator on to the celestial sphere. The celestial equator is used as the reference plane for the equatorial co-ordinates right ascension and declination. Its orientation changes over the years due to precession.

)))▶ *Declination, Precession, Right Ascension*

CELESTIAL SPHERE

An immense imaginary sphere with the Earth at its centre, on which celestial bodies appear to move. The celestial north and south poles lie directly over the Earth's poles and the celestial equator lies directly above the Earth's equator. The ecliptic marks the Sun's apparent yearly path against the background stars. The ecliptic is tilted at 23½° to the celestial equator, the amount by which the Earth's axis is tilted relative to its orbit. The ecliptic cuts the celestial equator at two points called the equinoxes. When the Sun is at these positions, in spring and autumn, day and night are equal in length the world over. The points where the Sun reaches its farthest position north or south of the celestial equator are known as the solstices. It reaches its most northerly point in June, when the northern hemisphere of Earth experiences its longest day and the southern hemisphere its shortest. At the Sun's southerly extreme, in December, the day lengths in the two hemispheres are reversed.

CEPHEIDS

An important category of pulsating stars are the Cepheids, named after their prototype Delta [δ] Cephei. These are yellow supergiants of spectral type F and G which oscillate on anything from a daily to monthly basis. As they do so their visible light changes as much as sixfold (two magnitudes), their temperature by over a thousand degrees and their diameter by about 10 per cent. Cepheids are highly luminous and so can be seen at great distances – even in other galaxies – and as their luminosity is related to their period of oscillation (the brightest ones having the longest periods), this makes them valuable as distance indicators despite their relative scarcity. If a star can be identified as a Cepheid, its absolute magnitude can be determined by measuring its period, and its distance can then be deduced.

)))▶ *Period–Luminosity Relation*

CERNAN, EUGENE (b. 1934)

American astronaut. The second American to walk in space, on flight Gemini 9. During a two-hour space walk, wrestling the umbilical cord and working against an over-stiff pressure suit, Cernan became dangerously overheated and tripled his heart rate to 180 beats per minute. He survived, but his mission had carried out contingency plans for re-entry attempts with a dead crew member abandoned in space. Cernan was also the last man on the moon, on Apollo 17, 1972.

CHALLENGER

The twenty-fifth shuttle flight – STS-51L – rose off the launch pad on 28 January 1986. On board the Shuttle Challenger were commander Dick Scobee, pilot Mike Smith, mission specialists Ellison Onizuka, Judy Resnik and Ron McNair, payload specialist Gregory Jarvis, and the first teacher to go into space, Christa McAuliffe, who was to broadcast live lessons into US schools from orbit.

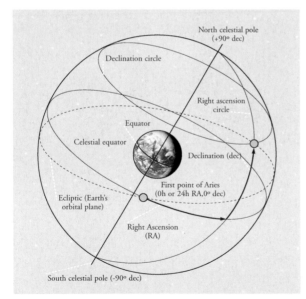

ABOVE: The imaginary celestial sphere is used in astronomical co-ordinate systems. Many principal astronomical reference points result from its concept.

BELOW: Astrophysicist Subrahmanyan Chandrasekhar.
BELOW RIGHT: A CCD camera contains a charge-coupled device, or CCD, an array of tiny electronic light sensors which, when activated, convert light signals into a pattern of electric charges.

It had been a cold night and the rubber joining rings on the solid rocket boosters had been weakened. Fifty-eight seconds into the flight, burning fuel began to leak from the bottom of the right booster. Flames burnt through the strut holding the booster in place and 72 seconds into the flight it crashed into the top of the external fuel tank, rupturing it. Burning fuel enveloped the whole Shuttle, tearing it into pieces. The crew cabin remained intact, continued upwards and then tumbled into the Atlantic Ocean. All seven astronauts were killed.

CHANDRASEKHAR, SUBRAHMANYAN (1910–95)

Indian theoretical astrophysicist. Chandrasekhar graduated in Madras in 1928 and went to Cambridge in 1930 to work on the application to stellar structure of a new theory of gases. He showed that the matter in the interiors of white dwarfs was degenerate and that, provided the mass was less than 1.4 Suns (now known as the Chandrasekhar limit), such a body could cool without further gravitational collapse. He was managing editor of The *Astrophysical Journal* for almost 20 years and recipient of numerous honours, notably a share of the Nobel Prize for physics in 1983.

CHANDRASEKHAR LIMIT

The maximum permitted mass of a white dwarf star if it is to avoid collapsing further to become a neutron star or black hole. The limit (around 1.4 solar masses) depends on the white dwarf's composition and rotation rate. Calculated by Subrahmanyan Chandrasekhar (1910–95).

CHARGE-COUPLED DEVICE (CCD)

When photographing through a telescope, specialized CCD cameras can record extremely faint images that are impossible with conventional film. The cameras use a charge-coupled device, a light-sensitive electronic chip that records an image as an electronic signal. The image is viewed immediately or stored on a computer and it can be enhanced using image-processing software.

Light falls on the CCD's tiny electronic sensors and produces a pattern of electric charges. Each is measured, converted to a number and transmitted consecutively for computer storage. When the computer reads the data, a reproduction of the brightness is displayed. Each sensor is of finite size and makes up one picture element or pixel of an image. A large chip has an array of 1,024 by 1,024 pixels. Many modern CCDs can handle a 13-magnitude difference in brightness. In addition, CCDs respond to light in a linear fashion; if double the light falls on the chip, the object is double in brightness.

CHARON

Only known satellite of the outermost planet, Pluto. Charon was discovered in 1978. The plane of revolution of the Pluto-Charon system is inclined at 99° relative to Pluto's orbit around the Sun, so every 124 years the plane lies along our line of sight, and the two bodies alternately eclipse each other. By good luck, mutual occultations began to occur soon after Charon's discovery, from 1985 to 1991. Observing the variations in the total reflected light during the eclipses gave insights into the two worlds.

Charon is 1,186 km (737 miles) across. The diameter of Pluto is less than twice that of Charon, making the system virtually a double planet. Their centres are separated by only about 1.5 Earth diameters (19,405 km/12,058 miles). Each world keeps the same side facing towards the other: from Pluto, Charon always appears in the same part of the sky.

CHAUCER, GEOFFREY (c. 1343–1400)

English poet. Although his fame rests on his poetry, Chaucer was the first man to write a scientific book in the English language, rather than in Latin. His *Treatise on the Astrolabe* (c. 1391) is a detailed manual for the use of that Arabic astronomical instrument, already commonplace across Europe, and which coordinated astronomy, angle measuring, and time finding. The brass astrolabe was used by calendar calculators, university teachers and students studying astronomy, in the same way that a modern person might use a planisphere or a computer. Chaucer is also believed to be the author of the *Equatorie of the Planets* (c. 1392),

ABOVE: The chromosphere can be glimpsed here in patches of glowing red around the dark edge of the Moon during this solar eclipse.

which describes a brass instrument, the equatorium, used for planetary calculation.

))))▶ *Astrolabe*

CHINESE ASTRONOMY

China's astronomical culture dates back to 2,000 BC or earlier. It was the dominant astronomical culture of Japan and Korea also. Chinese astronomy grew from its own roots, and while wrestling with many of the same problems that astronomers of other traditions confronted – such as reconciling the lunar and solar calendars – it developed independently from the cultures of India and the Middle East. In China, astronomy and politics were intimately connected, as it was an emperor's duty to organize Earthly affairs in conformity with the state of the heavens. This meant that from a very early date official sky-watchers were employed to record the appearances of comets or novae ('new stars'), while the ability to predict eclipses was of paramount importance to political stability. Chinese astronomers recorded a 'guest star' in AD 1054, which we now know to have been the explosion of the supernova whose remains are now visible as the Crab Nebula. The Chinese accurately determined the year to be 365¼ days, and divided the celestial equator into 365¼ degrees. This might be the reason that the Chinese never developed the flexible geometry that would be facilitated by a circle of 360°.

))))▶ *The 360° Circle*

CHONDRULES

Solidified droplets, composed mainly of silicates, found embedded in chondrites, which are a type of stony meteorite.

)))➤ *Meteorites, Classification of*

CHROMOSPHERE

A tenuous red glowing layer of gas, 2,000 km (1,200 miles) thick, lying above the photosphere, the bright white disk of the Sun that we see with the naked eye. The temperature of the Sun's atmosphere is at a minimum low down in the chromosphere, at about 4,100°C (7,400°F). The chromosphere comes into view during a total solar eclipse, glowing red around the dark edge of the Moon as the light of the photosphere is cut off. The red light is emitted by hydrogen ions recombining with electrons.

Above the coolest level the temperature starts to rise again, although the gas density continues to decline. Initially this rise is gradual, but at 2,200 km (1,400 miles) above the surface it increases rapidly through a thin 'transition region' before reaching temperatures of up to 2 million °C (3.6 million °F) in the outermost solar atmosphere, or corona.

When the chromosphere is viewed beyond the limb (the edge of the visible solar disk), its spectrum contains emission lines. When viewed against the bright background of the disk these lines appear dark owing to the absorption in the chromosphere of particular wavelengths of light emitted by the photosphere. Analysis of these lines reveals in detail the composition of the outer layers of the sun.

)))➤ *Fraunhofer Lines, Photosphere, Sun*

CIRCUMPOLAR STARS

A star that remains above the horizon at all times throughout the year. Observers at different latitudes will see different circumpolar stars. For a star to be circumpolar, its polar distance (90° minus its declination) must be less than the observer's latitude.

)))➤ *Declination*

CLARKE, ARTHUR C. (b. 1917)

British science writer and science-fiction author. The first person to propose geostationary communications satellites, Clarke's novels often reveal a realistic appreciation of orbital mechanics.

After working on wartime radar, Clarke published an article in *Wireless World* in 1945 in which he foresaw a global communications network, including worldwide television, linked by relay stations in geosynchronous orbits. This was 12 years before the first satellite was launched, 20 years before the first geosynchronous communications satellite (Early Bird), and more than 40 years before direct broadcast satellites fulfilled his prediction of beaming television straight into people's homes.

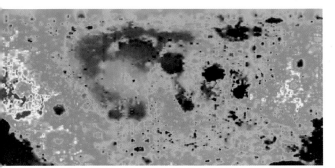

hydrogen nuclei into one helium nucleus with the emission of energy in the form of gamma rays. CNO stands for carbon-nitrogen-oxygen cycle. Nitrogen and oxygen are formed as by-products while carbon is used as a catalyst. Often termed the carbon-nitrogen-oxygen cycle or simply the carbon cycle.

CLEMENTINE

Clementine was built to investigate laser performance in space. The spacecraft reached lunar orbit on 20 February 1994 and spent 10 weeks mapping the whole Moon, recording its mineral composition and topography. An improvised experiment over the south pole, bouncing radio waves into an area of permanent shadow, hinted at the possible existence of water ice. Clementine spun out of control on its way to the asteroid Geographos after leaving the Moon. In July 1994 the craft swung by the Moon again and went into solar orbit.

CLUSTER MISSION

Mid-year 2000, two Russian Soyuz rockets, each carrying a pair of identical satellites were launched into space. The four Cluster spacecraft are part of an inter-national program to find out more information about how the Sun and Earth interact. The spacecraft will spend two years flying in formation, mapping Earth's magnetic field in three dimensions.

CNO CYCLE

A chain of nuclear reactions occurring in main sequence stars slightly more massive than the Sun. The overall effect of the CNO cycle is to fuse four

COALSACK NEBULA

The Coalsack Nebula is a pear-shaped blot of dust about 14 Moon diameters long and 10 Moon diameters wide, whose inky darkness hides a portion of the Milky Way from our view in the southern hemisphere. It lies at a distance of 600 light years.

COATHANGER CLUSTER

Brocchi's Cluster is more popularly known as the Coathanger because of its unmistakable shape – a line of six stars forming the hanger, with four more completing the hook. Lying in the constellation of Vulpecula, it is not a true cluster, but a chance alignment of unrelated stars at different distances from us.

COBE

The Cosmic Background Explorer (COBE) satellite was launched in 1989 to search for small variations in the cosmic background radiation. The results from the satellite confirmed that the spectrum of radiation had the shape of a black-body spectrum at a temperature of 2.725 K with a deviation of just one part in 10,000, but also that there were changes in intensity across the sky.

ABOVE: The moonprobe Clementine assessed the lunar surface at various wavelengths. The purple areas are basins, green indicates areas of average height and red marks the highest features, those over 7,500 m (25,000 ft).

RIGHT: NASA'S Cosmic Background Explorer (COBE) satellite produced a microwavable map of the whole sky, eventually collecting four years of data. Cosmology theory indicates that the density fluctuations observed could ultimately be responsible for the formation of galaxies.

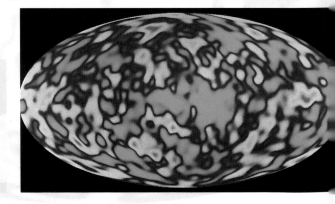

COLOUR INDEX

The difference in apparent magnitude of a star at two standard wavelengths used as a measure of the star's colour and hence temperature. The most commonly used indices are based on the UBV system, where the star is measured through different coloured filters, usually blue and yellow, giving the B-V index (B for blue, V for visual) or sometimes in the ultraviolet giving the U-B index.

))))▶ *Apparant Magnitude*

COMA

1. A defect in a telescope caused when light reaching the telescope at an angle to its axis is spread into a fan-shaped image instead of being focused to a point.
2. The globular cloud of dust and gas that forms around the nucleus of a comet as it approaches the Sun.

COMET SHOEMAKER–LEVY 9

Comet that collided with the giant planet Jupiter in July 1994. Carolyn and Eugene Shoemaker and their colleague David Levy had discovered the comet in 1993. Calculations showed that it had been in orbit around Jupiter for over 60 years and after a close approach in 1992 had broken into a chain of more than 20 fragments described as a 'string of pearls'. These hit the planet over a period of a week in July 1994. Dark spots were created in Jupiter's clouds up to 3,000 km (2,000 miles) across. These spots gradually merged into a dusky belt that took over a year to disperse. If the fragments of Comet Shoemaker-Levy 9 had fallen on Earth they would have blasted out craters 60 km (37 miles) across and caused significant climatic changes.

))))▶ *Near Earth Asteroids*

COMETS

A low-mass member of the Solar System, moving in a highly elliptical orbit and undergoing great changes in appearance as it approaches and then recedes from the Sun. Comets are highly insubstantial. Their only solid part is the nucleus, typically no more than a few kilometres across – a 'dirty snowball' of ice with a dusty crust.

Cometary nuclei spend most of their lives unseen in the outer reaches of their orbits, far from the Sun, but gravitational disturbances may send some of them on highly elliptical orbits towards the inner Solar System. As a comet nucleus approaches the Sun, the dirty snowball warms up and releases gas and dust to form a coma, perhaps 10 times the diameter of Earth, yet so tenuous that it is transparent. Gas and dust stream away from the coma to produce tails that, in extreme cases, could stretch from Earth to the Sun. Comets have two tails, one of dust and one of gas. Gas tails consist of ionized molecules and have a bluish colour; they are almost straight and are carried directly away from the Sun by the charged particles of the solar wind. Dust tails are curved because the dust particles lag behind the comet's motion; they appear yellowish because the particles reflect sunlight. Cometary dust disperses into space where it is eventually swept up by the planets or falls into the Sun. Dust particles from comets produce the bright streaks known as meteors when they burn up in Earth's atmosphere.

))))▶ *Asteroids, Meteorites, Meteors and Meteoroids*

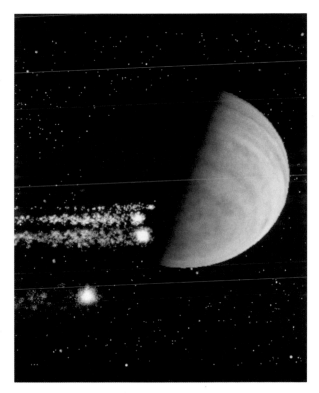

ABOVE: *Some comets, those moving on parabolic or hyperbolic orbits, have enough energy to escape from the Solar System.*

COMETS, CLASSIFICATION OF

Comets are divided into two broad categories, according to their orbital period (time taken to orbit the Sun). Short-period comets, which include the famous Halley's Comet, are defined as those with orbital periods less than 200 years. These come from a region beyond Neptune called the Edgeworth–Kuiper Belt (or sometimes simply the Kuiper Belt).

Long-period comets have orbital periods of thousands or even millions of years, and are thought to originate in a region named the Oort cloud, a hypothetical swarm of cometary nuclei surrounding the Solar System in all directions, roughly halfway to the nearest stars. The gravitational effects of occasional passing stars send some of these dormant comets towards the inner Solar System, where they develop comas and tails.

))))➤ *Comet, Edgeworth–Kuiper Belt, Oort Cloud*

COMMUNICATIONS SATELLITES

The concept of a communications satellite was proposed by Arthur C. Clarke (b. 1917) in 1945. He calculated that a satellite in orbit 35,880 km (22,295 miles) above the Equator would circle the globe in one day, appearing to hover over a point on Earth. With just three satellites in this geostationary orbit signals could be

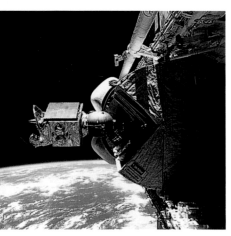

bounced to almost any point on the planet.

The first communication attempts were, however, conducted from a lower Earth orbit. In 1958 a US satellite called SCORE transmitted a tape-recorded Christmas message from President Eisenhower. Communication experiments continued with Telstar, in 1962. Although not in geostationary orbit, it transmitted live TV pictures and sound across the Atlantic.

))))➤ *Clarke, Arthur C.*

COMPTON GAMMA RAY OBSERVATORY

The Compton Gamma Ray Observatory (GRO) was launched in 1991 and re-entered Earth's atmosphere in 2000. GRO had four independent telescopes. The Burst and Transient Source Experiment (BATSE) monitored the whole sky for short bursts of gamma rays with energies between 50 keV and 600 keV. The Oriented Scintillation Spectrometer Experiment (OSSE) looked for the gamma-ray spectral lines expected from radioactive decay and electron-positron annihilation. The Imaging Compton Telescope (COMPTEL) surveyed the sky at gamma-ray energies from 1 MeV to 30 MeV, while the Energetic Gamma Ray Experiment Telescope (EGRET) was a spark-chamber detector sensitive to gamma rays from 20 MeV to 30 GeV.

CONJUNCTION

The alignment of two celestial objects (for example, of two planets or of a planet and the Sun) as seen from Earth. An inner planet – Mercury or Venus – is at 'inferior' conjunction when it lies between Earth and the Sun, and at 'superior' conjunction when it lies on

ABOVE: The Compton Gamma Ray Observatory, launched from the Space Shuttle Atlantis in 1991, increased the known number of gamma-ray sources tenfold before burning up in the Earth's atmosphere nine years later.
LEFT: A communications satellite is launched from the cargo bay of the Space Shuttle.

the opposite side of the Sun. An outer planet cannot pass between the Earth and the Sun. Therefore, when an outer planet is at conjunction it must lie on the far side of the Sun (superior conjunction).

CONSTELLATIONS

The sky is divided into 88 sections known as constellations, a combination of the 48 figures known to the ancient Greeks and others introduced more recently. Their names and boundaries were officially laid down by the International Astronomical Union in 1930. Constellations originated in the distant past as easy-to-remember patterns of stars, but nowadays astronomers regard them merely as areas of sky convenient for locating and naming celestial objects. The areas are bounded by arcs of right ascension and declination (epoch 1875). The patterns on which constellations were originally based are purely the product of human imagination – with very few exceptions, the stars in a constellation are unrelated and lie at widely differing distances from us.

CONTINENTAL DRIFT

The slow movement of the continents over the surface of Earth. The process of plate tectonics is responsible for continental drift. The decisive evidence for continental drift comes from magnetic studies of ancient rocks. When rocks are formed, iron-rich minerals in them become magnetized in the direction of the Earth's magnetic field. Once the rocks have formed, the direction of the magnetic field is frozen into them. Thus the rocks carry an indication of their position and orientation of the Earth's magnetic field at that time. Since Earth's magnetic field also reverses periodically, the time of a rock's formation can be revealed by its magnetism.

Putting together rock-magnetism studies from all over the globe reveals the motions of the continents. They show that land-masses that exist today once formed two large continents: Gondwanaland in the southern hemisphere, and Laurasia in the northern. Before this these two formed a single mass, named Pangaea.

))))➡ *Plate Tectonics*

CONTINUOUS SPECTRUM

Emitted by a hot, opaque object like a star. It looks like a smooth band of colours.

))))➡ *Spectrum*

COPERNICUS, NICOLAUS (1473–1543)

Polish astronomer. Nikolaj Koppernigk, latinized to Copernicus, was born into a prominent Polish family in 1473. Nicolaus's education was supervised by his powerful uncle, Lucas Waczenrode, Bishop of Ermeland, who no doubt recognized his nephew's abilities and saw their future use to Poland. Nicolaus was first sent to the University of Cracow in 1491, where he received a Latin training in classical literature, law and theology, and then, in 1496, to Italy. He studied in Italy until 1503, gaining doctorates in law and medicine, and acquiring skills that would be important to his perceived administrative career back in Poland. He also became fascinated with the new Greek learning of the Renaissance humanists, acquiring the familiarity with Greek astronomy and its problems that would one day make him famous.

Through his uncle's influence, Copernicus obtained the canonry of Frauenberg Cathedral, which gave him a comfortable income for life. Here, amidst his public and ecclesiastical duties, Copernicus was to spend the next 40 years of his life. And it was at Frauenberg Cathedral that he would study the pre-Ptolemaic Greek astronomers, make some observations, and quietly develop his extremely influential heliocentric theory.

ABOVE: Nicolaus Copernicus was the first to suggest a heliocentric model of the Universe, as opposed to the long-established and accepted geocentric model.

CORIOLIS EFFECT

An effect that influences the motion of objects on a rotating body such as Earth. Objects moving in the northern hemisphere are deflected to the right, while those moving in the southern hemisphere are deflected to the left. The Coriolis effect strongly influences the circulation of oceanic and atmospheric currents.

CORONA

A very tenuous outer layer in the atmosphere of the Sun and similar stars. Coronae are observed to reach incredibly high temperatures; the source of heating is not fully understood but processes that convert magnetic energy into thermal (heat) energy are believed to play a major role. The Sun's corona has a temperature of the order of a million degrees and can be seen at totality during a solar eclipse. Its high-temperature plasma emits extreme ultraviolet and X-radiation.

CORONAE (VENUSIAN)

Coronae (Latin: 'crowns') are circular volcanic structures, typically hundreds of kilometres across, with collapsed centres. Each corona marks a 'blister' on the crust where hot molten rock has welled up from below. Coronae, along with the hundreds of large volcanoes, are thought to have been important in allowing the planet's internal heat to escape.

CORONAGRAPH

An instrument used to observe the corona of the Sun, at other times than a total solar eclipse, by blocking out the photospheric light of the Sun with an occulting disk.

)))➤ *Corona*

CORONAL MASS EJECTION

Ejection of solar matter consisting of hot, electrically charged particles. In a coronal mass ejection, perhaps 10 billion tonnes of hot plasma are ejected into interplanetary space, pulling part of the coronal magnetic field with it. The cause of such ejections is still uncertain. Earth is not isolated from these violent events – the storms of energetic particles shot out by the Sun often wash across the near-Earth environment, affecting power lines and

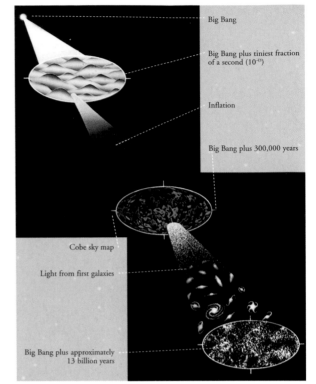

Big Bang

Big Bang plus tiniest fraction of a second (10^{-43})

Inflation

Big Bang plus 300,000 years

Cobe sky map

Light from first galaxies

Big Bang plus approximately 13 billion years

communications, generating auroral displays in the ionosphere around the north and south magnetic poles and damaging sensitive equipment on spacecraft.

)))➤ *Aurora, Corona*

COSMIC BACKGROUND RADIATION

The discovery in 1965 of the cosmic background radiation was an accident. Arno Penzias and Robert Wilson were working at the Bell Telephone Laboratories in New Jersey on the development of receivers for communication satellites. Investigating the problem of radio noise, they had found that the sky was unexpectedly bright at a wavelength of 7.3 cm (2.9 in), in the microwave region of the radio spectrum. They concluded that the noise from all over the sky corresponded to the glow of a black body at a temperature of about 3 K.

ABOVE: An artist's concept depicting crucial periods in the development of the Universe, from a tiny fraction of a second after the Big Bang up to the Universe as we see it today. The cosmic background radiation reveals the state of the Universe, 300,000 years after the Big Bang.

A few miles away at Princeton University, Robert Dicke and Jim Peebles had realized that radiation from the hot gas that filled the Universe in the first moments after the Big Bang should still be visible, but redshifted by the Hubble expansion from visible light to very weak radio waves. It would have a black-body spectrum at about 10 K. They had begun an independent search for this 'remnant' radiation in the microwave part of the radio spectrum when they heard of the discovery of Penzias and Wilson. Neither group knew that the radiation they had found had been predicted 20 years earlier by George Gamow.

The initial measurements of Penzias and Wilson indicated that the cosmic background radiation was isotropic – uniform across the whole sky. This implied that the radiation originated before galaxies had had time to form, in a Universe consisting only of a primordial gas of uniform density. However, theories of the origin of the Universe required that the density of the primordial gas could not be completely uniform. In order to form clusters of galaxies, small variations in density must have existed, and these would show up as very small variations in the brightness of the radiation. COBE confirmed the existence of changes in intensity across the sky. Although tiny, corresponding to differences of just a few parts in 100,000, the changes are consistent with the expected density differences within the primordial gas.

The cosmic background radiation is regarded as confirmation that the Universe did begin in a hot Big Bang.

⟫⟫ *Big Bang, Hubble's Law*

COSMIC RAYS

Cosmic rays are highly energetic charged particles that constantly bombard the Earth from space. Their energies range from 10^8 to 10^{19} eV. The majority are protons (hydrogen nuclei) and most of the remainder are alpha particles (helium nuclei), with a few per cent being electrons. These primary cosmic rays collide with molecules in the atmosphere to produce large numbers of other particles (secondary cosmic rays) which in turn decay to produce an extensive air shower covering several square kilometres of the Earth. A single energetic primary particle can produce up to half a million secondary particles.

Although cosmic rays were discovered almost 100 years ago, there is still no firm agreement on where they originate. They come equally from all directions and there are no obvious sources of cosmic rays because, being charged particles, the paths of the rays are bent by the magnetic fields of interstellar space and any trace of their original direction of motion has been lost. Cosmic rays can survive only a few million years before escaping from the Galaxy, so they must be regularly replenished. Some of the very low-energy cosmic rays are emitted by the Sun and it is possible that other lower-energy rays are emitted in supernova explosions, but as yet the origin of the higher-energy rays remains a mystery. They may even come from outside the Galaxy.

⟫⟫ *Electron, Proton, Supernovae*

COSMOLOGICAL CONSTANT

In order to overcome the problem of unstable static models of the Universe, Einstein introduced an extra term into his equations. He called it the cosmological constant. In essence the constant allowed for the existence of a very weak repulsive force, detectable only on the very large scales associated with cosmology, which would balance gravity and so allow a static Universe. Hubble's subsequent discovery of the recession of the galaxies removed the need for a static Universe and Einstein retracted his proposal for a cosmological constant. However some recent observations suggest the expansion of the Universe is accelerating and such an acceleration requires a repulsive force.

⟫⟫ *BOOMERanG*

COSMOLOGICAL PRINCIPLE

The view that there is nothing special about Earth, or the Sun, or even our own Galaxy has become enshrined in what is termed the 'cosmological principle'. This principle states that on the large scale the Universe is isotropic (it looks the same in all directions) and homogenous (it looks the same from all points). It follows directly from the principle of homogeneity that the Universe can have no edge. Despite the fact that the principle cannot, as yet, be justified by observation it has nevertheless played an important role in theoretical cosmology, as any cosmological model which does not conform to the principle is considered unsatisfactory.

))))▶ *Steady State Theory*

COSMOS SATELLITES

Cosmos was the name given to the series of Russian satellites that followed the early Sputniks. The first Cosmos was launched on 16 March 1962, followed by two more over the next two weeks. Since then, some 2,500 Cosmos satellites have been launched, conducting everything from military reconnaissance, space weapons research and communications to astronomy, Earth observations and biological research. The name has also been used as a cover for flights in other series that failed.

CRAB NEBULA

The Crab Nebula, M1, lies in Taurus about 6,500 light years away and is the wreckage of a supernova explosion that astronomers on Earth saw in 1054. The nineteenth-century Irish astronomer Lord Rosse (1800–67) thought it resembled a crab's claw. It can be

seen in small to moderate-sized telescopes, appearing as a faint, elongated smudge, with none of the bright filaments that are brought out on long-exposure photographs. The pulsar at its centre is far too faint to see through amateur telescopes.

CRATER

Scar left when a projectile slams into a solid surface at speeds of many tens of kilometres per second. The impact causes a violent shock wave, creating a pressure millions of times greater than that of the Earth's atmosphere. The projectile either melts or vaporizes. A crater starts to form when rapid decompression of the surface rocks occurs after the initial impact. The decompression 'frees' the recently struck compressed surface, allowing a cone of rebounding debris to be flung outwards from the impact site, forming an ejecta blanket. Very little, if any, of the projectile remains. The shape and size of a crater varies depending on the size and speed of the impactor, what it is made of (for example, ice, rock, or iron) and the type of surface it strikes (hard or soft). Icy comets are less dense than an iron asteroid and, all things being equal, inflict less damage on a planetary surface.

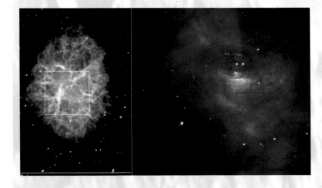

ABOVE: Craters such as this, which is known as Ptolemaeus, are a defining feature of the lunar surface. They are formed by the numerous impacts of other bodies on the Moon over billions of years.
LEFT: The Crab Nebula, M1 (left), the remains of a supernova explosion. At its heart is a pulsar (right), whose energy illuminates the entire nebula.

CYGNUS

Cygnus the swan contains a feast of interesting sights. Double stars include Albireo, Beta [β] Cygni, and Omicron-1 (o¹) Cygni. Chi [χ] Cygni is a pulsating red giant. Open star clusters include M29 and M39. Planetary nebulae include the Veil nebula and NGC 6826 (the Blinking Planetary). Other interesting objects include Deneb, the North American Nebula, Cygnus X-1 and Delta [δ] Cephei.

)))) *Double Stars, Open Clusters, Planetary Nebula*

CYGNUS X-1

One of the first cosmic sources of X-rays was discovered in 1964 in the constellation Cygnus. Observations of the spectrum of the X-rays from Cyg X-1 showed that they were probably produced from gas at an extremely high temperature, while later observations revealed variations in brightness on timescales down to a few thousandths of a second. Such rapid fluctuations

imply a very compact source, and the very high temperature implies the existence of an accretion disk. Cyg X-1 was therefore an extremely good candidate for a binary system

consisting of a 'normal' star paired with a neutron star or black hole. Although the compact source was invisible at optical wavelengths, astronomers were able to successfully identify the companion star: it was a hot, blue supergiant of spectral type O, of 9th magnitude as seen from Earth. The orbital period of the binary, revealed by the Doppler shift in the spectrum of the visible star, is 5.6 days. Analysis of the system shows that the compact object has a mass of more than eight times that of the Sun, too

ABOVE: Cygnus X-1, a strong X-ray source in the constellation Cygnus, was the first object recognized to contain a black hole.

great to be a neutron star and hence a strong candidate for a black hole.

)))) *Accretion Disk, Black Holes*

DARK HALO

The most massive – and most mysterious – component of our Galaxy is the dark halo. The Galaxy's overall mass is dominated by this surrounding halo of dark matter which probably extends out to more than 500,000 light years. The mass of this halo is 10 times greater than the mass in visible stars yet its composition remains a mystery. Possible components of the dark-matter halo include weakly interacting particles (WIMPS), relics of the Big Bang. Experiments searching for these elusive particles have not yet yielded clear results. Another possibility is that the dark halo is composed of dim stars, in particular white dwarfs, whose presence can be detected from the small-scale gravitational lensing effect they have on the light from background stars. Observations suggest that perhaps a quarter of the dark halo of our Galaxy is accounted for by faint, low-mass stars. Black holes are another possible component.

DARK MATTER

Most of the mass of the Universe seems to be in the form of invisible material known as dark matter. Studies of the rotation rate of galaxies show that most of a galaxy's mass lies in a halo perhaps 10 times the diameter of the visible galaxy, and although there are some stars in the halo they cannot account for all the mass, while observations of clusters of galaxies show that the galaxies are moving much faster than one would expect from the total mass of the visible galaxies. Some of the dark matter may be gas, dust and remains of burned-out stars, but there is not enough to account for the dark matter. Current estimates of the amount of dark matter in the Universe range from 10 times the amount of visible matter to as much as 300. There is also a strong theoretical reason why most of the dark matter cannot be made of ordinary baryonic matter: the present abundance of deuterium places strict limits on the density of matter in the early Universe and hence on the density today. There is too much dark matter for it to be baryonic.

)))) *Neutrinos, WIMPs*

DE REVOLUTIONIBUS

Abbreviated title of the epoch-making book *De Revolutionibus Orbium Coelestium* (*On the Revolutions of the Celestial Spheres*), published by a Polish churchman, Nicolaus Copernicus (1473–1543). It argued that a heliocentric (Sun-centred) system explained planetary motion more simply than the prevailing geocentric (Earth-centred) one. Nevertheless, like the ancients, Copernicus employed circular motions and a system of epicycles to reproduce the observed motions of the planets, Sun and Moon. He delayed publication of *De Revolutionibus* until the year of his death, fearing academic ridicule. The suggestion that the Earth was hurtling through space affronted common sense and the physics of Aristotle, which dominated the universities.

))》 *Epicycle, Heliocentric System, Ptolemaic System, Tychonic system*

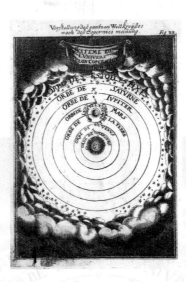

DECLINATION

One of the co-ordinates used in the equatorial co-ordinate system, the other being right ascension. The declination (symbol δ) of an object is its angular distance north or south of the celestial equator. Thus declination runs from 0° to 90° and is positive if north of the celestial equator, negative if southwards.

))》 *Celestial Equator, Right Ascension*

DEIMOS

The smaller of the two satellites of Mars. Deimos is potato-shaped and measures 15 x 12 x 10 km (9 x 7 x 6 miles). Like the other Martian moon, Phobos, Deimos almost certainly originated in the main asteroid belt, between Mars and Jupiter. In the distant past, Phobos and Deimos strayed too close to the red planet and fell under its gravitational influence, becoming satellites of Mars. Deimos has a dark grey, dusty surface covered with impact craters. It revolves around Mars in

1.262 days and rotates on its axis in the same time, so that one face is always towards Mars.

))》 *Mars, Phobos*

DELTA CEPHEI

Delta [δ] Cephei is the prototype of a class of regularly pulsating stars whose periodicity is directly linked to their inherent brightness, a valuable characteristic that allows them to function as standard candles for measuring distances. Delta Cephei varies every five days nine hours between magnitudes 3.5 and 4.4, easily visible to the naked eye. Binoculars and small telescopes show that this yellow supergiant is also an attractive double, with a bluish companion star.

))》 *Cepheids*

DELTA SCUTI STARS

Delta Scuti stars oscillate with periods of a few hours or even less, changing in brightness by only a few per cent, and are undetectable except with sensitive instruments. On the Hertzsprung-Russell diagram they lie at the bottom of the instability strip, joining it to the main sequence.

))》 *Hertzsprung–Russell Diagram*

DENEB

Deneb lies in the constellation of Cygnus and is a highly luminous supergiant, as bright as 250,000 Suns, and the most distant of the 1st-magnitude stars at over 3,000 light years from Earth. Its apparent magnitude is 1.25.

DENSITY WAVES

 A compressional wave moving through matter causing fluctuations in density. The density wave

ABOVE: Copernicus's seminal work De Revolutionibus *presented his heliocentric solar system, which correctly envisaged Earth and all the other planets revolving around the Sun.*

theory suggests that a density wave moving through material in a spiral galaxy causes bursts of star formation producing the spiral structure observed. Stars are slowed and are brought nearer together as they pass through the spiral arms, creating the enhanced density; interstellar gas is compressed by the density wave, leading to the formation of bright, young stars that light up the spiral arms, making them visually prominent. Although this theory elegantly explains spiral structure in galaxies, how a density wave is created in the first place and how long it persists remain unsolved issues.

))⟩⟩➤ *Spiral Galaxies*

DESCARTES, RENÉ (1596–1650)

French physicist. Descartes developed what became known as the Mechanical Philosophy, a comprehensive system of physics which argued that all movement was a product of impacts from corpuscles, or tiny physical bodies. Corpuscles of different size were the basis of everything, and space was filled with the smallest of these. Swirling 'vorticles' in this universe of corpuscles could move the planets and comets or transmit light, in accordance with exact mathematical laws. The drawback with Descartes' physics was its highly speculative character, as 'thought experiments' ultimately predominated over actual experiments.

DIFFERENTIAL ROTATION

The rotation of a non-solid body in which different regions rotate at different speeds. Differential rotation is observed in stars and the giant planets, which rotate in shorter periods of time at the equator than at the poles. Systems composed of many individual bodies – such as a galaxy, which is made up stars, as well as gas and dust – also exhibit differential rotation.

DINOSAURS, DEATH OF

Sixty-five million years ago the majority of existing species, including the dinosaurs, died out remarkably suddenly – over a few million years. This event occurred at the K/T boundary, the transition from the Cretaceous Period to the Tertiary Period. In 1978 Luis and Walter Alvarez discovered a thin layer of brown clay, rich in the element iridium, at the K/T boundary. Iridium is rare on Earth's surface but more abundant in the interior and in asteroids and comets. Probably there was both a huge volcanic eruption and a major impact of an extraterrestrial body, temporarily altering Earth's climate. This could have hastened the demise of the dinosaurs, which had probably already started to die out.

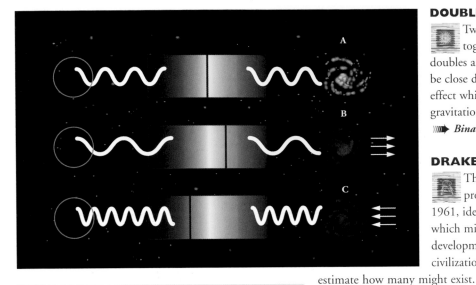

ABOVE: *The Doppler effect changes the wavelengths of light from stars and galaxies in motion. Galaxy A is at a constant distance from Earth so the Doppler effect does not occur. Galaxy B is receding from Earth and the wavelengths of light from it are 'stretched', shifting them towards the red end of the spectrum ('redshifted'). Galaxy C is approaching Earth and the light is squeezed to shorter wavelengths ('blueshifted').*

DOPPLER EFFECT

The Doppler effect applies to any kind of wave motion and occurs whenever the observer is moving with respect to the source of the waves. There is a change in frequency of electromagnetic radiation that arises as a result of the relative motion between the source of radiation and the observer. When the source moves away from the observer the frequency is decreased (and the wavelength correspondingly increased) and any spectral lines produced by that source will be redshifted relative to the corresponding lines from a stationary source. Conversely, the observed frequency is increased (and the wavelength decreased, or 'blue-shifted') when the source is approaching the observer. For speeds that are small compared with the speed of light, the amount of change (the Doppler shift) of an electromagnetic wave is given by:

$$\lambda_1 = \lambda_0 \left(1 + \frac{v}{c}\right)$$

where λ_1 is the emitted wavelength, λ_0 is the observed wavelength, v is the relative speed of the source away from the observer, and c is the speed of light.

DOUBLE STARS

Two stars that appear close together in the sky. Optical doubles are stars that appear to be close due to the line-of-sight effect while physical doubles are gravitationally bound.

))))▶ *Binary Stars*

DRAKE EQUATION

The Drake Equation, proposed by Frank Drake in 1961, identifies specific factors which might influence the development of technological civilizations and allows us to estimate how many might exist.

$$N = R^* \times f_p \times n_e \times f_i \times f_i \times f_c \times L$$

N = Number of communicative civilizations in the Milky Way whose radio emissions are detectable.

R^* = Rate of formation of stars with a large enough 'habitable zone' and a lifetime suitable for the development of intelligent life.

f_p = Fraction of sun-like stars with planets; this is currently unknown, but seems to grow with discoveries made.

n_e = Number of planets in the stars habitability zone for each planetary system.

f_i = Fraction of planets in the habitability zone where life develops.

f_i = Fraction of life-bearing planets where intelligence develops. Life on Earth began over 3.5 billion years ago. Intelligence took a long time to develop. On other life-bearing planets it may happen faster, take longer, or not develop at all.

ABOVE: *The yellow and blue components of the double star Albireo.*

f_c = Fraction of planets where technology develops, releasing detectable signs of existence.

L = Length of time such civilizations release detectable signals into space. The number of detectable civilizations depends strongly on L. If L is large, so is the number of signals we might detect.

DREYER, JOHN (1852–1926)

Danish-born astronomer. Dreyer worked as an assistant at the observatory of Lord Rosse in Ireland, where he observed faint nebulae and star clusters with Rosse's huge telescope, and then at the Armagh Observatory, where he was director from 1882 to 1916. At Armagh, Dreyer continued his interest in what are now termed deep-sky objects, publishing in 1888 the *New General Catalogue of Nebulae and Clusters of Stars* (popularly known as the NGC), a revision and expansion of a catalogue published earlier by John Herschel which contained 7,840 objects. In 1895 and 1908 Dreyer published two supplements, called the *Index Catalogues*, which added over 5,000 newly discovered objects.

DUMB-BELL NEBULA

M27, the Dumb-bell Nebula, one of the closest planetary nebulae to us, lies in the constellation of Vulpecula, some 1,000 light years away. Being relatively close it also appears quite large, about one-quarter the diameter of the full Moon, but this makes it more difficult to see since its light is spread over a greater area. Its shape supposedly resembles a body-builder's dumbbell – although a better comparison would be a figure eight or an hourglass.

DWARF SPHEROIDAL GALAXIES

Dwarf spheroidals are the most common galaxies in the universe – half the members of the Local Group belong to this type – but, being small and faint, they are not easy to see. A typical dwarf spheroidal has a diameter of a few thousand light years and a mass of a few million

RIGHT: A fantastically sculptured column of gas in the Eagle nebula, illuminated by hot young stars off the top of the picture. Finger-like protrusions contain denser knots of gas where stars are forming.

suns. The first examples were not discovered until after Hubble had drawn up his classification scheme, so they do not fit on to the tuning fork diagram. They are similar in shape to ellipticals but are much less centrally condensed – in fact, they appear as little more than a loose scattering of stars. Dwarf spheroidals contain little or no gas or dust so there is no present-day star formation.

⫸ *Elliptical Galaxies, Local Group*

DYNAMO MODEL

A long-standing theory of how a planet generates a magnetic field. According to the model, the planet has a fluid core that rotates differentially, with the interior spinning fastest. Any slight magnetic field that arises in this fluid will be coiled up by rotation and convection, and will be strengthened.

For Earth and most of the outer planets, this dynamo model works adequately. But Mercury, with a slow spin rate and inactive interior, should have almost no magnetic field. Yet it does have one, although weak. Venus has a slow rotation rate but a fluid core and should have a weak magnetic field, yet none has been detected.

EAGLE NEBULA (M16)

M16, the Eagle Nebula, lies in Serpens Cauda. On long-exposure photographs its full magnificence becomes apparent: it spreads wings of nebulosity that give rise to the popular name. Images obtained by the Hubble Space Telescope have shown stars that are forming from the dust-laden gas in this nebula.

EARTH

Largest of the terrestrial (rocky) planets, lying third from the Sun. Earth is a dynamic planet, with active volcanoes and areas of mountain-building. Beneath the thin crust lies the rocky mantle and an iron core. Earth's location in the inner Solar System means it has the ideal temperature for large oceans of liquid water to exist. These cover two-thirds of its surface, and a moist atmosphere supports its delicate ecosystems. It is the only place in the Solar System where life is known to exist.

Interior and Surface

By studying shock waves (seismic waves) from earthquakes, scientists can create a picture of the interior of our planet. Recording the velocities of earthquake waves, and noting positions where their velocity changes, has revealed distinct layers and boundaries in Earth's interior.

Earth's core can be divided into two parts: a solid inner core of iron and an outer core of molten iron. The radius of the entire core is about 3,500 km (2,200 miles). Above the core sits the mantle, 2,900 km (1,800 miles) thick, and consisting of iron- and magnesium-containing rocks. The mantle is not completely fluid; it acts more like putty, in that it can easily be deformed if a pressure is applied.

On top of the mantle is the crust, made of less dense granitic and basaltic rocks. The crust is divided into rigid plates that ride on the mantle. The thickness of the crust varies from about 15 km (9 miles) under the oceans to as much as 40 km (25 miles) under the continents. The overall structure of the Earth was determined early in its history. When the planet was still molten, the least dense materials rose to the surface, forming the crust, while the densest materials sank towards the centre, forming its core.

Earth's Atmosphere

Life on Earth would not be possible without the blanket of air that provides warmth, protection and the oxygen we need to breathe. The atmosphere consists of 77 per cent nitrogen, 21 per cent oxygen, and 2 per cent other gases, including water vapour. Air pressure and density decrease with height. Very high up, the atmosphere becomes so rarefied that gas particles collide less often and are able to escape into space.

The atmosphere has several distinct layers. From Earth's surface to a height of approximately 12 km (7 miles) is the troposphere, which comprises 75 per cent of atmospheric gas. Weather occurs here and the temperature drops with increasing altitude. The stratosphere continues to 50 km (31 miles) and contains the ozone layer, which absorbs most of the harmful ultraviolet radiation from the Sun. The

ABOVE: *The enchanting sight of Earth from space.*
BELOW: *Earth's atmospheric layers. The temperature of Earth's atmosphere varies greatly with increasing altitude. These changes are shown by the curved orange line as it passes through the principal layers of the atmosphere.*

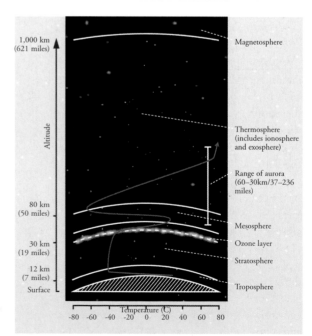

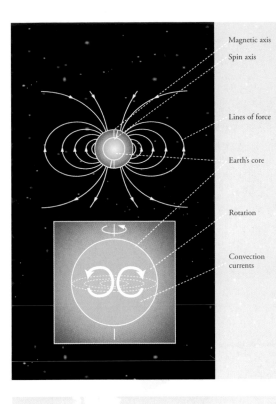

Magnetic axis

Spin axis

Lines of force

Earth's core

Rotation

Convection currents

ABOVE: Earth's rotation combines with convection currents to drive fluid motions in the molton core. These motions generate the Earth's magnetic field, whose lines of force extend beyond the surface out into space. The magnetic axis is tilted around 12° from the spin axis of the planet.

mesosphere, from 50 to 80 km (31 to 50 miles), is the coldest layer. Up to about 1,000 km (600 miles) is the thermosphere. This layer includes both the ionosphere, which reflects radio waves, and the exosphere. Beyond this lies the magnetosphere, a magnetic bubble around the Earth that traps solar particles.

Atmospheric Circulation

Earth's rotation and heat from sunlight combine forces to affect atmospheric circulation. Through the process of convection, heated air rises while cooler, denser air sinks to replace it. Locally, convection in the atmosphere produces fluffy cumulus clouds and stormy thunderheads. On a global scale, the sunlight that falls nearly vertically on equatorial regions creates hot air, while farther north and south the air is heated less strongly by the slanting

sunlight and so is colder and denser. Consequently an atmospheric flow between the equator and the poles is generated.

Oceans, Climate and Weather

Earth's oceans may be thought of as huge storage heaters, which regulate Earth's climate and day-to-day weather. Because the sea takes time to warm up and cool off, it has a warming effect during the winter, and a cooling effect during the summer. Large continental landmasses experience a greater diversity of temperatures than a small landmass surrounded by the sea.

Blue Skies, Red Sunsets

Sunlight entering Earth's atmosphere is scattered by air molecules. Since the shorter-wavelength blue light is scattered more than the longer-wavelength red light, the sky appears blue. At sunset and sunrise, when the Sun is near the horizon, the light from the Sun must pass through more atmosphere. In doing so, blue light undergoes far more scattering, so that less reaches the ground. However, red light is relatively unaffected and this results in crimson sunsets and sunrises.

Earth's Magnetic Field

Earth's magnetic field can be compared to that of an immense bar magnet. The north and south magnetic poles lie deep within the Earth, 12° askew from the corresponding north and south spin axes. Magnetic field lines, or lines of force, flow out from the south magnetic pole and loop inwards at the north magnetic pole. The field is thought to arise by from currents in the fluid outer core. The field exerts a force on any electrically charged particle moving through it. Particles are redirected from their original paths and spiral along the field lines. The region of space occupied by the Earth's magnetic field is called the magnetosphere.

Measurements in rock show that Earth's poles have swapped round 171 times in the last 71 million years. During a reversal, the magnetic field's strength drops to zero.

))))▶ *Aurora, Continental Drift, Coriolis Effect, Dynamo Model, Greenhouse Effect, Magnetosphere, Ozone Layer, Tectonics, Van Allen Belts*

EARTH, AGE OF

Measurements from the radioactive decay of elements put the formation of the oldest rocks on Earth at just under four billion years ago. The dates have been obtained from metamorphic rocks, those formed by the baking of precursor rocks under very high temperatures and pressures, deep within Earth. From the dating of other Solar System material, such as meteorites and the Moon, the modern consensus is that the Solar System as a whole formed about 4.55 billion years ago. Earth is likely to have started forming at this time as well. Current theories suggest that it continued to grow through the bombardment of planetesimals for some 120 to 150 million years. At that time, 4.44 to 4.41 billion years ago, Earth's atmosphere began to develop and its core began to form. The rocks that formed at this stage are likely to be those that were later baked to form the oldest metamorphic rocks known today.

EARTH ORBIT

Satellites following paths round our planet are in Earth orbit. A spacecraft is accelerated to an appropriate speed and height to reach Earth orbit. This requires sufficient energy to lift it against Earth's gravitational pull and accelerate it to orbital speed. A typical low Earth orbit is around 200 km (120 miles), which corresponds to a speed of 7.8 km/s (4.8 mi/sec) and an orbital period of about 88 minutes. A greater expenditure of energy is required to reach a higher orbit. A launch rocket's engines shut down at the correct height and speed for the intended orbit. The satellite is placed in a circular orbit, or by higher speed into an elliptical orbit.

ECCENTRICITY

The mathematical measure of the extent to which an orbit differs from a circle. A circle has eccentricity 0, while a parabola has eccentricity 1. The most strongly elliptical planetary orbit, that of Pluto, has eccentricity 0.25.

ECLIPSE, ANNULAR

A solar eclipse in which the Sun's apparent disk in the sky is larger than the Moon's. In such an eclipse, a ring (Latin: annulus) of photosphere is visible around the

ABOVE: A total lunar eclipse can occur only when the Moon is full and Earth is lying directly between the Moon and the Sun.

Moon. The bright light of this annulus drowns out the faint light of the corona. An annular eclipse occurs when the Moon is near apogee, the farthest point from the Earth in its elliptical orbit.

ECLIPSE, LUNAR

A lunar eclipse occurs when the Moon passes into the shadow of Earth. This can happen only at full Moon. However, a lunar eclipse does not occur every time the Moon is full, because the Moon does not orbit in the plane of the ecliptic, the Sun's apparent path in the sky; it dips above and below it by about five degrees. So the two conditions of full phase and the Moon crossing the ecliptic must be met before a lunar eclipse can occur.

Lunar eclipses are visible from any place at which the Moon is above the horizon. Because Earth is much larger than the Moon, it can take up to three hours or more for the Moon to pass all the way through Earth's shadow. First the Moon enters the penumbra of Earth's shadow, the less intense outer region, which begins to dim the lunar surface. The Moon then passes into the darker umbra. If the Moon is totally immersed in the umbra, a total eclipse is seen. At this point the Moon often appears to glow orange-red. This is due to light passing through Earth's atmosphere and bending towards the Moon. The duration of totality can be up to as much as 1 hour 44 minutes.

)))➤ *Eclipse, Solar; Phases of the Moon*

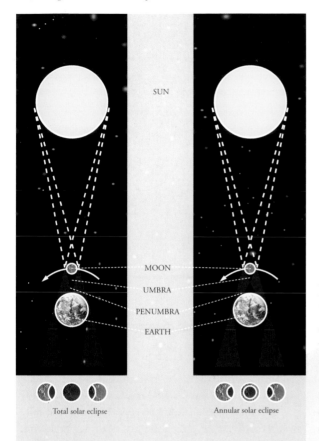

Total solar eclipse

Annular solar eclipse

SUN

MOON

UMBRA

PENUMBRA

EARTH

ECLIPSE, SOLAR

Blocking of the Sun's light by the Moon. The eclipse may be partial, when even at the height of the eclipse a crescent of the Sun remains visible; annular, when the Sun can be seen as a thin ring around the edge of the dark Moon; or total, when the Moon completely blocks out the Sun.

The eclipse begins when the Moon first touches the Sun's western limb (edge). Progressively, the Moon

ABOVE: A total solar eclipse can only be viewed within the area covered by the umbra. An annular solar eclipse occurs when the Moon is near its apogee and its shadow cone does not reach Earth's surface.

covers the Sun and the light level dims until the eastern edge of the Moon touches the Sun's eastern limb.

In a total eclipse, when the last bit of the photosphere (the bright disk of the Sun) is visible, it shines out like a diamond ring. Small sections of the photosphere may still shine through gaps in the mountains at the lunar limb, an effect known as Baily's beads.

Once the photosphere has been completely cut off, there is a brief opportunity to see the chromosphere, or inner atmosphere of the Sun, glowing red around the edge of the Moon. Then only the ghostly white corona can be seen streaming out into space. After only a few minutes the Moon begins to uncover the Sun, and the reverse process begins.

)))➤ *Eclipse, Annular; Eclipse, Lunar; Phases of the Moon*

ECLIPSING BINARIES

The orbits of some spectroscopic binaries are orientated side-on to us, so that one star periodically passes in front of the other, causing an eclipse and reducing the total light we receive from the binary for a while. Such a system is termed an eclipsing binary. A light curve (a graph of brightness versus time) can be plotted of the brightness variations caused by the eclipses which gives valuable information about the binary, including the shape of the stars, for it turns out that they are not always spherical: when the components are close together, they can deform each other into egg shapes which leads to additional variability as the observer sees the star either side-on or end-on. In the closest pairings the stars seem to be touching: these are termed contact binaries.

ECLIPTIC

The projection onto the celestial sphere of Earth's orbit around the Sun, and thus the apparent path of the Sun in the sky through the year. As the Earth's axis is inclined at an angle of about 23.5°, the ecliptic is inclined by this amount to the celestial equator. This angle is known as the obliquity of the ecliptic. The equinoxes are the points where the ecliptic crosses the celestial equator; the positions of these points change over the years because of precession.

)))➤ *Precession*

EDDINGTON, ARTHUR (1882–1944)

English astrophysicist. A brilliant student, Cumbria-born Eddington became Plumian Professor at Cambridge in 1913, where he spent the remainder of his career. One of the early and most authoritative proponents of Albert Einstein's (1879–1955) theory of relativity, he was closely involved in one of the expeditions to photograph the solar eclipse of 1919 which demonstrated the bending of light by a gravitational field, in this case the Sun's. Eddington worked in many areas of astronomy, such as stellar dynamics and the nature of the interstellar medium, but one in which he played a major role was in the application of physical and mathematical principles to describe the structure of a star.

This was encapsulated in his benchmark book *The Internal Constitution of the Stars* (1926). Towards the end of his life he devoted his considerable intellectual powers to a search for connections between the fundamental constants of nature.

EDGEWORTH–KUIPER BELT

A region beyond the orbit of Neptune containing KBOs (Kuiper Belt Objects), pieces of debris consisting of a mixture of rock and ice. Short-period comets are thought to originate from the belt. The planet Pluto is sometimes regarded as the largest member of the belt. Triton, the largest satellite of Neptune, was probably once a KBO.

))⏵ **Oort Cloud**

EINSTEIN, ALBERT (1879–1955)

Physicist. Einstein was born in Germany, but took first Swiss and then US citizenship. He devised the two theories of relativity and made important contributions to quantum physics. As a boy he questioned what a beam of light would look like if he could catch up with it. In 1905, while working in the Swiss patent office, Einstein published three landmark papers: one in which he introduced the concept of the photon (which won him the Nobel Prize in 1921) and one in which he set out the theory of special relativity. The third was on Brownian motion which contained evidence for the atom. But it was not until 1909 that he secured his first academic post, at Zurich University, and became an established member of the scientific community.

The general theory of relativity, published in 1916, explained gravity not as a force between particles but as a distortion in the fabric of space–time. The latter part of his life was spent unsuccessfully trying to unify gravity with electromagnetism. In 1933 Einstein left Nazi

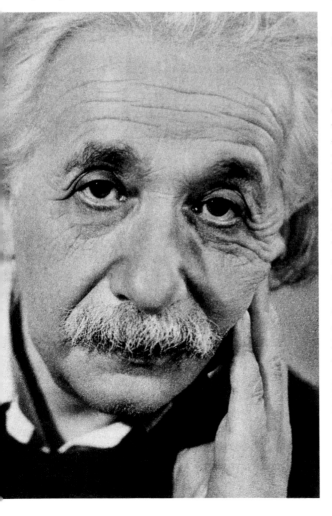

LEFT: Einstein saw that gravity should be understood not as the force between masses but as the effect of distortions in the four-dimensional fabric of space-time.
RIGHT: Visible light occupies only a fraction of the electromagnetic spectrum. The bands of shorter wavelength radiation (ultraviolet, X-ray and gamma ray) and longer wavelength radiation (infrared, microwave and radio wave) are all studied in modern astronomy.

Germany for Princeton, where he was to remain. In 1939 he alerted the US government to the possibility of the Nazis developing an atomic bomb and later campaigned for nuclear disarmament.

ELECTROMAGNETIC SPECTRUM

The electromagnetic spectrum is the range of possible frequencies and wavelengths of electromagnetic waves. While there is a continuous gradation in these properties through the spectrum, they are conventionally classified into a small number of ranges. Gamma rays, at the extreme short-wavelength end of the spectrum, have wavelengths shorter than 0.01 nm. X-rays have wavelengths between 0.01–10 nm. Ultraviolet radiation lies beyond the short-wavelength end of the visible band, between 10 and 400 nm. Visible light lies between 400 nm (violet) and 700 nm (red). Infrared radiation lies beyond the long wavelength end of the visible spectrum and stretches between 700 nm and 1 mm. Radio waves extend beyond wavelengths of about 1 mm.

)))➡ *Gamma Rays, Radio Waves, X-Rays*

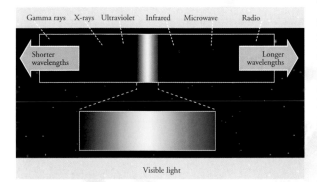

Gamma rays   X-rays   Ultraviolet   Infrared   Microwave   Radio

Shorter wavelengths

Longer wavelengths

Visible light

ELECTROMAGNETIC WAVES

Electromagnetic waves were predicted by Maxwell, who showed that varying electric and magnetic fields could sustain each other and travel through space at the speed of light. The spread of wavelengths is known as the electromagnetic spectrum. Electromagnetic waves are emitted by vibrating electrons and absorbed when they cause other electrons to vibrate in sympathy with them, or they may be emitted and absorbed in changes of the electronic state of atoms and molecules.

)))➡ *Electromagnetic Spectrum, Maxwell, James Clerk*

ELECTRON

A fundamental particle that is a constituent part of every atom. An electron orbiting an atomic nucleus may occupy any one of a series of distinct energy levels dictated by quantum mechanics. Each electron has a negative charge of 1.602×10^{-19} coulomb and a mass of 9.109×10^{-31} kg.

ELLIPTICAL GALAXIES

Elliptical galaxies are almost featureless conglomerations of old stars arranged into spherical or elliptical shapes, bright at their centres and fading to obscurity in their outskirts. The only obvious distinguishing feature of an elliptical galaxy is its overall shape: some appear almost completely round, while others are squashed and elongated. These shapes reflect the angle of view as well as the intrinsic morphology – for example, a galaxy shaped like a rugby ball (or an American football) would appear round if viewed end-on, but flattened if viewed from the side. Observations have shown that the flattening of elliptical galaxies is due to the fact that their stars move faster, and hence travel farther, in one direction than the other, not to rotation as for spiral galaxies. Elliptical galaxies rotate little, if at all. Elliptical galaxies display a wider range of luminosities than spirals: at the lower end are dwarfs containing a few million stars, like oversized globular clusters, while the largest are supergiants (known as cD galaxies) that can be 20 times as luminous as our own Galaxy. The stars in ellipticals are mostly old and there are usually no clouds of cold gas from which new stars can form.

ELONGATION

1. The angular distance between the Sun and a Solar System object (usually a planet) measured from 0° to 180° east or west of the Sun. A planet with elongation 0° is at conjunction. An inferior planet has a greatest elongation that is less than 90° east or west of the Sun. A superior planet with elongation 180° is at opposition; with elongation 90° or 270° it is at quadrature.

2. The angular distance between a planet and one of its satellites, measured from 0° east or west of the planet.

)))➡ *Conjunction, Opposition*

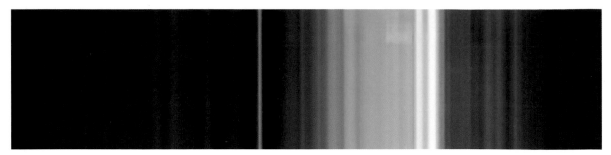

EMISSION LINE

A bright line or band in a spectrum, produced by the emission of electromagnetic radiation at certain wavelengths. One example is the pink glow often seen in photographs of nebulae. This is caused by a red emission line in the spectrum of hydrogen gas, the H-alpha line, which has a wavelength of 656 nm.

EMISSION LINE SPECTRUM

An emission line spectrum is emitted by hot, low-pressure gas. It consists of a number of bright lines (emission lines) of different colours. It is created when atoms and molecules in the object change their states, emitting light of certain particular wavelengths.

EMISSION NEBULA

A cloud of interstellar dust and gas that shines by its own light. The nebula is composed primarily of hydrogen that has been ionized. There are three main types of emission nebula: HII regions, planetary nebulae and supernova remnants.

EPHEMERIS TIME

By the 1930s it was clear that the Earth does not rotate smoothly, so that the length of the day is not constant. In the 1950s astronomers therefore introduced ephemeris time (ET), defined in terms of the predicted positions of the Sun, Moon and planets. Such predictions are listed in a table called an ephemeris. In 1984 ET was replaced for astronomical purposes by Terrestrial Time (TT) and Barycentric Dynamical Time (TDB), both of which are defined in terms of International Atomic Time (TAI), which is determined by the electromagnetic radiations given out by certain atoms.

))▶ *Greenwich Mean Time, Sidereal Time*

ABOVE: The technique of spectroscopy is used by physicists and astronomers. Coloured emission lines, such as these from a Wolf-Rayet star, can yield information about the object's composition, temperature and other properties.

EPICYCLE

In early theories of the motions of the solar system, a small circle in which a celestial body moves, whose centre in turn revolves around the Earth by travelling along the perimeter of a larger circle called the deferent. First introduced by Ptolemy, epicycles persisted into the heliocentric (Sun-centred) theory of Nicolaus Copernicus (1473–1543), but were abandoned by Johannes Kepler (1571–1630).

))▶ *Equant, Planetary Motion, Kepler's Laws of*

EQUANT

One of two points equally spaced from the Earth in Ptolemy's geocentric (Earth-centred) model of the solar system. Viewed from the equant, the centre of the planet's epicycle would appear to move at a constant angular rate. The other point was the 'eccentric', about which the centre of the planet's epicycle revolved.

))▶ *Epicycle*

EQUATOR

The great circle on the surface of a near-spherical body such as a planet or star, situated halfway between its poles. The equatorial plane is perpendicular to the body's axis of rotation and passes through the centre of the body.

EQUINOX

Either of two points on the celestial sphere where the ecliptic crosses the celestial equator; or either of

BELOW LEFT: By measuring the distance on the ground between Syene and Alexandria and multiplying it by 50, Eratosthenes obtained the circumference of the Earth, 250,000 stadia.
BELOW RIGHT: A Landsat image of the Nile Delta.

the times at which the Sun passes through those points. The vernal (or spring) equinox occurs about 21 March, when the Sun crosses from south to north; the autumnal equinox occurs about 23 September, when the Sun crosses from north to south. At the equinoxes the Sun rises due east and sets due west, and the durations of daylight and night are equal.

))))▶ *Celestial Sphere*

EQUIPOTENTIAL SURFACE

A boundary around a celestial body or system at which the gravitational field is constant. In a close binary system the equipotential surface forms two regions called Roche lobes, each of which contains one of the stars. Material from either star can pass through either of two Lagrangian points. Mass transfer takes place at the inner Lagrangian point, while mass is lost from the system at the outer Lagrangian point.

ERATOSTHENES (c. 276–195 BC)

Greek astronomer. Eratosthenes pioneered a technique which measured the size of the Earth. He knew that at midsummer the Sun shone right to the bottom of a deep well in the town of Syene, near the

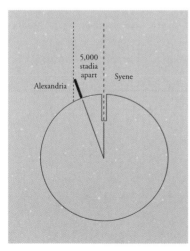

modern Aswan, and hence was directly overhead. Yet in Alexandria, just over 7° to the north, the Sun cast shadows. Eratosthenes also knew that as the rays of the Sun striking the Earth were parallel, the shadow angle cast in Alexandria must be the same as that

produced by radial lines drawn from Syene and Alexandria to the centre of the Earth. As Syene and Alexandria were 5,000 Greek stadia apart, he deduced that they were one-fiftieth of a circle apart, so the circumference of the Earth must equal 250,000 stadia. Although there is some debate about the exact length of Eratosthenes' stadia, his figure produces an Earth circumference of about 47,000 km (29,000 miles). The modern value is 40,074 km (24,902 miles).

ERIDANUS

Eridanus, the river, meanders from the borders of Taurus and Orion deep into the southern sky, ending at Achernar (Alpha [α] Eridani), a 1st-magnitude star which was below the horizon from ancient Greece. Eridanus contains two double stars of note: Theta [θ] Eridani and p Eridani.

ERTS

NASA launched their first Earth Resources Technology Satellite (ERTS) on 23 July 1972. Its 900-km (560-mile) Sun-synchronous polar orbit provided a constant Sun angle on the Earth to aid comparison of images taken on different days and in different wavelengths of light. ERTS 1 was completely successful and the program, renamed Landsat, continues today.

ESCAPE SPEED

The minimum speed at which a projectile must be fired in order to continue to recede indefinitely from a massive body without any further form of propulsion. A comet moving in a parabolic orbit has just sufficient energy to leave the Solar System and never return. At any point in its orbit it is moving at the local escape speed.

The speed required to escape the gravitational pull of a body of mass M at a distance r is given by:

escape speed = $\sqrt{\frac{2GM}{r}}$, where G is the gravitational constant.

The escape speed is 11.2 kps (7 mps) from the surface of the Earth, and 2.4 kps (1.5 mps) from the Moon. The escape speed drops the farther a rocket gets from the surface.

ETA CARINAE

One of the most remarkable luminous blue variables found in the southern sky, is Eta [η] Carinae, which has an estimated mass of around 120 Suns, near the upper limit physically possible for a star. Early in the nineteenth century it began to brighten, attaining a peak of magnitude -1, second only to Sirius, in 1843. It subsequently declined, by seven magnitudes over 14 years, sinking below naked-eye visibility. Since the 1940s it has slowly been on the rise again, reaching 5th magnitude in 1998. Eta Carinae itself is difficult to see, being embedded in thick nebulosity expelled during its outbursts.

))))➤ *Luminous Blue Variables*

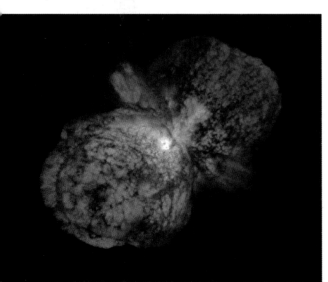

EUDOXUS (407–355 BC)

Greek astronomer. Eudoxus tried to explain the observed motions of the planets by devising a geometric model which contained 27 spheres, representing the motion of the planets in relation to the zodiac, while rotating around the Earth. The path taken by a planet against what was then thought to be a fixed background of stars could be observed in this model as a figure-of-eight curve, which Eudoxus termed a *Hippopede* (Greek: 'Horsefetter'). Eudoxus' system was the ancestor of the epicycle and eccentric circles system later developed by Hipparchus (fl. 160–125 BC).

EUROPA

One of the four largest satellites of Jupiter. Europa has a cracked, icy surface with very few impact craters, evidence of reworking of the satellite's entire surface by geological processes. Recent data from the Galileo spacecraft suggest a water ocean may exist below the frozen surface, possibly harbouring life.

EVENT HORIZON

The sphere around a black hole at the Schwarzschild radius is termed the event horizon. The event horizon is often thought of as the surface of the black hole, but it is not a material surface. Rather, it marks the location where the distortion of space–time by gravity becomes extreme. It is called a horizon because no information from within it can reach the outside world. However, there is nothing to stop things from falling inside the event horizon.

))))➤ *Black Hole, Schwarzschild Radius, Space–Time*

EXOPLANETS

Extrasolar planets or exoplanets are planets around other stars. Most of the first exoplanets to be discovered were the size of Jupiter or larger and orbited closer to their parent star than Mercury does to the Sun because they are the planets that are easiest to spot with the radial velocity technique used. Such planets, known as 'hot

LEFT: Eta Carinae, a supermassive star that flared up in the 1840s to become the second-brightest star in the sky. It threw off two lobes of gas and a large thin equatorial disk, shown in this Hubble Space Telesocope photograph.

Jupiters', may have formed farther out and then moved inwards as they were slowed by drag from the gas in the surrounding disk. Many of the exoplanets that lie farther away from their parent stars have orbits that are highly elliptical, unlike the near-circular orbits of the planets in our Solar System. Not until many more exoplanets are known can we tell whether our own Solar System is unusual. However, we can already draw important conclusions, notably that planets are common in the Galaxy and that perhaps the majority of stars have planets orbiting them. Several cases of multiple planets orbiting a single star have been found, confirming that entire planetary systems can arise. Planets tend to be found only around stars that, like our own Sun, are particularly rich in heavy elements. Most of the planets known have masses no more than a few times that of Jupiter, and as searches continue the number of lower-mass planets is increasing.

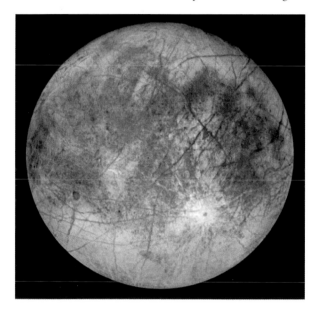

ABOVE: Jupiter's satellite Europa has a fractured and icy crust. Evidence suggests that beneath the icy surface there may be an ocean of liquid water.

EXPLORER SPACE PROGRAM

On 1 February 1958, Project Orbiter lived up to its name, placing Explorer 1 into a 360 x 2,534-km (224 x 1,575-mile) orbit. The first US satellite had been launched. James Van Allen (b. 1914), a physicist from Iowa University, had argued for placing a Geiger-Müller counter inside Explorer to detect cosmic rays. Explorers 3 and 4 detected regions of trapped radiation around the Earth. These regions were later named the Van Allen belt. Explorer 1 beamed back its discoveries until 23 May, but remained in orbit until March 1970. The earliest TV pictures of Earth's cloud were provided by Explorer 6 in August 1959.

FAR SIDE OF THE MOON

The Moon always keeps the same face towards Earth hence from Earth we can never see the far side of the Moon. The far side is miscalled the 'dark' side of the Moon – all areas of the Moon experience two-week days followed by two-week nights. The large, dark maria – plains of solidified igneous rock – which are common on the near side are lacking on the far side. The crust there is thicker, and it was more difficult for magma to escape to the surface in the past. The far side is a nearly continuous stretch of craters of all sizes.

FLANDRO, GARY (b. 1934)

American physicist. Whilst working at the Jet Propulsion Laboratory in California in 1964, Flandro was interested in planetary positions and computed a series of theoretical sling-shot missions. He discovered that at the end of the 1970s, a 175-year planetary alignment would enable a spacecraft to visit all the outer planets in one 12-year flight. From these calculations, the 'Grand Tour' of the Solar System emerged, later becoming a successful Voyager mission.

FOUR CORNERS OF THE WORLD

All the ancient Near-eastern cultures saw the cosmos as being built in tiers, or levels. The sky was flat and supported in some remote place by pillars at the 'four corners of the Earth'. Above the sky were the 'waters above the firmament', which broke forth to cause the Great Flood of Noah. Then there were the 'waters beneath the Earth', as well as the realms of the dead. This cosmology was shared, in its basic principles, by the ancient Egyptians, Babylonians, Sumerians and Jews. Astronomical bodies were seen as passing beneath the flat Earth at night.

FRAUNHOFER, JOSEPH VON (1787–1826)

German physicist and instrument-maker recognized as the founder of astronomical spectroscopy. In 1814 he devised a way of measuring the optical properties of glass by using the bright yellow emission line in the spectrum of sodium as a standard. He devised the modern spectroscope by using a telescope to study the spectrum produced by a prism. He found that the spectrum of the Sun was crossed by numerous dark lines, one of which corresponded in wavelength to the emission line found in the spectrum of sodium. Fraunhofer went on to catalogue more than 500 of these absorption lines – now known as Fraunhofer lines – and the system of letters he used to label the more prominent lines is still used. In 1821 he constructed the first diffraction grating and used it instead of a prism to form a spectrum and make precise measurements of the wavelengths of the solar absorption lines.

FRAUNHOFER LINES

Dark absorption lines in the Sun's spectrum caused by the presence of various elements in the Sun's outer atmosphere. The most prominent lines were first noticed in 1802 by a British chemist, William Wollaston (1766–1828), but he failed to recognize their significance. They were rediscovered in 1814 by the German physicist Joseph von Fraunhofer, who recorded several hundred of them. More than 30,000 Fraunhofer lines have now been mapped in the solar spectrum.

)))⯈ *Absorption Line, Fraunhofer, Joseph Von*

FREEDOM 7 SPACECRAFT

Alan Shepard was America's first astronaut. His spacecraft Freedom 7, was launched from Cape Canaveral, Florida on 5 May 1961. A Redstone rocket propelled them to 8,214 kph (5,103 mph) before shutting down on schedule and separating from the capsule. Shepard manoeuvred Freedom 7 and tested the reaction control systems. They reached a peak altitude of 187 km (117 miles), before splashing down in the Atlantic Ocean 15 minutes and 22 seconds after launch.

FRIEDMANN, ALEKSANDR (1868–1925)

Russian mathematician. Friedmann developed cosmological models based on general relativity. He saw cosmology as an exercise in

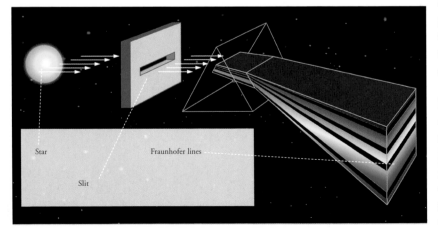

Star

Slit

Fraunhofer lines

mathematics and did not attempt to relate it to the physical Universe. It is said that he only became interested in cosmological models after noticing an error in Einstein's 1916 work, which Einstein first disputed and then later accepted. Today, cosmological models with a cosmological constant of zero are termed Friedmann universes.

FRIENDSHIP 7 SPACECRAFT

On 20 February 1962 John H. Glenn Jr (b. 1921), became the first American to orbit Earth. His Mercury capsule was called Friendship 7. Minor problems delayed the launch several times, but the countdown was completed at 9.47 a.m. Five minutes later Glenn was in orbit. Near the end of his first orbit, Friendship 7 was drifting slowly to the right and Glenn switched to manual to correct the problem. The re-entry retrofire began after four hours and 33 minutes. Friendship 7 splashed down 22 minutes later.

GAGARIN, YURI (1934–68)

Russian astronaut. The first man to fly in space, orbiting the Earth in his Vostok 1 capsule on 12 April 1961, just a few weeks before the first proposed American manned space flight. The 27-year-old Russian pilot climbed into his Vostok 1 spacecraft and at 04:10 UT was blasted into orbit by Korolev's SL3 rocket. Seventy-eight minutes into the flight, mission control fired the retrorockets and Gagarin began his descent. The Vostoks had no retrorockets for a soft-landing, and so 8,000 m (26,250 ft) above the ground Gagarin ejected from the capsule and parachuted to Earth, landing on the banks of the Volga not far from Engels. Gagarin was killed in a plane crash in 1968.

))))➤ *Vostok 1*

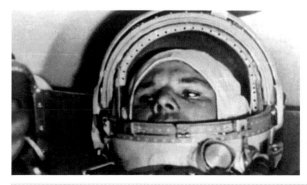

GAIA

ESA is planning the GAIA (Global Astrometric Interferometer for Astrophysics) mission for launch by 2012. GAIA will provide accurate distances and radial velocities on every object in our Galaxy brighter than 20th magnitude – roughly a billion stars – revealing the three-dimensional structure of our Galaxy all the way to its central bulge.

GALACTIC BARS

Bars are rapidly rotating, elongated structures composed of stars and gas which occur in nearly half of all spiral galaxies. The Galactic bulge is really a bar, viewed almost end-on down its long axis so it looks almost spherical in projection. Confirming evidence for a bar comes from small but unmistakable asymmetries in the distribution of stars around the Galactic centre, as well as distortions in the motions of gas detected at 21-cm (8-in) wavelengths. The size of the bar is uncertain but it probably extends out to about 10,000 light years from the centre.

))))➤ *Barred Spiral Galaxies, Galactic Bulge*

GALACTIC BLACK HOLE

Many galaxies are known to have objects at their centres with masses ranging from a few million solar masses, in the case of our own Galaxy, to several billion solar masses in other galaxies. Yet these enormous masses are crammed into remarkably small volumes, in some cases less than the size of the Solar System. It is widely believed, although there is as yet no definitive proof, that these objects are gargantuan black holes, and they are thought to provide the power sources for active galactic nuclei, including quasars. They may have been produced in the early Universe, acting as seeds around which the primordial gas condensed to form galaxies, or they may have built up inside galaxies as a result of gravitational interactions between stars. With the subsequent addition of more stars and gas the black hole would continue to grow.

))))➤ *Active Galactic Nuclei, Black Holes, Quasars, Stellar Black Hole*

LEFT: The Russians won the race to put the first man in space – Yuri Gagarin orbited Earth in Vostok 1 in April 1961.

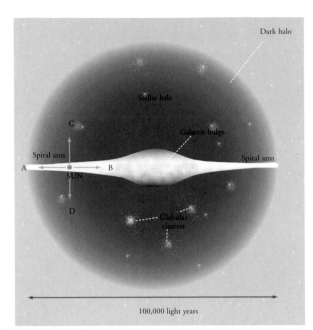

Dark halo

Stellar halo

C

Galactic bulge

Spiral arm

A   B

SUN

Spiral arm

D

Globular
clusters

100,000 light years

the rotation speed remains almost constant out to distances of 150,000 light years from the centre at least. This is evidence for the existence of a dark-matter halo The galactic halo rotates more slowly at 50 km/s^{-1}.

GALACTIC BULGE

Enveloping the Galactic centre marked by the radio source Sagittarius A* is a bulge of some 10 billion stars with a profile like a flattened ball (a shape known as a spheroid). Dust obscures the Galactic bulge from view at optical wavelengths, except in a few places, most notably the area termed Baade's Window in Sagittarius. Baade's window apart, the bulge is best studied at infrared and radio wavelengths, which can penetrate the obscuring dust. One significant discovery in recent years has been that the Galactic bulge is actually a rotating bar, seen nearly end-on from Earth.

))))▶ *Sagittarius A**

GALACTIC DISK

Outside the central bulge, most of the stars and gas in the Galaxy lie in a flat disk about 2,000 light years thick, concentrated into spiral arms coiled around the hub. The disk also contains abundant atoms of neutral (non-ionized) hydrogen. Using radio observations of hydrogen the Galaxy's speed of rotation has been measured. Atoms of hydrogen in the Galactic disk move on circular orbits with a speed of about 220 km/s (140 mi/s) irrespective of their distance from the galactic centre. Analyses of the velocities of satellite galaxies suggest that

GALAXIES

Dotted like islands throughout space, galaxies are collections of many billions of stars bound together by gravity. They are built up from a few major components – stars, gas, dust, dark matter and a central black hole – but the mix of these ingredients, and their individual characteristics, varies between galaxies. Galaxies are generally classified according to their optical appearance and their output of radiation at other wavelengths. Our own Galaxy, the Milky Way, is believed to be a barred spiral. Although enormous and highly luminous, galaxies are so far off that almost all of them are invisible to the naked eye, and even the brightest appear as little more than faint smudges through a small telescope. Galaxies are not uniformly distributed across the sky, but are found in clusters and the clusters of galaxies are themselves arranged in superclusters.

GALAXIES, CLASSIFICATION OF

One of the first systematic attempts to classify galaxies according to their appearance was made by Hubble in 1925. In Hubble's 'tuning fork' classification, elliptical galaxies are designated by an E followed by a number that indicates how flat the galaxy appears, from E0 (perfectly round) to E7 (the most elongated). Spiral galaxies are designated S and barred spirals SB. The letters a, b or c impart further information about the appearance of the spiral, progressing from galaxies with large central bulges and tightly wound spiral arms to those with small bulges and a well-defined, open spiral structure. Lenticular galaxies are termed S0, the '0' indicating the absence of spiral structure. Irr is used for the irregular galaxies that do not fit within this scheme. Other, more sophisticated,

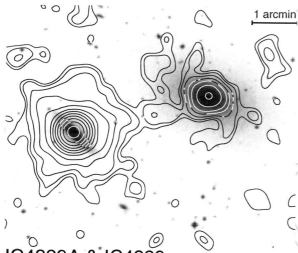

1 arcmin

IC4329A & IC4329

ROSAT HRI

schemes have since been introduced. For example, unbarred and barred galaxies are sometimes termed SA and SB, with those containing only weak central bars designated SAB. A spiral galaxy may have 'r' added if it is seen to be surrounded by a faint ring of light or 'pec' if it is in some way peculiar in appearance. However, the simplicity of Hubble's original scheme means that it is still widely used today to give a shorthand description of a galaxy's appearance.

▶▶▶ *Tuning Fork Diagram*

GALAXIES, CONTENTS OF

Stars are the most obvious component of all galaxies. In spiral galaxies, the oldest stars are found in an extended halo of globular clusters and the central bulge, while the disk contains stars with a wide range of ages. The youngest stars lie in the spiral arms. In elliptical galaxies, the stars are all older and irregular galaxies often exhibit very vigorous star formation.

ABOVE: Contents of galaxies. X-ray emission from extremely hot gas in the huge elliptical galaxy IC 4329 (right), overlain with contours on an optical image. To the left is IC 4329A, an edge-on spiral with an active nucleus.
RIGHT: The coma star clusters, an open cluster in Coma Berenices. Clusters like this consist of relatively young stars and lie in the spiral arms of galaxies.

The density of gas in the space between stars is incredibly low, but galaxies are so large that this can add up to a great deal: in a large spiral like the Milky Way, the total gas mass is several billion times the mass of the Sun, about 5 per cent the mass of its stars. In spiral galaxies the gas is cool while in elliptical galaxies, the gas is so hot – tens of millions of degrees – that it forms an ionized plasma which emits X-rays.

Dust is found in the disks of spiral galaxies, producing the dark lanes running across spiral galaxies seen edge-on and also causing the dark patches seen in our own Milky Way. Dust is also plentiful in irregulars but is not found in elliptical galaxies because the very high temperature gas in these systems bombards the dust grains, rapidly destroying any that form.

Stars, gas and dust comprise only about 10 per cent the mass of a typical galaxy. The remaining 90 per cent is 'dark matter'. The motions of stars and gas indicate that dark matter is distributed in an extended halo stretching well beyond the luminous limit of all galaxies.

1 arcmin

Most, possibly all, galaxies have black holes at their centre, with masses ranging from 100,000 to a billion suns. Central black holes are thought to provide the energy sources of quasars and active galaxies. Most galaxies do not behave like quasars because they lack the infall of gas and stars that powers active galactic nuclei.

GALAXIES, DEATH OF

The overall morphology of galaxies is not affected by the evolution of individual stars so as stars die, galaxies will become systems of dead stars. Over a long period of time galaxies can evaporate their stars: if two stars approach each other close enough to exert strong gravitational pulls on each other, one star can occasionally be flung out of the galaxy. The second star loses energy and moves towards the galactic centre. Stars may also migrate towards the centre of the galaxy as they radiate gravitational radiation. As a result a black hole forms at the centre (if one does not already exist) and increases in mass until it eventually contains all the mass of the galaxy.

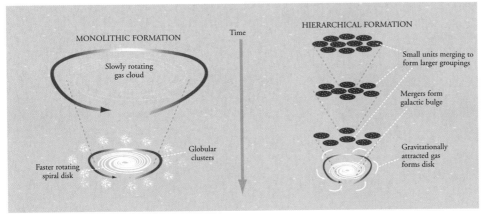

MONOLITHIC FORMATION

Time

Slowly rotating gas cloud

Faster rotating spiral disk

Globular clusters

HIERARCHICAL FORMATION

Small units merging to form larger groupings

Mergers form galactic bulge

Gravitationally attracted gas forms disk

GALAXIES, FORMATION OF

There are two main theories for the formation of galaxies. The first was developed in the 1960s when it was thought that galaxies were born when a large cloud of primordial gas collapsed under the inward pull of its own gravity. As the cloud contracted it left behind smaller lumps of gas which formed a halo of globular clusters. The speed of rotation of the cloud dictated whether it became an elliptical or spiral galaxy: if it was rotating fast enough, its outer regions would spread into a disk which would develop spiral arms.

More recently, an alternative scenario has arisen. In this view, the large galaxies seen today grew from the mergers of smaller galaxies which, in turn, had been the products of earlier mergers between still-smaller units. This hierarchical system would first produce an elliptical galaxy. If that elliptical galaxy were to gravitationally attract a new disk of gas it would develop arms and hence turn into a spiral. A mounting array of evidence now supports this hierarchical picture. For example, it has been found that around a quarter of all elliptical galaxies contain groups of stars that orbit quite rapidly near the centre of the galaxy in a direction unrelated to the majority of stars in the galaxy. These features appear to represent the partially digested remains of a small galaxy in the final stages of being absorbed by the elliptical galaxy.

One way of studying galaxy evolution involves comparing nearby galaxies with those far away – because of the time light takes to reach us, we see distant galaxies as they appeared long ago. Using this technique reveals that distant clusters of galaxies contain a greater proportion of spirals than do nearby clusters. The spirals must, it seems, have collided and merged to create elliptical galaxies, explaining the prevalence of the latter in nearby clusters. The Hubble Space Telescope has revealed other evolutionary effects: for example, in the past the Universe contained many more irregular galaxies than now; these were presumably the building blocks that merged to form the galaxies we see today.

GALAXIES, NAMES OF

Galaxies may have individual popular names, but are generally identified by catalogue numbers. Many of the brighter ones have M, NGC or IC as prefixes. These relate to the objects' listing in either Charles Messier's catalogue (the so-called Messier objects, of which there are 110), the New General Catalogue (NGC, 7840 entries) and the Index Catalogues (IC), two supplements to the NGC adding over 5,000 more objects.

GALAXY CLUSTERS

Galaxies are not uniformly distributed across the sky, but are found in clusters, collections of galaxies held together by gravity. Clusters contain from a few to a few thousand member galaxies, small clusters – containing up to a few dozen members – being known as groups. Our own Galaxy, the Milky Way belongs to a small cluster, the Local Group. Structure on scales larger than clusters is difficult to discern from two-dimensional images of the sky and so cosmologists use measurements of redshifts as an indication of distance and prepare maps of

ABOVE: Monolithic model of galaxy formation: a slowly rotating cloud of primordial gas collapses to form a faster-spinning spiral disk with a surrounding residue of globular clusters. Heirarchical theory: a sequence of small units merge into ever-larger groupings to form a galactic bulge.

RIGHT: Galileo with his telescopes, the development of which marked a turning pont in astronomical discovery and understanding.
BELOW: Galilean satellites. Galileo discovered the four major satellites orbiting the giant planet Jupiter in 1610. From the left they are Io, Europa, Ganymede and Callisto.

slices of the sky with redshift distances drawn radially from the centre. Such maps show that the clusters of galaxies are themselves arranged in superclusters. On even larger scales these superclusters link to form filamentary structures with vast voids separating them. Galaxy clusters are probably the largest bound structures in the Universe.

GALILEAN SATELLITES

The four largest satellites of the giant planet Jupiter. They are so called after Galileo Galilei (1564–1642), who observed them when he made his first telescopic observations of the sky in 1609–10. In order outwards from Jupiter they are named Io, Europa, Ganymede and Callisto, after mythological figures associated with Zeus, the Greek equivalent of Jupiter.

))))➤ *Callisto, Europa, Ganymede, Io*

GALILEI, GALILEO (1564–1642)

Italian astronomer. Galileo studied at Pisa University and, after abandoning medical studies, took to mathematics, becoming a lecturer at Pisa in 1588. It was in Pisa that Galileo made his first researches into swinging pendulums and falling bodies. In 1591 he became professor of Mathematics at Padua, which was then the finest scientific university in Europe. It was here, in 1609–10, that he made telescopic discoveries which, when published in his *Siderius Nuncius* ('Starry Messenger'), revolutionized astronomy and made him an international celebrity. His disputed co-discovery and anti-Aristotelian interpretation of sunspots with Christopher Scheiner after 1612 made him many enemies

amongst the intellectual Jesuit order, which was probably instrumental in engineering his trial in 1633.

GAMMA RAY ASTRONOMY

Gamma rays are photons with energies higher than about 100 keV and wavelengths shorter than 0.01nm. Like X-rays, they are stopped by the Earth's atmosphere, although the highest energies can be detected on the ground by their effects on the upper atmosphere. The first satellite to carry a gamma-ray telescope was the American SAS-2, launched in 1972. In 1975, the ESA COS-B satellite was launched, and it operated for several years. One of the most significant spacecraft dedicated to the study of gamma rays was the US Compton Gamma Ray Observatory, which operated from 1991 to 2000 and observed over 300 gamma-ray sources for each year of its operation. Major sources of cosmic gamma rays include solar flares, pulsars, supernova remnants, quasars and active galaxies. Thousands of sudden bursts of gamma rays have been detected from all parts of the sky. Although the origin of these 'gamma-ray bursts' is still uncertain, they appear to occur in distant galaxies and are thought to be produced by violent events such as the collision of pairs of neutron stars or the detontaion of hypernovae (powerful supernovae).

))))➤ *Compton Gamma Ray Observatory*

GAMMA RAYS

Gamma rays were identified in 1900 by a French chemist, Paul Villard (1860–1934), but it was not until 1912 that they were recognized as the most energetic form of electromagnetic radiation, with extremely short wavelengths of less than 0.01 nm. In many ways they behave like high-energy X-rays, and there is no consensus on the wavelength at which X-rays end and gamma rays begin. A useful distinction is their source: gamma rays proper are emitted from the nuclei of atoms either during nuclear reactions or as a result of spontaneous radioactive decay. Gamma rays are detected by counting them one by one. In that sense, they behave more like particles than like waves.

GAMOW, GEORGE (1904–68)

Russian physicist. Trained in nuclear physics in Leningrad (now St Petersburg), Gamow moved to the United States in 1933. He spent several years working on radioactivity and the quantum theory of the atomic nucleus. This led him to study the nuclear reactions that supply the energy for stars.

In the late 1940s, while researching the physics of the Big Bang, Gamow realized that the radiation emitted when the Universe was a hot, uniform gas should still be detectable, but redshifted to a temperature only a few degrees above absolute zero. It took a further two decades for the American physicists Arno Penzias (b. 1933) and Robert Wilson (b. 1936) to discover cosmic background radiation, and then only by accident.

GANYMEDE

One of the four large satellites of the giant planet Jupiter. It has two distinct surface components: areas with abundant craters, and others which are far less cratered, where melting and refreezing have modified the surface. The satellite's diameter is approximately 5,268 km (3,273 miles); its mean distance from Jupiter is 1.07 million km (665,000 miles).

⟫⟫ *Galilean Satellites*

GEMINI

The constellation of Gemini the twins is dominated by Castor and Pollux. It also contains two variable stars of note: Zeta [ζ] Geminorum, a Cepheid variable ranging from magnitude 3.6 to 4.2 every 10.2 days, and Eta [η] Geminorum, a red giant that fluctuates between magnitudes 3.1 and 3.9 every eight months or so. It also contains the planetary nebula, NGC 2392, which has been christened the Eskimo Nebula because on photographs it resembles a face with a faint outer fringe like a parka.

GEMINI SPACE PROGRAM

After two unpiloted Gemini flights in early 1964, 10 manned missions followed, pioneering complex techniques which would carry NASA to the Moon. The first manned flight, Gemini 3 on 23 March 1965, was commanded by Gus Grissom (1926–67) – the first man to fly to space twice, along with John Young. In another first for the mission, Gemini 3 used its manoeuvring engines to change orbit.

The Gemini 4 flight on 3 June 1965 kept Jim McDivitt (b. 1929) and Edward White (1930–67) in orbit for a record four days and White became the first American to walk in space. Gemini 6 carried Walter Schirra and Thomas Stafford (b. 1930) to orbit where they

LEFT: The Galilean satellite Ganymede.

the satellite will remain at all times directly above a fixed point on the equator.

The first attempt at a geosynchronous orbit was NASA's Syncom series, first launched in 1963. An international organization called Intelsat was established the same year to manage geosynchronous orbit and launch the world's first commercial communications satellite, Early Bird, in April 1965. The Early Birds could relay 240 telephone calls or one TV channel. By 1969 they covered the whole globe and transmitted worldwide television coverage of the first Moon landing. The current Intelsat-7 generation, built by Ford Aerospace, can simultaneously relay 18,000 telephone calls and three TV channels.

In the USSR the geostationary orbit was considered less useful because of the nation's extreme northern latitudes, so they pioneered an alternative communications satellite system using an orbit inclined at 65° to the Equator. As one satellite vanished over the horizon, the ground-tracking dishes could lock on to one another. Their Molniya constellation became the world's biggest domestic satellite network.

))))▶ *Communications Satellites*

manoeuvred to within 2 m (7 ft) of Gemini 7 launched 11 days earlier. The two craft flew in formation for 20 hours. Gemini 7's Frank Borman (b. 1928) and James Lovell (b. 1928) set a duration record of almost 14 days.

Gemini 8 came close to disaster in March 1966 when a thruster began to misfire. The resulting spin nearly caused the crew to black out. In June 1966 Stafford and Cernan on board Gemini 9 tried unsuccessfully to dock with an Agena rocket. Geminis 10–12 perfected the spacewalking technique and achieved perfect practice dockings with the Agena rocket boosters. On Gemini 11 Charles Conrad (1930–99) and Richard Gordon (b. 1929) used the Agena to set a new altitude record of 1,369 km (851 miles) from Earth. On his second flight, on board Gemini 12, Lovell became the most travelled man in space – completing a total of 265 orbits.

GEOSYNCHRONOUS ORBIT

A satellite placed in a geosynchronous orbit will revolve round the Earth in the same period of time (23h 56m) as the Earth takes to rotate on its axis. If the plane of the orbit coincides with the plane of the Earth's equator, the orbit will be geostationary and consequently

GIACCONI, RICCARDO (b. 1931)

Italian astronomer who discovered the first cosmic X-ray source and built two X-ray satellites. In 1959 Giacconi joined American Science and Engineering, a small research company which discovered the first source of cosmic X-rays, Scorpius X-1, in 1962. His group went on to build the Uhuru satellite, launched in 1970, which made the first complete survey of the X-ray sky and in 1973 he played a key role in developing the Einstein X-ray observatory.

THE GIANT PLANETS

Beyond the inner rocky planets and the asteroid belt lie four huge planets, separated by enormous distances. The inner planets, Mercury, Venus, Earth and Mars, all lie within 250 million km (155 million miles) of the Sun. But Jupiter, the next planet, orbits the Sun over three times farther out than Mars. Then comes the magnificent ringed planet Saturn, at nearly twice the distance of Jupiter.

Uranus, the next planet, is 19 times Earth's distance from the Sun. The next planet, Neptune, is half as far again as Uranus from the Sun. Beyond these four lies the outermost planet, Pluto, another tiny, rocky world.

The Gas Giants

The four giant planets are not at all like Earth. They are much larger and more massive. Jupiter has a diameter 11 times that of Earth and could contain every other planet and moon in the Sun's family. Saturn is smaller, with 57 per cent of the volume of Jupiter. Uranus and Neptune are very similar to each other, with about four times the diameter of Earth.

Rather than being rocky worlds, like those of the inner Solar System, these giants are composed mostly of gas, predominantly hydrogen and helium. The interiors of Jupiter and Saturn consist mainly of liquid hydrogen, but at their very centres there are thought to be relatively small rocky cores, perhaps the size of Earth. Uranus and Neptune are composed mainly of water, ice, methane and ammonia, with perhaps 10–15 per cent less hydrogen and helium than their larger siblings.

The Birth of the Gas Giants

When the planets were forming, over 4.5 billion years ago, the inner part of the Solar System was too close to the Sun for substances such as water and methane to solidify as ice. Consequently, the inner planets are formed from rock and metal. Farther out, there was a boundary beyond which it became cold enough for ices to condense. The outer planets formed by accumulating these ices as well as the rock, and thus grew to the huge masses that they have today. Hydrogen gas in the solar nebula was also swept up by the powerful gravity of these growing gas giants, swelling them further.

The Moons of the Giant Planets

The giant planets of the outer Solar System are attended by over 60 known moons, and it is likely that more await discovery. Many are small, irregularly shaped objects, probably captured asteroids. The larger moons display great variety. These worlds formed far from the Sun, in an environment rich in ices, and their relatively low densities suggest that they are largely made of ices.

)))▶ *Galilean Satellites, Jupiter, Neptune, Saturn, Uranus*

GIBBOUS MOON

Describing the phase of the Moon, planet or satellite when more than half, but less than the whole of its disk is illuminated as seen from Earth.

GIOTTO MISSION

A European spaceprobe, Giotto, flew to Halley's Comet in 1986, recording dust and the comet's chemistry. It found that the comet's nucleus was much darker than had been expected but, just as predicted, it was composed mainly of ice. Giotto's camera was disabled as it flew through the comet tail, but enough

BELOW: Gas giants, from left, Neptune, Jupiter, Uranus and Saturn. Jupiter and Saturn are the true giants, being 11 and 9 times wider than Earth respectively. Uranus and Neptune are around four times that of Earth.

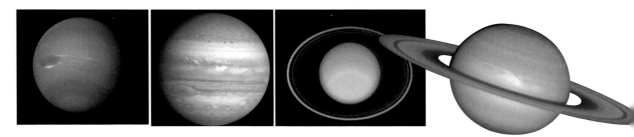

instruments survived to make it worth sending Giotto on to a second comet, Grigg-Skjellerup, in 1992. Giotto is still following a 10-month orbit around the Sun.

GLENN, JOHN (b. 1921)

American astronaut and the first American to orbit Earth. On 20 February 1962, Glenn boarded his Mercury capsule Friendship 7. Minor problems delayed the launch several times, but the countdown was completed at 9.47 a.m. Near the end of his first orbit, Friendship 7 was drifting slowly to the right and Glenn switched to manual to correct the problem. On the third orbit, mission control noticed a signal suggesting that the heat shield and landing bag were loose. Glenn was told to keep the retrorocket package on after firing so that its straps would hold the heat shield in place. By the time the pack burned away, aerodynamic pressure would keep the shield from slipping. The retrofire began after four hours and 33 minutes and during re-entry Glenn observed large chunks of the retrorocket package ablating. Friendship 7 splashed down 22 minutes later.

GLITCH

A temporary speeding up in the rotation of a pulsar. Pulsars gradually slow down over time and these glitches are believed to be due to adjustments occurring in the core or crust of the neutron star.

)))▶ *Pulsars*

GLOBAL POSITIONING SYSTEM

The Global Positioning Satellites (GPS) were developed by the US Department of Defense and launched in the early 1990s. Twenty-four satellites in six circular 20,200-km (12,550-mile) orbits are spaced so that at any one time at least six are visible from the ground. Ground stations around the world keep in constant contact with the satellites, computing precise orbital information and relaying this to each satellite so they continually know where they are and can act as precise positional reference points. Each GPS satellite transmits its position and a synchronized time signal. A hand-held GPS receiver can calculate its

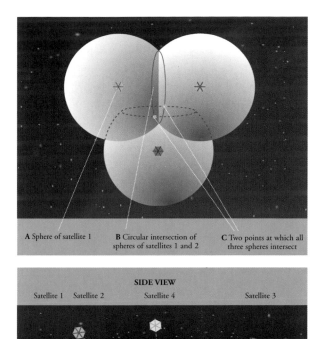

A Sphere of satellite 1   **B** Circular intersection of spheres of satellites 1 and 2   **C** Two points at which all three spheres intersect

SIDE VIEW

Satellite 1   Satellite 2   Satellite 4   Satellite 3

ABOVE: How a GPS receiver finds its position: A. By using time measurements to calculate the distance of satellite 1 it knows that it is somewhere on an imaginary sphere (with the satellite at its centre) with a radius equal to that distance. B. By measuring the distance to satellite 2, it confines its position to somewhere on the circular intersection of two spheres. C. After measuring the distance to satellite 3, it could only be on either of two points at which the three spheres intersect. A fourth satellite gives a more accurate result.

location anywhere on Earth by measuring the time delay of the signals reaching it from several satellites. The signals arrive at the GPS receiver at slightly different times depending on how far away a satellite is. Once the receiver has used these times to calculate the distances to at least four satellites it can calculate its position in three dimensions on Earth's surface.

gasoline-powered machine flew just over 60 m (200 ft), reaching a height of 13 m (43 ft) at an average speed of 96 km/h (60 mi/h). Goddard continued to refine his liquid-fuelled rockets, reaching a maximum height of 2,530 m (8,300 ft) and a speed of 500 km/h (300 mi/h) with his A-series liquid rockets.

GLOBULAR CLUSTERS

Globular clusters are the largest individual components of our Galaxy – huge spheres 100 light years or so across, typically containing hundreds of thousands of old stars (but little or no gas or dust). There are about 150 globular clusters arranged in a roughly spherical halo around our Galaxy, the most distant of them over 300,000 light years from the Galactic centre. Globular cluster ages are estimated by calibrating the turn-off point of their stars from the main sequence on the Hertzsprung-Russell diagram, from which we deduce that their ages are comparable with the age of the universe itself – 10 billion years or more. Globular clusters swarm around other galaxies, too, particularly giant ellipticals.

)))⯈ *Herzsprung–Russell Diagram*

GOULD'S BELT

Many of the brightest stars in our night sky lie in a broad band inclined at about 16° to the Galactic plane, called Gould's Belt after the US astronomer who studied it in the late nineteenth century. Gould's Belt seems to be a conglomeration of several associations or open clusters, including ones in Orion, Scorpius and Centaurus – signs of a recent burst of star formation in our region of the Galaxy.

GRANULATION

The small granular markings observable on the Sun's photosphere, or surface. They are the areas where hot gas is being brought to the surface by convection. Cells are around 1,000 km (600 miles) across and are part of a larger 'super-granulation' pattern.

GODDARD, ROBERT (1882–1945)

American scientist who pioneered the use of liquid fuels to power rockets. In 1915 he was the first to show experimentally that the rocket could work in a vacuum, and hence outer space. His key publication, *A Method of Reaching Extreme Altitudes* (1919), pointed out the possibility of sending a small rocket to the Moon. In 1921, recognizing that liquid fuels carried more energy potential, Goddard began to tackle problems such as fuel injection, ignition and engine cooling.

On 16 March 1926, Goddard launched the world's first liquid-propelled rocket. In a flight lasting 2.5 seconds, the liquid oxygen- and

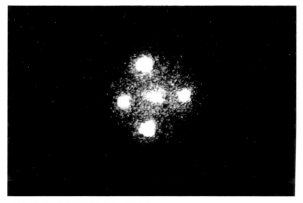

LEFT: A gravitational lens. The central blob is a foreground galaxy while the four surrounding blobs are four gravitationally lensed images of a quasar behind the central galaxy. This X-shaped effect is known as an Einstein Cross.

GRAVITATIONAL LENS

A gravitational lens is caused by the bending of the paths of rays of light and other radiation from a distant background object by a massive body such as a black hole or massive galaxy. The image of the background object is consequently split into multiple images and magnified. If the background object is an extended object like a galaxy, the image can be spread into arcs or occasionally into a complete ring, known as an Einstein ring.

GRAVITATIONAL WAVES

Gravitational waves are ripples in space–time predicted by Einstein's general theory of relativity. In the 1960s, experiments in the US appeared to show that gravitational waves were coming from the centre of the Galaxy. Other experiments failed to confirm this and it is now thought that the claims were mistaken. Several research groups are nonetheless constructing highly sensitive instruments which they hope will be the first to catch gravitational waves. The most ambitious project is the Laser Interferometer Gravitational Wave Observatory (LIGO) which is being built on two sites in Louisiana and Washington in the US. Each installation is an L-shaped structure with 4-km (2.5-mile) arms. Masses suspended at the corner of the 'L' and at the ends of the arms will move in response to a passing gravitational wave. Laser beams directed along the arms will sense these tiny motions of no more than one thousandth the diameter of a proton. Similar, though smaller-scale, observatories include VIRGO and GEO in Europe. An international proposal called LISA (Laser Interferometer Space Antenna) envisages a space-borne interferometer consisting of three spacecraft forming an equilateral triangle with sides measuring 5 million km (3 million miles) long. Lasers shining between the spacecraft will monitor their separation and so detect passing gravitational waves. Possible sources of gravitational waves include very close binaries, colliding neutron stars, and stars collapsing into black holes.

GRAVITY, DISCOVERY OF

In 1666 the young Isaac Newton gained his first insight into gravitation. According to his own account, it was triggered by his realization that the force that pulls an apple from a tree is the same as that which makes the Moon revolve around the Earth. Around 1684 Edmond Halley (1656–1742) visited Newton in Cambridge, and discovered that he had solved the problem of why the Moon moves around the Earth in an elliptical orbit. Halley urged the secretive Newton to publish his findings, and in 1687 *Philosophiae Naturalis Principia Mathematica* (*Mathematical Principles of Natural Philosophy*) appeared, setting forth Newton's revolutionary ideas not only on gravitation but also on mechanics.

))))➤ *Newtonian Cosmology, Planetary Motion, Kepler's Laws of; Relativity, General Theory of*

GREAT DARK SPOT

A storm on Neptune, observed during the 1989 Voyager 2 encounter with the planet, which has subsequently dissipated. The Great Dark Spot appeared to be a region where gases were welling up. White clouds rimming the storm system suggested that methane was being forced up from warmer depths, and then froze to create cirrus clouds of ice crystals. There were other, similar storms on the planet. Unlike Jupiter's Great Red Spot, the storm moved north and south as well as east and west. Recent images from the Hubble Space Telescope show no trace of this feature but reveal new dark spots.

))))➤ *Great Red Spot, Neptune*

GREAT DEBATE

The Great Debate was a public debate staged in Washington, DC in 1920 between Harlow Shapley and Heber D. Curtis (1872–1942), two proponents of the opposing theories of the nature of galaxies, or 'spiral nebulae' as they were then known. Well into the twentieth century, astronomers were deeply divided over their nature; some thought that they were separate 'island universes' comparable to our Milky Way, while others argued that they were smaller, nearby structures, perhaps other solar systems in the making. At the time, the Great Debate was inconclusive, but the issue was resolved in the following decade, when Edwin Hubble (1889–1953) demonstrated that spiral nebulae do indeed lie far outside our Milky Way and that their recession can be explained by the overall expansion of the Universe.

GREAT PYRAMID AT GIZA

Good surveys of the Great Pyramid of Giza (built *c.* 2700 BC), revealing its accurate astronomical alignment, date from AD 1638. They showed that the pyramid was accurately aligned north–south. It also contains finely cut shafts that point to spiritually significant star positions. The purpose behind these alignments, however, is impossible to know. Nor do we know how many alignments discovered by computer analyses from modern surveys of this and other ancient buildings were ever intended by the original builders. Far-fetched theories about these ancient structures and their builders abound.

GREAT RED SPOT

Enormous storm system on Jupiter that has been observed since telescopes were first strong enough to see it, in the seventeenth century. The colour may come from trace molecules (possibly sulphur) dredged up from below. The spot extends 23,000 km (14,300 miles) east–west, roughly twice the diameter of Earth, and 12,400 km (7,700 miles) north–south. There is a windspeed difference of 350 km/h (220 mi/h) across the north—south dimension of the spot. Constant replenishment from below and lack of a solid surface to disrupt the flow allow the Red Spot and other oval weather systems on the planet to exist for centuries or longer.

)))➤ *Great Dark Spot, Jupiter*

ABOVE: A Romanticized nineteenth-century picture showing Hipparchus using a large-aperture refracting telescope – actually invented 2,000 years later.

GREEK ASTRONOMY

In the hands of the ancient Greeks, astronomy took great strides as a rational science. In 585 BC Thales is said to have successfully predicted an eclipse, and by 480 BC, Parmenides and others were speaking of a spherical Earth. By 430 BC, the Athenian Meton had elucidated the 19-year cycle of solar eclipses. Eudoxus (407–355 BC) tried to explain the complex motions of the planets with a purely geometric model which contained 27 nested rotating spheres. By 280 BC Aristarchus (*c.* 310 BC–*c.* 230 BC) had devised a Sun-centred system, though it could not prevail against the physics of Aristotle (384–322 BC). Aristotle argued that the heavens (which began at the sphere of the Moon) were changeless; comets and new stars must be atmospheric phenomena.

Greek astronomy came to its zenith when it was infused with Babylonian computation techniques and planetary tables in the time of Hipparchus (fl. 160–125 BC). Hipparchus calculated that the Moon's maximum distance was 67.5 earth radii, astonishingly close to the true value of 63.8. He is said to have discovered the precession of the equinoxes and he further developed the system of epicycles of Eudoxus. The system was still further elaborated in the second century AD by the greatest figure of Greek astronomy, Claudius Ptolemy of Alexandria. His geocentric system went unchallenged for 1,400 years.

)))➤ *Epicycle, Hipparchus, Ptolemaic System*

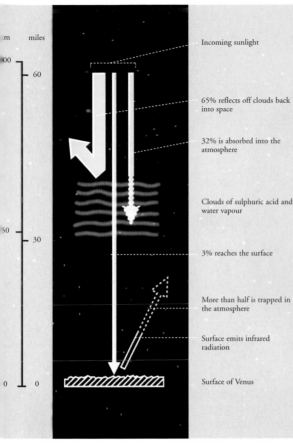

m miles

100 — 60

50 — 30

0 — 0

Incoming sunlight

65% reflects off clouds back into space

32% is absorbed into the atmosphere

Clouds of sulphuric acid and water vapour

3% reaches the surface

More than half is trapped in the atmosphere

Surface emits infrared radiation

Surface of Venus

temperature on Venus has built up to the searing level of 460°C (860°F) recorded today.

Earth, too, experiences a degree of greenhouse warming, resulting in a global surface temperature about 33°C (91°F) greater than if it had no atmosphere at all.

GREENWICH MEAN TIME

Mean solar time (in which time is measured with reference to a hypothetical 'mean Sun', which moves at a constant rate) at Greenwich, UK, on longitude 0°. It was renamed Universal Time (UT) for scientific purposes in 1928.

GREENWICH OBSERVATORY

The Royal Observatory, Greenwich, was founded in 1675, in the hope that an astronomical solution to the problem of finding longitude at sea could be found. The Reverend John Flamsteed became the first Astronomer Royal at Greenwich, though he had to provide the clocks and instruments from his own resources. Between 1675 and his death in 1719, Flamsteed began an entirely new catalogue of the northern heavens. He was a meticulous observer, and devised and established working procedures for the observatory that have survived to the present day.

GREENHOUSE EFFECT

The warming of a planet due to the trapping of solar energy by its atmosphere. The greenhouse effect is extremely intense on Venus. Although approximately two-thirds of the sunlight reflects off the planet's thick clouds with no heating effect, the remainder is absorbed in the atmosphere or penetrates to the surface. The energy of the absorbed sunlight is re-emitted at longer wavelengths, as infrared radiation. The dense carbon dioxide atmosphere is more effective at trapping this longer-wavelength radiation and is heated by it. The

ABOVE: The greenhouse effect on Venus. Although only 3% of the Sun's visible light reaches the surface of Venus, this is enough to cause the surface to emit heat as infrared radiation. More than half of this radiation is trapped, causing a greenhouse effect. As most of the atmosphere on Venus is carbon dioxide, this effect results in an average temperature of 464°C.
RIGHT: The famous Royal Observatory at Greenwich.

HALE, GEORGE ELLERY (1868–1938)

American astronomer. Hale developed the first spectrohelioscope for studying the solar surface in the light of calcium and hydrogen. In 1892 he became first director of the University of Chicago's Yerkes Observatory, when he persuaded streetcar magnate Charles Yerkes to pay for what is still the world's largest refracting telescope, with a 1-m (40-in) lens. Hale used this telescope to make observations of the Sun's chromosphere, but atmospheric conditions at Yerkes were not ideal for solar work and Hale eventually relocated to Mount Wilson near Los Angeles. There he built two major solar-tower observatories and began important programs of photographic observation of the Sun. More significant for astronomy in general, he had a flair for gaining funds to build large optical telescopes and his legacy is the 2.5-m (100-in) Mount Wilson and the 5-m (200-in) Palomar telescopes. He was also a founder, in 1895, of the prestigious Astrophysical Journal.

))))➤ *Mount Wilson Observatory*

HALLEY, EDMOND (1656–1742)

English astronomer. In 1715 Halley published a paper describing six stars that had altered considerably over time. Brahe's supernova of 1572 had disappeared altogether, whereas others, Mira, for example, varied in brightness. In 1716 he drew attention to the existence of six 'lucid spots' or telescopic nebulae. In 1718 he further discovered that three bright stars – Aldebaran, Sirius and Arcturus – had shifted position in relation to other stars since Ptolemy's time. Halley went on to question how stars could be found to have changed in position and brightness, and how they related to the nebulae. And why, if the Universe contained uncountable millions of telescopically visible stars in all directions, did the sky ever go dark at night? This problem would later be redefined as Olbers' Paradox. Best-known for his successful prediction that the comet which now bears his name would return in 1758 or 1759, Halley was instrumental in encouraging Newton to publish his *Principia*.

))))➤ *Olbers' Paradox, Newton, Isaac*

HALLEY'S COMET

Before the seventeenth century many astronomers thought that comets were atmospheric phenomena. But Sir Isaac Newton's *Principia, Book III* (1687), showed that comets were astronomical bodies moving in mathematically definable orbits. In 1705, Edmond Halley (1656–1742) published an analysis of cometary records, and argued that the bright comets of 1682, 1607 and 1531 were apparitions of the same body, moving in an elliptical orbit around the Sun. Halley predicted that it would return in 1758 or 1759. A German amateur astronomer, Georg Palitzch, caught the first glimpse of the returning comet on Christmas night, 1758. It has been known as Halley's Comet ever since.

ABOVE LEFT: Edmond Halley, whose observations of the changing positions of stars forced astronomers to reassess their belief in the fixed nature of the Universe.

ABOVE: Halley's Comet, seen from Australia at its last return in 1986. The fuzzy ball to its upper right is the galaxy NGC 5128.

HARRISON, JOHN (1693–1776)

English chronometer maker and carpenter from Yorkshire, who developed a chronometer, or sea clock, capable of keeping time to the one minute of error per month allowed by the Longitude Act of 1714. This was a huge task, for Harrison had to design mechanisms to compensate for temperature changes and the rolling of the ship. By 1761, he had produced four chronometers, each one an improvement on the one before, and while the Admiralty backed the cheaper lunar method, Harrison eventually earned himself a £20,000 prize in 1773 for inventing an accurate timekeeping mechanism for use at sea.

HAWKING RADIATION

In 1974, theoretical physicist Stephen Hawking showed that a black hole, even without an accretion disk, will emit thermal radiation. This represents a loss of energy, and therefore mass, so the black hole will slowly evaporate, eventually disappearing in a burst of radiation. According to quantum mechanics, space is not an empty vacuum in the conventional sense but is a 'soup' of so-called virtual particles which are continually popping in and out of existence. The virtual particles are created as pairs – one a particle and the other an antiparticle – and if such a pair is created just outside the event horizon of a black hole, one may be captured by the black hole while the other escapes. The separation process extracts energy from the gravitational field and this may be sufficient to convert the virtual particles into real particles. These pairs are continuously annihilating and producing Hawking radiation.

)))➤ *Accretion Disk, Antimatter*

HAWKING, STEPHEN (b. 1942)

English theoretical physicist. Hawking was born in Oxford (on the 300th anniversary of Galileo's death). Having graduated from Oxford University he

RIGHT: Stephen Hawking, who demonstrated that naked black holes (those without accretion disks) can also emit thermal radiation. The smaller the black hole, the greater the gravitational tidal force it produces. This explains why a smaller black hole is capable of greater radiation than a larger black hole.

moved to Cambridge to study for his PhD. He was made Lucasian Professor of Mathematics at Cambridge in 1980. Two of the eminent theoretical physicists who had previously occupied this chair were Newton (1642–1727) and Paul Dirac (1902–84). Hawking's work has been an attempt to synthesize the interests of gravity and quantum mechanics. After early work on relativity, Hawking concentrated on the problems of gravitational singularities, publishing important work on black holes and the Big Bang. In particular he has shown that black holes are not an irreversible energy sink, but by the processes of quantum mechanics slowly evaporate by the emission of thermal radiation. The rate of evaporation is inversely proportional to the mass of the black hole, so as the black hole diminishes in size the rate of mass loss increases. In 1988 Hawking published *A Brief History of Time*, a

outstandingly successful account of the current thinking in cosmology. It was another major achievement for a man afflicted by a crippling motor neurone disease, which has confined him to a wheelchair and requires him to talk by means of a voice synthesizer.

)))➤ *Big Bang, Black Holes, Hawking Radiation*

HELIOCENTRIC SYSTEM

Any theory in which the planets, including the Earth, are held to revolve around the Sun. Aristarchus of Samos (310–230 BC) formed a heliocentric theory, but the geocentric (Earth-centred) theory of Claudius Ptolemy dominated astronomy from the second to the sixteenth century. Nicolaus Copernicus (1473–1543) proposed a heliocentric theory in 1543 to explain the variations in the apparent motions of the planets, Moon and Sun. Though it was favoured by increasing numbers of scientists, its final victory depended on new discoveries by Johannes Kepler, Galileo Galilei and Isaac Newton.

)))➤ *Gravity, Discovery of; Planetary Motion, Kepler's Laws of; Tychonic System*

HELIOS MISSION

In December 1974, the first of two joint German-US solar spacecraft called Helios was propelled to within 46.4 million km (28.8 million miles) of the Sun to study the solar wind, magnetic fields and cosmic radiation. The second followed in January 1976. They flew closer to the Sun than previous probes.

HELIUM FLASH

An event whereby helium-burning starts explosively in the core of a lower mass star of around 1 to 2 solar masses. When the core of a star has finished burning hydrogen, it collapses and becomes 'degenerate' (a densely-packed state of matter in which the relationship between temperature and pressure that occurs in normal stars no longer applies). This causes the temperature to rise rapidly and the helium flash to occur. The helium flash is a short-lived event, for the core soon ceases to be degenerate and settles down to producing helium in a steady way. In stars of greater mass, higher temperatures allow helium fusion to commence more gradually.

HELIX NEBULA

The Helix Nebula (NGC 7293) lies in southern Aquarius and being the closest planetary nebula to us, only about 300 light years away, it is also the largest. It is known as the Helix because the gaseous ring appears to be shaped like two overlapping turns of a coil.

)))➤ *Planetary Nebula*

HERCULES CLUSTER

M13, the Hercules Cluster, is the most impressive globular cluster in northern skies, consisting of some 300,000 stars crowded into a ball over 100 light years across. Even so, at a distance of 25,000 light years all that starlight has faded to the limit of naked-eye visibility. For a sighting of M13 binoculars are needed.

HERSCHEL, SIR WILLIAM (1738-1822) AND CAROLINE (1750-1848)

German-born astronomers who were based in England. William's great discovery was the previously unknown planet Uranus in March 1781. His sister Caroline also revealed herself to be an astronomer of great talent. As well as assisting William, she discovered eight comets in her own right, and after his death in 1822 Caroline was honoured by the Royal Astronomical Society, receiving its prestigious Gold Medal, for completing his work.

HERTZ, HEINRICH (1857-94)

German physicist who discovered radio waves and showed that they travelled at the speed of light. In 1888, in order to test Maxwell's theory, Hertz generated electromagnetic waves by causing an oscillating spark to jump between two electrodes at the focus of a parabolic reflector. He detected them with a similar apparatus that produced a small spark in response to the waves. This new type of electromagnetic radiation, now called radio, was the first to be discovered after light, infrared and ultraviolet radiation.

ABOVE: William Herschel and his sister Caroline, observing the stars and planets. William is credited with the discovery of the planet Uranus.

RIGHT: The Hertzsprung-Russell diagram is a graphical way of comparing the different types of stars. It plots their surface temperatures (or spectral types) against their luminosities (or absolute magnitudes). Most stars lie along the band that runs from top left to bottom right, called the main sequence. Red giants and supergiants are at upper right, and white dwarfs at lower left.
BELOW: Heinrich Hertz and a model of the machine with which he proved the existence of electromagnetic waves.

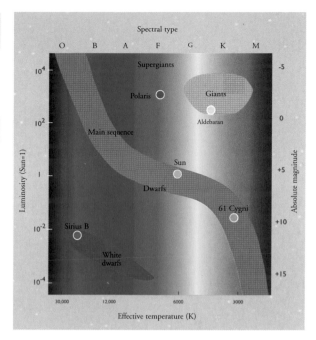

Hertz not only confirmed that Maxwell's theory was correct, but also laid the foundations of radio communications. The SI unit of frequency is named the hertz (Hz) in his honour.

HERTZSPRUNG, EJNAR (1873–1967)

Danish astronomer born in Roskilde, Denmark, a late-comer to astronomy at the age of 29. He produced a wealth of valuable results on magnitudes, colours, parallaxes and proper motions of stars, including visual binaries and variables. He was the first to realize that for stars of a particular colour there was a wide range in luminosity – he therefore discovered giants and dwarfs.
)))⟩ *Luminosity*

HERTZSPRUNG-RUSSELL DIAGRAM

In a Hertzsprung-Russell (HR) diagram, the intrinsic brightnesses of a sample of stars are plotted against some measure of their surface temperatures. Various parameters can be used: the vertical axis could be the star's apparent magnitude, absolute magnitude or luminosity. The horizontal axis might be spectral type, surface temperature or colour index (when the diagram is referred to as a colour–magnitude diagram). The outcome is not merely a random scattering of points. Stars populate very specific regions of the diagram, and this provides us with clues to their physical nature and their stage of evolution.

The well-populated band running across the HR diagram from top left to lower right is known as the main sequence. The diagram reveals that stars of similar surface temperature can have very different luminosities. To take this into account, stars are assigned a luminosity class which is appended to their spectral type. Above and to the right of the main sequence are stars of greater luminosity than dwarfs of similar temperature. These stars are giants or, in the top and upper right of the diagram, supergiants. At the other extreme, in the lower left part of the diagram, are to be found the white dwarfs.

Plotting the apparent magnitude against the spectral types of stars contained within open clusters, the standard pattern of an HR diagram emerges. If a second cluster is plotted on the same diagram, then its pattern will be the same but vertically displaced from the first. This vertical difference is because of the difference in distance of the two clusters, and the amount of displacement tells us the difference in distance. If the distance of one cluster is known, the distance to the other can be found by this process, which is known as main-sequence fitting. Additionally, it is possible to estimate the age of a star cluster from the turn-off point that stars have reached on the main sequence.

)))⟩ *Hertzsprung, Ejnar; Horizontal Branch, Instability Strip, Russell, Henry Norris*

HI AND HII REGIONS

Clouds of hydrogen in interstellar space. HI regions are composed of neutral atomic hydrogen while HII regions are composed of primarily ionized hydrogen. The hydrogen in HII regions is ionized by ultraviolet radiation from hot young stars. The Orion Nebula is a prime example of an HII region.

)))) *Emission Nebula, Orion Nebula*

HINDU ASTRONOMY

While Indian culture itself dates from earlier than 2000 BC, the basic elements of its astronomy are similar to those of Egypt and Mesopotamia. Before *c.* 1000 BC, the Hindus worked with a 360-day year. The great developments in Hindu astronomy, however, took place at the same time as those of the Babylonians, and it is quite likely that Babylonian astronomical techniques were conveyed to India along trade routes. These techniques included intercalation (the insertion of a period in the calendar to harmonize it with the solar year) and planetary table-making. Following the development of Greek planetary theory, Indian astronomers began to make use of epicycles (circles whose centres move around the circumference of greater circles) in solving problems involving variable planetary speeds. The sophistication of Hindu astronomy by 300 BC is evidenced by the quality of their lunar tables and by parallel developments in mathematics, which included the form of notation subsequently called 'Arabic' numerals. By this time, the modified Egyptian 365-day year had come into use, along with a properly intercalated calendrical cycle. By the Hellenistic, Roman and early Christian periods, trade began to flourish between the Mediterranean and India, and texts of Greek and Babylonian authorship began to be translated into Sanskrit.

HIPPARCHUS (190–120 BC)

Greek astronomer. One of his most remarkable achievements was the construction of the Hipparchian Diagram, from which he attempted to calculate the distances and respective sizes of the Moon and the Sun, from the ways in which the fast-moving (and hence closer) Moon exactly covers the slower-moving Sun during a total eclipse. Hipparchus calculated

HESS, VICTOR (1883–1964)

Austrian physicist who discovered cosmic rays in 1912. In 1910 Hess investigated the origin of background radiation that appeared in radioactivity experiments, even within lead-shielded containers.

Hess demonstrated in a series of experiments involving hazardous balloon ascents that the background radiation was due to extremely powerful cosmic rays coming from space. This illustrated that the cosmic rays were far stronger than those generated in laboratories and so penetrating that they could be detected through a metre of lead or a 500m (1,640ft) depth of water. Investigation of the nature of cosmic rays led directly to the discovery of the positron by Carl Anderson, and he shared with Hess the Nobel Prize for physics in 1936.

ABOVE: Victor Hess made several ascents in balloons up to 5 km (3 miles) to discover whether the background radiation varied with height.

that the Moon's maximum distance was 67.5 earth radii, which is astonishingly close to the correct value. He is said to have discovered the precession of the equinoxes, and constructed the first star catalogue. As an observer, a theoretician, and a utilizer of Babylonian science, Hipparchus consolidated and redirected Greek astronomy.

HIPPARCOS SATELLITE

Hipparcos, a European Space Agency satellite, measured accurate positions, parallaxes and proper motions for over 100,000 stars in our Galaxy between 1989 and 1993. It revolutionized our knowledge of the Sun's neighbourhood by providing – for the first time – large samples of stars with accurate distances and velocities, from which we were able to build up a three-dimensional picture of the Galaxy around us.

HOLMBERG, ERIK (1908–2000)

Swedish astronomer. Holmberg developed techniques for measuring basic properties of galaxies such as their brightnesses and sizes. In 1941, before the invention of the computer, he undertook the first N-body simulation. Since the strength of a gravitational force decreases with distance in the same way as the apparent brightness of a light source,

Holmberg used 74 light bulbs to represent a scale model of two galaxies. The amount of light arriving at the location of each bulb represented the gravitational pull on that part of the system. Holmberg was thus able to simulate the motions of the galaxies and demonstrate that colliding systems produce tidal tails and eventually merge.

HORIZON PROBLEM

When we measure the cosmic background radiation from any direction we are looking at gas which is so far away that the radiation from it has taken almost the age of the Universe to reach us. Looking in the opposite direction, we find that the same is true. Obviously no radiation can have passed between these two regions to equalize their temperatures and so physical contact between the two appears to violate the principle of causality. This is the 'horizon problem'.

)))))➤ *Inflationary Era*

HORIZONTAL BRANCH

The horizontal strip on the Hertzsprung–Russell diagram to the right of the main sequence and to the left of the red giant branch. Stars on the horizontal branch are low-mass stars that have passed through the helium flash and are now burning helium in their core.

)))))➤ *Hertzsprung–Russell Diagram*

HOUR ANGLE

The angle measured westwards (opposite to right ascension) along the celestial equator from an observer's meridian to the hour circle of a celestial object.

HOUR CIRCLE

A great circle on the celestial sphere along which declination is measured. The hour circle of an object thus passes through the object itself and both celestial poles.

ABOVE LEFT: The Hipparcos Satellite.
LEFT: 'Horizon Problem'. The solid circle drawn around our Galaxy represents our cosmic horizon. This is the limit to the distance we can see, set by how far light can have travelled during the lifetime of the Universe. No radiation can have passed between points A and B, on opposite sides of the horizon.

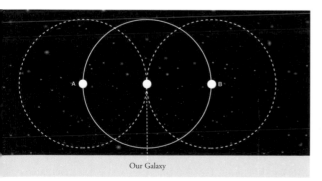

Our Galaxy

HOYLE, SIR FRED (1915–2001)

English astrophysicist and cosmologist. In 1948, together with Hermann Bondi and Thomas Gold, Hoyle proposed the Steady State theory of the Universe. Hoyle was also responsible, together with Margaret (b. 1919) and Geoffrey Burbidge (b. 1925) and William Fowler (1911–95), for the theory of nucleosynthesis, the production of the heavy chemical elements in nuclear reactions in stars. The theory – known by the acronym B^2FH after the initials of the four – applied nuclear physics to astrophysics, and argued that the synthesis of the elements found on Earth was the result of a series of nuclear reactions which occur in supernova explosions and the final stages of evolution of red giant stars.

HUBBLE DEEP FIELD SURVEY

The deep field survey carried out by the Hubble Space Telescope in 1995 revealed galaxies much farther away than any previously studied. Over 300 exposures were made in the direction of the north galactic

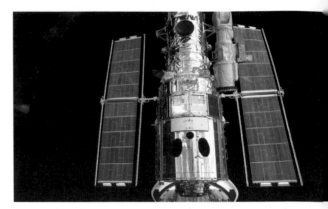

pole, each with an exposure time of 15-40 minutes and each in four colours to cover the electromagnetic spectrum from infrared to blue. More than 1,500 separate galaxies were identified. A large number of faint blue galaxies were observed which were present in the early Universe but are not present now. One explanation is that the present elliptical galaxies were formed from mergers of these early, smaller galaxies.

HUBBLE SPACE TELESCOPE

Ground-based telescopes are limited in resolution by atmospheric turbulence, which degrades the quality of the image. One solution is to place telescopes in space. The Hubble Space Telescope (HST) was launched into a 600-km (370-mile) high orbit around the Earth in April 1990. Named after the pioneering US astronomer Edwin Hubble (1889–1953), the HST features a 2.4-m (94-in) primary mirror and several cameras and spectrographs to cover the ultraviolet, visible and near-infrared bands. It is operated jointly by both NASA and ESA.

Soon after launch, it was discovered that the HST's primary mirror had been incorrectly figured and could not produce sharp images. Visiting astronauts inserted correcting optics in December 1993 and upgraded the

ABOVE: The Hubble Space Telescope (HST) is seen here in the cargo bay of the Space Shuttle during one of its service visits by astronauts.
LEFT: The sky as seen in the Hubble Deep Field (HDF) observation, the deepest-ever view of the distant Universe, like a cosmological core sample. These views capture an assortment of galaxies at various stages of evolution, some dating back to within a billion years of the Big Bang.

instruments further in 1997 and 1999. Although the 2.4 m (94-in) primary mirror is modest by modern standards, the freedom from atmospheric distortion allows the HST to achieve a resolution of better than 0.1 arcsecond, a tenfold improvement on most ground-based telescopes. With further servicing missions, the HST is expected to continue in operation until 2010.

Its replacement, the Next Generation Space Telescope (NGST), due for launch in 2009, may be as large as 8 m (315 in) in diameter and will concentrate on the near-infrared part of the spectrum.

HUBBLE, EDWIN POWELL (1889–1953)

American astronomer. Using Cepheid variable stars, Hubble determined the distance to the Andromeda galaxy in 1924. He proposed an evolutionary sequence beginning with near-circular elliptical galaxies and moving through increasing ellipticity to reach a basic form of spiral galaxy. The sequence, he believed, continued as two parallel forms of spiral, forming the famous tuning fork diagram. Although the evolutionary part of this classification is no longer believed to be correct, Hubble's basic forms are still used to define galactic types. In 1929 Hubble proposed what is now known as Hubble's law, implying that we live in an expanding Universe.

))))➤ *Tuning Fork Diagram*

HUBBLE TIME

From Hubble's law, if the expansion of the Universe has been steady, then the time which has elapsed since the Big Bang can, in principle, be calculated by using $1/H_0$ where H_0 is Hubble's constant. This is often referred to as the Hubble time. If we know Hubble's constant we also know the Hubble time. The current best estimate of the Hubble time is 15 billion years.

))))➤ *Hubble's Constant, Hubble's Law*

BELOW LEFT: Edwin Hubble determined that the Universe is composed of a multitude of galaxies of stars, and that they are moving apart from each other at a speed that increases with their separation. The Hubble Space Telescope is named in honour of his contribution to cosmology.

HUBBLE'S CONSTANT

By 1925, the American astronomer Edwin Hubble had shown the Andromeda 'nebula' to be a galaxy beyond our own, though his estimates for its size and distance were much smaller than those accepted today. With his colleague, Milton Humason, Hubble began to collect data on the distances and motions of similar objects. In 1929, Hubble presented evidence indicating that the farther away such galaxies are, the faster they are receding from us. This was the observational germ of the later Big Bang theory. During the 1930s, Hubble and Humason collected data from increasing numbers of galaxies, and confirmed the correlation. The ratio of speed to distance is called Hubble's constant, and recent measurements indicate that its value is likely to lie in the range 18–24 km/s (11–15 mi/sec) per million light years. Conventionally, the constant is expressed in units of kilometres per second per megaparsec (km/s/Mpc), where 1 megaparsec (Mpc) = 3,260,000 light years. The Hubble Space Telescope Key Projects team has obtained a value of 72 km/s/Mpc (22 km/s per million light years).

HUBBLE'S LAW

Edwin Hubble (1889–1953) noticed that while a few bright galaxies had blueshifts, the fainter galaxies had only redshifts. He also noticed that galaxies with the largest redshifts tended to have the smallest images, and so were farther away. Using this limited data, he proposed that the galaxies were receding from us at a rate that was proportional to their distance. The implication of this was profound – at some finite time in the past the whole observable Universe must have been concentrated into a very small region, i.e. the Universe had a beginning.

Hubble's law states that the recessional velocity, V_r, of any distant galaxy is proportional to its distance, d, and is normally expressed as a simple equation:

$$V_r = H_0 d$$

The value H_0 is known as Hubble's constant.

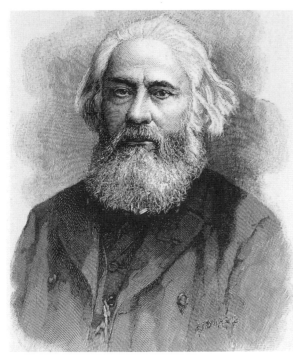

HUGGINS, SIR WILLIAM (1824–1910)

English astronomer. Huggins showed in 1863 that stars are made of the same elements as the Sun and detected gas in six nebulae in 1864. The difference between stellar and gaseous nebulae became obvious when examining them through a spectroscope. Huggins and his wife Margaret, together with Henry Draper (1837–82) in New York, photographed the spectra of thousands of objects over four decades, and played a major role in establishing the new science of astrophysics.

HUYGENS, CHRISTIAAN (1629–95)

Dutch mathematician and astronomer who proposed that light was a form of wave motion. In 1690 Huygens showed that each point on a wavefront, (the surface connecting crests of a wave), could be regarded as a source of 'secondary wavelets' that spread

ABOVE: Sir William Huggins, who was a pioneer in recording stellar spectra photographically during his 40-year career. By 1880, the new science of astrophysics was transforming cosmology.
RIGHT: Hyperion is a 400-km moon of Saturn whose chaotic axial rotation cannot be predicted even by the most powerful computers.

out in all directions. Huygens' principle provides a powerful model for the propagation of light and is still used in teaching the physics of diffraction.

Huygens was the first to realize (in 1659) that Saturn is surrounded by a ring and, in 1655, he discovered Titan, the largest satellite of that planet. He was also the first astronomer to sketch genuine features on the surface of Mars and to make a reasonable estimate of the planet's rotation period.

HYPERBOLIC ORBIT

An orbit that has the form of the open curve called a hyperbola, rather than an ellipse. It is the path of a celestial body that passes another but is not captured gravitationally, and thus does not enter into an orbit around the second body.

))))➤ *Planetary Motion, Kepler's Laws of*

HYPERGIANTS

The hypergiants are among the most luminous stars in the Galaxy, perhaps 100,000 times brighter than the Sun in the visual part of the electromagnetic spectrum. They have masses above about 30 Suns but below the 45 solar-mass threshold of the luminous blue variables. They have spectral types ranging from B to M and have been allocated the luminosity class Ia+ or even 0, setting them above the brightest normal supergiants. Hypergiants often move around the Hertzsprung–Russell diagram even within a human lifetime, these excursions being accompanied by sporadic events of mass-loss which generate shells of material around the star. A well-known example, Rho Cassiopeiae, is to be found near the familiar W-shape of stars in Cassiopeia.

))))➤ *Hertzsprung–Russell Diagram*

HYPERION

A small satellite of Saturn with a maximum diameter of about 370 km. Its main interest is that it follows a markedly elliptical orbit, under

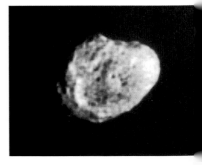

the influence of the large moon Titan, instead of rotating smoothly around a single axis. Its irregular shape and chaotic motion suggest that Hyperion was once a larger body that suffered a number of catastrophic collisions.

))))➤ *Planetary Motion, Kepler's Laws of*

INFLATIONARY ERA

A solution to the horizon problem was proposed by Alan Guth. He suggested that during its earliest stages – between roughly 10^{-34} s and 10^{-32} s – the Universe underwent a period of extremely rapid expansion, during which the expansion rate was actually accelerating. This period is known as the inflationary era (often shortened to 'inflation'), and during it the Universe's size increased dramatically. Although this solution may appear contrived, inflation simultaneously explains several features of our observed Universe.

))))➤ *Horizon Problem*

INFRARED ASTRONOMY

Most infrared radiation is absorbed by the Earth's atmosphere, although certain wavelengths penetrate through to high altitudes. Most objects glow brightly at infrared wavelengths, including Earth's atmosphere and telescopes. Detectors subtract background noise, and are cooled by liquid nitrogen to reduce their own emissions.

Amongst the largest infrared telescopes are the 3.8-m (150-in) UK Infrared Telescope (UKIRT) and the 8.2-m (323-in) Subaru Telescope, both to be found at Mauna Kea Observatory, Hawaii. These telescopes are used to observe relatively cool objects, such as dust clouds and newly forming stars. Since infrared waves are longer than those of ordinary light, they do not bounce off particles in dusty regions, but pass through, revealing stars hidden at visible wavelengths. Other infrared sources include active galaxies and starburst galaxies.

))))➤ *Active Galaxies, Infrared Rays, Infrared Satellites,*
Starburst Galaxies

INFRARED RAYS

The infrared region of the electromagnetic spectrum lies to the long-wavelength side of visible light and was discovered in 1800 by the German-British astronomer William Herschel, who placed a thermometer beyond the red end of a spectrum of sunlight formed by a prism. The thermometer rose, indicating that it was being heated by radiation invisible to the eye. Infrared radiation, which extends from 700 nm to 1 mm, is sometimes known as 'radiant heat' because it is emitted by objects at normal temperatures and can be felt as warmth on the skin. This term can be misleading, since all forms of electromagnetic radiation, including visible light, can warm matter if they are absorbed. Radiation at infrared wavelengths is readily emitted and absorbed by vibrating or rotating molecules. Absorption by carbon dioxide and water molecules make the atmosphere opaque in most of the infrared band. These molecules are also largely responsible for the greenhouse effect. The infrared region of the spectrum is roughly divided into the near, mid and far infrared.

INFRARED SATELLITES

The far-infrared region of the spectrum was first explored by high-altitude aircraft and balloon-borne telescopes in the 1970s, but the first comprehensive surveys awaited the arrival of infrared telescopes on board satellites. The first of these, the Infrared Astronomical Satellite (IRAS), was a Netherlands-UK-US spacecraft that surveyed the whole sky in 1983, detecting a quarter of a million individual sources. The European Infrared Space Observatory (ISO) followed in 1995. These spacecraft had short lifetimes because of the need to carry supplies of volatile liquid helium to cool their detectors. When ISO's coolant ran out after three years observing had to stop. More infrared spacecraft are planned, including the US Space Infrared Telescope Facility (SIRTF) and ESA's 3.5-m (138-in) Herschel Space Observatory. Herschel will be launched by Ariane 5 in 2007 and for a minimum of three years. It will help solve the big questions of how stars and galaxies form.

INSTABILITY STRIP

The narrow region of the Hertzsprung–Russell diagram in which pulsating variable stars (e.g. Cepheid variables, RR Lyrae stars etc.) are located. Most stars pass through this region at some time in their lives, the type of pulsating variable the star becomes depending on the star's mass.

)))) **Delta Scuti Stars**

INTERCALATION

Intercalation is the insertion of extra days or months into the calendar in order to harmonize it with the solar year. In the Gregorian calendar, which is used worldwide today, the extra day added every leap year is an intercalated day.

INTERFEROMETER

Radio astronomers use two or more telescopes together to form an interferometer, which achieves a resolution similar to that of a single dish of diameter equal to the maximum spacing (or baseline) between the telescopes. Detailed images are formed by aperture synthesis (the technique of combining the telescopes' signals to produce an image) where two or more

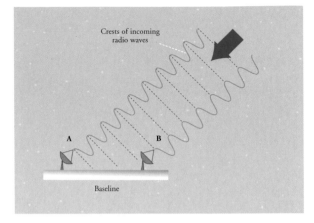

Crests of incoming
radio waves

A   B

Baseline

ABOVE: In a simple two-element interferometer, radio waves from a distant source arrive at one telescope (B) slightly before the other (A). The interferometer effectively measures this tiny delay and uses it to calculate the precise direction of the source in the sky. With more telescopes and extended observations a detailed picture of the source can be built up.
BELOW: The Very Large Array (VLA) in New Mexico is an aperture synthesis telescope made up of 27 dishes each 25 m in diameter.

telescopes are pointed at the same source for 12 hours as the Earth rotates. By successively altering the spacing between the telescopes, data is obtained as if a complete larger radio dish has been used. The Very Large Array (VLA) in New Mexico is an aperture-synthesis telescope, with 27 movable dishes. In

very long baseline interferometry (VLBI), telescopes are separated by hundreds or thousands of kilometres.

INTERNATIONAL COMETARY EXPLORER (ICE)

The International Cometary Explorer (ICE) was originally called ISEE-3 (International Sun-Earth Explorer). Once its original mission was completed it was reactivated and diverted, utilizing the Moon's gravity to flip it into a new orbit. ICE passed through the tail of comet Giacobini-Zinner on 11 September 1985 and observed Halley's Comet in March 1986.

INTERNATIONAL GEOPHYSICAL YEAR

On 29 July 1955, the US announced that a goal of the International Geophysical Year (IGY) – a global collaboration to study the physics of Earth from 1 July 1957 through to 31 December 1958 – would be to place an artificial satellite into Earth orbit. Both the US Army and Navy submitted plans for launch vehicles. Despite the Army's careful plan, and the potential of von Braun's rockets, which had already reached altitudes of 1,098 km (682 miles), it was the Navy's Vanguard project that was approved. By 2 August 1955, the Soviet Union had also declared its desire to launch an artificial satellite during the IGY.

INTERNATIONAL SPACE STATION (ISS)

The plans for an International Space Station were announced in 1984, when the US president Ronald Reagan declared that NASA would build a large space station for use by astronauts from the US and other nations. The former Soviet Union also joined the program in 1993 and the first component – the 19,320-kg (42,600-lb) Zarya ('Sunrise') module – was launched in November 1998.

A month later the Shuttle Endeavour attached the Unity docking module, a unit allowing other modules to be attached. A second Russian component, Zvezda ('Star'), containing living quarters and a propulsion

ABOVE: How the International Space Station should look when fully assembled in 2005.

system docked in July 2000. Other nations, including Brazil, Japan, Canada and the European Space Agency (ESA) are participating in the project. At 37 m (120 ft) in length and with a wingspan of 28 m (95 ft), the ISS is one of the brightest objects in the night sky.

The first crew arrived in November 2000 for an extended stay of four months. More than 40 flights will complete construction by 2006 at the earliest, when it will serve as a permanent orbiting science institute for research in a nearly gravity-free environment. By then the ISS will be three times the volume of a two-floored house and able to support a crew of seven.

INTERPLANETARY DUST

Fine grains of matter that permeate the space between the planets. When interplanetary dust particles enter Earth's atmosphere at high speeds, they burn up by friction at around 100 km (60 miles) altitude, creating a trail of ionized air that glows briefly to create a meteor or 'shooting star'. Some of this dust comes from asteroids and some from comets. Each time Earth crosses a comet orbit it encounters a swarm of dust particles and we see a meteor shower.

)))) *Meteor Showers, Meteorites*

INTERSTELLAR ABSORPTION

Absorption of light by gas and dust in interstellar space affects measurements of the colour and luminosity of stars. Interstellar gas produces an absorption-line spectrum which is superimposed on a star's own spectrum while the dust not only dims starlight but also reddens it by preferentially absorbing blue light, altering a star's colour index. The effect of reddening on a Hertzsprung-Russell diagram where apparent magnitude is plotted against colour index is to slide the points downwards and to the right. However, the spectral type is not changed and so the amount of reddening can be estimated and corrected for.

))))▶ *Aborption Line Spectrum*

INTERSTELLAR MEDIUM

The space between the stars is not as empty as it may at first appear – it contains gas, dust, magnetic fields and cosmic rays. Collectively, this is termed the interstellar medium, or ISM. The composition of the gas in the ISM ranges from simple hydrogen atoms to complex carbon-containing molecules; it also has a wide range of temperature and density. Some of it is very cold and relatively dense, with a temperature of about 20 K (-425°F) and a concentration of about a thousand molecules per cubic centimetre, as exemplified by the giant molecular clouds from which stars form. Less cold and dense are clouds of neutral (i.e. non-ionized) hydrogen, termed H I regions, which have a temperature of 100 K (-280°F) and a concentration of about 20 atoms per cubic centimetre – these clouds give out the 21-cm radiation that is detected by radio astronomers. Most impressive visually are the clouds of hot, ionized gas known as H II regions, at a temperature of a few thousand degrees K (or F), familiar to observers as the bright nebulae surrounding young stars, such as in Orion. Finally, there is a very hot (million-degree) gas of low density, heated by the blast waves from supernovae, which fills two-thirds of the volume of interstellar space. Dust always occurs with gas in the ISM. Interstellar dust is akin to soot and very fine sand, consisting of tiny grains of carbon, silicon and even small ice crystals. These dust grains absorb and scatter starlight, not merely dimming the light from stars but also reddening it. When dense,

ABOVE: The satellite Io. Scientists have recently discovered new details of a giant crater on its surface which contains a multi-coloured lake of molton lava.

dusty clouds are illuminated by nearby stars, light scattered by the dust can be directly observed as a bluish reflection nebula.

IO

Innermost of the four large satellites of the giant planet Jupiter. Unlike the other satellites, Io's surface is a cauldron of geological activity, where active volcanic vents coat the surface in red and yellow sulphur lava. Io's slightly noncircular orbit takes the satellite through constantly changing strengths of Jupiter's gravity field and constantly flexes it. The tidal forces heat the interior and trigger volcanic activity.

IRAS

The Infrared Astronomical Satellite (IRAS), a collaboration between the Netherlands, the UK and the USA, was launched in January 1983 to conduct the first sky survey at far-infrared wavelengths. The 60-cm (24-in) telescope and detectors were cooled to just three degrees above absolute zero by liquid helium to prevent their own radiation swamping the weaker signals from space. When the last of the helium had evaporated, in November 1983, the highly successful mission came to an end. The IRAS survey highlighted the location and structure of stellar nurseries, recorded more than a quarter of a million individual sources and discovered five comets and numerous asteroids.

IRREGULAR GALAXIES

Irregular galaxies are any galaxies which do not fit in any other category. They lack the symmetry of spirals and ellipticals, giving them a ragged appearance. Their lack of aesthetic beauty, combined with the fact

that they tend to be smaller and fainter than other galaxy types, means that irregulars do not feature prominently in most popular books on astronomy. However, they are very common, accounting for more than a third of all galaxies. Two of our closest galactic neighbours, the Magellanic Clouds, are both irregulars. The Large Magellanic Cloud has a noticeable bar-shape and so is classified as a barred irregular.

))))▶ *Large Magellenic Cloud*

ISLAMIC CALENDAR

The Islamic calendar is basically a lunar one, which means that observation of the new Moon – at its thinnest crescent – is a fundamental event for time reckoning. However, neither the lunar nor the solar cycles form neatly divisible numbers and from the very start, Muslims, like other peoples, faced the problem of reconciling the two. Although the prophet Mohammed ruled against intercalation on theological grounds,

ABOVE: Irregular galaxies – the Large Magellanic Cloud (LMC) is one of the Milky Way's closest neighbours.
ABOVE RIGHT: The Copernican Universe, showing the Sun at the centre encircled by Earth and other planets.

astronomers could not escape the problem; a lunar year of 12 months is roughly 11 days shorter than the solar year.

ITALIAN RENAISSANCE

The origins of the sixteenth-century Copernican revolution lie less in errors found in practical astronomy than in the growth of Renaissance humanism. There was an influx of scholars and original Greek manuscripts into Europe following the Turkish occupation of Constantinople in 1453. This meant that European scholars now had access to Ptolemy in the original Greek, rather than through Arabic-to-Latin translations. The Constantinople-educated cardinal and scholar Johannes Bessarion was a major driving force in this movement, and his collection of

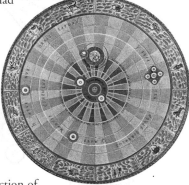

Greek manuscripts was important in enabling Georg Peurbach (1423–61) and Regiomontanus (1436–76) to produce the *Epitome*, or abridgement, of Ptolemy's *Almagest* (published 1496). It was these accurate Greek interpretations of Ptolemy which truly started the astronomical Renaissance.

))))▶ *Copernicus, Nicolaus*

JEANS, SIR JAMES (1877–1946)

British mathematician and physicist. In 1902 he showed that a cloud could only condense under gravity if it met certain initial conditions of density, size and temperature. His findings remain the basis for all modern work on the formation of stars and galaxies. Rejecting the idea that the Solar System had condensed in a similar fashion, he preferred the view that the material which formed the planets had been drawn out of the Sun by the gravitational pull of a passing star.

In 1928, 20 years before the development of the Steady State theory, he proposed that matter was continually created in the centres of spiral galaxies.

))))▶ *Spiral Galaxies, Steady State Theory*

JUPITER

The fifth planet from the Sun and by far the largest in the Solar System. It is twice as massive as all the other planets combined, and so voluminous that 1,300 Earths would fit inside it. Made mainly of hydrogen and helium, Jupiter has no solid surface. Its turbulent atmosphere extends downwards until extreme temperatures and pressures form a liquid core of metallic hydrogen, inside which there may be a rocky core. Jupiter orbits the Sun once every 11.9 years, accompanied by a large entourage of satellites.

Jupiter's Atmosphere

Jupiter's rapid rotation speed – 45,000 km/h (28,000 mi/h) at the equator – flattens the planet at the poles and creates a bulging equator. It also organizes the outer atmosphere into regions of alternating wind jets, decreasing in strength towards the poles and creating a banded cloud structure. Eastward winds reach 400 km/h (250 mi/h) in the equatorial region, while at 17° latitude westward winds blow at 100 km/h (60 mi/h).

The Magnetosphere

Jupiter has the largest magnetosphere of all the planets. It stretches for some 650 million km (400 million miles) on the side away from the Sun. Within the magnetosphere are radiation belts similar to Earth's Van Allen belts, but far more intense. As with the other gas giants, the origin of Jupiter's mighty magnetosphere lies within its liquid interior, where a continuous churning driven by internal heat produces a dynamo effect, creating the magnetic field.

ABOVE: Despite its massive size (1,300 times the size of Earth), Jupiter is simply an enormous globe of gas, mainly hydrogen and helium.
RIGHT: Each of Jupiter's four Galilean satellites has its own distinctive features. The surface of Io pictured here is sculpted by volcanic activity.

Jupiter's Interior

In December 1995 the Galileo orbiter released a small atmospheric probe that made a one-way trip into the clouds. The Orbiter sent back a wealth of data for 57 minutes before being crushed and then vaporized by the ever-increasing temperature and pressure, just 320 km (200 miles) beneath the visible surface.

The Jovian atmosphere comprises three principal cloud decks. The uppermost of these decks is composed of cold, wispy cirrus clouds of ammonia ice. In an atmosphere whose initial mixture of elements was similar to that of the Sun, hydrogen has combined with nitrogen and carbon to form ammonia and methane. At -150°C (-238°F), the ammonia condenses and forms Jupiter's opaque upper cloud deck.

The middle cloud deck is made of ammonium hydrosulphide, formed by water vapour combining with sulphur. The pressure is about 1 bar (1 bar is the atmospheric pressure at sea level on Earth).

In the lowest cloud deck temperatures hover close to the freezing point of water. The clouds are composed of

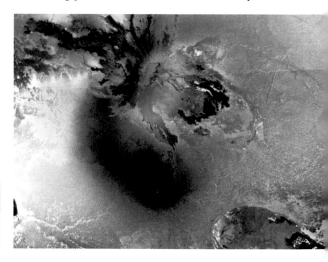

water in the form of ice crystals or possibly liquid droplets. Farther down, the temperature, pressure and wind speed increase rapidly as Jupiter's immense gravity crushes the atmospheric gases. The Galileo atmospheric probe's dying signal recorded a temperature of 300°C (572°F) and a pressure of 22 bars, 150 km (93 miles) below the height at which the probe began taking data. Wind speeds had increased from 360 km/h (224 mi/h) near the top of the atmosphere to 540 km/h (336 mi/h) and powerful lightning strikes were recorded.

Only theory can tell us what lies deeper within Jupiter. The models suggest that a huge hydrogen- and helium-rich envelope exists, thousands of kilometres deep, becoming increasingly compressed with depth.

Eventually, the atmosphere gives way to a global sea of hydrogen, crushed to such a degree that it is liquid even though it is at temperatures of many thousands of degrees. Deeper down, hydrogen behaves like a liquid metal (liquid metallic hydrogen) which conducts electricity. Circulating flows within the liquid metallic hydrogen zone generate Jupiter's powerful magnetic field. It is estimated that the central core must be at a temperature of 20,000°C (36,000°F) and a pressure of 100 million bars.

Rings and Minor Satellites

Jupiter's collection of moons can be subdivided into four sets. The innermost set comprises four small irregular satellites (Metis, Adrastea, Amalthea and Thebe). Then come four large satellites discovered by Galileo, there are also two outer sets of moons.

The Innermost Satellites

Metis and Adrastea, the two innermost satellites, have diameters of less than 50 km (30 miles). They are closely associated with a system of tenuous rings, so thin and dark that they were not observed until the spacecraft flybys. Among the outer satellites, orbital similarities suggest that the satellites are fragments of larger bodies. For example, they revolve around Jupiter in a retrograde direction (that is, in the opposite direction to the other satellites and opposite to the direction of Jupiter's own rotation). Satellites born together with the parent planet and other satellites would share the same direction of revolution.

Seeing Jupiter and its Satellites

Jupiter is one of the brightest objects in the sky, outshone only by the Sun, the Moon and Venus. Through a telescope Jupiter is a fine sight. Its complex cloud systems are clearly visible as light and dark bands, running parallel with the planet's equator. Perhaps the most readily distinguishable feature on the disk of Jupiter is the Great Red Spot.

Accompanying Jupiter are four easily observed satellites: Io, Europa, Ganymede and Callisto. These are known as the four Galilean satellites, named in honour of Galileo Galilei (1564–1642), who discovered them in 1610.

)))➤ *Galilean Satellites, Giant Planets, Great Red Spot, Magnetosphere, Planetary Rings, Van Allen Belts*

KANT, IMMANUEL (1724–1804)

German philosopher. In his *Theory of the Heavens*, published in 1755, Kant argued that the stars of the Milky Way were a rotating disk maintained by gravity. He also argued that some of the nebulae, the diffuse patches of light in the night sky, were elliptical, and 'systems of the same order as our own'. He conjectured that those other milky ways might form clusters and that such clusters might be found throughout the Universe. Kant considered the Universe as a whole, concluding that 'there is here no end but an abyss of a real immensity, in the presence of which all the capacity of human conception sinks exhausted'.

KAPTEYN, JACOBUS (1851–1922)

Dutch astronomer who in 1906 set out to map the structure of the Galaxy. Collaborators counted the numbers of stars of different brightness in some 200 selected areas of sky and measured their motions. Kapteyn wrongly concluded that the Sun lay close to the centre of the Galaxy. However, Harlow Shapley (1885–1972), a US astronomer, later demonstrated around 1918 that the Sun lay well away from the centre

))))⯈ *Shapley, Harold*

ABOVE: *Immanuel Kant speculated that some elliptical nebulae were separate systems of stars like the Milky Way.*
ABOVE RIGHT: *Johannes Kepler's investigations into the orbit of Mars revolutionized planetary theory.*

KECK TELESCOPES

At the time of writing, the world's biggest telescopes are the twin 10-m (390-in) Keck telescopes in Hawaii, whose mirrors are each made from a mosaic of 36 hexagonal segments rather than a single piece of glass. The light-collecting area of each telescope is 17 times greater than the Hubble Space Telescope.

KEPLER, JOHANNES (1571–1630)

German astronomer. A Lutheran Protestant from Weil in Catholic South Germany, Kepler's talent won him a place to train for the ministry at Tübingen, and while never ordained, his love of astronomy was imbued with a powerful religious conviction. After lecturing at Gratz in Austria (where the idea of the geometrical solids and the planets came to him), Kepler was taken up by Tycho Brahe (1546–1601), one of the leading astronomers of the Renaissance. Following Tycho's death he succeeded Tycho as Imperial Mathematician. He became Mathematics professor at Linz in 1612, and at Ulm in 1627 he published his *Rudolphine Tables*, based on Tycho's observations. From his analysis of Tycho's observations, he established three laws of planetary motion. He predicted the transits of Mercury in 1630 and Venus in 1631. Kepler's optical researches also led him to invent the telescope eyepiece that bears his name.

))))⯈ *Planetary Motion, Kepler's Laws of*

KIRKWOOD GAPS

Regions within the asteroid belt where few, if any, asteroids are found. The gaps result from periodic disturbances by Jupiter, which make stable orbits impossible. They occur at distances from the Sun at which the orbital period is a simple fraction of Jupiter's orbital period: for example, ¼, ⅓, ⅖, ½ etc. They are named after Daniel Kirkwood (1814–95), who first explained them.

KOROLEV, SERGEI PAVLOVICH (1906–66)

Russian rocket scientist. Korolev was an active member of the Moscow Group for the Study of Rocket Propulsion, with whom he helped to develop the first liquid-fuelled rockets launched in the USSR. Imprisoned by Stalin in 1938, he was forced to work in a scientific labour camp during the Second World War. Once freed, Korolev returned to rockets, working to improve the design of the captured V-2 missile and turning it into the first Soviet intercontinental ballistic missile, which carried the Sputnik satellites into orbit. Korolev later went on to mastermind the development of manned Vostok and Voskhod spacecraft and a series of robotic missions to the near planets.

LAGRANGIAN POINTS

Neutral points in the combined gravitational fields of a system of celestial bodies at which a small body will experience effectively zero net gravitational force. In a system of two massive orbiting bodies, the Lagrangian points are positions at which a smaller body can lie in equilibrium. For example, the Trojan asteroids are groups of asteroids that reside at two of the Lagrangian points in the Jupiter–Sun system, 60° ahead of and behind Jupiter in its orbit. In a system of close binary stars, the Lagrangian points are places where material can pass from one star to the other.

⟫⟫➤ *Equipotential Surface, Roche Lobes*

LARGE MAGELLANIC CLOUD

Second closest galaxy to the Milky Way, about 170,000 light years from the Sun, the Large

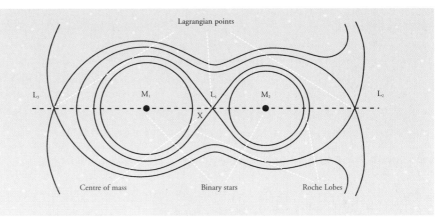

ABOVE: The combined gravitational influences of the two masses (M_1 and M_2), is effectively zero at the Lagrangian points.

Magellanic Cloud is an irregular galaxy visible to the naked eye in the southern sky. It has about a hundredth the total mass of our Galaxy and is about 35,000 light years wide. Together with the Small Magellanic Cloud, it is enveloped in a cloud of hydrogen gas from which emerges a swathe of gas called the Magellanic Stream. Close approaches between the Magellanic Clouds and the Galaxy are thought to have occurred about 300 million years and five billion years ago. The Small Magellanic Cloud was probably broken off the Large Cloud during one of those approaches. Both Magellanic Clouds are expected to suffer the same fate as the Sagittarius Dwarf, spiralling in to the Galactic centre in another 10 billion years or so.

LATE HEAVY BOMBARDMENT

Bombardment of the bodies in the inner Solar System by debris left over from the formation of the planets which took place between the time of their formation until about 3.9 billion years ago. The oldest surfaces in the inner Solar System, those of Mars, Mercury and the Moon, bear scarring that is a record of the Late Heavy Bombardment. Between 3.9 and 3.4 billion years ago the number of impacts declined greatly. It is between these dates that the earliest known fossils are found on Earth, indicating that, as soon as the period of heavy bombardment ceased, life was able to gain a foothold.

LATITUDE

1. On a near-spherical body such as a planet, the angular distance north or south of the equator.
2. Celestial (or ecliptic) latitude is the angular distance of a body north or south from the ecliptic.
3. Galactic latitude is the angular distance north or south of the galactic equator.

LE VERRIER, URBAIN (1819–77)

French astronomer whose analysis of the motion of the planet Uranus led to the discovery of the planet Neptune in 1846. A similar calculation was made by John Couch Adams. Le Verrier's analysis of the motion of Mercury led him to predict, erroneously, the existence of a planet closer to the Sun than Mercury.

LEAVITT, HENRIETTA (1868–1921)

American astronomer. Between 1908 and 1912, Leavitt, in her analysis of photographic plates of the Small Magellanic Cloud taken by the Harvard Observatory's telescope in Peru, discovered a curious thing: all the variable stars which showed a light-output curve similar to Delta [δ] Cephei – or Cepheid variables – shared a mathematical relationship. The brighter the absolute magnitude of the Cepheid, the longer it took for the particular star to go through its light cycle. Because all the stars in the Magellanic Cloud were virtually the same distance from Earth, they provided an ideal laboratory in which to quantify the period-luminosity patterns of bright and dim Cepheids.

LENTICULAR GALAXIES

Lenticular (lens-shaped) galaxies appear to form a transition between spiral galaxies and ellipticals. Like spirals, these galaxies have disks and central bulges; they can also contain central bar features. However, they lack any spiral structure and so have the smooth, featureless appearance of ellipticals. If a lenticular galaxy happened to be oriented face-on to us it would be difficult to distinguish from a round elliptical. Lenticular galaxies contain mostly old stars and little gas or dust, and are more common in rich clusters of galaxies. Whether lenticulars are former spirals that have somehow lost their gas or whether they formed as they are today is uncertain.

LEO

Leo the lion's most distinctive feature is a hook shape of six stars called the Sickle. In the arc of the Sickle of Leo lies one of the finest double stars for small telescopes, Gamma [γ] Leonis. Other double stars include Regulus (Alpha [α] Leonis), Zeta [ζ] Leonis and Iota [ι] Leonis. Galaxies in Leo include M65, M66, M95, M96 and M105. All five of these seem to be part of the same cluster, about 35 million light years from us. Leo also contains R Leonis, a variable red giant.

LEONOV, ALEXEI (b. 1934)

Russian astronaut. The first man to walk in space when he floated outside the Voskhod 2 spacecraft for 10 minutes on 18 March 1965. After attending an air-force school Leonov served as a fighter pilot before being selected as a cosmonaut in March 1960. Initially a candidate for the first Vostok spaceflight, Leonov was discounted in favour of Gagarin and Titov, who were several inches shorter than him.

After his Voskhod 2 flight, Leonov went on to train for the Russian manned circumlunar and lunar landing missions, and could have become the first man to walk on the Moon. The rest of his cosmonaut career was spent on

LEFT: Lenticular or lens-shaped galaxies such as NGC 3115 exhibit characteristics midway between those of spirals and ellipticals. They have a nucleus surrounded by a disk, but no spiral structure.

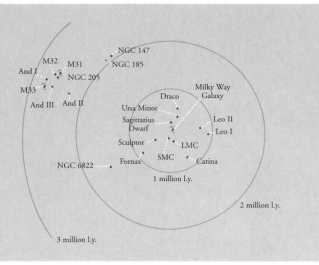

NGC 147

M32 M31 NGC 185
And I NGC 205
M33
And III And II

Milky Way
Galaxy
Draco
Ursa Minor
Sagittarius Leo II
Dwarf Leo I
Sculptor
NGC 6822 Fornax LMC
SMC Carina

1 million l.y.

2 million l.y.

3 million l.y.

ABOVE: The Local Group. Its largest members are two spiral galaxies of similar size and mass: the Milky Way Galaxy and the Andromeda Galaxy (M31). Both galaxies have clusters of dwarf galaxies associated with them. BELOW: Light pollution causes the night sky to glow orange but even in the brightly lit skies of towns it is still just about possible to spot stars and planets.

Earth orbital missions, but he did not fly again until the Apollo–Soyuz test flight in 1975. Leonov served as deputy director of the Gagarin Center for cosmonaut training until his retirement in October 1991.

))))▶ *Apollo–Soyuz Mission*

LIGHT POLLUTION

With the spread of urban light, the problem of 'light pollution' has become the bane of astronomers. With artificial light reflecting off surfaces or shining directly into the sky, the night starts to glow, often with an orange hue because of the type of lamp used in street lighting. Any light shining into the sky reflects off water droplets and dust particles, causing this 'sky glow'. As the background sky becomes lighter, the fainter stars are drowned out as a result. For years astronomers have campaigned for better lighting, asking that the minimum amount of light necessary should be used, and that the light should be directed where it is needed, not up into the sky.

))))▶ *Astronomy, Seeing for Yourself*

LIGHT YEAR

The distance travelled by light or any other form of electromagnetic radiation in a vacuum over one year. Symbol l.y., one light year is about 9.4605×10^{12} km; 0.3066 parsecs; 63,240 astronomical units.

LOCAL GROUP

The Local Group is the name given to the cluster of about three dozen galaxies, all bound together by gravity, to which our home Galaxy belongs. All galaxies within about three million light years of our own are generally considered members. Two spiral galaxies dominate the Local Group: one is our own, the other is the Andromeda Galaxy (M31). The Andromeda Galaxy is similar in size and mass to our Galaxy, but its central bulge and disk are larger and it has less gas. The most common galaxies in the Local Group are dwarf spheroidal galaxies, which cluster around the two big spirals – our Galaxy has an entourage of 12 dwarfs, ranging from the nearby Sagittarius Dwarf to the distant Leo I and Leo II. The Andromeda Galaxy has a similar number of dwarf companions, although here the sample is probably still incomplete.

))))▶ *Andromeda Galaxy*

LOVELL, SIR BERNARD (b. 1913)

English astronomer who conducted radar research during the Second World War. In December 1945 he installed ex-military radar equipment at the University of Manchester's botanical research station at Jodrell Bank in Cheshire, and studied radar echoes from daytime meteor showers, and cosmic rays from the Milky Way and beyond.

Lovell's project to construct a vast 76-m (250-ft) steerable dish gained momentum with the imminent birth of the Space Age and was rushed to completion by 1957 – just in time to track Sputnik 1's carrier rocket. The Russians were delighted when Lovell used the telescope to confirm that their Luna 2 probe had reached the Moon, and NASA used it to contact their first deep-space probe, Pioneer 5. Lovell directed the observatory until 1981 and the telescope has since been named after him. Refitted in the 1990s with a new reflective surface, it is still among the most powerful radio telescopes in the world.

LONGITUDE

1. On a near-spherical body such as a planet, the angular distance east or west of a reference meridian.
2. Celestial (or ecliptic) longitude is the angular distance of a body east of the vernal equinox, measured along the ecliptic.
3. Galactic longitude is the angular distance east of the Galactic centre, measured along the Galactic equator.

)))⟩ *Latitude*

LOOK-BACK TIME

The cosmological redshift from a distant galaxy is a measure of how long the radiation has been travelling through expanding space. It is, therefore, a measure not only of the distance to the galaxy, but also of the age of the Universe when the radiation was emitted. The difference between the present age of the Universe and its age at the time of emission is known as the look-back time. The relationship between the redshift and the look-back time depends on how rapidly the Universe has expanded in the past which is still very uncertain.

)))⟩ *Cosmological Redshift, Universe*

ABOVE: Sir Bernard Lovell, one of the pioneering fathers of radio astronomy, in front of the Jodrell Bank radio dish he campaigned for in the 1950s.

LOWELL, PERCIVAL (1855–1916)

American astronomer who founded the Lowell Observatory in Flagstaff, Arizona. He became famous for his observations of the planet Mars. He observed the 'canals' seen by Giovanni Schiaparelli and believed

that they were immense artificial structures, built by a native Martian civilization in order to irrigate their vast deserts with water from the polar caps. However these canals were an optical illusion, and few of them corresponded to real features on the Martian surface. Lowell also initiated the search for the planet Pluto. Although his calculations were spurious, they led the way to Clyde Tombaugh's discovery of the ninth planet in 1930, 14 years after Lowell's death.

LUMINOSITY

The total (or absolute) brightness of an object given by the total energy radiated per second. The luminosity (L) of a body over all wavelengths is the bolometric luminosity which is related to the body's effective (or surface) temperature (T_{eff}) by the Stefan–Boltzmann law: $L = 4\pi R^2 \sigma T_{eff}^4$ where R is the radius of the body and σ is the Stefan–Boltzmann constant

LUMINOUS BLUE VARIABLES

The most massive stars, of spectral type O, are forever losing huge quantities of gas from their surfaces, but when they leave the main sequence matters become far worse and they become luminous blue variables (LBVs). Violent instabilities set in, resulting in episodes of huge mass loss, probably every few hundred or thousand years, which cause the star to brighten by several magnitudes, and for its spectral type to change as its outer envelope of gas lifts off into space. The expanding shell will produce striking emission lines in the spectrum, with adjacent absorption lines where the shell absorbs light from the star below. Such dual structures are known as P Cygni lines since they were first identified in the spectrum of one of the most famous LBVs, the high-luminosity blue supergiant P Cygni.

))))▶ *Eta Carinae*

LEFT: Percival Lowell, known for his theories about mythical Martian 'canals'.
ABOVE: The vast Eta Carinae nebula is a glowing gas cloud that appears four times wider than the Moon, and contains in its brightest portion, just above centre, the peculiar eruptive luminous blue variable star Eta Carinae.

LUNA 9

Russian attempts to reach the Moon safely paid off on 4 February 1966, when Luna 9 touched down in the Ocean of Storms. Luna 9 ejected a lander sphere, which rolled to a halt before unfurling to start work. In Britain, Bernard Lovell was tracking the mission with the Jodrell Bank radio dish. When the signal changed on landing, he suspected it was a picture streaming back and connected a teletype machine to the signal. Lovell was astonished to see the first images of the Moon's surface. They appeared in the *Daily Express* the next day, before many of the Russian mission scientists had seen them.

LUNA SPACE PROGRAM

On 2 January 1959, Luna 1, the first Soviet lunar craft was launched to the Moon but missed its target. Luna 2 lifted off on 12 September 1959 and hit the Moon – the first human object to land on another world. On 4 October 1959 Luna 3 was launched for a flight around the Moon, photographing the far side for the first time. The next first – a soft-landing – was more difficult. Lunas 4 and 6 missed the Moon, Luna 5 crashed while attempting to land, and Lunas 7 and 8 crashed on to the surface. Luna 9 was the first to land safely, on 4 February 1966. It achieved another first when it sent back the first images of the Moon's surface.

On 3 April 1966, Luna 10 became the first spacecraft to go into orbit around the Moon. Three more orbiters began detailed mapping to help select sites for a manned Russian landing. In the late 1960s the USSR were developing an unmanned craft to return a sample of lunar material. Rushing to beat the Americans, the first few launch attempts failed. It was not until 13 July 1969 that Luna 15 took off successfully. On 21 July, just as Apollo 11 was preparing to lift off, Luna 15 crashed into the Sea of Crises. Over a year went by before Luna 16 attempted the same mission: this time returning with 101 g (4 oz) of lunar dust from the Sea of Fertility.

ABOVE RIGHT: The Russians finally soft-landed on the Moon with Luna 9, after five failed attempts. This is part of the panorama it sent back.
RIGHT: Lunakhod 1, the first unmanned rover vehicle, which arrived on board the Luna 17 craft in 1970 and roamed the lunar landscape for 321 days while operators monitored its progress through its cameras from Earth.

Just six weeks later, Lunakhod 1 an unmanned rover arrived on board Luna 17. Lunakhod 2 followed in January 1973, on board Luna 21. A final sample return mission, Luna 24, in August 1976, recovered samples from 2 m (6.6 ft) below the surface of the Sea of Crises. Eighteen years passed before another spacecraft was sent to explore the Moon.

LUNAKHOD ROVER VEHICLE

In November 1970 Lunakhod 1 – the first unmanned rover vehicle to operate on the surface of another world – arrived at the Moon on board Luna 17. The small car-sized, eight-wheeled wagon roamed over the lunar surface for 321 Earth days, travelling around the Bay of Rainbows where it had landed, while operators on Earth watched through its cameras. A second, faster Lunakhod arrived near the crater

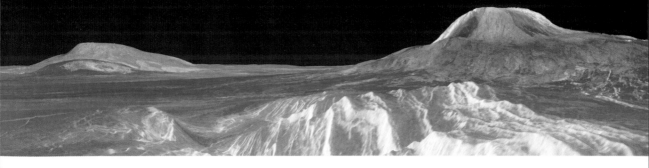

Lemonnier in January 1973, exploring mountainous terrain to the south.

LUNAR PROSPECTOR

The tantalizing hint of water ice at the lunar south pole revealed by the Clementine spacecraft in 1994 rekindled an interest in the Moon. Four years later, in 1998, NASA returned with a mission called Lunar Prospector. The mission carried no cameras, but instead studied chemical signatures of the lunar crust. Concentrations of hydrogen were detected at the poles, which some scientists interpreted as further evidence of water ice.

In an improvised experiment, Lunar Prospector crashed into the southern polar region and the world's telescopes were trained on the impact cloud that was thrown up, scrutinizing it for evidence of water vapour. However, no water vapour was found.

MACH'S PRINCIPLE

Ernst Mach (1838–1916), an Austrian physicist and philosopher, argued that the laws of physics and the physical constants, such as the speed of light, were determined by the matter in the Universe. Therefore, if the overall properties of the Universe, such as its density, changed then the laws and the constants should also change. In particular he argued that the inertial mass of a body, i.e. its reluctance to be accelerated, is not a property of the body itself, but is an interaction between the body and the rest of the matter in the Universe. For this inertial effect to be true, i.e. so that it is not solely the matter in the Solar System which affects local objects, but distant matter as well, then the force must be very long range.

)))➤ *Steady State Theory*

MAGELLAN MISSION

Mapping Venus with the same success as achieved with Mars was difficult. Venus's thick cloud cover meant little was known about its geology other than what had been gleaned from the Pioneer Venus inspection and Russian Venera orbiters, and an advanced radar mapper was called for. Magellan arrived at Venus in August 1990. To save money, the spacecraft had to record the data from each polar orbit on a tape recorder, then turn round to face Earth and use the same mapping antenna to beam its discoveries to Earth. Within one Venusian day (243 Earth days), 84 per cent of the planet had been mapped.

Magellan's radar maps reflected the roughness of the surface, the brighter areas being rougher than the darker ones. The images revealed that Venus was a vulcanologist's dream – smothered in vast sheets of lava flows, with volcanic craters of all shapes and sizes, and dominated by huge circular volcanic features called coronae, measuring hundreds of miles in diameter. Sinuous lava channels 4,000 km (2,500 miles) long meandered over the surface and tectonic fractures and cracks criss-crossed the plains and formed wrinkled regions called tesserae. Despite such intense volcanism and clues that the whole surface was relatively young, no eruptions were witnessed. In October 1994, Magellan burnt up in the Venusian atmosphere.

MAGELLANIC STREAM

The Magellanic Stream is a swathe of hydrogen gas emerging from the common cloud that surrounds the Large and Small Magellanic Clouds. The Magellanic Stream extends over more than 100° of the southern sky and is material which was probably torn from the Clouds by our Galaxy's gravitational forces during a past close encounter.

MAGNETIC FIELD

The pattern of magnetic influence around a magnetized body, such as a lodestone or a current-carrying wire. The direction and strength of the field at each point are defined in terms of the force that a moving charged particle would experience at that point. Magnetic fields are produced by electric currents. The magnetic field of a bar magnet, for example, arises from the motions of electrons within the iron atoms of which it is made.

MAGNETOSPHERE

The region around a celestial body in which its magnetic field, if it has one, is stronger than that of the surrounding space. A body's magnetosphere buffers that body against the solar wind, a stream of charged particles that constantly flows from the Sun. The solar wind compresses the sunward side of the magnetosphere and draws out the opposite side, forming the 'magnetotail'.

)))⟫ *Aurora, Jupiter, Magnetic Field, Solar Wind*

MAIN SEQUENCE STARS

Stars spend most of their lives on a region of the Hertzsprung-Russell diagram known as the main sequence. Here they 'burn' their initially plentiful hydrogen fuel by nuclear reactions in their core. During this time they will maintain a steady surface temperature and luminosity. The star's position on the main sequence and how long it will spend there depends on its mass. The most massive stars (up to about 100 times the mass of the Sun) populate the upper end of the main sequence and the least massive stars, the lower end. Stars on the main sequence are termed dwarfs even though the largest of them are 15 times bigger than the Sun.

)))⟫ *Hertzsprung–Russell Diagram*

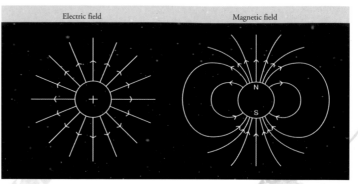

Electric field   Magnetic field

MANNED MANOEUVRING UNIT (MMU)

The first Gemini spacewalks in the 1960s had revealed how difficult it is to manoeuvre accurately in space, and an astronaut propulsion backpack was developed for Gemini 9, but proved hard to test. Skylab's second crew successfully flew a similar system without spacesuits inside Skylab's vast main chamber. The third generation backpack, called the Manned Manoeuvring Unit (MMU), was built to fly on the tenth Space Shuttle mission in 1984. Bruce McCandless was the first pilot and flew it out to 100 m (330 ft) from the Shuttle's cargo bay during a one-hour 22-minute flight, becoming the first untethered human spacewalker.

A series of daring satellite rescues using the MMU followed. Astronaut George Nelson attempted to rescue the ailing Solar Maximum Mission in April 1984, but a flaw with the docking mechanism designed to grab the satellite meant that in the end the Shuttle's robot arm

ABOVE RIGHT: Electric and Magnetic fields. A charged sphere (left) produces a radially symmetric electric field. A magnetized sphere always has two poles which are connected by loops of magnetic field lines. This is similar to the magnetic field of a star or planet.

RIGHT: Mariner 10 shown against Mercury's cratered surface.

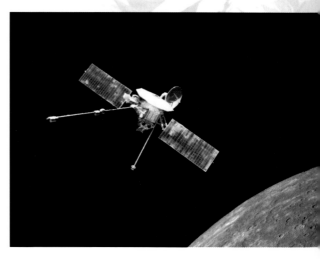

caught it. In November of that year, astronauts Joe Allen and Dale Gardner used an MMU to successfully capture two communication satellites. The USSR had their own MMU, or 'space motorcycle', which was first flown from Mir in February 1990 by cosmonaut Alexander Serebrov. Both US and Russian versions of this have now been abandoned.

))))➤ *Skylab*

MARINER SPACE PROGRAM

NASA developed a series of planetary missions called Mariner. The first – two identical spacecraft – were built to meet a tight launch window to Venus in 1962. Mariner 1 was destroyed during a launch attempt but Mariner 2 escaped from Earth successfully and, on 14 December 1962, became the first spacecraft to fly past Venus. Another pair of Mariners was ready for lift-off in 1964, this time bound for Mars. Once again the first attempt was unsuccessful, but Mariner 4 set off on 28 November. Seven months later, humankind got its first close-up views of Mars. Carrying no rocket to slow it down, however, Mariner 4 had time to snap just 21 pictures before rushing on into space. The images revealed an apparently dead, cratered world reminiscent of the Moon.

On 19 October 1967, Mariner 5 sailed past Venus, and Mariners 6 and 7 flew past Mars in the summer of 1969. Mariners 8 and 9 were designed to go into orbit around Mars. On 9 May 1971, Mariner 8 failed to reach Earth orbit and fell back into the Atlantic. Mariner 9 was launched successfully and reached Mars in November. After sitting out a dust storm, it mapped the planet – discovering a series of giant volcanoes and a vast valley stretching 5,000 km (3,000 miles) across Mars's surface. Everywhere there were old, dry river channels and gullies.

ABOVE: The Manned Manoeuvring Unit (MMU) allowed a series of daring satellite rescue missions.

Mars looked like a promising place to hunt for life and determination to land on the planet grew.

After flying by Venus, Mariner 10 reached Mercury in March 1974, photographing 40 per cent of the surface. Mercury looked very like our dead, cratered Moon. Looping around the Sun on its own orbit, Mariner 10 re-encountered Mercury twice. This last Mariner flight remains the only mission to Mercury.

MARS

The fourth planet from the Sun, with a striking red colour that led the ancients to name it after the Roman god of war. One-and-a-half times farther from the Sun than Earth, Mars takes 687 days to complete one orbit. Mars is a rocky planet with only about half the Earth's diameter and one tenth of its mass. It is colder than Earth, being farther from the Sun and wrapped in a much thinner atmosphere. There are enormous volcanoes and canyons, and there is strong evidence that liquid water once flowed across its now barren surface. The existence of water suggests that there may be life on Mars.

Seeing Mars

At its closest approach to Earth, Mars can be only 56 million km (35 million miles) away, and brighter than any star. Earth, Mars and the Sun line up once every 780 days on average. Through a moderate amateur telescope, it is possible to see darker patches on the surface, and the bright polar caps.

ABOVE: The Hubble Space Telescope has regularly monitored Mars and its atmosphere. Dust storms, cyclones and weather fronts are common throughout the Martian year.

RIGHT: Orbiting space probes have revealed volcanoes such as Olympus Mons, which may have been active as recently as 10 million years ago.

Like Earth, Mars has seasons. Its axis is tilted with respect to its orbit at almost the same angle as Earth's but, owing to the length of the Martian year, its seasons last twice as long. As Mars's poles are alternately illuminated by the Sun, the bright polar caps can be seen to wax and wane.

The Great Martian Volcanoes

Four huge volcanoes dominate Mars and are the largest in the Solar System. Arsia Mons, Pavonis Mons, Ascraeus Mons and Olympus Mons, the largest of them all, dwarf any volcano on Earth.

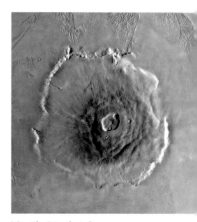

The summit of Olympus reaches up more than 27 km (17 miles) above mean surface level, and its base is 550–600 km (340–370 miles) across. In comparison the largest volcano on Earth, Hawaii's Mauna Loa, measures 120 km (75 miles) across its base and 9 km (6 miles) in height.

Olympus Mons and the other giant volcanoes are similar in nature to the shield volcanoes of the Hawaiian Island chain, formed by magma welling up from a 'hotspot' formed by a rising plume of material beneath the crust. On Mars, it seems that there has been little plate tectonics – the crust has never been in horizontal movement – so a volcano above a hotspot would stay there, and keep on growing to the staggering proportions we see today.

Not all Martian volcanoes are the same. Alba Patera, north of the Tharsis bulge, is some 1,500 km (930 miles) across but shows very little vertical relief. The large number of craters peppering it suggest that its activity was at a maximum around 1.7 billion years ago. Around the volcano can be seen solidified lava flows and collapsed lava tubes.

Other volcanoes, such as Tyrrhena Patera, show evidence that their eruptions were explosive in nature. It is likely that explosive volcanic activity on Mars was

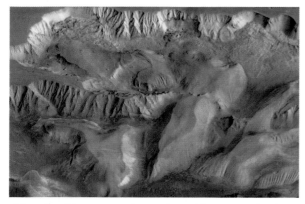

LEFT: This close-up image shows part of the vast Valles Marineris which stretches for 4,000 km (2,500 miles).
BELOW: Evidence that water once flowed on Mars comes from networks of channels on the planet's surface that resemble dried-up river beds.

driven by rising magma interacting with water or ice in the crust, creating a volatile mixture that erupted furiously at the surface.

Although Mars shows little signs of Earth-like plate tectonics, geological faulting has played a major part in shaping the planet's surface. Rifts and faults can be seen around many volcanoes, but the most imposing such feature is the Valles Marineris system. This is an enormous system of canyons, 4,500 km (2,800 miles) long, that would stretch from coast to coast of the USA. It is up to 7 km (4.3 miles) deep and, in places, is 600 km (370 miles) wide.

Signs of Water

Chunnels are distributed across the planet showing a variation in shape and size. Many of these channels are very similar to river valley networks on Earth. They show tributaries and increase in size downstream. But, in keeping with Mars' large-scale geology, there are other features that dwarf any terrestrial counterparts. For example, there are channels closely resembling landscapes formed by huge floods on Earth, only much larger. The presence of chaotic, jumbled terrain at the upper reaches of these Martian channels strongly suggests that the water erupted from under the ground.

The Interior

Mars' dense, iron-rich core has a diameter of around 2,900 km (1,800 miles). This is surrounded by a mantle 3,500 km (2,200 miles) thick, and in turn by a thin, light rocky crust whose average thickness is roughly 100 km (60 miles). A very weak magnetic field, around 1/800th the strength of Earth's, is most likely the remnant of a strong field that Mars once had, before its core cooled and solidified.

Atmosphere and Weather

The atmosphere on Mars has a pressure at the surface less than 1 per cent of sea-level pressure on Earth. It is composed of more than 95 per cent carbon dioxide, with the rest consisting mainly of nitrogen and argon. Water vapour, oxygen and carbon monoxide are also present.

Thin clouds of water-ice crystals form high in the atmosphere, often capping the summit of Olympus Mons.

Dust devils frequently criss-cross the surface. But the most spectacular phenomena which will confront any future Martian meteorologist are the great dust storms, which can engulf the surface of the whole planet.

⠀⠀⠀▶ *Mars, Life On; Martian Polar Caps*

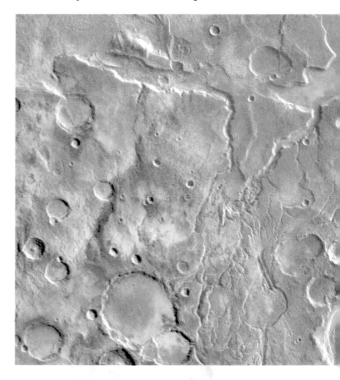

MARS, LIFE ON

In July 1976 Viking 1 reached the surface of Mars carrying a mechanical scoop, with which it collected Martian soil to be analyzed in a number of on-board experiments. The initial results showed oxygen was produced by the soil, as if microbes were digesting the nutrient liquid provided in the experiment. But this was a false alarm, triggered by a simple chemical reaction. Since the Viking missions, the quest to understand life on Mars has focused on Earth life in extreme environments. In Antarctica living organisms have even been discovered inside rocks, forming a green layer just below the rock's surface. If life could adapt to these conditions, then why not to Martian environments?

In 1996 NASA scientists announced that in a meteorite from Mars they had discovered microscopic structures that looked similar to Earth bacteria. However, many scientists now believe that these potential fossil microbes contaminated the rock after it landed on Earth, 13,000 years ago.

MARS, MISSIONS TO

By July 1969, with Apollo 11 en route to the Moon, US vice-president Spiro Agnew called for a human mission to reach Mars by the year 2000. Proposals were explored and dates for a mission in the early 1980s were drawn up to take advantage of launch and return windows. The mission would use a Venus slingshot, returning to Earth after a 30-day stay on Mars during August 1983. Only a year after the first footprints on

LEFT: Martian meteorite ALH84001 caused a stir in 1996 when scientists announced it contained a number of minute structures thought to be evidence for ancient Martian life. Later, other researchers disputed these claims. BELOW: The Mars Pathfinder's rover, Sojourner, became the first roving vehicle on the planet's rocky surface. Seen here examining a rock named Yogi, Sojourner carried instruments to analyze both Martian soil and rock.

the Moon, with the Apollo program truncated, dreams of reaching Mars were put aside. Three decades on, human spaceflight remains trapped in Earth orbit. The relevant powers have not been idle, but the priorities are to maintain the Shuttle program and, more significantly, complete the International Space Station. The more assured benefits of these goals may well keep missions to Mars just a dream for some time to come.

MARS GLOBAL SURVEYOR (MGS)

In March 1999, NASA's Mars Global Surveyor (MGS) achieved its planned orbit round Mars after a risky period of aerobraking. The most detailed mapping of the planet and monitoring of its atmosphere began. A number of images revealed gullies on cliff and crater walls which implied that liquid water had seeped on to the surface recently – within a million years or so.

MARS PATHFINDER

On 4 July 1997 Mars Pathfinder, with its rover, Sojourner, landed on the Martian surface, in an

area called Ares Vallis, a huge flood plain created billions of years ago by a vast torrent of liquid water. Sojourner was able to reach and analyze different rock types that had been deposited by that great flood. Many of the rocks around the landing site appeared to be similarly oriented, as if they had been laid down by water.

MARS SPACE PROGRAM

The Soviets achieved many space firsts. One they were keen to get was to be the first to reach the planets. Their first two attempts to send a spacecraft to Mars in 1960 failed, as did later missions in the 1960s. However, in 1971 three craft were ready for Mars and, after a launch failure, Mars 2 and 3 set off, just ahead of the US Mariner 9 mission. Mars 2 and 3 were designed to land on Mars, with the upper part going into orbit. When

ABOVE: An artist's impression of a human base on Mars. Although the first humans might visit Mars in the next 30 years, such extravagant bases are still many centuries away.

they arrived, in November 1971, a global dust storm was raging round the planet. Mars 2 vanished without trace. Mars 3 began to transmit a picture, but after 20 seconds the first Martian broadcast stopped. Above the planet, the orbiters waited for the dust to clear. The Russian craft transmitted data for nine months, but Mariner 9 was already beaming back high-quality images of the entire planet.

MARTIAN POLAR CAPS

The bright polar caps of Mars shrink and grow with the Martian seasons. When they are at their smallest, the northern cap is the larger of the two, around 600 km (373 miles) across, and represents a residual cap of water ice, left behind after a carbon dioxide seasonal cap has evaporated. The southern residual cap is only around 400 km (250 miles) across and is thought to be composed mainly of carbon dioxide. Both caps have been layered and cut by canyons over millions of years, as ice and dust are deposited and stripped away over the changing seasons.

MAUNDER, E.W. (1851–1928)

British astronomer who created the 'Butterfly Diagram', which depicts how the latitude and size of sunspots changes during the sunspot cycle (a phenomenon recorded by the German astronomer Gustav Spörer, 1822–95). This led to comparing different sunspot cycles and to the realization, first noted by Spörer, that historical records indicated long periods when there seemed to be essentially no sunspots at all. We now recognize the Maunder minimum (1645–1715) and the Spörer minimum (1450–1540), confirmed by radiocarbon dating of tree rings, as being times of low solar activity. The Maunder and Spörer minima also coincide with prolonged cold spells, hinting at the Sun's influence on Earth's climate.

MAUNDER MINIMUM

A period from about 1645 to 1715 when few sunspots were visible on the Sun. Identified by E. Walter Maunder (1851–1928), the Maunder minimum is believed to be a genuine period of low solar activity.

⫸ *Solar Cycle, Sunspots*

MAXWELL, JAMES CLERK (1831–79)

Scottish physicist. Maxwell devised a mathematical representation of the electric and magnetic fields and how they depended on each other, written today as four simple equations called Maxwell's equations. He showed how all the observed phenomena of electricity and magnetism could be understood. By thinking of space as an

LEFT: James Clerk Maxwell's theory of electromagnetism predicted the existence of electromagnetic waves more than 20 years before their discovery.

ABOVE: Astronomers contemplating the Universe, taken from a medieval manuscript. In the twelfth century, translations of Ptolemy and Aristotle brought classical science to northern Europe for the first time.

elastic medium, he discovered that electric and magnetic fields could travel through space in the form of a wave. The speed of the wave could be predicted and came out to be very close to the speed of light. Maxwell proposed in 1864 that light was nothing less than one form of electro-magnetic wave, and that an infinite range of 'invisible light' of longer and shorter wavelengths should also exist.

MEDIEVAL ASTRONOMY

In medieval Europe some of the ideas of the Greek scientists survived in Latin poetic digests or encyclopedic works, most notably by Macrobius (*c.* AD 400), Cassiodorus (*c.* AD 550) and Boethius (AD 480–524). The most important astronomical writer of this period lived in England: the Venerable Bede (AD 675–735) of Northumbria, the first known English astronomer.

After the Crusades had brought Western Christians into contact with the Arab world there was a twelfth-century revival of physics, philosophy, medicine, architecture and astronomy. Latin translations of Ptolemy's *Almagest* and Aristotle's *Physics* brought classical Greek science into northern Europe for the first time. Around 1460 Regiomontanus (Johannes Müller, 1436–76) began to measure celestial angles with a set of Ptolemy's Rulers, three graduated rods around 2 m (6 ft) long. Müller's colleague Bernhard Walther compiled the first long run of accurate original positional observations by a north European, between 1475 and 1504.

Following the establishment of Europe's great universities – Bologna, Paris, Oxford, Padua and Montpellier – astronomy became part of the curriculum. By the last quarter of the thirteenth century the scholars of Paris had begun to discuss the possibility of other worlds, while around 1370 the French scientist-bishop Nicole de Oresme suggested the concept that the Earth itself might be spinning on its axis.

)))➡ *Arabic Astronomy, Greek Astronomy*

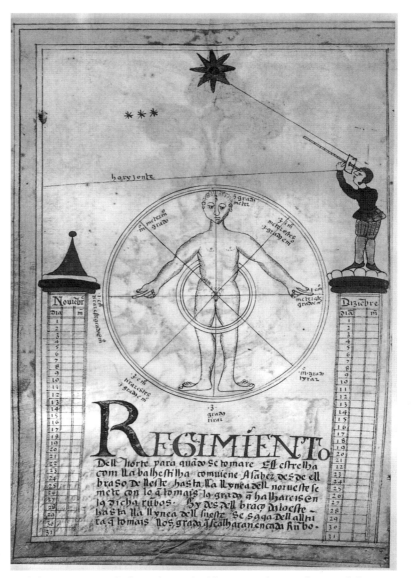

ABOVE: By Medieval times, observational astronomy was becoming a more defined science, sparking a revolution in astronomical knowledge.

MERCURY

The planet closest to the Sun. Mercury swings around its orbit faster than any other, once every 88 days. This diminutive world, less than half the diameter of Earth, is the second-smallest planet in the Solar System. It is an airless, waterless ball, with a rocky, cratered surface resembling the Moon in appearance.

Seeing Mercury

Mercury can be spotted in the evening or morning sky on only a handful of occasions each year, shining near the horizon for no more than two to three weeks at a time before vanishing again into the twilight. The best time to see Mercury is in the evening sky in the early spring, when it is setting after the Sun, and in the morning sky in the early autumn, when it rises before the Sun. Even then, a pair of binoculars will probably be necessary to pick it out against the twilight glow, looking like a bright, slightly yellow star. **Warning: use binoculars to observe Mercury only when the Sun is below the horizon.**

So difficult is Mercury to observe through even the largest telescopes that no reliable maps of its surface features existed until the American space probe Mariner 10, which made three flybys in 1974–75. Not surprisingly for a body only 40 per cent larger than our own Moon, Mercury turned out to look very Moonlike, its surface gouged by craters of all sizes. These craters are the legacy of the Late Heavy Bombardment by interplanetary debris after the formation of the planets, around four billion years ago. Mercury was especially open to such strikes because it has no atmosphere to speak of – just an exceedingly tenuous envelope of gas, some of it temporarily captured from the Sun and the rest exuded from the surface rocks, with a surface pressure around a thousand million-millionth that of Earth's atmosphere.

ABOVE: The planet Mercury has a heavily cratered surface. Its large core is surrounded by a mantle of rock.

Mercury's Surface

Mariner 10 encountered Mercury three times at six-monthly intervals between March 1974 and March 1975, photo-graphing about half the planet's surface and revealing details down to 100 m (330 ft) across. Much of Mercury's surface in the Mariner 10 photographs could easily be mistaken for the cratered highlands of the Moon. However, there are subtle differences, a result of Mercury's stronger gravity: secondary craters, formed by debris from the main impacts, are found closer to the parent crater than they are on the Moon, and crater walls are not as high.

Between the large craters lie smoother areas called intercrater plains, the origin of which remains uncertain. They may be sheets of debris thrown out by vast impacts early in Mercury's history, or they may result from widespread vulcanism while the crater-forming bombardment was under way. Surface features unique to Mercury are meandering faults, several hundred kilometres long and a kilometre or so high, resulting from a slight contraction in the planet's size as it cooled.

Overall, Mercury's surface rocks are dark grey, reflecting a mere 11 per cent of the sunlight hitting them, but – as on the Moon – young craters are surrounded by brighter splashes of pulverized and ejected rock. Mercury's craters are named after artists, musicians and writers: Beethoven, Dickens, van Gogh and Mark Twain are among those commemorated there.

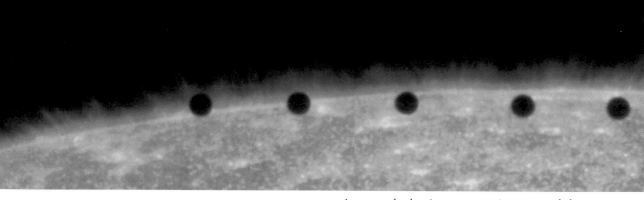

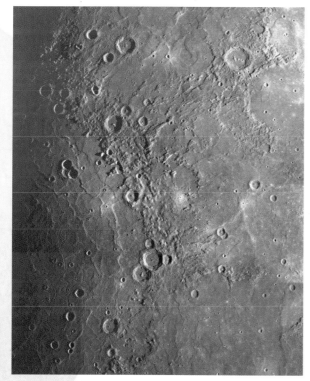

Furnace and Freezer

Mercury has a highly elliptical orbit that takes it between 46 and 70 million km (29 and 43 million miles) from the Sun. Seen from Mercury's surface, the Sun appears from two to three times larger than it does from Earth, depending on whether Mercury is at its farthest (aphelion) or closest (perihelion). At perihelion, Mercury's daytime surface temperature can exceed 400°C (750°F) on the equator – hot enough to melt tin and lead.

At successive perihelia, first one side of the planet and then the other is presented to the Sun. The two points on the equator that face the Sun at perihelion, receiving the

most intense solar heating, are sometimes termed the 'hot poles'. Yet, without an atmosphere to distribute heat around the planet, temperatures on Mercury's night side drop below -180°C (-292°F). Near the north and south geographical poles there may be permanently shaded regions where temperatures would remain sub-zero. So, surprisingly, Sun-scorched Mercury may have polar caps composed of ice accumulated from cometary impacts.

Mercury's Past

Clues to the nature of Mercury's interior, and also its evolution, come from its unusually high density, second only to that of Earth. This is due to a large iron core that accounts for two-thirds of the planet's mass. Motions of liquid iron in this core give rise to a weak magnetic field, about 1 per cent the strength of Earth's.

Why should Mercury, a dwarf among planets, possess such a disproportionately large iron core? At birth, Mercury may have been twice its present size, but suffered a hit-and-run accident with a stray body of similar size to our Moon, which blasted off most of its less dense, outer rocky layers. This collision could also have been responsible for knocking Mercury's orbit into its current elliptical shape.

))))➤ *Caloris Basin*

ABOVE: Occasionally, Mercury crosses in front of the Sun, where it can be seen in silhouette as a black dot, an event termed a transit. This series of images shows Mercury near the edge of the Sun during the transit of 15 November 1999, as seen by a Sun-watching spacecraft called TRACE.
ABOVE LEFT: The Caloris basin is the largest formation on the surface of Mercury. This massive lowland plain, partly visible at lower left of the picture, was created by an asteroid collision, and measures 1,300 km (800 miles) across.

MERCURY SPACE PROGRAM

The first US astronauts flew into space on board Mercury capsules. The first, on 5 May 1961, was Alan Shepard (1928–98), in his Mercury 3 capsule named Freedom 7. On 21 July 1961 Virgil 'Gus' Grissom (1926–67) made the second suborbital flight in his Liberty Bell 7 capsule. All went well until splashdown when the capsule's hatch burst off and water flooded in, nearly drowning Grissom and sinking Liberty Bell. On 20 February 1962 John H. Glenn Jr (b. 1921) on board Friendship 7 became the first American to orbit Earth. On 24 May 1962, Scott Carpenter (b. 1925) flew three orbits in Aurora 7 and, after a successful scientific mission, landed dangerously short of fuel, 350 km (216 miles) off target. He had to wait almost three hours to be recovered. On 3 October 1962 Walter Schirra (b. 1923) completed a six-orbit flight in Sigma 7, and on 15 May 1963, Gordon Cooper (b. 1927) flew the last Mercury flight in the bold 22-orbit mission of Faith 7.

MERGING GALAXIES

A collision between galaxies is not as destructive as it might sound, since galaxies consist mostly of empty space – their collections of stars can pass freely through each other, but at such close quarters the stars from the two galaxies feel each other's gravitational pulls.

Disrupted from their well-ordered orbits, the stars are drawn away from their parent galaxies into huge tidal tails that can stretch for hundreds of thousands of light years. Unlike stars, the gas in galaxies will collide directly in an encounter. Such collisions compress the gas, sparking the formation of large numbers of stars. In extreme cases star formation can spread across the entire galaxy simultaneously, producing a highly luminous starburst galaxy Another consequence of collisions is that stars and gas can end up being dumped on to the massive black holes at the centres of the original galaxies, so mergers are also associated with activity in the nuclei of galaxies.

LEFT: The Mercury 7 astronauts, who took part in the first US program for human spaceflight. The missions' objectives were to place manned spacecraft in orbital flight around Earth and investigate man's performance capabilities in a space environment.

BELOW: Two spiral galaxies merging. Strong tidal forces from the larger and more massive galaxy, NGC 2207 (left), have distorted IC 2163, flinging out stars and gas into long streamers stretching for 100,000 light years.

Ultimately, after hundreds of millions of years, the original stars from the progenitor galaxies, along with new stars created in the collision, will settle down to form a single elliptical galaxy.

))))▶ *Active Galactic Nuclei, Quasars*

MERIDIAN

1. An imaginary great circle on a near-spherical body such as a planet running perpendicular to its equator through the north and south poles.

2. Abbreviation of celestial meridian which is the great circle on the celestial sphere that passes through an observer's zenith, nadir (the opposite point to the zenith) and the two celestial poles. It intersects the observer's horizon at the north and south points.

MESSENGER PROBE

The US agency NASA intends to launch a probe called Messenger (short for Mercury Surface, Space Environment, Geochemistry and Ranging) to Mercury in 2004. It will fly past Mercury twice before going into orbit around it in 2009. It will send back the first global images of Mercury and study its shape, interior and magnetic field.

MESSIER CATALOGUE

A catalogue of non-stellar astronomical objects compiled by Charles Messier (1730–1817) to distinguish them from comets for which he was hunting. With additions by others, the total number of objects is 110. Objects are often known by their Messier number, e.g. the Orion Nebula is M42.

METEOR SHOWERS

Event in which many meteors, or 'shooting stars', are seen over the course of a few nights. The meteors are caused by dust from a comet. Comets release trails of dust as they pass through the inner Solar System and this dust spreads out along their orbit. As Earth moves around the Sun each year it passes through the orbits of several comets. All the members of a shower appear to originate from a small area of sky, termed the radiant, and the meteor shower is named after the constellation in which the radiant lies: for

example, the Perseids of August appear to radiate from Perseus and the Geminids of December diverge from Gemini. A 'shower' usually consists of no more than one or two meteors per minute, although occasionally much higher rates can occur if Earth encounters a particularly dense stream of dust, as happens every 33 years or so with the Leonids, seen in November.

)))➤ *Interplanetary Dust, Meteorites, Meteors, Meteoroids*

METEORITE ALH84001

Meteorite discovered in Antarctica that almost certainly originated on Mars, and which has been claimed to harbour signs of Martian life. NASA scientists announced in 1996 that they had discovered microscopic structures that looked similar to bacteria on Earth. However, many scientists now believe that these contaminated the rock after it landed on Earth, 13,000 years ago.

ABOVE: The Leonid meteor shower of 1999, shown on a composite image. The meteors (or shooting stars) appear to stream away from a point in the sky, known as the radiant, in the Sickle of Leo.
ABOVE RIGHT: Meteor Crater, near Flagstaff, Arizona, USA. The crater was formed around 50,000 years ago when an iron meteorite struck the ground creating a hole 1.2 km (three-quarters of a mile) in diameter.

METEORITES, CLASSIFICATION OF

Meteorites are divided into stones, irons and stony-irons, on the basis of their composition. Stony meteorites are subdivided into chondrites and achondrites. Chondrites, the most common meteorites of all, contain chondrules, rounded objects 1 mm (1/25 in) or so in size, which were once suddenly melted and then rapidly cooled, which could have happened either in the dust cloud surrounding the young Sun or in impacts on the surface of planetesimals.

Achondrites are stony meteorites that have been melted. Their parent bodies must therefore have been large enough to retain heat. In most cases this means a large asteroid, but some rare types come from the Moon or Mars.

Iron and stony-iron meteorites are also thought to have come from large asteroids that became sufficiently hot to separate into an iron-rich core and a rocky outer layer.

METEORITES, METEORS AND METEOROIDS

Most interplanetary matter is in the form of fine dust particles, termed 'meteoroids'. If these encounter Earth, they either burn up high in the atmosphere to produce a 'shooting star' (a meteor) or, in the case of microscopic particles, settle gently through the atmosphere to Earth's surface as 'micrometeorites'. An object heavier than about 1 g (c. 0.04 oz) can survive its fiery passage and reach the surface of the Earth. The fragments are called 'meteorites'.

ABOVE: The Nomad explorer vehicle, which was designed to search for meteorites in the frozen wastelands of the Antarctic, a favourite place for meteorite searches.

Orbits of certain incoming meteorites have been calculated from eyewitness descriptions and photographs of their passage through the atmosphere. All turn out to have come from the asteroid belt – they are fragments of asteroids.

Almost all meteorites are 4.5 billion years old and hence date back to the formation of the Solar System. But a handful are younger than this. Some, which contain the same minerals as the surface of the Moon, have ages between 4.0 and 2.8 billion years; these were ejected from the Moon by impacts.

A group of meteorites of volcanic composition, all but one of which have ages of 1.3 billion years or less, contain bubbles of gas which exactly match the composition of the Martian atmosphere. These gases became trapped within the rocks when they were blasted off the surface of Mars by an impact; the rocks subsequently orbited the Sun for a few million years before finally encountering Earth.

A meteorite weighing more than a few hundred tonnes forms a crater when it hits Earth. A crater-forming impact happens on Earth every 5,000 years or so, causing localized destruction. The very largest impacts have global consequences, chiefly because they throw a dust cloud into the upper atmosphere that can envelop Earth, blocking out sunlight for years. Events such as this appear to have happened a few times during Earth's lifetime. One huge strike may have caused the death of the dinosaurs.
)))➧ *Dinosaurs, Death of; Meteorites, Classification of*

MILKY WAY

1. The galaxy to which the Sun belongs. It is believed to be a barred spiral and the Sun lies in the Orion arm, two thirds of the way out from the centre.
2. The faint band of light visible in a dark sky composed of millions of stars lying in the plane of the Galaxy.
)))➧ *Galaxies*

MILKY WAY GALAXY

An arc of faint light spans the sky from horizon to horizon on a clear, moonless night. This band is the Milky Way, composed of many billions of distant stars arranged in a flattened disk. The richest part of the Milky Way is the great cloud of stars towards Sagittarius, where lies the hub of this huge, slowly spinning disk. Enveloping the disk in a faint halo is an entourage of old stars, some of them grouped into globular clusters, as well as a still more massive halo composed of invisible dark matter. Together, these constituents comprise the Galaxy – the name is written with a capital G to distinguish it from other galaxies.

A Spiral of Stars

Our Galaxy is built on a massive scale. Its disk contains about 100 billion stars fashioned into a spiral shape like a Catherine wheel, extending out to about 75,000 light years from the Galactic centre. It is classified somewhere between b and c in the spiral sequence; since it is almost certainly barred, its classification would be SBbc. Along with the stars in the disk are atoms and ions of gas (mostly hydrogen, the simplest and most abundant substance), curtains of obscuring dust and giant gas clouds containing complex molecules. Star formation continues in these gas clouds even today.

Rotation and Mass

The Solar System lies roughly 25,000 light years from the centre in one of the Galaxy's spiral arms. The Sun follows a roughly circular orbit around the centre, once every 220 million years, at a speed of about 220 km/s (140 mi/s). Our spiral arm is known as the local, or Orion, arm – the arm closer to the centre is called the Sagittarius arm, while the one farther out is the Perseus arm.

The Galaxy's overall mass is dominated by its surrounding halo of dark matter. Possible components of the dark-matter halo include black holes, dim stars, or elementary particles that are relics of the Big Bang. The centre of the Galaxy is marked by an unusual radio source called Sagittarius A*, probably the site of a super-massive black hole. Enveloping the Galactic centre is a bulge which is actually a rotating bar, seen nearly end-on from Earth.

Outside the central bulge, most of the stars and gas in the Galaxy lie in a flat disk about 2,000 light years thick, concentrated into arms coiled around the hub. The spiral pattern is traced out most vividly by young, hot stars, open clusters and glowing nebulae like the one in Orion. The disk also contains abundant atoms of hydrogen in its so-called neutral state, i.e. not ionized. Hydrogen atoms have the useful property for astronomers of giving out radio waves at a wavelength of 21 cm (8 in), which can be easily detected by radio telescopes. Radio observations of hydrogen have enabled astronomers to trace the spiral arms of the Galaxy and to measure the Galaxy's speed of rotation at various points between the Sun and the centre. Atoms of hydrogen in the Galactic disk move on circular orbits with a speed of about 220 km/s (140 mi/s) irrespective of their radial distance. Analyses of the velocities of the satellite galaxies, including the Large Magellanic Cloud, suggest that the rotation speed remains almost constant out to distances of 150,000 light years from the centre at least. This is surprising: if most of the mass in the Galaxy were confined to the visible stars, then the rotation speed would be expected to fall off with increasing distance in accordance with Kepler's laws. It is this behaviour of the Galaxy's rotation that provides evidence for the dark-matter halo. Enshrouding the disk of the Galaxy is the stellar halo, a halo of luminous matter, distinct from the dark halo.

⫸ *Dark Halo, Galaxies, Classification of; Stellar Halo*

ABOVE: Our Galaxy, the Milky Way, is a spiral galaxy approximately 150,000 light years across. Our Solar System lies in one of the Galaxy's arms. RIGHT: Star fields of the Milky Way, overlain by dark clouds of dust that lie in the spiral arms of the Galaxy. The star fields become denser and brighter towards the centre of our Galaxy in Sagittarius, at the bottom.

MINOVITCH, MICHAEL (b. 1936)

American mathematician. While working as a vacation student at the Jet Propulsion Laboratory (JPL) in 1962, Minovitch independently discovered a solution to the problem of how to accelerate and redirect a spacecraft by means of a close encounter with a planet. Although the English scientist Derek Lawden is credited with first solving the basic problem in 1954, it was Minovitch's work that brought this 'sling-shot' technique to prominence in the US.

))))▶ *Flandro, Gary*

MIR SPACE STATION

The Russian space station Mir (meaning 'a community living in harmony and peace'), with its modular design, docking ports and solar panels, provided the means for the first permanent human presence in space. The first module was launched on 20 February 1986 and less than a month later Mir's first guests, Leonid Kizim (b. 1941) and Vladimir Solovyev (b. 1946), arrived. A new crew arrived in February 1987 and kicked off almost three years of continuous occupancy.

The longest stay – a whole year – was completed by Musa Manarov (b. 1951) and Vladimir Titov. Their marathon saw a number of Progress supply flights and three visits by other teams, including medical doctor Valery Poliakov (b. 1942), and Frenchman Jean-Loup Chrétien (b. 1938), who became the first European to spacewalk. Chrétien left with Manarov and Titov in December 1988. Poliakov remained with two other crew who had arrived with Chrétien. All three returned to Earth on 27 April 1989 and Mir was empty for the first time in almost three years.

The first crew to return to Mir arrived on 7 September 1989, starting a second phase of occupation. The first new crew, Alexsandr Viktorenko and Alexsandr Serebrov, worked on a new Kvant-2 module which arrived on 6 December 1989. On 1 February 1990 Serebrov flew 33 m (108 ft) from Mir, untethered during the first flight of the Russian 'space motorcycle', a machine similar to NASA's Manned Manoeuvring Unit. During crew exchanges, foreign visitors made one-week trips to Mir. The first was Japanese journalist Toyohiro Akiyama, and another was Helen Sharman (b. 1963) – the first Briton into space. The long-duration spaceflight record was extended to 679 days, spread over two flights by Valery Poliakov.

In 1993 NASA, preparing for the International Space Station, signed a deal to fly up to 10 Shuttle flights to Mir, taking US astronauts for longer-duration stays. In the late 1990s faults plagued Mir. Fire broke out while Michael Foale was on board in 1997. Only a few days later a Progress supply craft crashed into the Spektr module, puncturing the station. After the last Shuttle left in June 1998, a commercial company called MirCorp was set up to save the station, turning it into a space hotel – with a one-week stay costing $20 million. Wealthy businessmen signed up, but not enough to cover the estimated $250 million annual running costs. Russia demobilized Mir in March 2001, bringing the 137-tonne craft down to Earth.

LEFT: The Space Shuttle about to dock with the Mir space station. Nine Shuttle flights took place to Mir, delivering astronauts for long-duration stays in weightlessness to prepare for the launch of the International Space Station.

MIRA

Mira 'the amazing one' (Omicron [o] Ceti) was the first variable star to be observed. Since then many thousands of similar stars have been discovered, known as Mira variables. They are stars with similar masses to the Sun that have swollen up late in their lives, becoming pulsating red giants. Mira is easily visible to the naked eye when at its brightest, achieved every 11 months or so, but in between fades to 9th or 10th magnitude. It is about 400–500 times the diameter of the Sun.

MIRA VARIABLES

Long-period variables or Mira stars (named after their prototype, Mira or Omicron [o] Ceti) are pulsating cool red giants or supergiants. They change by up to 11

BELOW: Star-forming clouds of hydrogen gas in the spiral arms of our Galaxy show up as pink patches against the starry background of the Milky Way. The most prominent clouds are the Lagoon Nebula (M8), below centre, the Omega Nebula (M17) and the Eagle Nebula (M16), above centre.

magnitudes, being about two or three times larger when at their biggest than at their smallest. During the pulsation cycle their surface temperatures range from about 1,600°C (2,900°F) to 2,300°C (4,200°F) – that is, if their tenuous outer layers can be thought of as a surface, since they have densities lower than a vacuum produced in an Earth-bound laboratory. It is mainly the change in temperature rather than size that is responsible for the variations in the visible light from Miras; at minimum, much of their energy is emitted in the invisible infrared. Another feature of this phase of evolution is extensive mass loss in a 'wind' of particles from the star's surface; half the star's mass, or more, can seep into space in this fashion. Equally significantly, huge convection cells in the star's outer layers can dredge carbon from the star's core to the surface. Carbon is blown off by the stellar wind and condenses into solid dust grains in interstellar space.

)))➧ *Red Giant, Supergiant*

MOLECULAR CLOUDS

In the space between the stars lie cold, dark clouds of gas and dust that can be seen only where they are silhouetted against a brighter background. Hydrogen is the main constituent of these clouds, much of it in the form of molecules (H_2). Many other molecules, some of considerable complexity, are also to be found within them; hence they are known as molecular clouds. The largest examples, the giant molecular clouds (GMCs), contain a million solar masses or more of gas and are hundreds of light years across. It is from these GMCs that stars are born. A GMC can become unstable and collapses, eventually fragmenting, each portion undergoing its own continued collapse. Perhaps 100,000 years after the GMC started to collapse the individual fragments turned into protostars.

MOON

Earth's only natural satellite. With a diameter of about one-quarter of Earth, the Moon is large compared to the planet it orbits – the Earth-Moon system is often referred to as a double planet. It is the only world beyond the Earth to have been visited by human beings – in the Apollo missions (1968–1972).

Observing the Moon

With the unaided eye, two principal landforms can be seen: dark patches, which are the *maria*, and the brighter highlands, called *terrae*. Through a pair of binoculars or a small telescope, the Moon is a fascinating object to study, revealing myriads of craters and mountain ranges, as well as smooth lava flows covering the lowland plains. The best time to pick out craters and mountain ranges is when they lie close to the terminator, the line which divides day and night. The low-angled illumination helps throw the topography of the lunar surface into stark relief.

Occasionally, the Moon will pass in front of a bright star or planet. This is called an occultation. Because the Moon has a negligible atmosphere, stars passing behind it will wink out instantaneously when they encounter the limb of the Moon, while planets take longer to disappear.

The Formation of the Moon

The Moon probably formed from the debris created when a Mars-sized object impacted Earth, about 50 million years after the formation of Earth. Further material was pulled onto the Moon gravitationally from around 4.5 billion years ago. Leftover debris continued to impact the Moon, heating and melting the newly formed crust. Slowly, the impacts ebbed and the crust had a chance to cool and solidify, approximately 4.3 billion years ago. Debris that impacted the surface after this time formed the many craters seen today on the surface. The interior was still hot and molten, and some of the larger impacts fractured the lunar crust and allowed magma to flow outwards, creating the dark *maria* and lowland basins. The vulcanism which formed the *maria* lasted from 3.9 billion years ago to 3.0 billion years ago, and ended when the Moon's interior cooled so much that the crust became thick and impermeable, trapping the magma permanently below the surface.

The Surface of the Moon

The Moon's surface consists of mountainous highlands (called *terrae*) and smoother lowlands (called *maria*). The maria are lowlands flooded with basaltic lava, and many of them formed when the lunar surface was fractured by large asteroid impacts relatively early in the Moon's history.

Craters are most common on the lunar highlands, resulting from the relentless bombardment of space debris billions of years ago. There are ghostly remnant craters

ABOVE: Although the Moon has no water on its surface, evidence suggests that water ice may exist in the deep craters at the lunar poles (centre, in blue). ABOVE CENTRE: A close-up of the Moon in its crescent phase. Being so close to us, the Moon is ideal as a first target for the amateur astronomer – a pair of binoculars will reveal its most prominent features.

and youthful ray craters, which retain bright streaks radiating outwards.

Craters are termed 'complex' if they have flat floors, terraced walls and central peaks – huge mountains of material thrown upward during the last stages of the crater's formation. These are typically tens of kilometres to a few hundred kilometres in diameter. Two beautiful examples of complex craters are Tycho and Copernicus, each about 90 km (55 miles) in diameter. Tycho has a distinctive pattern of bright rays composed of debris sprayed thousands of kilometres across the lunar surface. Rays are typical of young craters. The ejecta has not had time to be darkened by the action of microscopic dust and cosmic rays which rain down onto the lunar surface.

Craters larger than about 320 km (200 miles) across are called impact basins and are the largest impact structures on the Moon. Most are over 800 km (500 miles) in diameter and result from truly cataclysmic collisions. They are typically flooded by smooth basaltic lava that either welled up through fractures in the lunar crust, or formed from melting of the crust when the asteroid-sized impactor struck.

Surface Composition

The surface of the Moon is covered with an ancient soil called the lunar regolith. The regolith consists of rock fragments and finer particles which have been ground down through billions of years of bombardment by micrometeorites. Round, glassy spherules are also common within the regolith. These drops are the remains of impacts that melted the surface rocks, and materials flung from volcanoes when the Moon was still geologically active.

Moon rocks can be divided into three main categories: anorthosites, basalts and breccias. The anorthosites are common in the hilly regions and are more numerous than the other types; they are pale, igneous rocks containing aluminium and calcium. Basalts are dark, dense rocks containing iron, titanium and magnesium. The basalts formed when lavas erupted on to the lunar surface and cooled between 3.9 and 3.0 billion years ago. These rocks form the maria. Breccias are rocks reconstituted from fragments of anorthosites and basalts, shattered during violent impacts and cemented together by later impacts.

Rocks on the Moon contain no water. However, the Lunar Prospector probe found tentative evidence for water-ice mixed in with the lunar regolith at the edges of steep crater walls at the poles. If there is water there, it is likely to have come from comet impacts.

How Earth and the Moon affect each other

As with many satellites in the Solar System, the Moon is locked into a rotation pattern in which its orbital period is the same as the time it takes to turn once on its axis. This relationship is called 'synchronous' or 'captured rotation'. Synchronous rotation explains why we always see the same side of the Moon from Earth.

The same gravitational tug-of-war is also slowing the rotation of Earth. Eventually the length of the day on Earth will match the length of the month. When this happens the Moon will appear to hang permanently in the same part of the sky.

Another result of this orbital dance is that the Moon is very slowly moving away from the Earth. A small amount of gravitational energy is transferred from Earth to the Moon, causing it to recede from Earth by almost 4 cm (1.5 in) a year.

)))▶ *Far Side of the Moon, Phases of the Moon, Tides*

MOON LANDINGS

MEN WHO WALKED ON THE MOON

Mission	Landing date	Astronauts who walked on the Moon
Apollo 11	21 July 1969	Neil Armstrong, Edwin (Buzz) Aldrin
Apollo 12	19 November 1969	Charles (Pete) Conrad, Jr., Alan L. Bean
Apollo 14	5 February 1971	Alan B. Shepard, Jr., Edgar D. Mitchell
Apollo 15	30 July 1971	David R. Scott, James B. Irwin
Apollo 16	20 April 1972	John W. Young, Charles M. Duke, Jr.
Apollo 17	11 December 1972	Eugene A. Cernan, Harrison H. Schmitt

The Apollo missions (1968–72) were the first, and to this date the only human spaceflights to orbit another body in space, land on its surface and return. The feat of engineering required to accomplish these goals are among the pinnacles of human achievement. The missions greatly increased our knowledge about the Moon. A large sample of lunar materials collected for analysis, as well as first-person accounts of the lunar environment, have gone a long way in furthering our knowledge of the Solar System.

))))▶ *Apollo Space Program*

MOUNT WILSON OBSERVATORY

There has been an observatory on Mount Wilson, high above Los Angeles in the United States, since 1904. In 1917, the 2.5-m (100-in) Hooker reflector came into operation there, and was the world's largest telescope until 1948. Today, Mount Wilson is entering a new era with CHARA (Center for High Angular Resolution Astronomy), an array of six 1-m (3 ft 3 in) telescopes which will work together.

MU CEPHEI (GARNET STAR)

Mu [μ] Cephei was named the Garnet Star by William Herschel on account of its reddish hue,

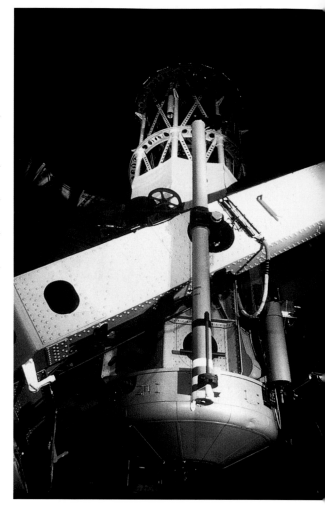

ABOVE: *The 100-in (2.5-m) reflector at the Mount Wilson Observatory.*

which is readily noticeable through binoculars. A pulsating red supergiant, it is a semiregular variable, stars which have less well-defined periods than regular pulsators. Mu Cephei varies in magnitude from about 3.4 to 5.1 over about two years.

NASA

America's divided approach to rocket-powered flight through the three branches of its military cost the country the first round of the Space Race. President Eisenhower was severely criticized for his

penny-pinching policies, which had lost America its
technological leadership. Unifying US rocket research and
development into a single program was essential if they
were to regain the lead. In early 1958, a Space Act was
drawn up by Congress and the National Advisory
Committee for Aeronautics (NACA), which had already
been secretly researching the feasibility of orbital flight,
became the National Aeronautics and Space
Administration (NASA).

On 1 October 1958, NASA officially opened for
business, with an annual budget of $340 million.
Project Mercury – to place the first American in space –
began within a week, and NASA took delivery of its
first Mercury capsule on 1 April 1960. After a long fight,
the Army's Ballistic Missile Agency was finally transferred
to NASA on 1 July of that year, bringing with it the
million-pound thrust engine of the Saturn rocket which
would win the Americans the race to the Moon. Today,
NASA is a billion dollar industry employing many
thousands of people in the United States, as well as
others around the globe.

NEAR EARTH ASTEROID RENDEZVOUS (NEAR)

NASA's Near Earth Asteroid Rendezvous (NEAR)
mission encountered two asteroids. It flew past
Mathilde as it journeyed to its main target, Eros. The

renamed NEAR Shoemaker became the first spacecraft to
orbit an asteroid when it moved into orbit around Eros
on 14 February 2000. Almost one year later, on 12
February 2001, the craft landed on the asteroid.

NEAR-EARTH ASTEROIDS

Asteroids that have been thrown out of the main
asteroid belt by the gravitational influences of
Jupiter and Mars into orbits that can bring them closer to
Earth. There are three such groups of near-Earth asteroids
(NEAs): the Amor asteroids cross the orbit of Mars but
not that of Earth, while the Apollo and Aten groups cross
Earth's orbit. Astronomers are on the lookout for NEAs
because of the collision threat they pose to Earth.

NEBULAE

Astronomers have traditionally used the term
nebula (Latin for 'mist') to refer to any diffuse
patch of light in the night sky. As early as 1781 Charles
Messier (1730–1817) had drawn up a catalogue of about
100 nebulous-looking objects. With improved telescopes
many of the nebulae proved to
be clusters of stars, but others
remained enigmatic. For many
years a Great Debate raged over
the nature of these misty
objects. Some astronomers
argued that they were clouds of
gas between the stars of the
Milky Way, while others

maintained that they were huge star systems far outside
our Galaxy. Interestingly, both views are now known to be
correct. Some objects, such as the Orion Nebula, are
indeed gas clouds within the Milky Way (and in modern
usage a 'nebula' is such a cloud), but others are distant
galaxies, far removed from our own.

)))▶ *Messier Catalogue, Milky Way, Orion*

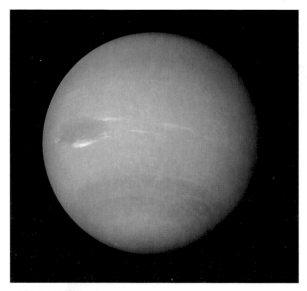

NEPTUNE

A blue-green gas giant, the eighth planet from the Sun. Its discovery was a triumph for Newton's theory of gravitation. The planet's existence and position had been independently predicted by an English mathematician, John Couch Adams (1819–92), and a French astronomer, Urbain Le Verrier (1811–77), on the basis of its gravitational perturbation of the movements of Uranus, the seventh planet. The planet was seen through the telescope in 1846. Neptune is smaller than Jupiter or Saturn, but still approximately four times larger than Earth. Neptune is too faint to be seen without the aid of a telescope or good pair of binoculars. Even the largest telescopes only reveal a small blue-green disk and occasional vague markings. Neptune has a system of rings and a suite of eight known moons.

The Atmosphere of Neptune

Neptune is composed mainly of hydrogen and helium, with its distinctive colour arising from small amounts of methane, which absorbs red light.

Owing to the incredibly low temperature, most clouds on Neptune form at significantly lower altitudes than

ABOVE: The Voyager 2 spacecraft flew past Neptune in 1989, revealing a Great Dark Spot rimmed with white cirrus clouds.

those on Jupiter and Saturn, where temperatures and pressures are greater. The lower altitude means the cloud decks are harder to spot through the upper atmospheric methane haze. Once the clouds had been discovered, scientists tracked their movement, finding wind speeds of up to 580 km/h (360 mi/h).

Voyager 2 encountered Neptune in August 1989. Surprisingly, Neptune's atmosphere was found to be highly active. There is a high haze of frozen methane as well as high white cirrus clouds. But the most startling discovery was a series of high-pressure storm systems in the southern hemisphere. The largest was the Great Dark Spot, a large 'hurricane' which whipped around the planet in a little over 18 hours. Further south was the 'Scooter', another smaller storm travelling even faster, revolving around Neptune once every 16 hours. Some of the strongest winds in the Solar System were recorded close to the Great Dark Spot, a staggering 2,000 km/h (1,250 mi/h). Although the Great Dark Spot was similar to Jupiter's Red Spot, ground-based infrared observations indicate that, like storm systems on Earth, it has dissolved. Storms on Neptune are powered by heat rising from the warmer interior.

The Interior of Neptune

Neptune is denser than Jupiter and Saturn. Owing to its greater density, scientists have speculated that beneath its hydrogen atmosphere an ocean of water with ammonia and methane may exist, over a central rocky core.

➤ *Great Dark Spot, Uranus*

NEUTRINOS

Neutrinos are tiny, fundamental particles that are emitted in certain kinds of nuclear reaction. They possess little or no mass, interact extremely weakly with other matter and always move at, or very close to, the speed of light. Their interest to astronomers is that they are generated in the nuclear reactions that occur in the cores of stars like the Sun. They stream unhindered out of the Sun and pass straight through the Earth. Several large detectors have been constructed to search for solar neutrinos. In one type, chlorine atoms are turned into argon on the very rare occasions on which they collide with a neutrino. In another, gallium atoms are turned

ABOVE: The Sudbury Neutrino Observatory in Ontario is located 2,000 m
(6,800 ft) below ground in a nickel mine. It consists of a 12-m (40-ft)
spherical tank containing 1,000 tonnes of heavy water. Neutrinos colliding
with the water molecules emit flashes of light which are picked up by an array
of 9,600 photomultiplier tubes.

into germanium. In a third type, neutrinos occasionally
collide with water molecules to produce flashes of light.
Results so far indicate that fewer neutrinos are being
caught than theory predicts, but this is more likely due to
subtleties in the nature of the neutrino than failings in
our understanding of the solar interior. Other possible
sources of neutrinos are supernova explosions (neutrinos
from Supernova 1987A were detected by chance) and
active galaxies. Neutrinos created in the Big Bang may
form part of the dark matter that cosmologists believe
accounts for a large part of the mass of the Universe.

))))➡ *Active Galaxies, Big Bang, Supernovae*

NEUTRON

A fundamental particle that is a constituent part of
all atoms except those of common hydrogen.
Neutrons are part of the nucleus with no charge and a
mass of 1.6749 x 10^{-27} kg.

NEUTRON STARS

If a dying star retains too much mass to qualify as
a white dwarf it will collapse further, into a
neutron star. Under extreme gravitational pressure,
electrons combine with protons to form the chargeless
particles called neutrons. The bulk of the star becomes a
'sea' of free neutrons with a density over a million times
greater than that of a white dwarf, topped by a solid crust
consisting of a latticework of atomic nuclei.

Neutron stars are probably left behind by many
supernovae, although if their weight-loss routine is insuf-
ficient to take them below about three solar masses then
further collapse awaits, into the oblivion of a black hole.
Some neutron stars may arise from the addition of gas to
a white dwarf from a companion star in a binary system,
tipping it over the Chandrasekhar limit.

Neutron stars were predicted theoretically in the 1930s
but the first was not discovered until 1967, when radio
astronomers detected rapidly pulsating sources that were
dubbed pulsars. Neutron stars have since been found in
binary systems where gas from a companion falls on to
the neutron star, heating up and emitting X-rays and at
the centres of supernova remnants.

))))➡ *Black Hole, Chandrasekhar Limit, Pulsars, Supernova
Remnant, Supernovae*

NEW GENERAL CATALOGUE (NGC)

A catalogue of nebulous objects (nebulae, star
clusters and galaxies) compiled by J. L. E. Dreyer
and published in 1888. This was a revision and expansion
of a catalogue published earlier by John Herschel and
contained 7,840 objects. Many of these turned out to be
galaxies, the existence of which was not recognized at the
time. In 1895 and 1908 Dreyer published two
supplements, called the Index Catalogues, which
added over 5,000 newly discovered objects. Objects
in these catalogues are still widely referred to by their
NGC and IC numbers.

NEWTON, ISAAC (1642–1727)

English scientist. A great mathematical genius, Newton was also an experimental scientist, as his work on optics testifies. He was elected to the Royal Society in 1672, and after solving the gravity problem, in *Principia* (1687), he rapidly won international renown and became the archetype of a scientific genius. Taking the positions of Master of the

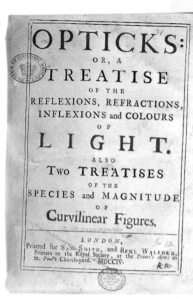

Mint and President of the Royal Society, he was at the time the most powerful figure in British science, although he remained difficult to deal with throughout his life.

NEWTONIAN COSMOLOGY

Isaac Newton (1642–1727) attempted to devise a physical model of the Universe on the basis of his theories of mechanics and gravitation. He recognized that gravity would dominate the Universe on the largest scale, but this led to a problem. If the Universe were finite, everything in it would 'fall down into the middle of the whole space and there compose one great spherical mass'. The fact that this had not happened and apparently was not happening led Newton to the view that the Universe was infinite. However, in an infinite Universe even the slightest unevenness in the distribution of stars would also quickly lead to collapse.

From telescopic observation William Herschel (1738–1822) found that the Milky Way, which at that time seemed to comprise the whole Universe, had the shape of a millstone, with the Sun near the centre (it is in fact about two thirds of the way out). It did not collapse

because it was rotating. In the 1920s it was discovered that the Milky Way is just one of billions of galaxies, all rushing apart from each other. By this time Einstein's theories of relativity had supplanted Newton's physics and made modern cosmology possible.

⟫⟫ *Big Bang, Relativity, General Theory of*

NODE

One of the two points where an orbit intersects a reference plane – for example, the orbit of a planet with the ecliptic. The ascending node is the point at which the body moves from south to north and the descending node is where it moves from north to south.

NORTH AMERICA NEBULA (NGC 7000)

Lying in the constellation of Cygnus and seemingly close to Deneb in the sky – although in reality only about half as far away – is a cloud of gas and dust, NGC 7000, known as the North America, Nebula because of its resemblance to the shape of that continent. Visually it is elusive; under the best conditions it can be detected with the naked eye as a brighter patch in the Milky Way, but its full magnificence is apparent only on photographs.

ABOVE LEFT: Newton's great work Opticks, *in which he laid out his theories on the properties of light, most notably the breaking up of a beam of light into its constituent colours through the use of a prism.*

ABOVE: The North America Nebula (NGC 7000), a softly glowing cloud of gas named for its resemblance to the shape of the continent of North America. It lies in the constellation Cygnus near the 1st-magnitude star Deneb.

NORTH CELESTIAL POLE (NCP)

The point on the celestial sphere which would be cut by extending the Earth's rotation axis through the north pole. At present it is near the star Polaris in Ursa Minor but, due to precession, the position of the NCP moves in a circle over about 25,800 years.

)))▶ *Celestial Sphere, Precession*

NOVAE

The name 'nova', Latin for 'new', was given in ancient times when astronomers saw stars appear where none had been seen before and concluded that they were indeed new arrivals in the firmament. They are now known to be cataclysmic binaries. Dozens of novae are thought to occur in our Galaxy each year, although only occasionally does one become bright enough to be visible to the naked eye. A typical nova brightens by 10 magnitudes (a factor of 10,000) or more in a few days and then declines slowly back to its original luminosity.

NUCLEOSYNTHESIS

An understanding of the synthesis of the lightest elements in the first few minutes after the Big Bang is considered to be one of the cornerstones of modern cosmology. The abundance and distribution of the nuclei of hydrogen, helium and lithium provides a detailed record of conditions in the early Universe. As the Universe cooled down, these light elements began to coalesce under the action of gravity to form stars. The synthesis of nuclei continues within stars as the lighter nuclei fuse to form heavier elements such as carbon and oxygen. Additional nucleosynthesis occurs in supernovae. The products ejected in supernovae spread out into the interstellar medium, where they can form the raw material for a subsequent generation of stars and planets. Indeed, all the heavier elements in our bodies were 'cooked' inside an earlier generation of stars.

NUCLEUS

Generally, the inner part of an object. 1. In a comet, the nucleus is the solid body, composed mainly of water ice, which lies within the coma. 2. In a spiral or barred spiral galaxy, the nucleus is the concentration of material (stars, gas and dust) at the centre.

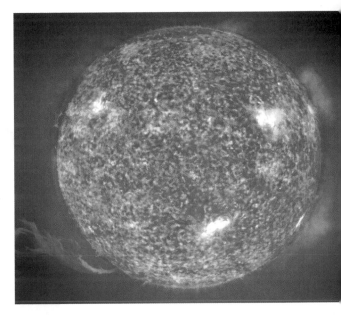

ABOVE: Nucleosynthesis occurs when lighter nuclei fuse to form heavier elements. This process stokes the power of all stars, including the Sun.

OB ASSOCIATIONS

Loose groups of young massive stars of spectral types O and B, thought to be the result of comparatively recent star formation. A whole range of lower-mass stars may be present, but they are drowned out by the light of the hotter stars.

)))▶ *T Association*

OBSERVATORIES

Observatories house and protect telescopes. Optical telescopes are located on mountain-top sites around the globe and take advantage of the observing conditions such locations offer. The telescopes are above the clouds, away from manmade pollution, where the air is dry and stable. By contrast, radio telescopes are unaffected by altitude and are often near universities. A remote observatory requiring access, accommodation and workshops, as well as powerful telescopes, is an expensive project and countries often join together to own and run one. Some planetariums, universities or astronomical societies offer open nights at their local observatories which are excellent places to discover the night sky.

OCCULTATION

The obscuring of a celestial body by another. A solar eclipse is an occultation in which the Moon passes in front of the Sun as seen from Earth. Occultations also occur when the Moon, or a planet, passes in front of stars. Grazing occultations occur when a body skims the limb (edge) of another.

OLBERS' PARADOX

Why is the sky dark at night? This problem is known as Olbers' paradox, after the German astronomer Heinrich Olbers (1758–1840). Although stars are far away, if we draw a line of sight outwards from Earth in an infinite Universe, every line would eventually reach a star. Since stars are similar to the Sun, the night sky would appear as bright as the surface of the Sun and given enough time the Universe would heat up to the surface temperature of the Sun. Olbers thought that the explanation for the dark night sky was that light from distant stars was absorbed by interstellar material such as dust clouds. But given enough time, the absorbing material would itself heat up and become luminous.

The night sky remains dark because the Universe has a finite lifetime. Because the speed of light is finite, we can see no farther than light can travel in the age of the Universe. Whether or not the Universe as a whole is infinite, the observable Universe is always finite and bounded. Stars beyond that distance cannot be seen because their light has not had time to reach us.
)))➤ *Hubble Time*

OMEGA NEBULA (M17)

The Omega Nebula (M17) lies in Sagittarius, an irregularly shaped patch of nebulosity whose shape will depend on the instrument you are using. Through larger telescopes it has an arch shape that William Herschel likened to a Greek capital letter Omega. There is no obvious cluster associated with M17; the illuminating stars must be hidden from our view.

OORT CLOUD

A reservoir of icy debris surrounding the entire Solar System from which long-period comets are thought to originate. Long-period comets are those that have orbital periods of thousands or even millions of years. Although the Oort cloud has yet to be observed, it is believed to surround the Solar System at a distance of 100,000 times Earth's distance from the Sun – roughly halfway to the nearest star. Gravitational disturbances by neighbouring stars occasionally put a dormant comet into an orbit that takes it into the inner solar system. As it approaches the Sun it develops a coma and a gas tail and dust tail.
)))➤ *Edgeworth–Kuiper Belt*

OORT, JAN HENDRIK (1900–92)

Dutch astronomer who made many significant contributions to galactic astronomy. By analysing the motions of distant stars, he was able to quantify the rotation of the Galaxy and determine the Sun's distance from its centre. He discovered there is a spectral line at radio frequencies that we can detect, and his student Hendrik van de Hulst (1918–2000) calculated that it is emitted by atomic hydrogen at a wavelength of 21 cm (8 in). This is valuable because atomic hydrogen is common in the disks of galaxies and because absorption is

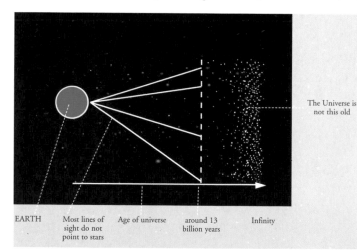

EARTH | Most lines of sight do not point to stars | Age of universe | around 13 billion years | Infinity

The Universe is not this old

ABOVE: The resolution to Olber's Paradox lies in the fact that light from the most distant stars cannot have travelled for longer than the age of the Universe – between 13 and 15 billion years – and that light from an infinite number of stars could not have reached Earth.

negligible at radio wavelengths. In the 1950s Oort and collaborators used 21-cm (8-in) hydrogen observations to make the first map of the spiral arms of our Galaxy. Oort is also famous for his proposal in 1950 that there is a cloud of comets around our Solar System, now termed the Oort Cloud.

OPACITY

A measure of the ability of a body to absorb or scatter radiation.

OPEN CLUSTERS

Young stars in the Galactic disk often belong to associations or open clusters, having formed together from a giant molecular cloud. Open clusters are smaller and denser than associations, containing up to a few thousand stars in a volume no more than 50 light years across. They are among the most conspicuous tracers of spiral arms, in our Galaxy and others. Prominent nearby examples are the Hyades and Pleiades. Young open clusters are often still embedded in the remains of the gaseous nebulae from which they formed.

OPPOSITION

The position of a planet when it is directly opposite the Sun as seen from Earth. The outer planets – Mars, Jupiter, Saturn, Uranus and Neptune –

are at their apparent brightest when they reach opposition and are best observed then. The planet then rises as the Sun sets and sets at dawn, allowing for optimum viewing and maximum viewing time.

)))) *Conjunction*

ORBIT

The path of a celestial object moving in a gravitational field. The planets follow elliptical orbits about the Sun with the Sun at one focus. Seven orbital 'elements', or pieces of data, define an orbit precisely (see below): the eccentricity, e; the semi-major axis, a; the inclination of the orbital plane to a reference plane, i; the longitude of the ascending node, W [Ω]; the longitude of perihelion, p; [ω] the epoch (time of perihelion passage), T; and the period, P.

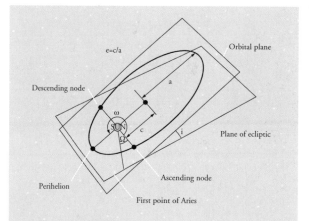

ORBITAL PERIOD

The time taken for a body to complete one revolution about another body or about the centre of mass of a system. The orbital period of the Moon is the month; that of a planet about the Sun is its 'year'.

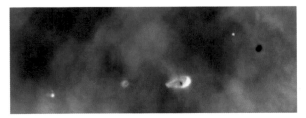

ORION

Straddling the celestial equator, Orion the hunter is visible equally well from the northern and southern hemispheres on Earth. Three stars in a row comprise the hunter's belt, while below this is the famous Orion Nebula and some star clusters, which together represent his sword. Betelgeuse marks his left shoulder, while Rigel marks the lower right of his tunic.

The Orion Nebula breaks down into several components. The main one is M42, a cloud of gas glowing with the light of a cluster of young stars within it. It is more than two Moon diameters wide and is faintly visible to the naked eye even over a distance of 1,500 light years. The brightest star within it is actually a quadruple called the Trapezium, or Theta-1 [θ^1] Orionis. Nearby lies Theta-2 [θ^2] Orionis, a wide double star separable with binoculars. Other interesting doubles include Iota [ι], Delta [δ], Sigma [σ] and Zeta [ζ] Orionis.

To the north of M42 is M43, an extension of the same cloud. Further north still is NGC 1977, an elongated patch of nebulosity surrounding two stars. Completing the northernmost extent of this complex is NGC 1981, a loose open star cluster visible in binoculars.

)))▶ *Celestial Equator, Rigel*

OWL NEBULA (M97)

The Owl Nebula, M97, lies in Ursa Major and is one of the closest planetary nebulae to us, some 1,500 light years away. One of the faintest objects in Messier's catalogue, through larger apertures you can start to make out the owlish countenance, resulting from two dark hollows, like eyes, that give this wisp its name.

)))▶ *Messier Catalogue, Planetary Nebula*

OZONE LAYER

A region of the atmosphere about 30 km (19 miles) above the surface of Earth, in which the greatest concentration of the gas ozone occurs. Potentially deadly ultraviolet radiation strikes oxygen and is absorbed in creating O_3, or ozone. The threat to human beings from ultraviolet radiation ranges from sunburn to skin cancer.

Concern is growing over human activities which alter the amount of ozone in the stratosphere. Since the 1950s, measurements over Antarctica have shown an intensification of the regular decrease in ozone that occurs in the spring.

Chlorofluorocarbons (CFCs), which are substances found in aerosols, refrigerants and other materials, are the leading pollutants that result in the depletion of ozone. CFCs can remain in the stratosphere for over 100 years. Ultraviolet rays break up CFCs, releasing chlorine, which in turn breaks down ozone. One chlorine atom destroys about 100,000 ozone molecules before it is rendered harmless by being combined with nitrogen dioxide.

P CYGNI LINES

Double lines in a spectrum consisting of absorption lines adjacent to an emission feature, indicative of an outflow of absorbing gases from a central star.

)))▶ *Absorption Line, Luminous Blue Variables, Spectrum*

ABOVE LEFT: This Hubble Space Telescope close-up of part of the Orion Nebula reveals newborn stars surrounded by disks of gas and dust.
ABOVE: The extent of the hole in the ozone layer is shown here by the blue area – this image shows the continent of Antarctica and the South Pole.

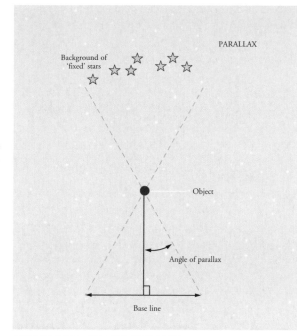

PARALLAX

Background of 'fixed' stars

Object

Angle of parallax

Base line

LEFT: Diagram illustrating how parallax works. Astronomers use parallax to measure distances to stars by taking bearings from two different places.

PALOMAR OBSERVATORY

The 5-m (200-in) Hale telescope, which came into operation at the remote Palomar Observatory on the Palomar Mountain, California in 1948, is one of the most famous telescopes ever built. It remained the largest and finest in the world for decades. Other telescopes on the mountain include the 1.2 m (48-in) Schmidt telescope used for the 1950s photographic sky survey.

))))➤ *Telescope, Reflecting; Telescope, Refracting*

PANSPERMIA THEORY

The Panspermia theory claims that in the early Solar System, before the inner planets took on their present environments, life was likely to have started on all of them. The blizzards of asteroids and comets in those first few hundred million years ensured that impacts were common and oblique collisions would have blasted rocks housing simple bacteria between planets. Support for the Panspermia theory grew in the 1970s with the discovery of dormant bacteria on Surveyor 3's camera brought back after three years on the Moon. Over two decades later the discovery of bacteria in a Martian meteorite, although now discredited, kicked off the Panspermia debate again.

))))➤ *Mars, Life on*

PARABOLIC ORBIT

An open orbit with the shape of the open curve called a parabola, followed by a object under the gravitational influence of another body. At every point on a parabolic trajectory, the speed of an object is precisely equal to the escape speed of the massive body at that point. Some comets move in parabolic orbits around the Sun. In a parabolic orbit, the object does not return to pass the other body again.

PARALLAX

The angular distance an object appears to move against a background of more distant, apparently 'fixed' objects due to being observed from two widely spaced points. The distance of an object can be determined from its parallax provided the distance between the observation points is known. Trigonometric parallax uses a base line such as the Earth's radius (diurnal parallax) or radius of Earth's orbit about the Sun (annual parallax). Other methods of using parallax to determine distance include spectroscopic parallax, moving cluster parallax and statistical parallax. The nearest star, Proxima Centauri, has a parallax of 0.77 arcseconds. Distance measurement was revolutionized by the Hipparcos satellite.

))))➤ *Hipparcos Satellite, Parsec*

PARSEC

The distance at which an object would have a parallax of one arcsecond. Symbol pc. One parsec is about 30.857×10^{13} km; 3.2616 light years; 206,265 astronomical units.

PAYNE-GAPOSCHKIN, CECILIA (1900–79)

British-born astronomer. Author of a thesis, *Stellar Atmospheres*, in which she used the calculations of the Indian astrophysicist Meghnad Saha (1893–1956) to interpret the spectra of stars according to temperature and to deduce their chemical compositions. She later demonstrated that hydrogen was the main constituent of stars, which had not been appreciated until then.

PEGASUS

The constellation of Pegasus, the winged horse, contains one of the landmarks of the sky, the Great Square of Pegasus. Halfway down the right-hand side of the Square is a faint star, 51 Pegasi, the first star discovered to have a planet. The constellation also contains the globular cluster M15, which lies over 30,000 light years away.

PENUMBRA

1. The lighter area surrounding the dark central part of a sunspot.
2. The lighter outer region of a shadow cast by a celestial object. An observer in the penumbral shadow of the Moon sees a partial solar eclipse.

))))➤ *Umbra*

PERIGEE

The point in an orbit about the Earth which is the nearest to the Earth.

PERIHELION

The point in an orbit about the Sun which is the nearest to the Sun.

PERIODIC COMET

A short-period comet (that is, one with a period less than 200 years) that has been observed to orbit the Sun more than once.

The official designation of a periodic comet is prefixed with 'P/', as in 'P/Halley'. Periodic comets 'wear out' as they lose gas and dust with repeated passages around the Sun.

PERIOD-LUMINOSITY RELATION

The Period-Luminosity Relation is the relationship between the period of light variation of a Cepheid variable and its luminosity. The luminosity of a Cepheid increases with its period of variation.

The period-luminosity relation enables Cepheid variables to be used as standard candles, as observing the period gives an indication of the absolute luminosity, and comparison with the apparent luminosity gives an estimate of distance.

))))➤ *Cepheids, Luminosity, Standard Candles*

PERSEUS

The constellation of Perseus contains a pulsating red giant, Rho [ρ] Persei, that changes in brightness between magnitudes 3.3 and 4.0 every seven weeks or so. Perseus also contains the open clusters M34, the Alpha Persei cluster and the Double Cluster, two open clusters side by side, NGC 869 and 884, also known as h and Chi [χ] Persei. Algol also lies in Perseus.

PERTURBATION

A small disturbance which causes an object or system to deviate slightly from equilibrium. Gravitational effects can perturb celestial bodies in their orbits. The existence of unseen companions to some stars can be inferred from perturbations in the star's proper motion. Neptune was discovered by its perturbation of the orbit of Uranus.

PHASES OF THE MOON

The changing appearances presented by the Moon throughout the month, to do with the relative position of the Earth, Sun and Moon. The Moon shines by reflected sunlight, and as it moves in its orbit, a varying amount of its illuminated side is visible from Earth. New Moon occurs when the Moon lies between the Sun and Earth and hence its unlit side faces us. During the next

ABOVE: The different 'phases', or shapes of the Moon result simply from the fraction of the sunlit half of the Moon that we see as it orbits the Earth.

seven days, the Moon is said to be waxing, or growing larger, and the phase is called a waxing crescent. A half Moon occurs seven days after new Moon. During the ensuing week, seven to 14 days after new Moon, more of the illuminated side becomes visible. A three-quarters illuminated Moon is called a gibbous Moon. Fourteen days after new Moon, the Moon lies on the opposite side of Earth from the Sun. The phase seen is the full Moon. Over the next two weeks the amount illuminated as seen from Earth diminishes: the Moon is said to be waning.

PHOBOS

The larger of the two satellites of Mars. Phobos is irregular in shape, being 27 km (17 miles) along its greatest axis. In the distant past, Phobos and Deimos strayed from the asteroid belt, coming too close to the Red Planet and becoming its satellites. Phobos has a dark, dusty, heavily cratered surface, marked by a series of almost parallel grooves. Their most likely origin is the impact that produced crater Stickney, 5 km (3 miles) across, the largest on Phobos. Phobos orbits less than 6,000 km (3,700 miles) from the surface of Mars, circling the planet three times in a Martian day.

)))) *Deimos*

PHOTOMETRY

Measurement of the light of stars is known as photometry and can be done with the naked eye, by estimating a star's brightness in comparison with others of known magnitude. More accurate measurements can be made photographically, but the most precise results are obtained electronically with a photoelectric photometer or a charge-coupled device (CCD) placed at the focus of a telescope. If special coloured filters are interposed between telescope and detector, then by comparing the light obtained through such different filters a star's colour index is obtained, from which certain properties of the star can be deduced.

PHOTON

A discrete 'packet' of electromagnetic radiation travelling at the speed of light. Electromagnetic radiation travels as waves but it interacts with matter as if it were composed of particles (photons). The energy (E) of the photon is directly related to the frequency (v) of the electromagnetic radiation: E = hv, where h is the Planck constant.

)))) *Electromagnetic Waves*

PHOTOSPHERE

The visible surface of the Sun. The photosphere has a temperature of about 5,500°C (9,900°F). Here the most common constituents, hydrogen and helium, are generally not ionized, although most of the heavier chemical species are at least partially so. This mixture of atoms and ions, plus some resilient, simple molecules, absorbs light emerging from the interior to produce a rich absorption-line spectrum in which the signatures of at least 65 chemical elements have been found. High-resolution photographs of the surface reveal a mottled appearance known as granulation, which changes on a timescale of 10 minutes or so. It is caused by rising and falling bubbles of gas. On a larger scale, supergranulation can be observed, in which vast convective cells, perhaps 30,000 km (20,000 miles) across, can be traced. The photosphere is marked by sunspots, regions that are relatively cool and dark compared with their surroundings.

)))) *Chromosphere, Corona, Granulation, Sunspots*

BELOW: *Loops of hot gas, which originate in active regions on the photosphere, follow the Sun's magnetic field lines in the inner corona.*

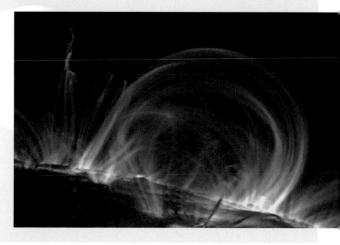

PIERRE AUGER OBSERVATORY

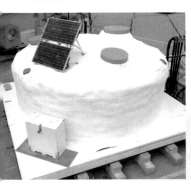

An international cosmic ray observatory, the Pierre Auger Observatory, named after the French physicist who discovered cosmic ray air showers, is under construction. It will consist of two arrays of detectors, one in the US and one in Argentina. Each array will contain 1,600 detectors spread over an area of 3,000 sq km (1,158 sq miles).

PIONEER SPACE PROGRAM

Announced in 1958, NASA's Pioneer program was to send five spacecraft towards the Moon. After one launch failure, Pioneer 1 lifted off on 11 October 1958, reaching 113,854 km (70,749 miles) before falling back to Earth. None of the next four Pioneers reached their destination – the closest missed the Moon by 60,000 km (37,000 miles). With such an embarrassing start, NASA changed tack.

The second generation of Pioneers would orbit the Sun, monitoring conditions in space. On 11 March 1960, Pioneer 5 lifted off to become NASA's first successful interplanetary mission, voyaging 60 million km (37 million miles) from Earth and testing communications in space. Pioneers 6–9, launched between December 1965 and November 1968, did equally well, flying to within 118 million km (73 million miles) of the Sun and mapping interplanetary conditions.

Pioneers 10 and 11 were humankind's first ventures through the asteroid belt and on to the giant planets. Pioneer 10 was launched on 3 March 1972, and reached a new record speed of 50,240 km/h (31,214 mi/h). It arrived at Jupiter on 4 December 1973, charting the

---

ABOVE: One of the 1,600 cosmic-ray detectors that will form part of the Pierre Auger Observatory. Each self-contained detector is solar-powered and contains 11,000 litres (3,000 gallons) of water.
RIGHT: Max Planck, one of the twentieth century's most influential physicists.

---

planet's powerful magnetic fields and radiation belts, and recording images better than anything previously seen.

Pioneer 11, launched on 5 April 1973, flew past Jupiter on 4 December 1974, and used the planet's gravity to move towards Saturn, arriving on 1 September 1979. As well as returning the first spacecraft images of Saturn, Pioneer 11 scouted a route through Saturn's rings for the Voyager missions already on their way. Pioneer 11's last communication was received in November 1995. Without power, it flies on towards the star Lambda Aquilae. Heading in the opposite direction at 12 km/s (7 mi/s) Pioneer 10, currently over 11.7 billion km (7.27 billion miles) from Earth, will pass the star Aldebaran in about two million years.

PLANCK ERA

A very early phase of the Universe covering the time to when the Universe was 10^{-43} seconds old and its temperature was about 10^{31} K. Before this Planck time, general relativity and quantum mechanics come into conflict, and our present laws of physics break down. There is, as yet, no satisfactory quantum theory of gravity that would guide us in understanding the development of the Universe up to the Planck time.
))))➤ *Universe*

PLANCK, MAX (1858–1947)

German physicist. Planck had proposed his radical quantum theory in order to solve the black-body radiation problem, however he half suspected that it was just a mathematical trick rather than a true description of the nature of radiation. Planck spent many years attempting to find a way around his own theory – unfortunately without success.

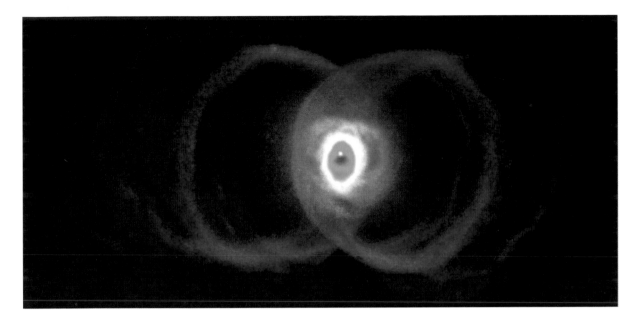

PLANETARIUMS

A good way to learn your way around the night sky is to have someone guide you for an initial orientation. This can be done in a planetarium where the night sky is reproduced on a domed ceiling. Modern planetariums utilize sophisticated star projectors to show simulations of the night sky, and produce three-dimensional views of constellations revealing the true distances of the stars.

PLANETARY MOTION, KEPLER'S LAWS OF

Johannes Kepler (1571–1630) formulated three laws of planetary motion based on the meticulous observations made by Tycho Brahe (1546–1601). The first two were published in 1609 and the third in 1619.

1. The orbit of a planet around the Sun is an ellipse with the Sun at one focus. (Mathematically, every ellipse is defined in terms of two points called the foci, at equal distances from the centre; the greater the separation between the foci, the more elongated the ellipse.) Until that time the planets had been assumed to move in circles.

2. The line connecting a planet to the Sun sweeps out equal areas in equal times. A planet will move much faster when it is closer to the Sun and slower when it is farther away.

ABOVE: A young planetary nebula, the Hourglass Nebula, showing different colours due to ionized nitrogen (red), oxygen (blue) and hydrogen (green).

3. The square of a planet's orbital period (its 'year' or the time it takes to go round the Sun) is proportional to the cube of the semi-major axis (half the greatest diameter) of the ellipse.

PLANETARY NEBULA

A cloud of gas that has been emitted by a star, often the envelope of a red giant. The misleading name comes from the fact that some of them resemble the small disks of planets when viewed telescopically; they have nothing to do with planets. The high-energy photons pouring from the surface of the star's core cause the ions in the expanding, low-density nebula around it to glow with wonderful colours. Planetaries show great diversity of structure. One reason is the differing angles at which we view them, but another is that the mass is often not ejected symmetrically, sometimes because of the influence of a binary companion. The material can also be twisted into beautiful shapes by magnetic fields. The light show lasts a few tens of thousands of years before the planetary nebula shell disperses.

)))➡ *Magnetic Field, Red Giant*

PLANETARY RINGS

Rings of debris, consisting of rock and ice, that orbit the four gas giants. The formation of planetary rings is still not fully understood. For many years it was considered that the rings formed when a moon or stray asteroid entered inside the Roche limit, a zone around a planet where the gravitational pull of the planet is strong enough to tear a body apart. The French mathematician Edouard Roche first proposed the idea over a century ago. For Saturn, the edge of the Roche limit does indeed lie close to the outer edge of the main ring system. However, a number of moons have now been found within the Roche limits of Saturn and other outer planets. Furthermore, the ring systems for some planets extend beyond their Roche limit. While the Roche limit is likely to play a significant role in the formation of planetary rings, by breaking up small moons and asteroids, ring formation is a more complex process and probably involves the 'shepherd moons' that orbit inside and outside the rings. The rings themselves are likely to be relatively young, geologically speaking, and are thought to be replenished by dust and fragments from the surfaces of small moons, as well as by cometary material.

))))▶ *The Giant Planets, Saturn, Roche Limit*

ABOVE: Saturn's rings are made from chunks of rock and ice, some as large as cities and some the size of smoke particles.

PLANETESIMALS

Small bodies, composed of dust, rock or ice and ranging in diameter from less than a millimetre to several kilometres, from which the planets formed in the early Solar System by the process of accretion (accumulation of material by gravitational attraction).

))))▶ *Accretion Disk*

PLASMA

At very high temperatures gases become plasmas in which the atoms are broken down into negatively-charged electrons and positively-charged nuclei. The attraction between these charged particles gives a plasma properties which are different from those of normal gases. For example, various forms of wave motion can arise in a plasma and these can be excited by the absorption of radiation. Consequently plasmas are opaque over a wide range of frequencies, unlike normal gases which absorb at specific frequencies, the so-called spectral lines.

PLATE TECTONICS

The processes by which Earth's crust is shaped, involving interactions between the large slabs called plates into which the crust is divided. The plates are supported by the denser mantle beneath. Plates can slide past each other, creating a fault zone such as the San Andreas fault line, where the Pacific plate slides past the North American plate. The release of pent-up energy as two plates grind past each other gives rise to earthquakes. Alternatively one plate may descend under another, creating a subduction zone. A subduction zone is also known as a destructive plate margin, since the plate which is sinking is destroyed in the process. Such plate boundaries are typically marked by strings of active volcanoes, mountains and earthquake activity.

When two plates converge with little or no subduction, significant mountain building often occurs, as one plate buckles against the other. The greatest mountain belt on Earth, the impressive Himalayas, is the result of India crunching into Asia.

At a constructive plate margin, crust is formed rather than destroyed. The crust beneath the oceans is formed by the eruption of lava along mid-oceanic ridges, such as the Mid-Atlantic Ridge. The new crust is carried away from the mid-oceanic ridges towards the continents, where it will eventually be subducted and melted.

PLEIADES

Lying in Taurus 380 light years away, the Pleiades, M45, is an open cluster. Popularly termed the Seven Sisters, sharp eyes are needed to see more than its six brightest members, which are arranged in the shape of a mini dipper spanning two Moon diameters of sky. The most prominent member is Alcyone, magnitude 2.9. Binoculars show dozens of stars in the cluster and small telescopes bring even more into view. All the brightest stars in the Pleiades are hot, bluish-coloured giants no more than a few million years old; the entire cluster has come into being since the dinosaurs died out on Earth.

PLUTO

The outermost planet of the Solar System, ninth from the Sun. This icy world orbits the Sun once every 248 years and has the most highly inclined and eccentric orbit of all the planets. At its nearest, Pluto strays closer to the Sun than Neptune does. Its size and peculiar orbital characteristics suggest it may belong to a group of small, icy bodies moving outside the orbit of Neptune and making up the Edgeworth–Kuiper Belt. In 1978, Pluto was found to have a large moon, Charon.

LEFT: The Pleiades, a nearby young open cluster easily visible to the naked eye in the constellation Taurus. Its brightest members are blue giants. BELOW: Pluto and its satellite Charon. Charon, discovered in 1978, is believed to be formed from ice thrown off Pluto when another object collided with the planet. The surface of the satellite itself is covered in water-ice.

Pluto is far too small and remote to be seen with the naked eye. Even large telescopes reveal it as nothing more than a faint point of light. It was discovered as late as 1930 by the US observer Clyde Tombaugh (1906–97).

The Structure of Pluto

Pluto and Charon are likely to be similar worlds in terms of surface and internal properties. The Hubble Space Telescope has been able to distinguish surface markings on Pluto, which are likely to be a combination of frost deposits and the result of collisions with smaller bodies which have modified the surface of the planet over time. An indication of what Pluto may be composed of comes from the planet's density, which is approximately twice that of water. The density indicates that Pluto is probably a mixture of rock and ice, much like Neptune's largest moon, Triton. The brighter areas distinguished by the Hubble Space Telescope are likely to be areas of frozen methane ice. Below an icy crust, Pluto and Charon may have large rocky cores.

The Atmosphere of Pluto

Pluto has a transient atmosphere. In the early 1980s methane gas was observed while the planet was nearing its closest approach to the Sun, the period of maximum warming. Because the heating power of the Sun varies by more than 60 per cent throughout Pluto's 248-year orbit, temperatures will drop considerably as Pluto moves away from the Sun and the methane gas should then condense and form fresh white ice on the surface.

Pluto is over seven times as massive as Charon, and has a brighter surface. Observations have also revealed that Charon loses methane from its surface by evaporation. Some is attracted toward Pluto, forming a frost on its surface. Nitrogen and carbon monoxide may also be present in the atmospheres of these two worlds.

))))➤ *Charon, Edgeworth–Kuiper Belt*

POLARIS

The North Pole Star, Polaris, the pivot around which the sky seems to turn as the Earth spins daily on its axis, lies in Ursa Minor. Currently Polaris lies three-quarters of a degree from the pole but is slowly getting closer because of the effect of precession; it will be at its closest around the year 2100. Polaris is a yellowish-coloured supergiant nearly 50 times larger than the Sun, giving out some 2,500 times as much light. It is a Cepheid variable – the closest one to us, 430 light years away, but its brightness variations are small, only a few hundredths of a magnitude. It is also a double star.

))))▶ *Cepheids, Double Star, Supergiant*

POPULATION I STARS

Galaxies contain two distinct populations of stars. Those in the spiral arms of our Galaxy are classified as Population I, the Sun being a typical example. Population I stars exhibit a variety of ages, and include the very youngest ones, but a common factor is that they are all comparatively rich in elements heavier than hydrogen and helium.

))))▶ *Population II Stars*

POPULATION II STARS

Stars belonging to the Galactic halo and central bulge are termed Population II – the constituents of globular clusters are typical examples. Population II stars are very old, often nearly as old as the Universe itself, and contain only a very small proportion of heavy elements – about 1 per cent the amount present in the Sun, consistent with them having been formed within the first billion years or so of the Galaxy's history.

POSITION ANGLE

A measure of the position of a celestial body on the sky relative to a reference point; for example, the position of the fainter star in a binary system relative to the brighter. Position angle is measured anticlockwise eastwards from north, from 0° to 360°.

PRECESSION

Slow wobble of the Earth in space like a spinning top, under the combined gravitational pulls of the

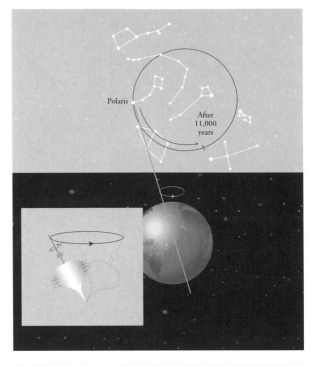

ABOVE: *The Precession of the Earth. Currently the North Celestial Pole lies near Polaris, the North Star. After about 11,000 years, it will be near Vega.*

Sun and Moon. As the Earth's orientation changes, the celestial poles (which are defined by the position of the Earth's poles) trace out a complete circle against the stars every 26,000 years approximately. Not only are the positions of the celestial poles affected, the coordinates of all objects on the celestial sphere gradually change. The steady march of precession means that the positions of all stars in a catalogue, or the coordinates on a chart, have to be referred to a set date, known as the epoch.

PRIMORDIAL BLACK HOLE

In the exceptionally hot and dense conditions of the early Universe, immediately after the Big Bang, it is possible that black holes were produced with an almost unlimited range of masses, from that of an atom to that of a cluster of galaxies. The very smallest ones would already have vanished due to evaporation by Hawking radiation, while those with an original mass of around a billion tonnes, would be in their final stages of evaporation (and hence at their most luminous) about now. The Hawking radiation from them would be in the X-ray region of the spectrum, but, so far, X-ray telescopes have failed to find evidence for black holes of this type.

))))➤ *Big Bang, Black Holes, Hawking Radiation*

PRIMORDIAL GAS

Stars condense out of the interstellar gas in a galaxy and the primordial gas is that from which the first stars condensed. The present interstellar gas has been enriched with new elements synthesized in earlier generations of stars, so to learn about the make-up of the primordial gas we must look for members of the first generation of stars to be formed. Such first-generation stars are found in globular clusters. These stars are composed of 75 per cent hydrogen and 25 per cent helium, with small traces of lithium. If these elements existed before the first stars were formed they must have been created in the high temperatures of the early Universe.

))))➤ *Interstellar Medium*

PRINCIPIA MATHEMATICA

Abbreviated title of *Philosophiae Naturalis Principia Mathematica* (*Mathematical Principles of Natural Philosophy*), epoch-making work of Isaac Newton, published in 1687. Edmond Halley (1656–1742) had urged the secretive Newton to publish, and paid for publication himself. One of the keys to Newton's achievement was his invention of 'fluxions', an early form of calculus. In the work, Newton dismissed the idea of saying what gravity was, and concentrated on elucidating the laws it followed.

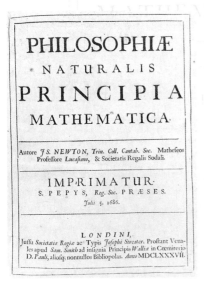

PHILOSOPHIÆ

· N A T U R A L I S

PRINCIPIA

MATHEMATICA·

Autore *JS. NEWTON*, *Trin. Coll. Cantab. Soc.* Mathefeos Professore Lucafiano, & Societatis Regalis Sodali.

IMPRIMATUR·
S. PEPYS, *Reg. Soc.* PRÆSES.
Julii 5. 1686.

L O N D I N I,
Juſſu Societatis Regiæ ac Typis *Joſephi Streater*. Proftant Venales apud *Sam. Smith* ad inſignia Principis Walliæ in Cœmiterio D. *Pauli*, aliofq; nonnullos Bibliopolas. *Anno* MDCLXXXVII.

PROMINENCES

Filaments of gas extending above the photosphere, the visible disk of the Sun. They can often be seen during a total solar eclipse, fringing the dark disk of the Moon. Observations at hydrogen and calcium wavelengths show them some 40,000 km (25,000 miles) above the photosphere and extending typically for 100,000 km (60,000 miles). They show a range of structures, especially loops and arches. Some quiescent prominences may persist for months, while active ones last only a short time and can sometimes be seen rising from the Sun's surface, occasionally to heights of several hundred thousand kilometres.

PROPER MOTION

The apparent angular motion of a star on the celestial sphere resulting from its transverse motion (motion across the line of sight) relative to the Solar System. Barnard's star has the greatest known proper motion of 10.3 arcseconds per year.

))))➤ *Barnard's Star*

PROTOGALAXY

An inhomogeneous cloud of gas created by gravitational fluctuations in the primordial matter formed at the beginning of the universe from which a galaxy may form.

PROTON

A fundamental particle that is a constituent part of every atom. Protons are part of the nucleus with a positive charge equal to that of an electron (1.602×10^{-19} coulomb) and a mass of 1.6726×10^{-27} kg.

PROTON–PROTON CHAIN

A series of nuclear fusion reactions occurring in the cores of main sequence stars with mass similar to the Sun or less. The overall effect of the proton–proton chain (pp chain) is to fuse four hydrogen nuclei into one helium nucleus with the emission of neutrinos and energy in the form of gamma rays.

LEFT: Newton's Principia *established the new science of classical mechanics. It covered the laws of motion, the theory of gravity and explained the tides.*

PROTOPLANETARY DISK

A disk of dust and gas around a young star, from which planets may form. Over 100 have been observed in the Orion Nebula by the Hubble Space Telescope. They are recognizable by their strong emission at infrared wavelengths.

PROTOSTARS

A stage reached by an embryonic star after it has fragmented from its parent cloud of dust and gas but before temperatures have become high enough for nuclear fusion to occur in its core. Still embedded in their parent cloud, protostars can be imaged in the infrared. If plotted on the Hertzsprung–Russell diagram a protostar would lie to the upper right. As it continues to collapse, the protostar progresses downwards on the HR diagram and to the left, joining the main sequence once the core is hot and dense enough to ignite hydrogen-burning nuclear reactions. This marks its transition into a true star.

PTOLEMAIC SYSTEM

The peak of Greek astronomical achievement is represented in the encyclopedic *Almagest* of Ptolemy (fl. AD 127–141). Using the works of earlier Greek and Alexandrian astronomers as his basis, Claudius Ptolemy (*c.* AD 120–180) produced a definitive catalogue

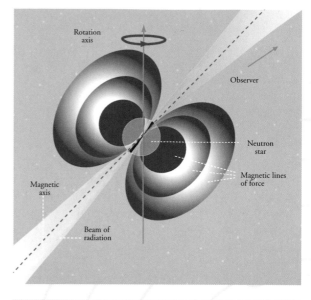

ABOVE: The lighthouse effect of a pulsar is caused by a rapidly rotating neutron star that emits radiation in two beams, directed along the opposite poles of its magnetic field. The beam swings round with the rotation of the star, giving the effect to a distant observer of a pulsing signal.

of 1,022 stars that fixed 48 constellations that we still use. His complex system of circular planetary motions known as the Ptolemaic System reconciled several centuries of recorded observations with the uniform circular motions required by Greek philosophers. Ptolemy firmly established a geocentric (Earth-centred) astronomy for the next 1,400 years.

⟫⟫ *Epicycle*

PTOLEMY, CLAUDIUS (c. AD 120–180)

Greek astronomer. Using Hipparchus's earlier works as his basis, Ptolemy produced *Magna Syntaxis* ('*Great Syntax*') or, in Arabic, the *Almagest of Ptolemy* and his celestial system, known as the Ptolemaic system. His Earth-centred cosmology harmonized with the physics of Aristotle, provided quantities from which calendars could be calculated, and was used equally by

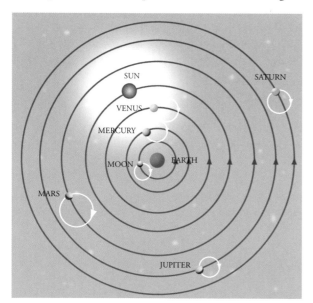

LEFT: Ptolemy's celestial system had the Earth at its centre, with the Sun, Moon and planets moving around it in perfect circular orbits.

CENTRE RIGHT: This Hubble Space Telescope image of a distant quasar reveals that it consists of at least two galaxies in the process of merging.

Christian, Jewish, Arabic and Hindu astronomers.

))))➤ *Ptolemaic System*

PULSAR

A rapidly rotating neutron star detected by pulses of radiation, usually at radio wavelengths. Neutron stars have strong magnetic fields, because the magnetic field of their parent star became concentrated when it collapsed.

Charged atomic particles race along the magnetic field lines, beaming high-energy radiation in their direction of travel. Since the field is particularly strong at the magnetic poles, the beam shines out most intensely from there. And because the magnetic axis is usually not aligned with the rotation axis, the beam sweeps around like a lighthouse as the star spins, from once every several seconds to hundreds of times a second depending on the pulsar concerned. The powerful radiation from a pulsar spans the entire electromagnetic spectrum; it is powered by the rotational energy of the star – so, over thousands of years, the pulsar gradually slows down. However, this spin-down is not always smooth; occasional sharp increases, called glitches, are recorded, apparently due to 'starquakes' in the pulsar's crust.

PYTHAGORUS (c. 580–500 BC)

Greek philosopher. The leisured society of Greece gave philosophers such as Pythagorus and Thales (c. 625–547 BC) the personal freedom to ask questions such as 'What is the substance out of which the Universe is made?' and 'Does the Universe have a central fire?'. Driven by the concept of the rational structure of creation, there seemed no reason why solutions should not be found.

The unification of these attitudes and intellectual freedoms with Babylonian mathematics caused a significant change of direction in human thought. In 585 BC Thales is said to have predicted an eclipse, and some 40 years later Pythagorus began to explore the properties of circles and triangles, producing the theorum which still bears his name.

QUADRANT

An astronomical instrument for measuring the altitude of a celestial object (its angular height above the horizon). It had a scale graduated from 0° to 90°. Used since ancient times, it was greatly developed by the Danish observer Tycho Brahe (1546–1601).

))))➤ *Brahe, Tycho*

QUASARS

In the early 1960s radio observations of the sky led to the identification of a baffling new class of object. The objects had large redshifts, much larger than had been seen in galaxies. These redshifts indicated huge distances to the objects, distances which implied correspondingly vast energy outputs. The optical images of the objects, which were star-like, coupled with other properties which were distinctly non-stellar, led the objects to be termed quasi-stellar sources, a name which was rapidly shortened to quasar. Today it is thought that

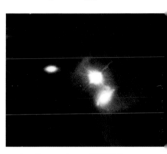

a quasar is just one form of active galactic nucleus (AGN), a term which is used to describe a variety of violent phenomena observed at the centres of some galaxies.

The most obvious property of quasars is their very large luminosities. This property is not confined to the optical part of the spectrum – they also produce large amounts of ultraviolet radiation and X-rays. They also exhibit rapid variations in brightness, especially at X-ray wavelengths, which implies that the emission source is small. In some cases, changes in brightness of a few per cent occur in a matter of minutes while others fluctuate by larger amounts over weeks or months. One quasar, 3C 446, increased in luminosity by a factor of 20 in a year. The variability of a source gives an indication of its size, demonstrating that many quasars are about one light-day in diameter, similar in size to the Solar System, while many others are no more than one light-month across. Although the variations in luminosity need not be associated with the entire source, changes by a factor of two or more imply that significant sections of the source must be involved.

))))➤ *Active Galactic Nucleus*

QUASARS, FEATURES OF

Maps of quasars at radio wavelengths can display three types of features. At the centre is a compact source which coincides with the star-like object seen by optical astronomers. On either side are two large radio-emitting lobes, arranged symmetrically about the central source but separated from it by many galactic diameters. The third feature, not always seen, is a single jet emerging from the central source and pointing to one of the lobes. The geometry of these features suggests that the energy of the quasar comes from the compact source at the centre, but the relative strengths of the features varies from quasar to quasar and even between frequencies in the same quasar.

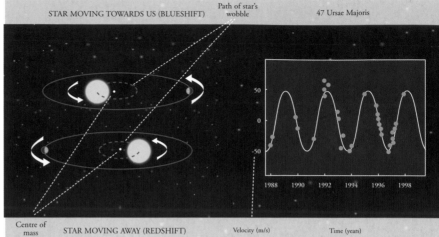

STAR MOVING TOWARDS US (BLUESHIFT)

Path of star's wobble

47 Ursae Majoris

Centre of mass

STAR MOVING AWAY (REDSHIFT)

Velocity (m/s)

Time (years)

ABOVE: Measuring the radial velocity of a star can reveal the presence of an orbiting planet. It can be detected by measuring the 'blueshift' or 'redshift' of the star's light. Here the dots show measured data of 47 Ursa Majoris, the line is the sinewave that best fits the data. Calculations from this graph have revealed the existence of a planet that takes about three years to orbit its star. BELOW: The 76-m Lovell Telescope at the Jodrell Bank Observatory.

R CORONAE BOREALIS STARS

Among the stranger types of variable, the R Coronae Borealis stars stand out. These are supergiants of spectral types F or G, rich in carbon. Atmospheric instabilities that occur every few years cause R Coronae Borealis stars to eject great clouds of carbon into space, where it immediately turns to soot and blocks the light from the star.

RADIAL VELOCITY

The component of velocity of an object in the line of sight, either towards or away from the observer. The radial velocity can be calculated from the Doppler shift of spectral lines.

RADIANT

The point on the celestial sphere from which the members of a meteor shower appear to originate. Usually the meteor shower is named after the constellation in which the radiant lies, e.g. the Leonids have their radiant in the constellation Leo.

))))▶ *Meteor Showers*

RADIO ASTRONOMY

In 1932 an American radio engineer, Karl Jansky (1905–49), accidentally detected radio emissions from the Sagittarius region of the Galaxy. In 1937, his compatriot Grote Reber (b. 1911) built a 9-m (31-ft) antenna to detect astronomical radio sources. It was the enormous advance in electronic engineering during the Second World War, however, that really made radio astronomy possible. Sir Martin Ryle (1918–84) at Cambridge pioneered radio telescopes consisting of large fixed arrays of aerials, while Sir Bernard Lovell (b. 1913) developed the steerable dish at Jodrell Bank, Manchester. Radio interferometry (the linking of widely separated telescopes) across the world

made it possible to identify the exact positions of radio sources, to match them up with visible light sources and to detect pulsars and other previously unknown objects. Major sources of radio waves include the Sun, interstellar gas clouds, nebulae, supernova remnants and radio galaxies.

RADIO GALAXIES

A galaxy that emits approximately a million times more strongly at radio wavelengths than an ordinary galaxy. Usually elliptical galaxies, they are a type of active galaxy similar to quasars. The source of the radio waves is thought to be synchrotron radiation (electromagnetic radiation emitted when charged particles (usually electrons) spiral around magnetic field lines with speeds that are a significant fraction of the speed of light) emitted by jets and clouds of gas that have been ejected from the galaxy's core during the accretion of matter onto a central black hole.

RADIO WAVES

The longest electromagnetic waves, from about 1 mm upwards, are known as radio waves. They were discovered by the German physicist Heinrich Hertz in 1888 while testing the predictions of Maxwell that electromagnetic waves should exist at longer wavelengths than those of light. Radio waves occupy the widest stretch of the electromagnetic spectrum and the region is often subdivided into standard bands for convenience. The shortest waves, less than about 10–30 cm, are called microwaves. The relatively long wavelengths and low frequencies allow radio waves to be generated under precisely controlled conditions by causing an electric current to oscillate in a suitable circuit.

)))) *Hertz, Heinrich, Maxwell, James Clerk*

RADIOACTIVE DATING

Radioactivity is the spontaneous disintegration of an atomic nucleus. Certain heavy elements are naturally radioactive and the decay of one of these nuclei (termed the 'parent') creates a nucleus of a different element (the 'daughter'). Often the daughter nucleus is itself radioactive, but occasionally the daughter is stable and serves as a tracer of the now-decayed parent nucleus. Radioactivity provides us with clocks which can be used over timescales ranging from a few thousand years to several million years.

RANGER MOON PROBES

The Ranger program was conceived by NASA to get a close look at the Moon's surface. After two unsuccessful test flights, Ranger 3 was developed to carry a small TV camera and a landing capsule containing a seismometer to record moonquakes. Neither Ranger 3 nor its clones 4

and 5 succeeded in their objectives and the lander was dropped from the remaining missions.

Early in 1964, all looked well with Ranger 6 until the cameras were switched on and no pictures appeared. Still blind, the probe hit the Moon 20 minutes later. More than 4,000 pictures were sent back by Ranger 7 in the last 13 minutes of its kamikaze flight, which ended with it crashing into the Sea of Clouds in July 1964. Rangers 8 and 9, launched in February and March 1965, repeated this success, revealing objects as small as 1 m (3 ft) across and contributing immensely to the selection of the first Apollo landing sites.

RED DWARF

A red dwarf is a star at the lower (cool) end of the main sequence with a surface temperature between 2,500 K and 5,000 K and a mass in the range 0.08 to 0.8 times that of the Sun. Red dwarfs are the most common type of star in the Galaxy, comprising at least 80 per cent of the stellar population.

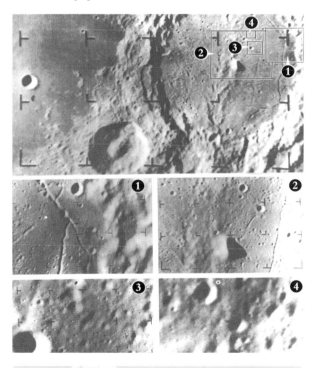

ABOVE: The pictures sent back to Earth by the Ranger probes from the Moon aided the selection of landing sites of the first Apollo missions.

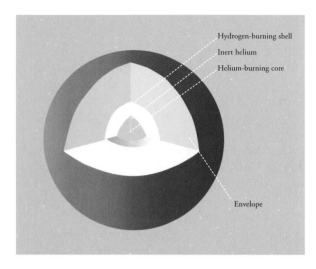

Hydrogen-burning shell
Inert helium
Helium-burning core

Envelope

ABOVE: By the time a star becomes a red giant, the nuclear fusion of hydrogen over billions of years has already made a core of burning helium, contained within a helium shell. Surrounding this is a further shell of burning hydrogen, beyond which is the tenuous envelope.

RED GIANT

A star which has finished burning hydrogen in its core and which is expanding due to burning hydrogen in a series of shells. In response to this, the star's outer layers expand and cool, making it appear red in colour. The swelling star moves off the main sequence and moves first to the right on the Hertzsprung-Russell diagram as its surface temperature drops and then upwards to reflect its increasing luminosity. Red giants have diameters 10 to 1,000 times that of the Sun with surface temperatures as low as 3,600°C (6,500°F). No energy is now being generated in the helium-filled core, which begins to contract and heat up. Stars of two solar masses reach this turning point in their evolution less than two billion years after birth, while for the smallest, the timescale is longer than the present age of the Universe, so none of those have yet left the main sequence.

REDSHIFT

The increase in wavelength of electromagnetic radiation emitted from a source, due either to the source's own movement away from the observer (Doppler effect) or to the expansion of the Universe (cosmological redshift). The opposite effect is blueshift.

)))) ➤ *Doppler Effect*

REFLECTION NEBULA

A cloud of interstellar dust and gas made visible by the reflection of starlight from the dust grains that it contains. Reflection nebulae often appear blue in photographs because the blue light is scattered more efficiently than red.

REFLECTION SPECTRUM

A reflection spectrum is seen when light from one source is reflected from another object, such as a planet or a dust cloud. Emission or absorption lines in the spectrum of the source may be seen in the reflection spectrum.

)))) ➤ *Absorption Line, Emission Line*

RELATIVITY, GENERAL THEORY OF

Physical theory proposed by the German-born physicist Albert Einstein (1879–1955) in 1915, building on his special theory of relativity of 1905. The general theory of relativity (GR) supplanted Newton's theory of gravitation.

Newton's first law is that free bodies move in straight lines. GR asserts that free bodies follow the equivalent of a straight line not in space but in space–time, a four-dimensional combination of three-dimensional space and the single dimension of time. Gravity, said Einstein, should be considered as a curvature of space–time caused by bodies with mass. Free bodies move in response to the local curvature of space. The theory can be summed up as: matter tells space–time how to curve, space–time tells matter how to move.

GR made the following predictions, among others, that were subsequently confirmed:
• In a gravitational field, time runs more slowly than in free space. For example, the frequency of light from a star is decreased.
• Light is deflected when passing near a massive object like the Sun.

)))) ➤ *Gravitational Lens, Relativity, Special Theory of; Space–Time*

LEFT: A manuscript showing Einstein's early search for his general theory of relativity, which revolutionized the way scientists thought about space and time. BELOW: Students are shown how to link up to the 0.6-m (24-in) Mount Wilson Telescope from the Carnegie Science Centre's control room in Pittsburgh.

REMOTE-ACCESS TELESCOPES

Professional astronomers use telescopes remotely and have done so for decades. Amateurs began gaining access to remote telescopes when the Mount Wilson Observatory's 'Telescopes in Education' project began in 1993. By combining a planetarium program with CCD camera control software on your home computer, a simple click on the star map can slew the telescope to an object, take a CCD image and download it to your computer. The Global Telescope Network plans for a system of sophisticated telescopes and CCD cameras which will allow anyone with an Internet connection to view and photograph the heavens, 24 hours a day. The current state of the project can be found by accessing the website www.globaltelescope.com.

))))► *Charge Coupled Device*

RELATIVITY, SPECIAL THEORY OF

Physical theory proposed by the German-born physicist Albert Einstein (1879–1955) in 1905 to solve problems in the existing theories of mechanics and electromagnetism. It uses the principle that the laws of physics – in particular, the speed of light in free space – are the same for any two observers that are moving at constant velocity (or are at rest) in relation to each other.

Relativity diverges sharply from Newtonian mechanics at speeds comparable with the speed of light. For example, a spacecraft moving close to the speed of light is reduced in length in relation to observers at rest on the ground. But to an observer in the spacecraft, lengths and distances on the ground are likewise reduced.

Processes on the spacecraft also run slow in relation to those on the Earth, and vice versa. This 'relativity' of space and time accounts for the fact that different observers, even though moving at different speeds, find the same value for the speed of light in free space.

))))► *Relativity, General theory of; Space–Time*

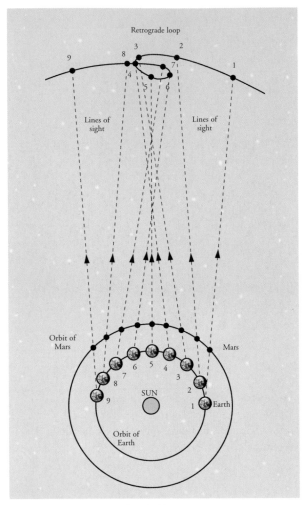

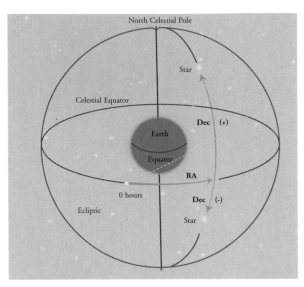

ABOVE: *Right Ascension. Objects in the sky are plotted using two co-ordinates comparable with longitude and latitude, called right ascension and declination. A star's right ascension is measured from west to east around the celestial equator in hours, minutes and seconds from 0-24 hours.*
LEFT: *While the Earth is overtaking Mars (points 4-6), the planets' apparent motion reverses, causing it to trace out a retrograde loop in the sky.*

RETROGRADE MOTION

Motion in the opposite direction to that which is considered positive or standard in a given frame of reference. Positive motion is called 'direct' motion.
1. The apparent backward (east to west) motion of a superior planet in the sky, due to the Earth overtaking it on its orbit. 2. Orbital or rotational motion opposite to that of the Earth.

RHO CASSIOPEIAE

Rho [ρ] Cassiopeiae is a hypergiant which rises and falls between 4th and 6th magnitude every 10 or 11 months, although the variations do not repeat exactly with each cycle.

RICHARD OF WALLINGFORD
(c. 1292–1336)

English astronomer. One of the first clock designers, Wallingford, Abbot of St Albans, built an extraordinary mechanism which not only told the time, but which also rotated circles to replicate the motions of the Ptolemaic Universe. To reproduce the complex motion of the Moon he used elliptical and differential gears some three centuries before Jeremiah Horrocks (1619–41) actually proved the lunar orbit to be elliptical. Astronomers and inventors across Europe began to build clocks, to tell the time and to replicate the celestial motions. In 1364, Giovanni de Dondi built an even more complex astronomical clock. Detailed descriptions of the Wallingford and Dondi clocks still survive.

RIGEL

Rigel, lying in the diametrically opposite corner of Orion from Betelgeuse, is a contrasting blue supergiant. With an apparent magnitude of 0.18, it is the 7th-brightest star in the sky. It has a 7th-magnitude companion, although you will need good conditions and high magnification on your telescope to see it because it is drowned in Rigel's glare. Rigel lies nearly twice as far away as Betelgeuse, some 770 light years from us.

RIGHT ASCENSION (RA)

One of the co-ordinates used in the equatorial co-ordinate system, the other being declination. Symbol [α], right ascension is the angular distance measured eastwards along the celestial equator from the First Point of Aries (the vernal equinox). It is expressed in hours, minutes and seconds (h m s) from 0 to 24h, where 1 hour is equivalent to an angle of 15°.

ROCHE LIMIT

The minimum distance at which a planetary satellite can remain in orbit without being pulled apart by the planet's gravitational field, first determined by Edouard Roche (1820–83). A planet's Roche limit is about 2.5 times its radius.

ROCKETS

Since our ancestors first stared up at the sky humans have dreamt of what lies beyond. But the laws of physics declared that we would need to travel at over 40,300 km/h (25,000 mi/h) to escape Earth's gravity. Although the reaction principle had been understood for many years, it would take the development of rocket motors to turn theory into any kind of reality. And before we embarked on missions to space our reaction engines would be put to more primitive uses: transporting our weapons of destruction across continents.

As early as AD 62, the Greek writer Hero described the 'reaction' principle of the rocket motor. Hero's reaction engine was a water-filled hollow metal sphere. A fire heated the water and steam, pushed from two opposite facing pipes in the sphere, caused the sphere to spin. By the seventh century, Chinese reaction devices had become more rocket-like – spitting fire from explosive chemicals such as gunpowder. Within 600 years such weapons had spread through Asia and into Europe and were being refined for more precise flight. During those same six

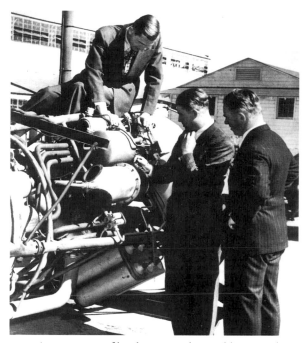

centuries, accounts of battles across the world reported an increasing use of rockets as effective weapons.

By the early twentieth century, rocketry had become more sophisticated. Instrumental in this evolution was the Russian prophet of space travel, Konstantin Tsiolkovsky (1857–1935). His first thesis on rocket propulsion, in 1903, suggested that super-cooled liquid hydrogen and liquid oxygen would provide the best reactive forces. Tsiolkovsky's challenge was not met until the mid-1920s, when the American engineer Robert Goddard launched a series of rockets from his research base in New Mexico. Others, inspired by Tsiolkovsky's ideas and Goddard's proof, were convinced of the merits of liquid rockets. Among them was an East Prussian aristocrat, Wernher von Braun (1912–77). The German army watched his early work with interest and, in 1932, provided him with funding to work on what was to become the world's first long-range ballistic missile. Von Braun's resulting liquid-fuelled V-2 missiles would touch the edge of space.

)))➤ *Von Braun, Wernher*

ABOVE: Wernher Von Braun (centre) with one of his V-2 missiles. These were originally developed as weapons and were used during the Second World War.

ROCKETS, HOW THEY WORK

All rocket motors work by burning fuels to produce gas that blows out in one direction, pushing the rocket forward in the opposite direction. The force does not come from pushing on air, but from the combined momentum of all the molecules in the gas moving in one direction. According to Isaac Newton's (1642–1727) third law of motion, the rocket's momentum in the opposite direction will match this. Typically, the gas molecules are blown out of a rocket at between 8,000 and 16,000 km/h (5,000 and 10,000 mi/h), but to escape Earth's gravity and reach orbit, a rocket needs to travel at around 28,000 km/h (17,400 mi/h). To attain this speed, multi-stage rockets are used with smaller, lighter rockets piggy-backing on larger ones. Each stage is jettisoned as its fuel runs out, but adds its own velocity cumulatively, so that the final speed of the last stage is several times that of a single-stage rocket, propelling it into orbit.

From the 1960s extra thrust was achieved by strapping extra solid-fuel powered rocket motors to a rocket's sides. Such rocket configuration launched the Viking spacecraft to Mars in 1975 and the two Voyager spacecraft to the outer planets in 1977. Strap-on-booster rockets are mounted on the Space Shuttle's main external fuel tank. They are jettisoned once their fuel is spent and tumble back into the ocean to be recovered and reused. Many of today's 25 expendable commercial launch vehicles use strap-on boosters to place extra-heavy payloads into orbit.

There are two types of rocket fuels. Solid rockets run on solid powdered fuels which can be chemically designed to burn very quickly without exploding, giving an even thrust. Solid rockets are relatively cheap, but the thrust they produce cannot be adjusted during flight and, once ignited, cannot be stopped. For its thrust to be controllable, a rocket needs to burn liquid fuel. Most liquid rockets use a fuel and a source of oxygen, which are pumped together into a combustion chamber where they

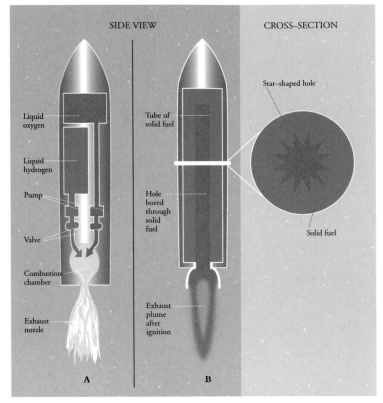

SIDE VIEW

CROSS–SECTION

Liquid oxygen

Liquid hydrogen

Pump

Valve

Combustion chamber

Exhaust nozzle

Tube of solid fuel

Hole bored through solid fuel

Exhaust plume after ignition

Star–shaped hole

Solid fuel

A

B

ABOVE: A Liquid -fuelled Rocket (A): These rockets usually combine two liquids, e.g. liquid oxygen and liquid hydrogen which are pumped through valves into a combustion chamber. The resulting exhaust gases are forced out of the nozzle to drive the rocket in the opposite direction.
A Solid-fuelled Rocket (B): This works by combustion inside a hole bored through the centre of a tube of solid fuel. Viewed in cross-section, the hole often has a star-shaped profile to maximize the surface area available to burn. The exhaust gases driven out of the nozzle gives the rocket its thrust.

burn, producing hot gases which are forced down, driving the rocket in the opposite direction. The fuel and the oxidizer are often super-cooled liquefied gases such as liquid hydrogen (LH2) or liquid oxygen (LOX).

Three types of electric rocket engines have already flown in space: the first, electrothermal, uses electric elements or plasma (electrically charged or ionized gas) to heat up a propellant; second is the electrostatic, which ionizes the propellant and then accelerates it through an electric field; and third, electrodynamic systems, which generate a plasma and then accelerate it with an electric

BELOW CENTRE: Henry Norris Russell, along with Ejnar Hertzsprung, revolutionized the study of stellar evolution.

BELOW RIGHT: Ernest Rutherford made numerous contributions to science, notably his demonstration of the existence of the atomic nucleus.

or magnetic field. Each can provide high exhaust velocities – very gradual accelerations which are only suitable once the craft is in space. The first practical ion engine to fly in space was tested on NASA's Deep Space 1 spacecraft, launched in October 1998.

Thermonuclear rocket engines have been developed and tested, but not flown in space. They pass the propellant through a nuclear reactor to heat it. In the distant future, nuclear fusion engines and even matter/antimatter systems may be used as ways of generating large amounts of energy to heat a propellant.

R-PROCESS

A method of creating heavy stable nuclei within the interiors of stars by successive capture of neutrons. In the r-process neutrons are added rapidly before the nuclei have time to decay, a process which occurs in supernovae.

RR LYRAE STARS

A type of pulsating variable star that varies over about 0.2 to 2 magnitudes in a period of less than one day, generally found in globular clusters. Fainter than Cepheids, they are still valuable as distance indicators.

They have a similar range of brightness variation to the Cepheids but much shorter periods, no more than about a day. In the HR diagram they are located on the horizontal branch between the main sequence and the red giants at spectral types A and F, and are stars of low mass, burning helium in their cores, following the helium flash.

▶ **Stars; Low-Mass**

RUSSELL, HENRY NORRIS (1877–1957)

American scientist. Russell made major contributions to laboratory and theoretical spectroscopy and to stellar astrophysics, interests he combined to make the first reliable determination of the abundances of the elements in the Universe. His pioneering work on stellar evolution, starting with the Hertzsprung-Russell diagram, was followed by equally seminal work on eclipsing binary stars, which provides one of the most fertile testing grounds for theories of stellar structure.

▶ **Hertzsprung-Russell Diagram**

RUTHERFORD, ERNEST (1871–1937)

New Zealand-born scientist. One of the most influential figures of twentieth-century science, by the time Rutherford had demonstrated the existence of the atomic nucleus, through his study of alpha-particle scattering, he had already won a Nobel Prize for chemistry (in 1908 for his work on radioactivity). Through his work on nuclear reactions he was the first scientist to realize the alchemists' dream of transmutation of the elements (changing one element into another). Rutherford's greatest mistake was the belief that nuclear power could never be realized. He famously described as 'moonshine' the notion that humanity could ever harness the energy trapped within atomic nuclei. He died in 1937, two years before the discovery of nuclear fission.

RYLE, SIR MARTIN (1918–84)

British astronomer. A pioneer of radio astronomy, in the 1950s, Ryle discovered how to use several small radio telescopes to imitate the performance of a larger instrument, a technique he called aperture synthesis. He built two major aperture synthesis telescopes at Cambridge, the One-Mile Telescope and the Five-Kilometre Telescope (which is now known as the Ryle Telescope).

He was a leading proponent of the Big Bang theory for the origin of the Universe, based upon his own surveys of distant radio sources which indicated that radio galaxies had been more powerful in the past and that the Universe must have been evolving.

ABOVE: The Lagoon Nebula, M8, in Sagittarius is a cloud of gas divided by a dark lane. The entire nebula spans three times the width of the full Moon.

SAGAN, CARL (1934–96)

American scientist. As a student in the 1950s Sagan's doctoral thesis included a section on 'The Radiation Balance on Venus'. Great minds such as Harold Urey (1893–1981), Fred Whipple (b. 1906), and Fred Hoyle (b. 1915), all disagreed about what existed under Venus's thick cloak of clouds. The confusion only increased when observations told of a blisteringly high temperature. Sagan's thesis, building on the work of those before him, pointed to a greenhouse effect as the logical culprit, a result that was confirmed when Mariner 2 flew past Venus in 1962.

One of the outstanding popularizers of astronomy, Sagan wrote many best-selling books, and his television series, 'Cosmos', drew the largest audiences ever for a public television series.

SAGITTARIUS A*

The centre of the Galaxy is marked by an unusual radio source called Sagittarius A*, whose diameter is about the same as that of Earth's orbit around the Sun. Using the motions of stars very close to the centre suggests the mass of Sagittarius A* is a few million times that of the Sun, implying that Sagittarius A* is probably the site of a supermassive black hole, such as seem to exist in the nuclei of other galaxies.

SAGITTARIUS

The constellation of Sagittarius the archer contains 15 Messier objects. These include M8, the Lagoon Nebula, a stellar nursery lying about 5,000 light years away in the Sagittarius spiral arm of our Galaxy. To the north of the Lagoon is M20, the Trifid Nebula. M22 is the third-best globular cluster in the sky, while variable star observers will want to look out for two Cepheids, W and X Sagittarii, both with pulsation cycles of a week.

SAGITTARIUS DWARF

Surprisingly, the nearest galaxy to ours was not discovered until 1995 because it is obscured from view almost directly behind the Galactic centre. Called the Sagittarius Dwarf, it lies about 80,000 light years from the Sun and is presently being broken up by the gravitational forces of the Milky Way.

SAKHAROV, ANDREI (1921–89)

Russian physicist. In 1967 Sakharov argued that a 'matter Universe' could have emerged from the initial creation process if that process had produced a very small excess of matter over antimatter. Matter and antimatter would later have annihilated, and at the end of the annihilation process the slight excess of matter would have remained to evolve into the Universe we see now.

The annihilation produces photons, and, recognizing that the microwave background contains around 1,000 million photons for every proton in the Universe, Sakharov concluded that the initial asymmetry needed only to be one part in 1,000 million. He also pointed out that such an asymmetry must arise from the decay or interaction of fundamental particles and should be detectable by experiments in particle accelerators.

)))))➤ *Annihilation*

SALYUT

The first space station, the Soviet craft, Salyut 1, was the modified upper stage of a rocket containing living and work room. The 19-tonne station was launched by a Proton rocket on 19 April 1971 and the first crew docked in Soyuz 10 on 23 April 1971. A malfunction prevented the crew from entering the station and they returned to Earth. In June a second crew arrived, staying for over three weeks. Salyut 1 was abandoned and burnt up on 11 October 1971.

Salyuts 2, 3 and 5 were military missions, placed into lower orbits for surveillance. Salyut 4, a civilian mission, carried a large solar telescope. Alexei Gubarev (b. 1931) and Georgi Grechko arrived in January 1975 for a month-long program of science and set a new Soviet space endurance record. After a failed attempt to reach Salyut 4 by a crew in April 1975, the last crew arrived in May 1975 and stayed for another record-breaking 63 days.

SAMARKAND OBSERVATORY

In 1420 Ulugh Beg (1394–1449), Mongol prince of Samarkand, in what is now Uzbekistan, built a three-storey drum-shaped observatory. It was 30 m (100 ft) high, and housed an enormous masonry sextant of 40-m (130-ft) radius. With this and other instruments at Samarkand, Ulugh Beg determined the length of the solar year to within a minute and compiled a table which gave the precise positions of 1,018 stars.

BELOW LEFT: Cosmonauts Piotr Klimuk and Vitaly Sevastyanov in the orbital space station Salyut 4.

BELOW: Allan Sandage, Edwin Hubble's former assistant and now one of the world's leading cosmologists.

SANDAGE, ALLAN (b. 1926)

American astronomer who was a major figure in observational astronomy. Sandage's early work was a continuation of Hubble's attempt to measure the geometry of the Universe using optical observations of distant galaxies. In 1960 he made the first optical identification of a quasar. With Thomas Matthews he found a faint optical object coincident with the compact radio source 3C48. Sandage noted the object's unusual spectrum, which was soon shown to be due to a large redshift. He continued to engage in a vigorous debate over the value of Hubble's constant and hence the age of the Universe, arguing for a low value of the constant and a large age for the Universe.

)))))➤ *Hubble's Constant*

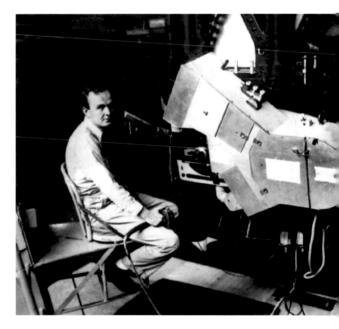

SATURN

The outermost planet that is easily visible with the naked eye, and the second largest in the Solar System. It is in many ways a smaller version of Jupiter, composed principally of hydrogen and helium and with a similar internal structure. While not unique to Saturn, its magnificent ring system is by far the most extensive, complex and brightest of all. Saturn boasts a large family of moons, including Titan, the only satellite in the Solar System to possess a thick atmosphere.

Seeing Saturn

Saturn is readily visible in the night sky. When viewed with a small telescope, it is a spectacular object. Faint bands of colour similar to those of Jupiter, but more subdued, can be seen crossing its yellow disk. The most striking feature is the planet's ring system, which, with a moderate-size telescope, may be resolved into several distinct parts. Titan, Saturn's largest moon, can also be seen as a bright point of light.

Images of Saturn show that the planet is flattened. This is because Saturn rotates on its axis in just over 10 hours, which results in an equatorial bulge: Saturn's equatorial diameter is nearly 10 per cent larger than the polar diameter.

Saturn's Atmosphere

Like Jupiter, Saturn has three main decks of cloud. However, Saturn's frigid environment causes water and

ABOVE: Saturn, the other true giant of the Solar System along with Jupiter, is famous for its complex and dramatic ring system and large number of moons.

ammonia clouds to form lower down than within Jupiter's atmosphere. Convective motion, fuelled by the outward transport of heat, is not strong enough to produce towering cumulus clouds in the Saturnian stratosphere. Individual clouds are far less common than on Jupiter and when they do occur they are generally short-lived. Many change rapidly in response to prevailing winds.

Measurements of the motion of the clouds reveal a broad equatorial region with eastward winds as high as 1,600 km/h (1,000 mi/h). These winds form alternating east-west jets, with wind speeds decreasing towards the poles. There are oval storms near 70° north latitude and 45° to 55° latitude, forming cloud systems similar to those on Jupiter. However, they are smaller, with diameters less than 5,000 km (3,000 miles).

Saturn's Interior

Although Saturn's mass is 95 times that of Earth, its average density is less than that of water. If it were possible to place Saturn on an ocean large enough, it would float. The low density and variation in gravity sensed by passing spacecraft indicate that Saturn, like Jupiter, has a small dense core surrounded by a compressed gaseous envelope which is rich in hydrogen and helium.

Saturn radiates 1.8 times more energy than it absorbs from the Sun. Decay of radioactive isotopes or slow overall contraction of the planet under its own gravity could account for the excess energy. In addition, there may be a region deep in the interior where convective mixing is so small that the heavier helium sinks toward the core, releasing energy. At shallower depths, where the magnetic field is generated, there is evidence of organized convection. Unlike Earth, Saturn's magnetic field is aligned along its rotational axis.

Storms on Saturn

In 1990, a white cloud in Saturn's equatorial region was discovered and its growth noted by amateur observers. Cameras on board the newly launched Hubble Space Telescope were used to study the development of the storm. Although ground-based observers had reported occasional storms, this was the largest storm in 57 years.

Most storms on Saturn are short-lived and disperse in a manner that suggests they are generated by convection, which transports heat from the interior. The convective activity carries material to high altitudes, where the temperature is so low that ammonia and water immediately freeze to form ice. As the rising mass encounters the prevailing winds, the ice clouds serve as markers to reveal the progress of the storm. As the 1990 storm developed, it became apparent that it was similar to two previous equatorial disturbances that had been observed within the previous 125 years. These three storms were spaced at intervals of 57 years, nearly two Saturnian years, implying that these storms may be cyclic in nature.

The Nature of the Rings

In 1610 Galileo observed Saturn with his low-power telescope and saw two protrusions, one at each side of the planet. In 1612 the protrusions had vanished. Continuing observations revealed that their apparent size waxed and waned over a period of about 15 years. Finally, in 1659,

ABOVE: A false-colour image of Saturn, taken by Voyager 2 in August 1981 from a range of 114.7 million km (9.1 million miles). Seen hovering by the planet are two of its satellites, Dione (above) and Enceladus (below).

Christiaan Huygens (1629–95), a Dutch astronomer, realized that there is a thin ring around Saturn's equatorial plane, which seemed to be larger or smaller according to its angle with the line of sight from Earth.

Coinciding with these discoveries, Johannes Kepler (1571–1630) had formulated his laws of planetary motion. Although the dimensions of Saturn's ring were not known, it was apparent that the distance around the outer perimeter of the main ring system was 1.5 times greater than that around the inner edge. Kepler's laws required the inner part of the ring to move faster than the outer part. Thus, the ring could not be a rigid sheet but must be composed of a swarm of particles revolving about the planet. Observational proof of this was not obtained until 1895, when James Keeler (1857–1900) used a spectrograph to show that the orbital speed of the particles decreased outwards across the rings.

)))➤ *Planetary Rings, Saturn's Rings, Uranus's Rings*

SATURN NEBULA (NGC 7009)

The Saturn Nebula, NGC 7009, is a planetary nebula lying in the constellation of Aquarius, near the border with Capricornus. It is so-named (by the nineteenth-century Irish astronomer, Lord Rosse) because of its resemblance to the planet Saturn. Small telescopes show NGC 7009 as an elongated ellipse similar in size to the globe of Saturn. But the 'rings' – actually long jets of gas ejected by the central star – become visible only in larger apertures.

SATURN'S RINGS

Saturn's ring system extends from about 7,000 km (4,000 miles) above the cloud tops out to 74,000 km (46,250 miles). They are made of fragments of dark ice and rock, ranging from bodies a few kilometres across to dust particles. The rings are in the plane of Saturn's equator, which is tilted by nearly 27° compared with the planets orbital plane.

Three distinct rings are visible from Earth: A, B and C, in order from the outermost to the innermost. A fainter inner ring, the D ring, was discovered in 1969. Farther out beyond the A ring, in order of increasing distance, are rings F, G and E, discovered by space probes. There are also gaps, filled with thousands of thin individual 'ringlets'.

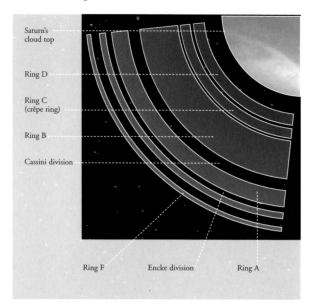

Saturn's
cloud top

Ring D

Ring C
(crêpe ring)

Ring B

Cassini division

Ring F   Encke division   Ring A

Braided and kinked rings, and strange, ephemeral spoke patterns are found. The F ring has gaps and regions that appear braided or twisted. The culprits are tiny 'shepherd moons', orbiting just inside and outside the F ring. The spokes may be electrically charged dust levitating above the rings.

SCHMIDT, BERNHARD (1879–1935)

Estonian telescope-maker. Schmidt designed a wide-field telescope that made possible large-scale photographic surveys of the night sky. One drawback of conventional reflecting telescopes is that they produce sharp images over only a narrow patch of sky. Schmidt's idea was to place a thin glass corrector plate in front of a deeply curved spherical mirror. The glass was subtly shaped to correct the distortions that the mirror would produce, resulting in a distortion-free image over several degrees of sky.

Schmidt produced his first telescope in 1930 and large Schmidt cameras with apertures of a metre or more have been in routine use in photographic sky surveys.

SCHWARZSCHILD RADIUS

According to general relativity, if a body's gravity is sufficiently strong, space–time becomes so highly curved around the body that light is unable to escape from it. The German physicist Karl Schwarzschild (1873–1916) showed that this occurs when the radius of the body is less than a certain critical value, which increases with the body's mass. This critical radius is now known as the Schwarzschild radius. In Newtonian theory it equates to the distance at which the escape velocity from the body becomes equal to the speed of light, equivalent to the Laplacian view that light has been slowed and fallen back to the object.

SCORPIUS

The heart of Scorpius the scorpion is marked by Antares. Near Antares is the globular cluster M4,

LEFT: Ring A is the outermost part of Saturn's ring system visible from Earth. The Cassini division, about 4,500 km (2,800 miles) wide, separates this from the brightest and widest part, ring B. The next ring is C, or Crêpe ring. The fainter rings D and F lie inside and outside the visible rings.

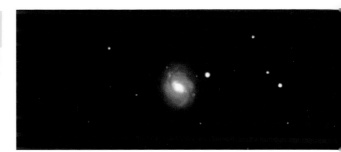

RIGHT: M77, in the constellation Cetus, a spiral with an active nucleus that is the brightest member of the class known as Seyfert galaxies.
BELOW: The giant Arecibo radio telescope has been employed by the SETI program to search for signals that might reveal life elsewhere in the Galaxy.

one of the closest globulars to us, 7,000 light years away. Double stars include Beta [β], Nu [ν], Xi [ξ] and Zeta [ζ] Scorpii. Open clusters include M6 (the Butterfly Cluster) lying 1,600 light years away, nearly twice as far as M7, and NGC 6231.

)))➤ *Antares*

SETI@HOME

SETI@home uses the processing power of millions of Internet-connected computers to analyze data from the radio telescope at Arecibo, Puerto Rico, looking for possible signals from extraterrestrial civilizations. Following its launch on 17 May 1999, SETI@home attracted over one million participants in the first three months. Using a smart screensaver program, each participant's computer downloads data, and while the computer sits unused, a background program sifts the data for suspect signals. The program halts any time the computer is in use, so the regular computer use is unaffected. The results are subsequently sent to the University of California at Berkeley and another block of data is returned.

SEYFERT GALAXY

A galaxy with a very luminous, compact nucleus. Seyfert galaxies contain active galactic nuclei (AGNs) with strong emission lines in their spectra. They are much less energetic than quasars and much more numerous. The great majority of Seyfert galaxies are spirals or barred spirals. In the unified model of AGNs, Seyfert galaxies are thought to be produced when the central engine is partially obscured (type 1 Seyfert or quasars) or totally obscured (type 2 Seyfert) by the disk of matter surrounding the supermassive black hole. Named after Carl Seyfert (1911–60) who first studied them.

)))➤ *Blazars, BL Lac Objects*

SHAPLEY, HARLOW (1885–1972)

American astronomer who demonstrated around 1918 that the Galaxy was far larger than the estimate of Jacobus Kapteyn (1851–1922), a Dutch astronomer, and that the Sun lay well away from the centre of the Galaxy. American Robert Trumpler (1886–1956), showed that Kapteyn's results were badly affected by interstellar dust, which dims the light from distant stars and gave the erroneous impression that their numbers fell off equally in all directions around us. Shapley's determination of the size of the Galaxy was based on the distribution of the globular clusters.

)))➤ *Kapteyn, Jacobus*

SHENZHOU SPACECRAFT

China is currently working on a manned space program. Successful unmanned test flights of their Soyuz-type Shenzhou-1 craft began in November 1999. Shenzhou 2 went through a more rigorous test-flight in January 2001 and the first 'taikonaut', or Chinese astronaut, is expected to be launched in the next five years.

SHEPARD, ALAN (1923–98)

American astronaut Alan Shepard was selected as America's first man in space. He named his spacecraft Freedom 7. The launch, from Cape Canaveral in Florida, was originally scheduled for 2 May 1961 but was postponed until 5 May because of bad weather. At 5.15 a.m. EST, Shepard entered Freedom 7 and over four hours later the Redstone rocket propelled him to 8,214 km/h (5,103 mi/h) before shutting down on schedule 142 seconds after lift-off and separating from the capsule. Shepard manoeuvred the craft about all three axes and tested the reaction control systems. Freedom 7 reached a peak altitude of 187 km (117 miles), before Shepard prepared for re-entry, splashing down in the Atlantic Ocean 15 minutes and 22 seconds after launch. Subsequently Shepard commanded the Apollo 14 mission which touched down in the Fra Mauro region of the Moon on 5 February 1971.

SHOEMAKER, EUGENE (1928–97)

American lunar geologist. Although best known for discovering a comet that hit Jupiter in July 1994, Shoemaker's signature work was his research on the nature and origin of the Barringer Meteor Crater in Arizona, which helped provide a foundation for research into cratering on the Moon and planets.

Shoemaker was an inspiration behind America's lunar exploration. He took part in the Ranger lunar robotic missions, was principal investigator for the television experiment on the Surveyor lunar landers, and led the geology field investigations team for the first Apollo lunar landings. He later conceived the 1994 Clementine lunar mission, but in 1997, at the age of 69, while doing field work in Central Australia with his wife, Carolyn, he was killed in a car crash. As a tribute to the father of lunar geology, some of Shoemaker's ashes were carried to the lunar surface on board the Lunar Prospector mission, which impacted there in 1999.

SIDEREAL TIME

Time based on the rotation of the Earth with respect to the stars. Local sidereal time is zero hours when the vernal equinox crosses the observer's meridian. When a celestial object is on the observer's meridian, its right ascension equals the local sidereal time.

SIMON, PIERRE, MARQUIS DE LAPLACE (1749–1827)

French mathematician and astronomer. In 1785 he was recognized as France's leading mathematician and between 1799 and 1825 he published the five huge volumes of his *Mécanique Céleste* ('*Celestial Mechanics*'), thought to be the finest work on the subject since Newton's *Principia Mathematica* (1687). Laplace believed that though God had created the Universe, it was now an ordered, self-running system, a belief which heralded the Age of Reason.

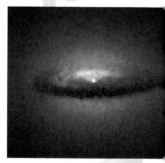

In an earlier book, *Système du Monde*, published in 1796, Laplace, noted that if a star was big enough or

ABOVE: A disk of gas and dust surrounding a black hole.

LEFT: Eugene Shoemaker specialized in the study of the Moon, asteroids and comets. His name is associated with a comet which hit the planet Jupiter in July 1994, jointly discovered by him, his wife and David Levy.

BELOW: Skylab built on the technology developed for the Apollo Space program. It contained private sleeping quarters and a zero-gravity shower.

heavy enough, the force of gravity acting on light particles would prevent them from escaping. As Laplace put it, 'the attractive force of a heavenly body could be so large that light could not flow from it'. Although his reasoning was wrong – Laplace assumed light consisted of particles which would be influenced by gravity – and he did not use the term, Laplace had defined the black hole.

SINGULARITY

Singularity is defined as a mathematical point where the laws of physics break down. Calculations predict that a singularity exists at the centres of black holes, a point of infinite density and zero radius. Anything falling into such a hole would in effect be crushed out of existence at the singularity. A rotating black hole would contain a ring-like singularity – a very thin (almost zero thickness) ring of matter with high, but not infinite, density surrounding empty space. Rotating black holes might have two separate event horizons – and, stranger still, if the black hole is rotating fast enough these might coincide and cancel each other out leaving a so-called 'naked' singularity, not hidden from view. Such naked singularities seem to defy the laws of physics, but some physicists have postulated that they might be produced not only by spinning black holes but may also be left behind when a black hole has completely evaporated by emission of Hawking radiation. The Big Bang theory proposes that the Universe started from a singularity.

))))➤ **Big Bang, Black Holes, Event Horizon, Hawking Radiation, Universe**

SKYLAB

Determined to build on technology developed for Apollo, NASA came up with the Apollo Applications Program, later renamed Skylab. This space station, a converted Saturn rocket stage, contained living quarters – a communal area, a toilet, a kitchen area, individual bedrooms and a larger area for exercising – and a laboratory for scientific experiments. A series of airlocks and docking modules allowed other experiments to be exposed to space and astronauts to climb outside. Skylab 1 was launched on 14 May 1973. Within seconds a thin meteoroid Sun shield opened too early and was torn off, dragging one solar panel with it and jamming a second panel shut. Once in orbit, four telescope solar panels were deployed and were able to generate enough power to switch all the systems on but, without the shield, temperatures began to rise and the first manned mission was postponed.

Charles Conrad commanded the first repair mission to Skylab on 25 May 1973. The crew entered the overheated chamber and pushed a thermal blanket out of one of the air locks to act as a temporary sunshade. During a three-and-a-half-hour spacewalk they managed to open the last solar panel and, with Skylab fully operational, the crew stayed for 28 days. Alan Bean's (b. 1932) crew arrived in July and undertook solar and stellar astronomy, Earth observations, material science and space medicine studies. During a 59-day stay they also deployed a more permanent Sun shield and undertook several spacewalks to change the film in the solar telescope. The third and final Skylab crew arrived in November 1973 and studied the effect of their 84-day stay on their bodies. Skylab crashed back to Earth on 12 July 1979. Most fell into the Indian Ocean but some fragments – including a one-tonne oxygen tank – landed in Australia.

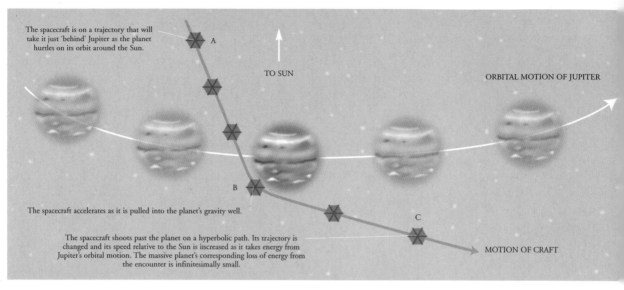

The spacecraft is on a trajectory that will take it just 'behind' Jupiter as the planet hurtles on its orbit around the Sun.

A

TO SUN

ORBITAL MOTION OF JUPITER

B

The spacecraft accelerates as it is pulled into the planet's gravity well.

C

The spacecraft shoots past the planet on a hyperbolic path. Its trajectory is changed and its speed relative to the Sun is increased as it takes energy from Jupiter's orbital motion. The massive planet's corresponding loss of energy from the encounter is infinitesimally small.

MOTION OF CRAFT

SLING-SHOT

The gravity-assist, or gravitational sling-shot technique (above) is a fuel-efficient means of sending a spacecraft to the planets, especially the outer planets. The spacecraft makes a close approach to a planet and uses its gravitational field to speed it on its way. Cassini, arriving at Saturn in 2004, will have been boosted by approaches to Venus, Earth, Venus again, and Jupiter.

SLOAN DIGITAL SKY SURVEY (SDSS)

The SDSS is a major project to map the large-scale distribution of galaxies, allowing cosmologists to refine their theories of how the Universe evolved. This five-year American-Japanese venture is based at the Apache Point Observatory in New Mexico. SDSS is actually two surveys, since both photometric and redshift information is being collected.

SMALL MAGELLANIC CLOUD

An irregular galaxy, third closest to the Sun at about 200,000 light years. With its companion, the Large Magellanic Cloud, it is visible to the naked eye in the southern sky. The Small Magellanic Cloud has about a thousandth the total mass of our Galaxy and was probably broken off the Large Cloud during a close approach to the Milky Way
))))➤ *Large Magellanic Cloud.*

ABOVE: Gravitational sling-shot technique:

A: Here the spacecraft is on a trajectory that will take it just 'behind' Jupiter as the planet hurtles on its orbit around the Sun.

B: The spacecraft accelerates as it is pulled into the the planet's gravity well.

C: The spacecraft shoots past the planet on a hyperbolic path. Its trajectory is changed and its speed relative to the Sun is increased as it takes energy from Jupiter's orbital motion. The massive planet's corresponding loss of energy from the encounter is extremely small.

SOJOURNER LANDER

After a seven-month journey, Mars Pathfinder bounced onto the Martian surface on 4 July 1997. Inside squatted a six-wheeled rover called Sojourner. The buggy gained global fame when it rolled successfully on to the red surface and spent 10 weeks probing the chemical make-up of nearby boulders. Pathfinder's camera allowed Earth-based scientists to follow Sojourner's progress.
))))➤ *Mars Pathfinder*

SOLAR AND HELIOSPHERIC OBSERVATORY

The 1990s saw a revolution in our observations of the Sun. A key part of this was the Solar and Heliospheric Observatory (SOHO), a joint ESA-NASA spacecraft launched in 1995 and positioned 1.5 million km (932,100 miles) from Earth. It studies the Sun 24 hours a day and records images in a variety of wavelengths.

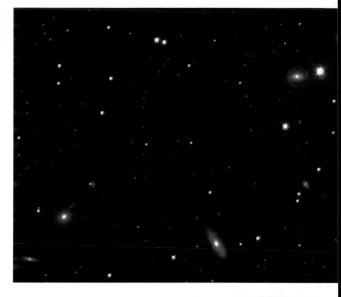

RIGHT: The Sloan Digital Sky Survey (SDSS) is a major project to map the large-scale distribution of galaxies in the Universe.
BELOW RIGHT: The Sun seen at extreme ultraviolet wavelengths, showing features in the solar corona at a temperature of about one million degrees, recorded by the Solar and Heliospheric Observatory (SOHO).

SOLAR CYCLE

The periodic variation in solar activity. The sunspot cycle has an approximately 11-year period. The magnetic solar cycle, however, is twice as long as this, because the magnetic polarity (field direction) in each solar hemisphere reverses after each sunspot cycle.

SOLAR DAY

1. Apparent solar day: the time between successive meridian crossings by the Sun. As the apparent motion of the Sun is not constant through the year, the apparent solar day varies in length.
2. The mean solar day uses a hypothetical 'mean sun', which moves at a constant angular rate.

SOLAR NEUTRINO

Neutrinos produced by nuclear reactions in the heart of the Sun. Neutrinos are electrically neutral particles of extremely small – possibly zero – mass. They are elusive, being able to pass through Earth with only a minute chance of interacting with any atom on the way. Fewer neutrinos than originally predicted arrive at the Earth from the Sun. This might have indicated a flaw in our understanding of processes in the Sun. However, a different explanation is almost certainly true: that the neutrino has a small mass, which results in some solar neutrinos turning into a different, undetected kind of neutrino before they reach Earth.

)))➤ *Neutrinos*

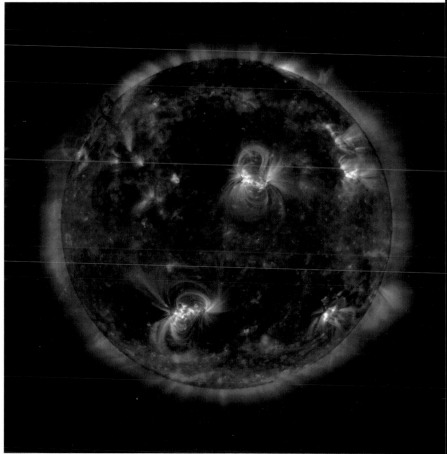

SOLAR SYSTEM

The Sun and the planets, satellites, interplanetary debris, gas and dust that orbit around it. The Sun is just one of a hundred billion stars which belong to the Milky Way Galaxy, a huge stellar system bound together by the force of gravity. The Sun shines by the release of energy in its core, in nuclear reactions which convert hydrogen into helium under immense pressures and temperatures. As hydrogen atoms fuse to form helium, energy is released.

The Birth of the Solar System

Around four and half billion years ago the Sun was enveloped in a disk of gas and dust born from a collapsing nebula, or cloud of gas and dust. Under the influence of gravity, material not swept up by the young Sun gradually accreted to form small rocky chunks called planetesimals. The inevitable collision of planetesimals gave rise to larger bodies, and within approximately 10 million years, a relatively short period of time astronomically speaking, the planets had formed.

What process triggered the initial collapse of our solar nebula is more of a mystery. One suggestion is that a massive nearby star ended its life in a huge explosion, producing a supernova. The shock waves slammed into a region of gas and dust and triggered its collapse, ultimately resulting in the formation of the Sun, the planets… and us.

BELOW: The Sun and the nine known planets of our Solar System; Mercury, Venus, Earth, Mars, Jupiter, Saturn, Uranus, Neptune and Pluto.

Earth and the Moon

The Moon is large in comparison to Earth and scientists often refer to Earth and the Moon as a double-planet system. The most likely cause of the Moon's formation was a cataclysmic glancing blow from an object the size of Mars. Owing to its smaller size, gravity on the Moon is only one-sixth of that on Earth. Any atmosphere the Moon may once have had has almost completely leaked away into space.

Earth is the only world we know of that teems with life. Carbon, hydrogen and oxygen, along with energy in the form of heat, are all essential for the origin and maintenance of life. These elements are found in abundance on other planets and satellites but it seems the balance was not quite right for the proliferation of life to arise there.

SUN	Venus 107.5 to 108.9 million km	Mars 206.6 to 249.2 million km	ASTEROID BELT	Jupiter 740.5 to 816.6 million km	Uranus 2,741.3 to 3,003. million km
	Mercury 46.0 to 69.8 million km	Earth 147.1 to 152.1 million km			

The Other Planets

The inner, or terrestrial, planets – Mercury, Venus, Earth and Mars – are relatively small and dense, with solid, rocky crusts. The outer planets – Jupiter, Saturn, Uranus and Neptune (excluding the oddball world of Pluto) – are larger and lighter, and are composed mostly of hydrogen and helium. They are referred to either as the gaseous planets or gas giants.

The distinction came about very early during the formation of the Solar System – perhaps during the first 10 million years. Originally, the gas and dust contained within the protoplanetary disk from which the planets formed was evenly mixed. However, as the Sun grew larger and radiated more energy, the lighter gases and ices closer in were vaporized and blown outwards, leaving behind denser material. The inner planets formed from the dense leftovers. The lighter gases moved outward until they condensed in regions of the outer Solar System where temperatures were cooler. Small rocky planets, already existing in the outer Solar System, became swamped with the lighter gases, which they readily swept up, forming the giant gaseous outer planets.

Compositions and Atmospheres

The terrestrial worlds have solid crusts with molten cores. Mercury and Mars have tenuous atmospheres, whereas those of Venus and Earth are much thicker and more dynamic. Earth is still geologically active, with erupting volcanoes, earthquakes and plate tectonics. Mercury's surface is covered with craters, evidence that its crust is much older and that geological activity ceased there billions of years ago. The surfaces of Venus and Mars reveal that powerful geological forces have been at play. Mars is home to the Solar System's largest volcanoes and has a huge rift valley. Venus has an abundance of volcanoes and volcanic plains. While present-day vulcanism on Venus is open to debate, Martian volcanoes are believed to be extinct.

The outer planets have no solid surface; they are much larger than the terrestrial planets and are composed mainly of hydrogen and helium. Each gas giant has a system of satellites and is girdled by a series of rings made of rock and ice.

The ninth planet, Pluto, is the smallest in the Solar System and is composed mainly of rock and ice as hard as steel. Recently astronomers have questioned whether Pluto represents a true planet, since it is likely to belong to a large swarm of icy planetesimals that populate the outer Solar System, forming the Edgeworth–Kuiper belt. Pluto is accompanied by its large moon, Charon.

Comets, Asteroids and Planetesimals

Apart from the planets, the Solar System is littered with the debris left over from its formation. The main asteroid belt lies between the orbits of Mars and Jupiter. More than 10,000 asteroids within the belt have been catalogued and many thousands more are likely to exist. Reservoirs of dormant comets lie in the Edgeworth–Kuiper belt, beyond the orbit of Neptune, and in the Oort cloud, which forms a sphere extending halfway to the nearest star.

))))➤ *Asteroid, Comet, Edgeworth–Kuiper Belt, Oort Cloud, Plate Tectonics, Supernovae*

ABOVE: A dense layer of cloud, composed of droplets of sulphuric acid completely obscures the surface of Venus from view.

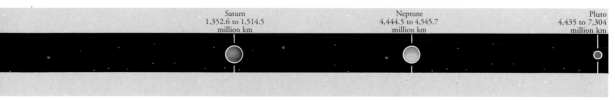

Saturn	Neptune	Pluto
1,352.6 to 1,514.5 million km	4,444.5 to 4,545.7 million km	4,435 to 7,304 million km

SOLAR WIND

The continuous, though highly variable, outflow of charged particles (mainly electrons and protons) from the Sun.

SOLSTICE

The most northerly or southerly apparent position of the Sun during the year, or either of the times when it passes through these positions. The summer solstice occurs about 21 June, when the Sun is 23.5° north, while the winter solstice occurs about 22 December, when the Sun is 23.5° south.

)))➤ *Equinox*

SOMBRERO GALAXY (M104)

A spiral galaxy lying in the constellation Virgo that is not a member of the Virgo Cluster, but lies about 10 million light years closer to us. Tilted almost edge-on to us, this galaxy looks rather like a wide-brimmed Mexican hat in photographs, hence its popular name the Sombrero, although small telescopes show it as only an elongated smudge. Larger apertures will bring into view a dark lane of dust crossing the galaxy's nucleus.

SOUTH CELESTIAL POLE

The point on the celestial sphere which would be cut by extending the Earth's rotational axis through the south pole. Unlike the North Celestial Pole, it is not marked by any nearby star at present. Due to precession, the position of the SCP traces out a circle over about 25,800 years, like the NCP.

SOUTHERN CROSS

Crux, the Southern Cross is the smallest of all 88 constellations but its distinctive shape and bright stars make Crux easy to identify. Double stars include Mu [μ] Crucis, Alpha [α] Crucis and Gamma [γ] Crucis, a red giant that forms an apparent double with an unrelated 6th-magnitude background star. Crux also contains the Coalsack Nebula and the spectacular open cluster NGC 4755, better known as the Jewel Box because the nineteenth-century astronomer John Herschel described it as resembling a cask of precious stones.

)))➤ *Coalsack Nebula, Double Stars, Open Cluster, Red Giant*

ABOVE FAR RIGHT: Shuttle Flight Program
ABOVE: The constellation Crux, the Southern Cross, contains the glittering Jewell Box (NGC 4755), an open star cluster.
BELOW: The Sombrero galaxy, M104, a spiral galaxy seen edge-on.

1 Having blasted-off using three main engines and two Solid Rocket Boosters (SRB), the SRBs are detached. Altitude: 45 km (28 miles). Flight time: 2 min.

2 Just before orbital insertion, the external tank separates. Altitude: 109 km (68 miles). Flight time: 8 min.

3 Orbital operations carried out. Altitude varies according to mission: 185–1,110 km (115–690 miles). Flight duration: 7–30 days.

4 Shuttle turns to backward angle and retro-fires engines to reduce speed.

5 After change of angle to reduce friction heat – the nose cap reaches 1,430°C (2,606°F) – the Shuttle enters terminal phase of re-entry.

6 Glide approach to airstrip, then landing at 343–364 km/h (213–226 mi/h).

SPACE DEBRIS

Hurtling round Earth at over 27,000 km/h (17,000 mi/h), even the tiniest fleck of paint can prove lethal to an astronaut or spacecraft. No one has been hurt by one of these space bullets but collisions have occurred. Shuttle windows have been pitted and, in 1981, Cosmos 1275 suddenly exploded into almost 300 fragments. It is suspected this Soviet satellite collided with an uncatalogued piece of space debris. Over 25,000 items of space debris are listed, many are large enough to be tracked with radar, but countless smaller fragments are not. Debris comes from craft that go wrong, old or dead satellites, run-down batteries, and left-over rocket parts. Many pieces of debris are pulled back toward Earth and burn up, others orbit in trajectories which will last for centuries. Space agencies are exploring possible ways of cleaning up Earth orbit and making missions less messy.

SPACE SHUTTLES

In the early 1970s NASA announced its intention to build a reusable Space Shuttle and the USSR began its own short-lived program which produced Buran. Funding for the American Shuttle – a versatile flying laboratory, a reusable launch vehicle, and a method of re-capturing and repairing satellites in orbit – was approved in 1972. The Shuttle consists of a delta-winged orbiter which sits on a large fuel tank. Strapped to the tank are two solid rocket boosters. The orbiter carries up to eight people in its nose. The lower level is for sleeping and eating while the upper floor houses the flight deck and an area for operating payload bay equipment. The bulk of the Shuttle's 56.1-m (184-ft) length houses the payload bay.

Columbia made the first shuttle flight on 12 April 1981. A second was completed seven months later, the world's first reusable space vehicle had arrived. Three Shuttles were added to the fleet and by 1985 launches were an almost monthly routine.

There have been over 100 Shuttle flights to date. The Shuttle fleet has recently been refitted and modernized and is expected to fly until 2030. Launches still cost around $400 million and expendable launch vehicles are cheaper for reaching space.

))))▶ *Buran, NASA, Spacelab*

SOYUZ SPACE PROGRAM

Soyuz was conceived as a three-module lunar spaceship by Soviet chief designer Korolev. In 1967 the Apollo program was in trouble, after a fire on the launch pad had killed the entire crew of Apollo 1. By April that year the Soyuz program was poised to regain the lead in the race to the Moon. The plan was to dock two Soyuz capsules in orbit and transfer two crew members between spacecraft. Soyuz 2's launch was postponed after Soyuz 1 struck trouble in orbit, eventually crashing when its landing parachutes failed, killing cosmonaut Komarov. Soyuz 2 eventually flew a year later, as an unmanned target for Georgi Beregovoi (1921–95) flying Soyuz 3.

In 1969, Soyuz 4 and 5 practised docking and crew transfer and are thought to have been a rehearsal for the Soviet's upcoming lunar missions.

But by July 1969 Apollo 11 had reached the Moon and Soyuz 6, 7 and 8 were launched together in October to practise manoeuvring. Soyuz 9, the following summer, set a new endurance record when its crew Andrian Nikoleyev and Vitaly Sevastyanov (b. 1935) remained in orbit for almost 18 days. Further Soyuz flights would be simple ferrying missions to the space stations, Salyut and – later – Mir.

SPACELAB

Spacelab was conceived in the 1960s when NASA was looking for international collaborations on its post-Apollo space programs. It was eventually decided that the US would develop a reusable Space Shuttle and Europe would build a modular laboratory to be carried in the Shuttle's payload bay. The laboratory called Spacelab consisted of a combination of one or two pressurized modules and up to three external pallets. Inside the modules was a shirtsleeve environment where scientist-astronauts could conduct experiments. They were linked to the main Shuttle cabin by a tunnel. Other experiments and astronomy or Earth-observation equipment was mounted outside on the U-shaped pallets. The Space Shuttle Columbia carried Spacelab-1 into orbit on 28 November 1983, along with the first European astronaut Ulf Merbold. The mission lasted 10 days and carried 38 different sets of experiments, supporting 73 investigations from 14 countries. Subsequent Spacelabs undertook astronomy, Earth-observation and biological experiments. Spacelab's last mission was in 1998.

SPACE–TIME

Einstein's special theory of relativity presented a new view of the nature of time and space. In Newtonian mechanics there are three dimensions of space and one of time. Any event can be located by specifying where it happened (three co-ordinates) and when (one co-ordinate). But while for Newton space and time exist independently

ABOVE: The Space Shuttle Colombia, which carried Spacelab-1 into orbit on 28 November 1983, was the first reusable launch vehicle.

of each other, for Einstein they do not. In Einstein's universe space and time are entwined in a four-dimensional entity called space–time. This means that changes in intervals of time for one observer are associated with changes in distance in space for another, but the separation between events in space–time is the same for both. It is in this sense that we live in a four-dimensional universe. It remains true, though, that space and time are different in kind. The equations of relativity treat space and time differently, but space and time are intimately interwoven.

⟫▶ *Relativity, Special Theory of*

SPECTRA

The band of colour produced by shining white light through a prism is known as a spectrum. It is caused by different wavelengths of light travelling at different speeds in the glass and being refracted by different angles at the surfaces. A similar effect is achieved by a diffraction grating, a simple device that splits white light into several coloured beams. Either can be used as the basis of instruments to form and study the spectra of astronomical objects. The general appearance of the spectrum depends upon the physical conditions in the source of light and any absorbing matter along the line of sight.

Several different types of spectrum may be distinguished according to the conditions in which the radiation is

LEFT: As a beam of white light enters a prism, the beam bends and fans out into different colours. It is bent again on leaving the prism, so creating the familiar band of colours known as a spectrum.

BELOW: A hot opaque object, such as a star, emits a continuous spectrum. A hot, thin gas emits light at certain wavelengths, forming an emission line spectrum. Where a cool, thin gas lies between the star and the observer, it absorbs light from the star, forming an absorption line spectrum.

Each chemical element produces its own characteristic set of lines, which may appear either in emission or absorption, thereby allowing analysis of the composition of celestial objects. The measured wavelengths of emission and absorption lines in astronomical objects often differ from the wavelengths of the same elements in the laboratory. This difference is due to the fact that the gas in which the lines arise is moving with respect to the observer because space is expanding, and the wavelengths of the lines are being changed by the Doppler shift.

The Doppler shift also affects the width of the spectral lines. The atoms in a gas are all moving at different speeds, and in consequence the emissions from each atom will have slightly different wavelengths. The result is that the line is slightly broadened, and the lines from a hot gas are broader than the lines from a cold gas, an effect known as Doppler broadening. The line width tells astronomers the temperature of the gas. Doppler broadening can also indicate turbulence in the gas or even that the whole source is rotating, expanding or contracting. Any of these conditions would broaden the lines.

emitted. These include continuous spectra, absorption spectra, emission line spectra and reflection spectra. More than one type of spectrum may be present at the same time. The spectrum of the Sun, for example, consists of a continuous spectrum together with bright emission lines and dark absorption lines. The entire solar spectrum may itself be observed as a reflection spectrum in the light reflected from clouds.

Sometimes single lines that appear broadened are actually split into two or more lines. This Zeeman effect is apparent in the light from sunspots and indicates that a strong magnetic field is present. The amount of splitting is a measure of the strength of the field.

An emission line from the hydrogen atom, with a wavelength near 21 cm, is the strongest feature in the radio spectrum. By measuring the precise wavelengths of the 21-cm lines coming from the Milky Way, astronomers can identify many gas clouds moving at different speeds and use them to map the spiral structure of the Galaxy.

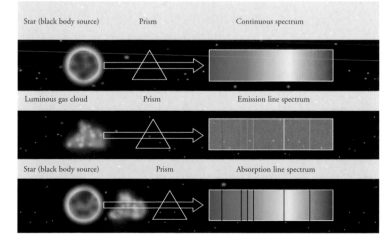

Star (black body source)	Prism	Continuous spectrum
Luminous gas cloud	Prism	Emission line spectrum
Star (black body source)	Prism	Absorption line spectrum

SPECTRAL TYPE

A shorthand description of a star's basic properties is provided by its spectral type, designated by one of seven capital letters: O, B, A, F, G, K, M, running from the hottest stars to the coolest. Such spectral types are allocated purely from the appearance of the star's spectrum; this is compared with a set of standard stellar spectra that are arranged so that the pattern of features (primarily absorption lines) changes progressively with surface temperature. The odd sequence of letters used in spectral classification is a legacy of early attempts to find a pattern among stellar spectra, before the effects of temperature were recognized. Sub-classes 0 to 9 were introduced to afford a finer distinction. On this scheme, the Sun is classified as a G2 star.

SPECTROGRAPHS

A device used to split light from an object into its component wavelengths. A slit placed in the focal plane of the telescope is used to isolate the object, such as a star or galaxy. Light passing through the slit falls on a diffraction grating (occasionally a prism), where it is spread out to form a spectrum of the object. Modern spectrographs sometimes use optical fibres to channel the light from many objects into the slit side by side. Spectral analysis can give information about chemical composition, temperature, radial and rotational velocities, and magnetic fields.

SPECTROSCOPE

A device that analyses light by splitting it into its component colours, using a prism or diffraction grating. In 1666, Isaac Newton (1642–1727) split sunlight into its spectrum, or band of component colours, using a prism. In 1802 William Wollaston (1766–1828) found a few inexplicable black lines in the spectrum of sunlight, each line representing the absence of a definite

colour. In 1814–15 Joseph von Fraunhofer (1787–1826) mapped the positions of 574 black lines seen in sunlight. Such lines in astronomical spectra reveal the identities of atoms and molecules in the bodies that are the sources of the light.

SPECTROSCOPIC BINARIES

Many stars are too close together to be resolved directly through a telescope, but they can be detected by spectroscopy. If the lines in a star's spectrum are moving cyclically back and forth in wavelength, it could be due to the Doppler shift as the star moves in

ABOVE RIGHT: Spectographs such as this model built c. 1919 were used to observe and measure electromagnetic radiation emitted by black bodies.
RIGHT: The sequence of changing spectral lines reveals the presence of a spectroscopic binary. When both stars move across the observers line of sight, the lines merge (1 and 3). When one star is approaching and the other is receding, the lines have become separated (2 and 4).

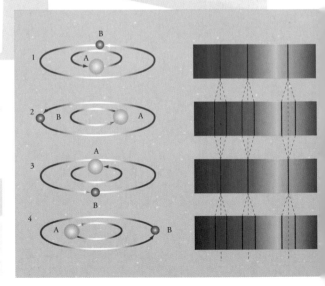

RIGHT: A faint object Spectograph on the William Herschel Telescope. Such devices are used to create a photographic or electric image of a spectrum.

orbit around its centre of mass with a companion (although it could be a single star that is pulsating in size). If the spectrum of only one component can be seen it is termed a single-line spectroscopic binary, but when the two are of comparable brightness a double-line spectroscopic binary may be observed. By monitoring such a spectroscopic binary throughout its orbital cycle, astronomers can calculate the orbital elements, quantities which describe the characteristics of the orbit: its period, shape, size and orientation in space, and the speed of the stars. This is one of the techniques used to discover many otherwise invisible planetary companions of stars.

SPECTROSCOPY

Spectroscopy is the branch of physics concerned with the formation and interpretation of spectra. Instruments used for observing spectra are variously known as spectroscopes, spectrometers, or spectrographs. Spectroscopic instruments use either a prism or a diffraction grating to form a spectrum. A diffraction grating is more common, as there is a simple relationship between the wavelength of the light and the angle through which it is diffracted. It is also effective over a wider range of wavelengths than a prism. In astronomy, where almost all objects have to be observed remotely, spectroscopy is a powerful tool for studying the physical conditions in planets, stars, galaxies and interstellar space. Among its many applications, astronomers use spectroscopy to measure the chemical composition of stars and planetary atmospheres, the temperatures of gaseous nebulae, the strengths of magnetic fields in space, the rotation speeds of galaxies, the expansion rate of the Universe, and the masses of black holes.

SPECTRUM

The distribution of intensity of electromagnetic radiation with wavelength. The spectrum of white light through a prism reveals the 'rainbow' band of colours. A continuous spectrum is an unbroken distribution, whereas a line spectrum contains emission and/or absorption lines.

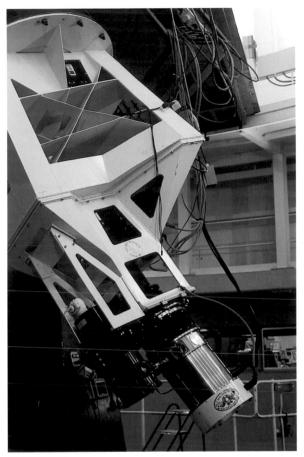

RIGHT: A faint object Spectograph on the William Herschel Telescope. Such devices are used to create a photographic or electric image of a spectrum.

SPICULES

Short-lived (around 5 to 10 minutes) narrow jets of solar material on the chromosphere, seen at the limb (the edge of the visible disc of the sun). They have temperatures in the region of 10,000 to 20,000 K and velocities of 20 to 30 km/s. They are located at the edges of supergranulation cells.

◗◗◗▶ *Chromosphere*

SPIN–ORBIT COUPLING

This effect is caused by tidal interactions between two bodies that causes the less massive body to match its spin period to its orbital period. When this effect occurs (as with the Moon), the body is described as having synchronous rotation and it always shows the same hemisphere towards the more massive body.

◗◗◗▶ *Orbital Period*

SPIRAL GALAXIES

Most visually striking of all galaxies are the spirals. They can take a wide variety of forms, ranging from impressive swirling 'grand design' systems in which two spiral arms unwind from their central hubs, to so-called 'flocculent' (or 'fleecy') systems that contain many short, disjointed segments of arms. Spirals have masses ranging from about a billion to a million million solar masses and diameters from 10,000 to over 200,000 light years.

Seen face-on, spirals display a whirlpool-like appearance that immediately conveys the impression of orderly circulation. Rotation regiments the stars into a fairly flat plane – confirmed by measurements of the Doppler shifts in the light from the stars and radio emissions from the interstellar gas. The side-on view of spirals clearly illustrates that their stars are arranged in a disk that is very thin by comparison with the galaxy's diameter, as in the case of our own Galaxy.

In addition to the eye-catching arms, most spirals possess a central bulge, shaped like a flattened sphere, in which the stars follow more random orbits about the galaxy's nucleus. The stars of a spiral galaxy's bulge are mostly old – Population II stars as in our own Galaxy – while the encircling disk contains stars with a mixture of ages, including highly luminous young supergiants, star

ABOVE: Spiral galaxy NGC 4603 is receding from us at a speed of nearly 2,500 km/s (1,550 mi/s).

BELOW: The spiral galaxy NGC 253 in the constellation of Sculptor is seen nearly edge-on and so appears elliptical in outline.

clusters and glowing clouds of star-forming gas, all highlighting the structure of the arms. A spiral galaxy is categorized according to how tightly its arms are wound and the size of its central bulge.

))))➡ *Doppler Effect, Galactic Bulge, Population II Stars*

SPOT SATELLITES

With support from Belgium and Sweden, France joined the Earth observation industry in 1986, with its polar-orbiting SPOT series (Satellite Pour l'Observation de la Terre). SPOT 1 was launched in February of that year. To date four SPOT satellites have been launched, the latest providing colour 20-m (65-ft) resolution stereoscopic ground views.

SPUTNIK I

On 4 October 1957 the R-7 rocket rose from its pad at Baikonur carrying Sputnik 1. In orbit between 228 and 947 km (142 and 589 miles) above Earth, the world's first artificial satellite (a polished 58-cm/ 23-in sphere) unfurled four rod-shaped antennae and began its broadcast. The Space Age had arrived. Sputnik 1 remained in orbit for 92 days, burning up in the atmosphere on 4 January 1958. By then Russia had successfully launched another satellite – carrying a dog called Laika – and was planning a recoverable surveillance satellite and capsules to carry the first humans into space.

SPUTNIK SPACE PROGRAM

The Space Age started with the launch of the satellite Sputnik 1 in October 1957. By November of that year the Soviet Union had achieved another space first with Sputnik. The first living creature in space, a dog called Laika, was sent onboard Sputnik 2. The Soviet Union continued to build on the successes of Sputniks 1 and 2, launching the massive Sputnik 3 on 15 May 1958. The polished metallic cone, covered in antennae and solar panels, spent 691 days in space, recording data on cosmic rays, the Van Allen belts and micrometeorite

collisions. In preparation for the first human spaceflight, later Sputnik missions flew a variety of biological cargoes into Earth orbit. These missions carried mainly dogs. After a day in orbit, Pchelka ('Little Bee') and Mushka ('Little Fly'), on board Sputnik 6, re-entered the atmosphere at too steep an angle and were killed. On 9 March 1961, Sputnik 9 orbited a dog called Chernushka ('Blackie') with a guinea pig, some mice and a dummy cosmonaut. Zvezdochka ('Little Star') on Sputnik 10 was the last dog to fly before the first human, Yuri Gagarin, lifted off in Vostok 1.

))))➡ *Animals in Space*

SS433

Optically faint, SS433 is a strong radio source and a variable source of X-rays. Its emission lines of hydrogen have three components: one is quite strong and moves slightly in a 13-day cycle, while the two weaker components show enormous shifts, corresponding to velocities of 40,000 km/s (25,000 mi/s), varying over 164 days. This suggests a relatively normal star is shedding material into an accretion disk around a neutron star or black hole. The binary has a period of 13 days and the strong hydrogen emission comes from the disk. Material approaching too close to the compact object is either sucked into it or ejected in jets perpendicular to the disk. The whole system is precessing like a top in a period of 164 days so that the jets end up spraying their material into space like a high-speed garden sprinkler. It is these jets that produce the weak but dramatically moving hydrogen lines.

STANDARD CANDLES

Astronomical objects of known luminosity which are therefore useful for determining astronomical distances. Cepheid variables are an example, since the easily observed period of brightness variation is related to the luminosity. Supernovae of Type Ia are another widely used class of standard candle.

))))➡ *Cepheids, Period-Luminosity Relation*

LEFT: Inside Sputnik 1:
1. Protective outer shell (top half). 2. Cone containing radio transmitter (this altered the pitch of its beeps according to the temperature registered by the themometer). 3. Sockets to hold four whip antennae. 4. Chemical batteries.
5. Themometer. 6. Protective outer shell (bottom half).

STARBURST GALAXIES

A small proportion of galaxies are undergoing an intense surge of star formation. In many cases, the activity in these so-called starburst galaxies seems to result from a collision or near-miss with another galaxy, which has compressed the gas clouds to form new stars. Starburst galaxies are particularly prominent in the infrared; this strong infrared emission comes from dust within them that has been heated by the young, luminous stars. An example of a starburst galaxy is M82 in Ursa Major, which appears to have been disturbed by an encounter with the nearby spiral M81 and other members of the small cluster to which they both belong.

STARS, COMPOSITION OF

Dark absorption lines in a star's spectrum are produced by atoms and ions (and, for the cooler stars, molecules) in the star's atmosphere. The precise pattern is determined by many factors but the dominant one is the temperature: the hotter the gas, the more violently the atoms, ions and electrons collide with one another. This influences how many electrons the atomic nuclei can retain (their state of ionization) and also the level of excitation of those electrons in their orbits. Density is another factor: the more rarefied the stellar atmosphere, the easier it is for electrons to avoid being captured by the positively charged ions. The composition of the gas in the star's surface layers can be determined from the signature of absorption lines in its spectrum once the temperature is known (from the star's colour) and its density has been estimated (from the degree of ionization of elements such as iron).

))))▶ *Absorption Line*

STAR MAPS

Star maps provide a positional layout of the constellations in the same way that maps of the Earth show roads. The co-ordinate system is analogous with that used for the Earth. On a star map, 'longitude' is called right ascension and 'latitude' is called declination. Locations of stars, galaxies, star clusters and nebulae are indicated by special symbols.

STARS, DEATH OF

The way stars end their life cycles depends upon their mass. Stars with masses similar to the Sun end as white dwarfs, while those which are much more massive die catastrophically in supernova explosions producing a neutron star if the core has a mass of less than a few solar masses or, if the core is more massive than this, a black hole. The rate at which stars go through their life cycle also depends upon their mass. Whereas a star comparable to the Sun will have a lifetime of about 10^{10} years, the highest mass stars have lifetimes of only a few million years, and the lowest mass stars have lifetimes which are greater than the current age of the Universe. But eventually – present estimates are that it will take 10^{14} years, that is about 10,000 times the present age of the Universe – the final generation of stars will have reached the end of their life cycles. The Universe will then consist of galaxies populated with white dwarfs, neutron stars and black holes.

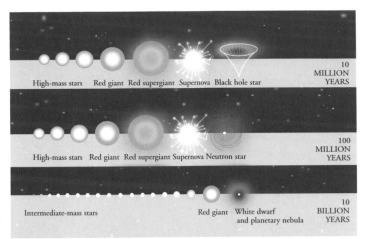

ABOVE: Very high-mass stars are profligate with their nuclear fuel, their eventual gravitational collapse results in a black hole. High-mass stars also burn fuel rapidly; they explode as supernovae and collapse to form neutron stars. Intermediate-mass stars, such as the Sun, fuse hydrogen for billions of years before swelling to become red giants and then white dwarfs.

STARS, HIGH-MASS

Massive stars burn their hydrogen in a set of reactions known as the CNO cycle at a faster rate than lower mass stars and so remain on the main sequence for a shorter period of time. The high luminosity of the most massive stars drives a strong stellar wind, a more extreme version of the solar wind which carries off considerable amounts of matter during the star's main-sequence lifetime. It is the ability of intense radiation to accelerate gas in the atmosphere of a star that limits the mass a star can have. If the energy generation rate is so high that the radiation pressure is greater than the surface gravity, then the star will literally blow itself apart. This maximum luminosity is known as the Eddington limit. It puts a ceiling on stellar masses in the region of 150 solar masses.

))))➤ *CNO Cycle*

STARS, LOW-MASS

A low-mass star such as the Sun will spend more than 10 billion years on the main sequence, undergoing only a small decrease in surface temperature and a small increase in size. This long-term stability is a consequence of the modest rate at which these stars consume their hydrogen fuel. At their centres, where temperatures are 15 million°C (27 million°F) and densities 150,000 kg/cubic metre (9,400 lb/cubic ft), the main nuclear reactions are the proton–proton chain. As the central store of hydrogen is used up, the core becomes richer in helium, leading eventually to a crisis in the star's life.

))))➤ *Proton–Proton Chain*

STARS, MOTION OF

Although stars appear to be fixed in their constellation patterns, precise measurements reveal that they do slowly move relative to each other. This transverse proper motion across the sky is larger for nearby stars than more remote ones. Stars also move towards or away from us in the line of sight, the speed being known as their radial velocity. These two components of motion arise from the stars' individual orbital movements around the centre of our Galaxy so the appearance of the constellations gradually changes over long periods of time.

))))➤ *Barnard's Star*

STARS, NAMES OF

Stars bear a variety of names, some traditional, others named after astronomers who discovered or studied them. All bright stars are identified by either a letter (usually Greek) or a number, along with the name of the constellation that contains them. For example, Sirius is also Alpha [α] Canis Majoris, – the genitive (possessive) case of the constellation name is always used in this context. In 1603 Johann Bayer (1572–1625) published an atlas in which the stars were identified by Greek letters, and so these are usually termed Bayer letters. A supplementary system identifies stars by numbers – called Flamsteed numbers, after the first Astronomer Royal of England. An example is 61 Cygni. Variable stars, if they are not already identified on one of the preceding systems, have a different style of nomenclature. Names of the brighter ones consist of one or two Roman letters, e.g. P Cygni, VV Cephei. Others are called V (for variable) with a three- or four-digit number.

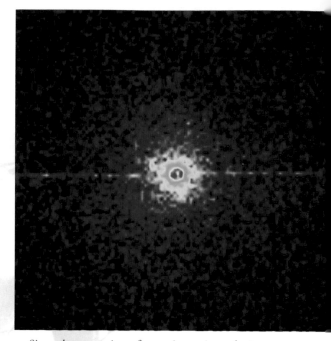

STEADY STATE THEORY

In the 1950s it was argued that the cosmological principle ought to be extended so that the Universe should not only be homogeneous in space, but also that its large-scale properties should not change with time. To differentiate such an extension from the basic principle, the extension became known as the 'perfect cosmological principle', which led to the development of the 'Steady State' theory of the Universe, primarily by Austrian-born English physicist Hermann Bondi (b. 1919), the Austrian Thomas Gold (b. 1920) and English astronomer Fred Hoyle (1915–2001).

Since the expansion of space is moving galaxies apart and, therefore, reducing the overall density of the Universe, the perfect cosmological principle requires that new matter is continuously created in space, this matter eventually condensing to form galaxies and so maintaining a constant density of the Universe. The required rate of creation is surprisingly low, about one hydrogen atom per cubic metre of space every 10^{10} years. The proponents of the Steady State theory were also influenced by Mach's principle, which implies that the laws of physics would change in an evolving Universe. However, despite its attraction most cosmologists abandoned the Steady State theory after the discovery of the cosmic background radiation in 1965. The radiation was a natural consequence of the Big Bang, but could not be explained by the Steady State theory.

➤ *Hubbles's Law, Mach's Principle*

ABOVE: An X-ray image of a stellar black hole. Most stars do not collapse to form black holes, as gravity is usually balanced by the degeneracy pressure of electrons or neutrons, causing them to become white dwarfs or neutron stars. LEFT: Austrian physicist Ernst Mach's principle argued that a body's inertial mass is a product of the interaction occuring between that object and the surrounding matter in the Universe. This influenced the Steady State Theory.

STELLAR BLACK HOLE

If the dying core of a star has more than about three solar masses, it has enough gravity to overcome the neutron degeneracy pressure (the immense pressure exerted by close-packed neutrons) within a neutron star and it becomes a stellar black hole. Such black holes are difficult to detect unless they are in binary systems accompanied by a normal star when an accretion disk of hot gas from the normal star accumulates around the black hole, creating a powerful X-ray source. Accretion disks can also form around neutron stars in binaries, so we cannot assume that every X-ray-emitting binary contains a black hole. In most known binary X-ray sources the compact object has a mass about that of the Sun, and so is probably a neutron star, but in a few cases the mass is much greater than three solar masses, beyond the theoretical limit for a neutron star. These must, it seems, be black holes.

))))▶ *Accretion Disk, Black Holes, Neutron Stars, X-Rays*

STELLAR DISTANCES

Since the apparent magnitudes of stars depend on their distances, to compare stars' brightnesses objectively we need to know how far off they are. For the nearest stars, distances can be measured by simple trigonometry, like that used by surveyors, while for those farther afield, comparisons can be made with similar stars nearby to deduce approximate values. Once a star's distance from our Sun is known, its apparent magnitude can be corrected to give its absolute magnitude, corresponding to the brightness it would have at a standard distance of 10 parsecs (32.6 light years).

))))▶ *Parallax*

STELLAR HALO

The stellar halo enshrouds the disk of the Galaxy but is much less massive than the flat disk and different in composition from the dark-matter halo. Visually, the most obvious features of the stellar halo are the 150 or so globular clusters, but there are also many individual stars. Stars in the halo have a low content of heavy elements and are therefore thought to be among the oldest objects in the Galaxy, formed before the Galaxy's interstellar hydrogen became enriched with the products of supernova eruptions. Whereas the stars in the disk are moving on roughly circular orbits around the Galactic centre, those in the halo (including globular clusters) have highly elliptical paths that plunge through the disk at all angles.

))))▶ *Globular Clusters*

STONEHENGE

Ritual monument on Salisbury Plain in southern England, dominated by concentric rings of huge standing stones. The outermost is 33 m (108 ft) wide. Stones were first raised on the site about 2200 BC, having been brought from south Wales. A processional roadway

called the Avenue, nearly 3 km (2 miles) long, leaves the site to the north-east, the direction of the summer solstice. Other points of astronomical significance may have been indicated by the alignment of stones.

SUBDWARFS

Stars that are less luminous by 1 to 2 magnitudes than main sequence stars of the same spectral type. Generally old, Subdwarfs are Population II stars with low metal content that lie below the main sequence on the Hertzsprung–Russell diagram.

))))▶ *Hertzsprung–Russell Diagram, Main Sequence Stars, Population II Stars*

BELOW: *The monoliths at Stonehenge in the UK are arranged along an axis that is aligned on the point of sunrise at the summer solstice.*

SUN

An ordinary star, one of countless millions of similar stars, situated two-thirds of the way out from the centre of a fairly ordinary spiral galaxy, which is itself just one among billions in the observable Universe. The Sun is special to us only because it is so close, a modest 150 million km (93 million miles) away. Its nearest competitor, Alpha Centauri, is 275,000 times farther away and 40 billion times fainter in our sky. The Sun is single and middle-aged, two attributes that are essential for the existence of life on Earth. If the Sun had been in a binary system (a double-star system), which is common among stars, Earth's orbit would probably have been disrupted long ago. And if the Sun's energy output were significantly variable, as it will be in its later development, life would not be able to adjust to the fluctuating conditions on Earth's surface.

Observing the Sun

The Sun is so brilliant that it can damage the eye within seconds. **Never look at the Sun directly through a telescope or binoculars, nor stare at it with the naked eye**. By far the safest way to observe the Sun is to use a telescope or binoculars to project its image onto a white card or sheet. When this is done, dark sunspots may be seen. Advanced observers may use specially made filters, consisting of a thin plastic sheet or glass with a metal coating. These filters are placed over the front of the telescope tube, not at the eyepiece (where they may burn or crack). Nonetheless one must be certain that the filters are of proper specification.

Evolution of the Sun

The Sun formed almost 4.6 billion years ago from a cloud of gas. It developed into its present status as a 'main-sequence' star, one that produces energy by converting hydrogen into helium in its core. The central supply of hydrogen is expected to last for a few billion years more, but when it runs out the Sun will undergo a restructuring: the core will shrink and heat up to 100 million degrees, hot enough for helium to be converted into carbon. Meanwhile, the outer layers will expand and the Sun will become a red giant, extinguishing all life on Earth. Ultimately, when the helium fuel is also depleted, the core will collapse further, the outer layers will be discarded as a planetary nebula and the remnant will become a white dwarf, a star bereft of energy sources, which slowly cools and fades.

The Sun's Core

The composition of the Sun is typical of stars of similar age in the Milky Way – almost 71 per cent hydrogen, 27 per cent helium and the remainder mainly carbon, nitrogen, oxygen and neon, with a smattering of other chemical elements. This means that the Sun has a rich supply of hydrogen fuel in its core, the region spanning the innermost 20 per cent of the Sun. Here, at a temperature of some 15 million°C (27 million°F) and a density of 150,000 kg/cubic metre (9,400 lb/cubic ft), the hydrogen atoms are stripped of their electrons. The nuclei collide with enough force and frequency to combine in a series of nuclear-fusion reactions to produce helium. The conversion of four hydrogen nuclei into one helium nucleus destroys a small amount of mass, m, which is transformed into a large amount of energy, E, via Einstein's famous equation $E = mc^2$, where c is the velocity of light. Around 4.3 million tonnes of matter disappear every second in the Sun, converted into pure energy.

Solar Structure

The high temperature and density at the centre of the Sun are maintained by the balance between energy generation heating the gas, so creating pressure to expand, and the forces of gravity trying to crush the outer layers in towards the centre. At the surface, the temperature is only 5,500°C (9,900°F) and the density less than 0.001

kg/m³ (0.00006 lb/ft³). The mechanisms of energy transport change throughout the Sun: in the volume within 70 per cent of the radius, energy is moved outwards by radiation in the form of photons, repeatedly absorbed and re-emitted in a zigzagging 'drunkard's walk' – the radiation takes tens or even hundreds of thousands of years to reach the surface from the centre. For the final 30 per cent of the way, energy is transported by convection, with currents of hot gas rising to the surface to be replaced by descending cooler gas.

The Active Sun

The visible surface of the Sun, or photosphere, appears as a blindingly bright white disk. The telescope reveals that relatively dark areas, or sunspots, are usually present at the lower latitudes. The numbers of these grow and shrink in an 11-year cycle. At their maximum sunspots can occasionally be seen with the naked eye.

During a total solar eclipse, when the light of the photosphere is briefly cut off, the glowing red chromosphere, or lower atmosphere of the Sun, appears around the edge of the dark Moon. Extending beyond the Chromosphere is the pearly-white corona, or outer atmosphere, extending far into space. Astronomical instruments now make it possible to study these features at any time.

The solar cycle controls a host of other activity on and above the Sun's surface. Bright regions called *faculae* frequently appear before sunspots emerge; these are hotter and denser than surrounding material. Filaments of gas called prominences rise from the photosphere. Among the more violent events occurring on the Sun are flares, in which a huge amount of energy – the equivalent of as much as 10 billion one-megaton bombs – is released in a short time (typically minutes to hours). Very occasionally these can be seen in white light, but they also give rise to X-rays and ultraviolet emission, together with the ejection of energetic particles. Passing through the corona, these create shock waves and produce strong bursts of radio emission.

||||➤ *Main Sequence Stars, Prominences, Sunspots*

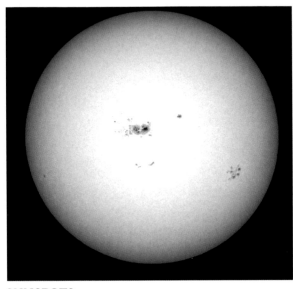

north magnetic polarity and the trailing spot a south polarity. In the southern hemisphere, the situation would be reversed, with the south-polarity spots leading.

SUPERCLUSTER

Grouped clusters of galaxies about 100 million light years across. The superclusters appear to be elongated around voids, like soap bubbles. The Local Group belongs to the Local Supercluster, which is centred on the Virgo cluster.

SUPERGIANT

The largest and most luminous stars known, with spectral types from O to M. Red (M-type) supergiants have the largest radii, of the order of 1,000 times that of the Sun. Supergiants lie above the main sequence and giant region on the Hertzsprung–Russell diagram and are often variable, due to instabilities created by radiation pressure.

SUNSPOTS

Relatively dark areas on the photosphere, or bright white surface of the Sun. They have a lower temperature than the rest of the photosphere, down to 3,700°C (6,700°F). Small spots, just a few hundred kilometres across, may last only a few hours, but some grow quite large, perhaps 10 times the diameter of Earth, and may last for months.

The number of spots waxes and wanes over an 11-year period. A cycle starts with a few spots at mid-latitudes. As it progresses, the number and size of the spots increase and they appear nearer the equator (although the region within two or three degrees of the equator is generally free of spots). At maximum, several groups can often be seen together and the larger ones may persist for a few complete rotations. Eventually the number declines to just a few above and below the equator, or occasionally to none, before the new cycle begins with high-latitude spots.

Spots behave as though they are magnets, with one pole descending into the Sun and the other protruding from the surface. They generally occur in pairs with, for example, those in the northern hemisphere during one cycle having the leading spot showing a

ABOVE LEFT: Dark sunspots on the Sun's surface.
BELOW: Birth of a supernova: When it runs out of hydrogen fuel, the core of a massive star begins to contract. This raises its temperature and initiates a sequence of nuclear reactions which create new elements, culminating in the formation of iron. The iron core collapses, triggering an explosion that sends shock waves, and a flood of neutrinos, outwards, blasting matter into space. All that remains is a city-sized neutron star.

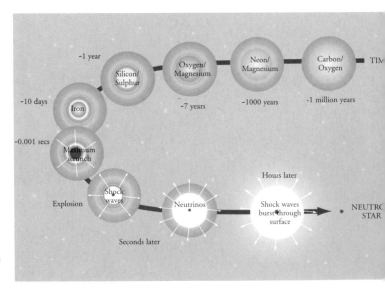

SUPERNOVA 1987A

On 23 February 1987 automatic detectors working deep underground registered an unexpected burst of neutrinos. The following morning a Canadian astronomer, Ian Shelton, noticed that his just-developed photographic plate of the Large Magellanic Cloud showed a bright star that had not been there the night before. This was the first naked-eye supernova since Kepler's Star of 1604. The star that had exploded was Sanduleak -69°202, a blue supergiant, not a red one as theory predicted. The star had been towards the lower level of the mass range for supernovae, perhaps initially about 20 solar masses, possibly on its final excursion to the left of the HR diagram when it exploded.

SUPERNOVA REMNANT

Material left over from the explosion of a supernova. These are a type of emission nebula that are heated either by interaction with the interstellar medium or by radiation from the pulsar formed in the supernova explosion.

))))▶ *Emission Nebula, Interstellar Medium, Pulsar*

ABOVE: A Hubble Space Telescope view of part of the Cygnus Loop, the remains of a star that exploded as a supernova some 30,000 years ago.

SUPERNOVAE

At the ends of their lives, the cores of massive stars successively contract as they burn their nuclear fuel. Eventually the temperature in the core is high enough to form iron, but, because of its atomic structure, iron will not fuse with anything to yield more energy. In a doomed attempt to extract yet more energy, the iron core tries to shrink further. However, as the core's mass is above the Chandrasekhar limit, gravity takes over and the star collapses. The energy created by this infall, instead of going to support the core against further collapse as previously, is soaked up by the iron nuclei, which disintegrate into alpha particles (helium nuclei). The implosion proceeds at incredible speed, with considerable amounts of energy being carried off on a tide of neutrinos in just a fraction of a second. At the star's centre, protons and electrons merge to become neutrons. When a ball of such nuclear material a few kilometres across has formed, the collapse halts. The impact of further infall is reflected in a huge shock-wave which races back through the outer layers of partially processed material. It is then that many exotic heavy chemical elements are produced by the process known as rapid neutron capture (the r-process). The shock-wave blasts the outer layers into space at speeds up to 20,000 km/s (12,500 mi/s). A supernova of Type II appears, shining with the luminosity of a billion Suns. The gas that is shot back out into space is highly contaminated with the heavy chemical elements forged in the explosion. Once it has dispersed into the interstellar medium, this gas can later be swept up into new generations of stars. These new stars will have an enriched chemical composition and will evolve slightly differently from their predecessors. The heavy elements made in a supernova explosion are essential for the creation of rocky planets – and of life.

There are two principal types of supernovae with distinctly different origins distinguished on the basis of features in its spectrum. After the explosion of a supernova, the core remains as a neutron star or if it is over about 3 solar masses, a stellar black hole, embedded in a supernova remnant.

))))▶ *Pulsar, Spectrum, Type I Supernova, Type II Supernova*

SURVEYOR MOON PROBES

The 1960s saw an intensive and ambitious study of the Moon, culminating in a first human visit in July 1969. Before that could be accomplished there was much to discover: how to go into a predictable orbit around the Moon; how to land softly; and what the astronauts would be stepping out on to when that moment arrived. The Ranger and the following Surveyor programs were to provide the answers.

Despite the success of the Rangers, a soft lunar landing eluded the Americans and many believed the Moon had a deep layer of surface dust into which any lander would sink without trace. Surveyor 1 proved otherwise when it touched down gently in the Ocean of Storms in June 1966. Six more Surveyors attempted to land on the Moon, the final one in January 1968. Four succeeded, beaming back thousands of pictures and providing invaluable surface data for the Apollo design team.

T ASSOCIATION

Groups of T Tauri stars, often still enveloped in material from which they have formed.

))))➤ *OB Associations*

T TAURI STARS

Very young stars with mass similar to or less than that of the Sun still settling down on to the main sequence. Named after the prototype in Taurus. Such objects are still surrounded by their birth clouds, which partially or totally obscure them at optical wavelengths, but they also exhibit surface activity of their own which causes erratic brightness changes. They often show evidence of strong stellar winds.

))))➤ *T Association*

TAURUS

The constellation of Taurus the Bull contains the first object in Messier's catalogue, the Crab Nebula. The V-shaped cluster of stars forming the face of the bull, with the red giant Aldebaran as its angry eye is the Hyades, the nearest large open cluster to us, 150 light years away. Aldebaran is not a true member of the cluster, but a super-imposed foreground star. Taurus also contains the Pleiades.

))))➤ *Crab Nebula, Pleiades*

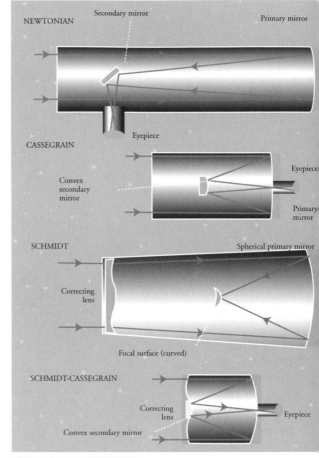

TELESCOPE MOUNTS

Most amateur telescope mounts are one of three types. 1. Altazimuth: the most basic of mounts. A horizontal and vertical axis allows movement up and down and from left to right. Both movements are required to follow a celestial object. 2. German equatorial: has a polar axis aligned to the Celestial Pole and a declination axis at 90° to the polar axis. Rotation around the polar axis alone will allow tracking of celestial objects. 3. Equatorial fork: a variation on the German mount in which the telescope lies inside a U-shaped frame. The two sides of the fork provide the declination axis, and its base is mounted at the upper end of the polar axis.

ABOVE: Light rays are directed along different paths in the four principal types of reflecting telescope: Newtonian, Cassegrain, Schmidt and Schmidt-Cassegrain.

BELOW: There are two methods of taking astronomical photographs with a refracting telescope; the piggy-back method involves mounting the camera on an equatorially-mounted telescope; the prime focus method means attaching the camera to the telescope in place of the eyepiece as shown here.

BELOW RIGHT: Valentina Tereshkova, the first woman in space.

TELESCOPE, REFLECTING

A telescope that uses a concave mirror, rather than a lens, to collect and focus light. Reflecting telescopes, or 'reflectors', do not suffer from colour distortions called chromatic aberration. The first reflector was invented by Isaac Newton (1642–1727). In the Newtonian telescope, the main mirror focuses the light onto a small mirror, called the secondary, which diverts the light to the side of the tube. Here an eyepiece magnifies the image.

In the Cassegrain reflector, the secondary mirror is convex and sends light back down the tube and through a hole in the main mirror. By folding the light path in this way, a telescope of long focal length can be accommodated within a relatively small tube. The effective focal length depends on the focal length of the main (primary) mirror and on the curvature of the secondary.

An important astronomical telescope design is the Schmidt–Cassegrain, which employs a weak lens to correct the aberrations intrinsic to the main mirror.

)))➤ *Telescope, Refracting*

TELESCOPE, REFRACTING

A telescope that uses a convex lens, rather than a mirror, as the main component that collects and focuses light. The image formed is then magnified by an eyepiece. Astronomical refracting telescopes, or

'refractors', use a combination of lenses made from different kinds of glass, of different refractive indices, which greatly reduce the colour distortions called chromatic aberration. However, all major astronomical telescopes in use today are reflectors.

)))➤ *Telescope, Reflecting*

TERESHKOVA, VALENTINA (b. 1937)

Russian astronaut. The first woman in space, on 16 June 1963, the 26-year-old was launched into orbit aboard Vostok 6 and in the next three days circled the Earth 48 times, more than the six American Mercury astronauts combined.

In September 1961, inspired by the Vostok flights, Tereshkova had written a letter to the space centre asking to join the cosmonaut team. With her application helped by a background in parachuting, she was selected in March 1962 and, along with four other women, reported to the training centre. Soviet Premier Krushchev personally picked her out for the Vostok 6 flight because of her working-class background.

Famed as a heroine of the women's movement in Soviet society, she went on to a career in politics and married fellow cosmonaut Andrian Nikoleyev. Tereshkova later earned a Candidate of Technical Sciences degree (in 1976) and was eventually promoted to the rank of major general, retiring in March 1997.

element interferometer developed by Martin Ryle (1918–84) and his colleagues. The survey had unexpected results, leading to the discovery of compact radio sources which, after optical identification, proved to be quasars. 3C48 was the first quasar to be identified. Many well-known sources are still identified by their number in the 3C catalogue, perhaps the best example being 3C273, the brightest quasar. Of course many objects occur in different catalogues: one such is the Crab nebula which is M1 in the Messier catalogue and 3C144 in the 3C Catalogue.

TERRESTRIAL PLANETS

The Earth and the three small, rocky planets that most closely resemble it: Mercury, Venus and Mars. Their location near the Sun is responsible for their similarities. The Sun and the planets formed from a large cloud of gas and dust called a nebula. When the solar wind – a stream of charged particles – first began to flow from the Sun, it blasted lighter gas and dust out of the inner Solar System. The denser material left behind finally amalgamated to form the inner planets. In each planet the densest materials, such as iron, sank inwards, while lighter elements migrated upwards to form a mantle and crust of lighter silicate rocks.

))))▶ *Earth, Giant Planets, Mars, Mercury, Moon, Venus*

THIRD CAMBRIDGE (3C) CATALOGUE

The *Third Cambridge (3C) Catalogue* is a widely used catalogue of radio sources which contains information on 471 objects measured by Cambridge radio astronomers in their attempt to use radio sources as a test of cosmological models. The data came from a survey of the sky visible from Cambridge made with a multi-

THOMSON, WILLIAM, LORD KELVIN (1824–1907)

British physicist who is best remembered for the introduction of the absolute scale of temperature which bears his name. His scale is independent of any physical substance, in line with his desire to create an international system of standards. Thomson's early work was in electromagnetism where he gave a mathematical basis to the discoveries of Michael Faraday, paving the way for James Maxwell's great synthesis.

Thomson also helped develop the theory of thermodynamics, and debated the age of Earth, which he estimated from its rate of cooling to be as low as 20 million years – no-one then knew that the temperature of Earth is maintained by radioactive decay.

ABOVE: The four terrestrial (also known as inner) planets: Mercury, Venus, Earth (shown with its only natural satellite, the Moon) and Mars.

THE 360° CIRCLE

Accurately determining the length of the year was not easy for early peoples. Most early cultures worked on the basis of a 360-day year, adding extra days after the error became obvious over a series of years. Of all the near-eastern peoples it was the Assyrians and Babylonians, occupying the regions of modern Iran and Iraq, who made the first great innovations in astronomy and geometry. Driven by an official culture which demanded the observation and calculation of astronomical cycles for divinatory purposes, the Babylonians developed the 360° circle (each degree corresponding to a solar day) and exploited its divisibility by 60.

TIDES

Rise and fall of the oceans under the gravitational influence of the Moon and Sun. Two high tides and two low tides occur each day.

The gravitational attraction of the Moon is stronger on the side of Earth closest to the Moon. Here the oceans are pulled in the direction of the Moon, creating a high tide. However, a high tide also occurs on the opposite side of Earth, the side that faces away from the Moon. This bulge of water forms because Earth is very slightly pulled toward the Moon, leaving an accumulation of water behind. As Earth rotates, so its land masses pass through the two bulges of water, and experience two high and two low tides a day.

In practice the tides occur slightly ahead of the Moon and not directly in line with it. Earth rotates faster than the Moon revolves and friction drags the ocean bulges ahead of the Moon. The friction also slows Earth's rotation slightly: over millennia the day is lengthening.

The gravitational attraction of the Sun also raises tides, but its effect is weaker, because the Sun is so much farther away than the Moon. The effect of the Sun's attraction is to enhance or to weaken slightly the attraction of the Moon. At full and new Moon, the Sun, the Moon and Earth are in alignment, resulting in a tidal force stronger than average. This creates spring tides, which have a

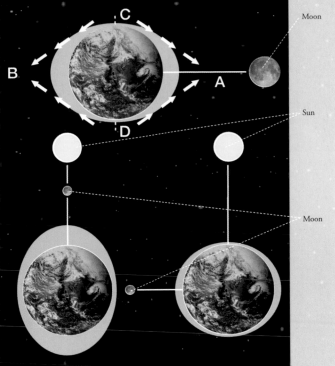

ABOVE: Tidal effects on Earth. 1. The gravitational pull of the Moon causes the oceans to bulge at points A and B, and to be reduced at points C and D. 2. When the Moon and the Sun are in line, their gravitational effects combine to produce greater tidal ranges ('spring tides'). 3. When the Moon and the Sun are at right angles, their influences partly cancel each other out, producing smaller tidal ranges ('neap tides').

greater range between high and low tides. At the Moon's first and third quarter phases, the three bodies form a right angle. With the Moon pulling in one direction and the Sun in the other, the effect on the oceans is less dramatic, resulting in less of a tidal range. These are called neap tides.

Much smaller, but finite, tides are raised in the solid body of the Earth and the Moon. Indeed, tidal forces are experienced by any body of finite size that is placed in a non-uniform gravitational field. Close binary stars (stars that orbit close to each other under their mutual gravitational attraction) are drawn out into egg shapes by tidal interactions.

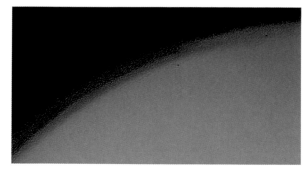

TITAN

Titan is Saturn's largest satellite. Its diameter is one and a half times that of the Moon. Titan revolves around Saturn at a distance of over a million km (625,000 miles). It is tidally locked and rotates on its axis in the same period, 16 days, in which it revolves around Saturn. Titan has retained a thick nitrogen-rich atmosphere that exerts a surface pressure approximately 50 per cent greater than that of Earth's atmosphere. Solar ultraviolet radiation has interacted with gases in the upper atmosphere, forming thick smog. The composition of Titan's atmosphere is believed to be similar to that of Earth's shortly after its formation.

))))➤ *Saturn*

TRANSFER ORBIT

The most economical route for sending a spacecraft to another planet without the aid of another celestial body's gravity is a Hohmann transfer orbit, named after Walter Hohmann, a German space-travel theorist of the 1920s. The transfer orbit is an ellipse that just touches the orbits of the Earth and the destination planet. Commonly used for probes to Mars and Venus, it requires a great deal of fuel to reach more distant destinations.

TRANSITS

1. The passage of an inferior planet (Mercury or Venus) across the disk of the Sun. 2. The passage of a planetary satellite or its shadow across the disk of its parent planet. 3. The passage of a celestial body across an observer's meridian.

TRIPLE-ALPHA REACTION

The nuclear fusion reaction which converts three alpha particles (helium nuclei) into carbon with a consequent release of energy. The triple-alpha process occurs at temperatures above 100 million K after stars have consumed all their hydrogen. Also called the Salpeter process, it is the dominant energy-producing process occurring in red giants.

TRITON

The only large satellite of Neptune. This exotic world is about three-quarters the diameter of our Moon. Triton revolves around Neptune in a retrograde fashion – that is, in the opposite direction to the rotation of the planet. This suggests it may have been captured by Neptune in the past. Even though it currently holds the record as having the lowest observed temperature in the Solar System, -235°C (-391°F), Triton has an extremely tenuous atmosphere and some geological activity at its surface.

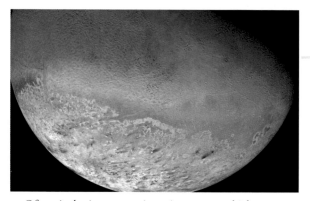

Of particular interest are its active geysers, which spray dark gaseous material up to 8 km (5 miles) into the atmosphere, where it encounters an airflow that sweeps the plume sideways. Fallout from the plumes can be seen as dark diffuse streaks on Triton's frozen surface. A proposed mechanism for the formation of the geysers involves transparent surface ices. Sunlight penetrates the transparent ice causing the surface beneath to sublime as the temperature increases slightly. The gas builds up under the ice and

ABOVE LEFT: The surface of Saturn's largest satellite, Titan, is obscured by a haze in the atmosphere.
ABOVE: Triton, Neptune's largest Moon, has a surface covered with frozen nitrogen and methane, with a temperature of -235°C (-391°F).

eventually the pressure ruptures the overlying ice, allowing the trapped gas to rush out, carrying fine, dark dust with it. Light is reflected from the surface of Triton in a way similar to that of Pluto and its moon Charon, indicating that these bodies may have a similar origin.

TROPICS

Two circles of latitude on the surface of the Earth which correspond to the maximum northerly and southerly latitudes at which the Sun can be vertically overhead at noon at some date in the year. The Tropic of Cancer (23.5° north) is reached by the Sun at the summer solstice about 21 June, while the Tropic of Capricorn (23.5° south) is reached at the winter solstice, about 22 December.

TSIOLKOVSKY, KONSTANTIN (1857–1935)

Russian rocket scientist. This visionary prophet of rocket travel published an explanation of how rockets could fly in the vacuum of space in 1883, and in *Dream of the Earth* (1895), he predicted artificial satellites positioned 300 km (190 miles) from Earth.

In 1903 selected chapters of his thesis, *The Exploration of Space Using Reaction Devices*, described multi-stage, liquid-fuelled rockets, stabilized by gyroscopes and steered by tilting rocket nozzles. The spacecraft was tear-shaped, with a passenger cabin in the rocket nose housing life-support systems and protected from extremes of temperature and the threat of meteoroids by a double skin. Tsiolkovsky even described details of the missions such as escape velocity, re-entry and the idea of a spacewalk, although he prophesied that these would not happen until the twenty-first century. Alexei Leonov's (b. 1934) first spacewalk was only 62 years later. In his 78 years, Tsiolkovsky never built a rocket, preferring to write and sketch his ideas.

TULLY–FISHER RELATION

In 1977, Brent Tully and Richard Fisher showed that the total luminosity of a spiral galaxy (contributed mainly by the stars in its disk and central bulge) is closely correlated with the rotation speed at large radii (which is dictated by the mass of the dark halo). The physical reason for this Tully–Fisher relation is unknown, but is presumably tied up with the complete history of the galaxy, including its creation and the subsequent formation of stars within it. The relation provides a useful method of estimating the true luminosity of a galaxy from its speed of rotation. An analogous phenomenon is observed in elliptical galaxies, where the luminosity of a galaxy can be deduced from its size, surface brightness and the random motions of its stars (whose velocities are dictated by its mass); this correlation is termed the Faber–Jackson relation, or the Fundamental Plane.

)))⮕ *Dark Halo, Galactic Bulge, Spiral Galaxies*

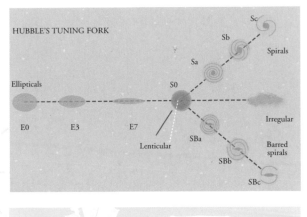

ABOVE: Hubble's Tuning Fork diagram.

TUNING-FORK DIAGRAM

Edwin Hubble set out the various classes of galaxy in a diagram resembling the shape of a musician's tuning fork. Hubble's arrangement started with elliptical galaxies, running from the roundest to the flattest, followed by the lenticular systems (S0). The diagram then divided into two branches, one for ordinary spirals (S) and one for barred spirals (SB). Along each branch the galaxies were arranged in increasing order of complexity, starting with those that contained smooth tightly-wound arms and working towards those with well-developed open arms dotted with clumps of hot young stars. The size of the central bulge of stars also decreases along this sequence of spiral galaxies; since a bulge looks much like an elliptical galaxy, this arrangement places the ellipticals very naturally next to the most bulge-dominated spirals. Irregular galaxies are added at the ends of the spiral galaxy sequences.

)))⮕ *Hubble, Edwin; Elliptical Galaxies, Spiral Galaxies*

TWIN PARADOX

The twin paradox is a famous puzzle arising from special relativity. Identical twins, Ann and Betty, are astronauts. Ann makes a return trip to Alpha Centauri, at 90 per cent of the speed of light. Betty is ground controller. When they meet again, 9.8 years have passed but Ann has aged only 4.3 years. Time dilation ensures that spaceship time passes more slowly than on the ground; Ann is now 5.5 years younger. This is strange, but not a paradox.

From Ann's ship she sees Betty receding and then approaching. If only relative speeds matter, time dilation should operate in the opposite sense, and Ann should find Betty is younger. While separated, they can disagree about the passage of time but together on Earth, they can't both be the younger! The twins' situation is not symmetrical. Betty remains in an inertial frame, while Ann changes frames – when she takes off, turns around, and when she lands. It is the changing frames that cause one to age more than the other.

TWO DEGREE FIELD (2DF) SURVEY

The 2dF survey measures 2,000 redshifts to distant galaxies each night. Begun in 1998 it uses the 3.9-m (12.8-ft) Anglo-Australian telescope in New South Wales, Australia. The survey aims to measure redshifts of 250,000 galaxies in the sky close to the north and south galactic poles.

TYCHONIC SYSTEM

Tycho Brahe (1546–1601) was impressed by the mathematical elegance of Copernicus's theory (1543) that the Earth was a planet that moved with the other planets around the Sun, but he could not believe in the physical reality of the Earth's motion. In 1583 he developed a system in which the planets (which did not include the Earth) revolved around the Sun, which revolved around the Earth. The new physics of Isaac Newton (1642–1727) ruled out the Tychonic system.

))))➧ *Brahe, Tycho; Newton, Isaac; Newtonian Cosmology*

TYPE I SUPERNOVA

Type I supernovae lack hydrogen in their spectra as the stars have no hydrogen left when they explode.

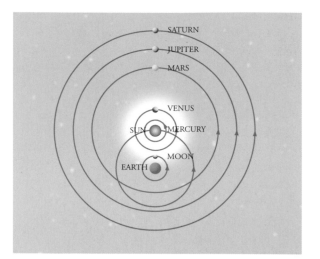

Type Ia is thought to arise from the detonation of a white dwarf in a close binary system when gas from the companion spills on to the white dwarf as the companion expands towards the end of its own life. This extra mass compresses and heats the white dwarf, igniting the carbon and oxygen in its core in a nuclear explosion. Subtypes known as Ib and Ic apparently result from the explosion of single massive stars that have lost their outer layers, probably Wolf–Rayet stars.

))))➧ *Type II Supernova*

TYPE II SUPERNOVA

Type II supernovae are the explosion of high-mass stars at the ends of their lives. They show the existence of hydrogen in their spectra, from the ejected outer layers of the star.

))))➧ *Type I Supernova*

ABOVE: The Tychonic celestial system was an ingenious compromise in which the Earth was central and yet all other planets orbited the Sun.
CENTRE: A Type Ia supernova (the bright spot at lower left) in the outskirts of galaxy NGC 4526.

UHURU SURVEY

By the late 1960s about 30 X-ray sources were known, and most had been discovered during flights by sounding rockets or satellites designed for other purposes. The need for a systematic survey of the X-ray sky was all too apparent. It came in 1970 when NASA launched SAS-1, the first Small Astronomical Satellite, renamed Uhuru after the Swahili word for 'freedom'. It carried two sets of proportional counters which picked up X-ray sources during its two-year mission. Important discoveries were that many X-ray sources are binary stars, and strong X-ray emission comes from hot gas in the centres of rich clusters of galaxies.

ULTRAVIOLET ASTRONOMY

The longer waves of ultraviolet light, between 310 and 400 nm, can be observed from the ground by conventional telescopes, but those between 10 and 310 nm can only be observed from above the atmosphere. Early observations of ultraviolet radiation were made from rockets and high-flying balloons. The first satellite observations were made with the US Orbiting Astronomical Observatory-2 (OAO-2) spacecraft in 1968. The most famous UV satellite, the International Ultraviolet Explorer, was launched in January 1978. It worked for 18 years, 15 years more than expected, and became the longest-lived of any scientific satellite. The extreme ultraviolet (XUV or EUV), covering 10^{-91} nm, was not studied until the early 1990s, when Rosat and the Extreme Ultraviolet Explorer (EUVE) conducted the first all-sky surveys. Major sources of ultraviolet radiation include hot, massive stars, the cores of active galaxies and, in the EUV, newly formed white dwarfs.

ULTRAVIOLET RAYS

A German pharmacist, Johann Ritter (1776–1810), investigated the region beyond the blue end of the visible spectrum. In 1801 he discovered an invisible type of radiation that affected photographic plates and became known as ultraviolet radiation (UV). The UV has wavelengths in the range 10–400 nm. UV waves carry more energy than visible light does, and the higher-frequency radiation is able to knock electrons out of atoms (ionization), break chemical bonds and damage molecules. Ultraviolet radiation from the Sun is responsible for sunburn and certain types of skin cancer and is most dangerous in the 290–320 nm region known as UVB. Most of the UVB from the Sun is absorbed by atmospheric ozone. When UV rays strike certain materials the energy is absorbed and re-emitted in the form of visible light, a phenomenon known as fluorescence if the re-emission is immediate, or as phosphorescence if it persists after the stimulating UV ceases.

ULYSSES MISSION

Launched by the Space Shuttle in 1990, the joint ESA/NASA Ulysses mission used Jupiter's gravity to sling-shot into a solar polar orbit, and provide our first observations of the Sun from above and below. Ulysses is adding to our knowledge of the Sun, how it works and its effect on the Solar System.

UMBRA

1. The dark central part of a sunspot.
2. The dark inner region of a shadow cast by a celestial object. An observer in the umbra of the Moon's shadow sees a total solar eclipse.

))))➤ *Penumbra*

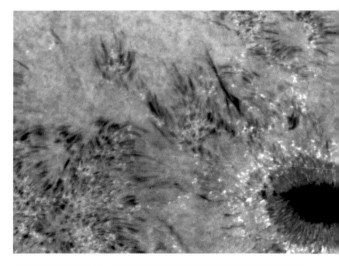

ABOVE: The dark central region of a sunspot that looks like a hole is known as the umbra. This area is the coolest part of the sunspot and is surrounded by a hotter outer region called the penumbra.

UNIVERSE

In Isaac Newton's (1642–1727) view the Universe was infinite in extent, the bodies within it moving under the influence of the mutual attraction of gravity. The bodies moved according to Newton's laws of motion. Newtonian cosmology lasted for 250 years until Albert Einstein (1879–1955) changed our understanding of space and time, showing that they are relative, and that gravity is caused by distortions of space–time rather than an attractive force in the conventional sense. Modern cosmologies are built around the framework of general relativity, but incorporate the ideas of quantum mechanics.

ABOVE: Celebrated English scientist Isaac Newton (1642–1727)
ABOVE RIGHT: Nicolaus Copernicus (1473–1543), Polish astronomer.

The Expanding Universe

Nicolaus Copernicus (1473–1543) did not need a telescope to understand that the Sun was the centre of the Solar System. The later development of the telescope showed that the Sun was just one of many stars. Earth was not the centre of the Universe, and neither was the Sun, nor even the Milky Way. It became apparent that our Galaxy was one of many galaxies. The problem for astronomers was measuring the distances to these far-off galaxies. Within the Milky Way, Cepheid variable stars are a useful 'standard candle' for measuring distances, but Cepheids are visible only in the nearby galaxies. It was during investigations of alternative methods of measuring distances to these galaxies that Edwin Hubble (1889–1953) proposed that, since the fainter galaxies had the larger redshifts, then the velocity at which they were receding was proportional to their distance. The implication of this simple statement was profound: the Universe was expanding. Current cosmological models suggest that the Universe is not just big, but that it may be infinite.

Hubble's discovery of an expanding Universe had a second, equally profound, implication. If the galaxies were receding then they must, at some time, have been concentrated into a small region of space. This means that the Universe must have a finite age. Hubble's law can be expressed simply; it relates the distance of a galaxy to its velocity of recession, via a value known as Hubble's constant. If the Universe has been expanding at a constant rate, then Hubble's constant is a direct measure of the age of the Universe. The problem is that measuring Hubble's constant is not straightforward, and that cosmological models allow for a variation of the expansion rate of the Universe with time. Present best estimates put it at about 13 billion years. Another effect of the Universe being of finite age is that it solves Olber's Paradox.

Hubble's results led some cosmologists, notably Lemaitre, to argue that the observable universe had begun by exploding from a highly-compressed initial state (perhaps a point of infinite density), a model which became known as the Big Bang.

Big Bang Theory Established

The discovery of the expansion of the Universe meant that the need for a static model was redundant. Yet despite the evidence for a single point of origin, cosmologists did not immediately adopt the Big Bang as their model. The Steady State theory, a model which involved the continuous creation of matter to account for the assumed large-scale homogeneity of the Universe, had many virtues – and

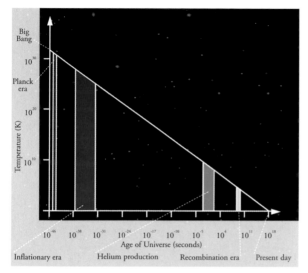

Temperature (K)

Big Bang

10^{30}

Planck era

10^{20}

10^{10}

10^{-46} 10^{-38} 10^{-31} 10^{-24} 10^{-17} 10^{-10} 10^{-5} 10^{4} 10^{11} 10^{18}

Age of Universe (seconds)

Inflationary era   Helium production   Recombination era   Present day

LEFT: Evolutionary eras of the Universe. The temperature and key evolutionary eras of the Universe are shown at different times after the Big Bang. This graph is not to scale.
BELOW: These two-dimensional models are commonly used to visualize the curvature of the Universe. The sphere has a closed, finite surface with no edge. The saddle, whose shape would extend geometrically, represents an open, infinite Universe. The intermediate model is the open Universe with a flat surface.

many proponents. Not until the discovery of the cosmic background radiation in 1965 was the theory finally abandoned by mainstream cosmologists in favour of the theory of the Big Bang.

Models of the Big Bang marry the two fundamental ideas of the physics of the twentieth century, quantum mechanics and general relativity. This juxtaposition is required because the huge mass of the primordial fireball makes consideration of gravity inevitable, while on the other hand the constituents of the fireball are the fundamental particles of matter and radiation, the temperature of the fireball being too high for atoms to form. The lack of a satisfactory theory combining the two means that the very earliest stages remain poorly understood, but cosmologists have been able to make precise predictions from within a second of the Big Bang onwards.

Future Evolution

Once the question of how the Universe began has been addressed, the other fundamental question of how it will end must also be considered. Since gravity is expected to slow the expansion of the Universe down, one factor which affects the future rate of expansion is the average density of the Universe. To determine the future of the expansion, we need to know how the density compares with the so-called critical density, which is the density for which the expansion will come to a stop in the infinite future. But to measure the density of the Universe, we need to know the amount of dark matter contained within it.

The density of the Universe also has a profound on its large-scale geometry. Modern cosmological models predict that there will be an overall curvature of space–time in the Universe, superimposed on the small-scale distortions due to the gravitational fields around local concentrations of mass. A universe with positive curvature would be a closed universe. A universe with negative curvature would be infinite – an open Universe. An intermediate state between these two extremes would be a flat universe.

)))▶ *Big Bang, Big Crunch, Hubble's Law, Olber's Paradox, Steady State Theory*

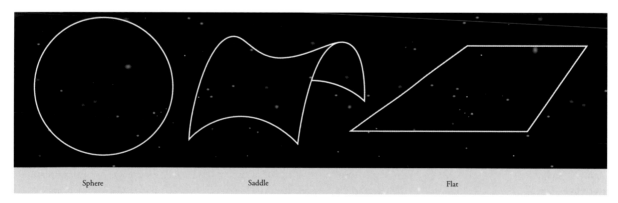

Sphere   Saddle   Flat

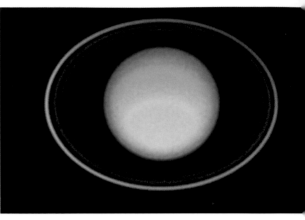

URANIBORG OBSERVATORY

Astronomical observatory on the island of Ven, founded by the Danish astronomer Tycho Brahe (1546–1601) in 1576. Here Tycho developed a succession of large and accurate instruments, including quadrants, sextants and armillary spheres. Uraniborg had its own craftsmen and workshops, so that instrument scales and observing procedures could be constantly monitored and improved. Tycho drew up new tables of planetary motion, and his instruments and observing procedures changed the direction of European astronomy.

ABOVE: The observatory at Uraniborg, where Tycho Brahe developed and improved a series of astronomical instruments, including sextants, quadrants and armillary spheres.
ABOVE RIGHT: Uranus with its faint rings and some of its satellites.

URANUS

A blue-green gas giant, the seventh planet from the Sun. It is considerably smaller than Jupiter or Saturn, but still approximately four times the diameter of Earth. Uranus is within the range of the naked eye on a moonless night, away from areas of light pollution.

The Structure of Uranus

The composition of Uranus is similar to that of Neptune. It is composed mainly of hydrogen and helium, together with methane and ammonia. It contains less hydrogen than Jupiter or Saturn. Some scientists have speculated that beneath its hydrogen atmosphere there may be an ocean of water, with methane and ammonia, over a central rocky core.

Cloud decks form deep in the atmosphere, below the upper atmospheric methane haze. The clouds are driven by wind speeds of hundreds of kilometres per hour.

The Rotation of Uranus

Uranus is unique among the Jovian planets in that its axis of rotation is tipped by more than 90°. It is possible that Uranus was struck by a large body, which 'flipped' the planet over on its side. Owing to this extreme axial orientation of Uranus, the Sun shines directly down on its North and South Poles in turn, as the planet makes its 84-year orbit. Each pole has repeated cycles of 42 years of daylight and 42 years of darkness.

The magnetic field of Uranus is tilted by 60° with respect to its rotational axis – more than any other planet in the Solar System. As with Earth, Jupiter and Saturn,

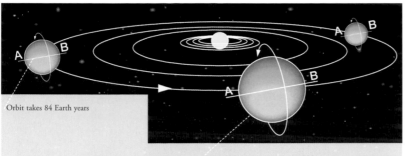

Orbit takes 84 Earth years

Uranus spins on its axis in 17.24 hours

URANUS'S RINGS

In 1977 astronomers organized an effort to observe Uranus as it passed in front of a star. Such an event is known as an occultation, and from it they hoped to measure the diameter of the planet more precisely and learn more about its upper atmosphere. Surprisingly, the brightness of the star abruptly dropped and returned to normal nine times before it was occulted by Uranus. When the star emerged from behind Uranus, a similar pattern of fluctuations recurred, indicating the existence of nine thin rings around Uranus. Additional analysis of the data revealed four more rings. In 1989 instruments on the Voyager space probe revealed two additional, faint rings. The amounts of light blocked by the rings revealed their differing thicknesses. The width of Epsilon, the densest ring, is about 100 km (60 miles) while the fainter rings are 12 km (8 miles) wide or less. The intervening gaps are hundreds of kilometres wide.

the solar wind distorts the magnetosphere, creating a magnetotail that stretches away from the planet for many millions of kilometres in the direction opposite to the Sun.

The Moons of Uranus

Before Voyager 2 arrived at Uranus, the planet was known to have five moons. Oberon and Titania, the outermost, are covered with impact craters and stress fractures. Umbriel and Ariel, a slightly smaller pair, have distinctly different characters. Umbriel's surface appears dark and old while Ariel displays a maze of fault lines and signs of melting and resurfacing – evidence that it has undergone tidal heating that helps keep its surface geologically young. Miranda, the smallest, innermost satellite, has a spectacular surface. Composed of seemingly unrelated structures, it appears to have been shattered by a major collision and then reconsolidated, resulting in the highly complex and disordered surface seen today. Voyager 2 discovered many smaller moons orbiting Uranus, bringing the planet's total complement of known moons to 21.

))))➤ *Giant Planets, Neptune*

URSA MAJOR

The constellation of Ursa Major, also known as the great bear, contains the asterism of the Plough or Big Dipper. The 2nd-magnitude stars Alpha [α] and Beta [β] Ursae Majoris (Dubhe and Merak), are the Pointers that guide the way to the north pole star, Polaris. Ursa Major contains the binary Xi [ξ] Ursae Majoris and also the planetary nebula M97, the Owl Nebula.

ABOVE LEFT: Rather than spinning like a top as it orbits the Sun, Uranus has a distinctive feature; its axis of spin is tilted almost parallel to its orbital plane. This means that the polar regions (points A and B) alternately point towards and away from the Sun as Uranus orbits. During an 84-Earth-year orbit, each pole experiences one 42-year day and one 42-year night.
ABOVE Uranus's innermost satellite Miranda.

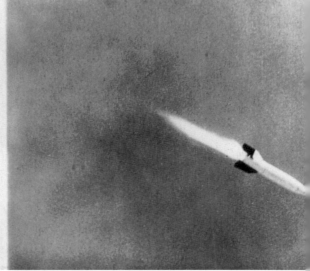

V-2 ROCKETS

The V-2 missiles, originally developed as weapons and used during the Second World War, were a turning point in rocket technology. Travelling on supersonic trajectories, they touched the edge of space. On 8 September 1944, a London suburb was shaken by a blast of high explosives. It was the V-2, the first of a new breed of supersonic Vergeltungswaffe, or Nazi 'vengeance' weapons. Once launched it climbed rapidly to 37 km (23 miles) and then arched down towards London.

)))) *Rockets*

VAN ALLEN BELTS

Two torus-shaped regions within the Earth's magnetosphere in which charged particles are trapped. The outer belt contains mainly electrons captured from the solar wind. The inner belt contains both protons and electrons. Within the lower belt is a radiation belt containing particles produced by interactions between the solar wind and cosmic rays.

)))) *Aurorae, Magnetosphere, Solar Wind*

ABOVE: A captured German V-2, the forerunner of the modern space rocket, veers off course shortly after launch during a test firing in 1946 from White Sands, New Mexico. Such failures were common during early rocket tests such as these.

VEGA MISSIONS

The primary purpose of the two Russian Vega missions was to investigate and photograph Halley's Comet. They used Venus for a gravity sling-shot to reach their target. While at Venus, in June 1985, each dropped off a Venera-style landing capsule and a French atmospheric balloon. These floated around the planet carrying instruments to record temperatures, pressures and lightning frequencies. They drifted over 10,000 km (6,000 miles) in Venus's powerful winds. The two craft encountered the comet in the following year, Vega 1 on 6 March and Vega 2 on 9 March, imaging its nucleus and studying its dust, gas and magnetic field.

)))) *Sling-Shot*

VEIL NEBULA

In the constellation of Cygnus lies the Veil Nebula, the filamentary remains of an ancient supernova explosion. While the nebula looks impressive on photographs, it is hard to track down visually; today the debris is thinly spread and hard to find. The brightest part of it is an arc labelled NGC 6992.

VELA

The constellation of Vela contains many double stars including Delta [δ], Gamma [γ], Lamda [λ] and Psi [ψ] Velorum, Dunlop 70 and Dunlop 88. It also contains the Vela supernova remnant, the Gum Nebula and NGC 3132, a bright elliptical planetary nebula.

))))▶ *Double Stars*

VENERA SPACE PROGRAM

The Russian Venera program to Venus began with a launch failure on 4 February 1961. Four more attempts were made to reach Venus before Venera 4 parachuted into its cloud tops on 18 October 1967, beaming back data for 94 minutes. Pressures of 22 Earth atmospheres and temperatures of 280°C (536°F) crushed the capsule 25 km (16 miles) above the surface. Despite redesigns, Veneras 5 and 6 failed to reach the surface as well. In 1970, Venera 7 survived the pressures of 90 Earth atmospheres and 475°C (887°F) to transmit the first signal from the surface of another planet.

Venera 8 lasted 50 minutes and revealed there was as much light there as a dull day in Moscow. It was June 1975 before Veneras 9 and 10 snapped the first pictures from the surface of another planet. Veneras 11 and 12 measured the chemistry of the atmosphere during descent and recorded possible lightning flashes. Then, in 1982, Veneras 13 and 14 returned the first colour pictures and drilled into the rocky ground. The following year, Veneras 15 and 16 went into orbit around Venus and mapped the planet by radar, covering 120 million sq km (46 million sq miles).

))))▶ *Venus*

VENUS

The second planet from the Sun and Earth's nearest neighbour. Venus has a mass and diameter similar to those of our own planet. Thick clouds constantly hide its surface. Once thought likely to be the most Earthlike of the planets, its true nature has been shown by visiting spacecraft: its dense, choking atmosphere makes the surface a hell of scorching heat and crushing pressure.

Seeing Venus

Venus moves within the Earth's orbit, and so never strays far from the Sun in our sky. Best seen shortly before sunrise or after sunset, it is commonly called the Morning Star or Evening Star. Its brilliance is a result of highly reflective clouds and its close proximity to Earth.

Because it moves inside Earth's orbit, Venus shows phases, like the Moon. These phases are apparent through binoculars or a small telescope.

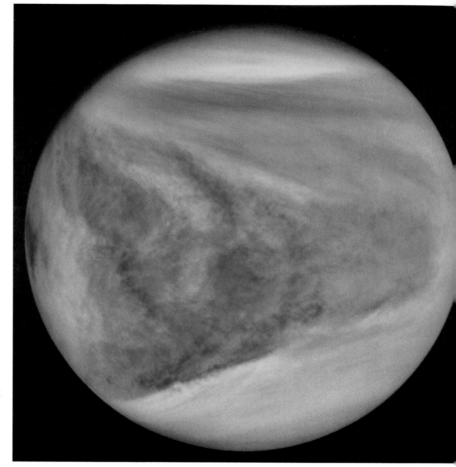

The Surface of Venus

Underneath the clouds lies a tortured landscape, preserving the scars of geological processes that have been at work for hundreds of millions of years. Venus is peppered with volcanoes of all sizes, cut by a maze of faults and ridges, and plastered with sheet-like lava flows hundreds of kilometres wide.

Eighty per cent of the Venusian surface has a range in altitude of no more than 1,000 m (330 ft), making it much smoother than Earth. Venus also lacks plate tectonics – the constant movement and recycling of large crustal regions that has shaped the Earth's surface.

Although heights are less extreme, mountains and valleys do exist on Venus, testament to huge forces resulting from the shifting of molten material beneath the crust. The most complex features of the deformed terrain on Venus are *tesserae* (Greek: 'tiles'), high-standing plateaux characterized by a lattice of faults and fractures. *Tesserae* may be formed where Venusian crust is dragged and rucked up very much like a carpet, by the sinking of molten rock below.

Over 900 impact craters exist on Venus, compared with fewer than 200 on Earth. Almost all the craters appear fresh; very few are cut by faults or flooded by lava.

ABOVE: This view of Venus, taken from orbit by the Pioneer Venus orbiter, shows the swirling mass of thick cloud that obscures its surface.

The number and degree of preservation of Venusian craters give an indication of the average age of the surface, which is estimated to fall between 200 and 600 million years – much younger than the Moon's, but slightly older than Earth's.

Vulcanism

The surface of Venus is dominated by volcanic landforms. More than 80 per cent of the planet is covered with undulating lava plains. Tens of thousands of small volcanoes a few kilometres across litter the surface. Larger shield-style volcanoes, similar to the Hawaiian Island volcanoes on Earth, have produced aprons of complex lava flows hundreds of kilometres wide. In general, Venusian volcanoes are lower and much wider than those on Earth.

Coronae (Latin: 'crowns') are large, circular volcanic structures, typically hundreds of kilometres across, with collapsed centres. They appear unique to Venus. Each corona marks a blister on the crust where heat and molten rock have welled up from below.

Inside Venus

Samples obtained by the Russian Venera landers show that Venus has a rocky crust made of basalts similar to those found under the oceans on Earth. Venus probably also has a thick mantle and a molten metallic core. Most

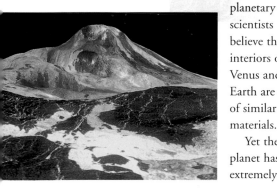

planetary scientists believe the interiors of Venus and Earth are made of similar materials.

Yet the planet has an extremely weak magnetic field. Part of the reason for this lack may be the slowness of the planet's rotation. It rotates once every 243 Earth days. Remarkably, Venus differs from the other planets in having a retrograde rotation: it spins from east to west. This rotation may be the result of a large impact early in its history.

The Venusian Atmosphere

The clouds responsible for the brilliance of Venus totally obscure its surface. Even modern telescopes show only faint, irregular cloud patterns and can never glimpse the surface below.

The Venusian atmosphere is 96.5 per cent carbon dioxide. There are three principal cloud decks, lying approximately 48–60 km (30–37 miles) above the surface, much higher than clouds on Earth. The clouds revolve around Venus at high speeds, carried by winds up to 350 km/h (220 mi/h), driven by energy from the Sun. The clouds are made from tiny droplets of sulphuric acid, making them as corrosive as an acid bath.

Although the temperature at the top of the atmosphere measures a chilly -45°C (-49°F), carbon dioxide is a potent greenhouse gas and the temperature rises steadily towards the surface. On the ground, temperatures soar to over 460°C (860°F), nearly twice as hot as a conventional oven and hot enough to melt lead. Furthermore, the atmospheric pressure at the surface of the planet reaches a crushing 90 times that experienced at sea level on Earth. Far from being Earth-like, the surface of Venus is one of the most hostile known.

VERY LARGE TELESCOPE (VLT)

The European Very Large Telescope of the European Southern Observatory in Chile consists of an array of four 8.2-m (323-in) reflectors, each housed in a separate dome. They can be used individually or interlinked to create the equivalent collecting area of a telescope of 16.4-m (645-in) aperture.

VIKING SPACECRAFT

Vikings 1 and 2, spacecraft sent to Mars, were both orbiters and landers. The orbiters carried television cameras to hunt for potential landing sites and the landers carried a suite of instruments to monitor weather conditions, photograph the surface and, most importantly, search for life. In the summer of 1976, landers from both Vikings 1 and 2 descended to the

ABOVE: The European Very Large Telescope (VLT) of the European Southern Obervatory in Chile consists of an an array of 8.2-m (323-in) reflectors.

surface, relaying views of their rubble-strewn landing sites beneath a dust-soaked, pink sky.

Robotic arms gathered soil that was tested for evidence of life. Initial results proved positive but were later attributed to chemical reactions in the soil rather than biological activity. The Viking landers survived on the Martian surface for four years, far longer than their 90-day design life. The Viking orbiters acted as relay stations for the landers, returning over 52,000 photographs and monitoring atmospheric circulation. It was over 21 years before another spacecraft – Mars Pathfinder – visited Mars.

)))➡ ***Mars, Missions to; Mars Pathfinder***

VIRGO CLUSTER

The Virgo Cluster contains over 2,000 galaxies. The most prominent members are all giant ellipticals, among them M84 and M86. It also contains M87, an active galaxy. The brightest spiral in the Virgo Cluster is M100. The Hubble Space Telescope has spied Cepheid variables within M100, from which we know that it – and hence the Virgo Cluster – lies about 55 million light years away.

VISUAL BINARIES

If both the components of a binary star are far enough apart as seen from Earth then it is known as a visual binary. The larger the telescope's aperture, the closer the stars that can be distinguished, although the ease of doing this will also depend on the relative brightness of the pair: a bright star may drown out the light of a feebler companion. Some apparent double stars are not connected and are simply viewed along a similar line of sight; these are called visual doubles, but they are much less common than true binaries. If a true binary is observed for long enough, signs of orbital motion will be detected, as the stars gradually change their separation and orientation relative to each other; careful measurement of these quantities can be used to determine the masses of the stars.

VON BRAUN, WERNHER, (1912–77)

German rocket scientist who advocated the use of rockets for spaceflight. Despite the success of the liquid rockets he designed for the German army during the Second World War, von Braun saw them as space

vehicles and designed larger rockets capable of orbiting a 30-tonne payload. After the War, he played a major role in developing Saturn 5, which took the Apollo astronauts to the Moon. Over 15 years of testing and flying for the US Army turned his V-2 into the rockets that would launch America's first artificial satellite and take the first American into space.

VOSKHOD

Once humans had flown in space the race was on to launch multi-crewed spacecraft. Russia's chance of beating the two-man American Gemini program into orbit was to modify their existing one-man Vostok so it could take three cosmonauts. Three couches replaced the single ejection seat and, after one unmanned test flight, three cosmonauts squeezed into the tiny Voskhod 1 capsule without pressure suits, and were blasted into orbit on 12 October 1964. Vladimir Komarov (1927–67) commanded the flight, which lasted just one day. With barely any space to move, very little of scientific value was accomplished.

Voskhod 2 was launched on 18 March 1965 with just two pressure-suited cosmonauts – commander Pavel Belyayev (1925–70) and Alexei Leonov. About 90 minutes after launch, Leonov passed through an airlock wearing a prototype moonwalking space suit and, tethered to Voskhod on a 5-m safety line, became the first person to 'walk' in space. Russia was still ahead in the race.

VOSTOK 1

The first spacecraft to take a human into orbit was a spherical capsule called Vostok: 2.3 m (8 ft) in diameter and coated in protective material so it could re-enter the atmosphere at any orientation without burning up. Five robotic Vostok flights from May 1960 paved the way for the first human mission. Just a few weeks before the first proposed American manned space flight a 27-year-old Russian pilot named Yuri Gagarin climbed into his Vostok 1 spacecraft. At 04:10 UT on 12 April 1961 he was blasted into orbit by the SL3 rocket. Seventy-eight minutes into the flight, mission control fired the retrorockets and Gagarin began his descent. The Vostoks had no retrorockets for a soft-landing, and so 8,000 m (26,250 ft) above the ground Gagarin ejected from the capsule and parachuted to Earth. It would be over 10 months before the Americans could improve on this pioneering flight.

))))➤ *Gagarin, Yuri*

LEFT: Wernher von Braun (right), Bill Pickering (left) and James Van Allen (centre) with the first US satellite, Explorer 1.

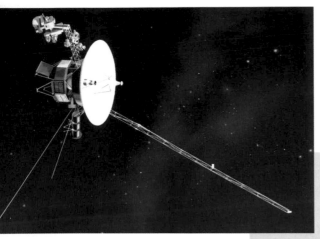

VOYAGER SPACE PROGRAM

Conceived to take advantage of a rare alignment of the outer planets, NASA planned its most ambitious robotic planetary expedition, and Voyagers 1 and 2 were launched from Cape Canaveral in the late summer of 1977. Voyager 1, which had started off after its twin, took a shorter route and was first to arrive at their joint target. It reached the realms of Jupiter in the spring of 1979 and beamed back the first clear, close-up views. These were used to make time-lapse movies of the planet's complex weather patterns. A thin ring around Jupiter was discovered and detailed images of the planet's four largest moons revealed an active sulphurous volcano erupting on Io, the smooth ice world of Europa, the complex ridged and grooved terrain of Ganymede and the crater-coated surface of Callisto. Voyager 2 flew past four months later and recorded more observations of the Jovian system.

Voyager 1 reached its next target, Saturn, in November 1980 and revealed intricate details of the planet's rings and weather patterns. Swinging past Saturn's largest moon, Titan, Voyager 1 was thrown out of the plane of the Solar System and away from the planets. When Voyager 2 reached Saturn in August 1981, it imaged more details of the rings, moons and cloud patterns, and permission was granted to extend the mission to the more distant and, so far, unexplored planets Uranus and Neptune. In January 1986 Voyager 2 imaged the giant planet Uranus and its moons. At Neptune, three-and-a-half years later, an Earth-sized dark storm spot was observed in detail, and nitrogen geysers on its moon Triton were photographed.

WEATHER SATELLITES

The US launched the first dedicated weather-watching satellite network called TIROS in the early 1960s. These were polar satellites and it was not until 1974 that the first US geostationary weather satellite series was operational. Today the whole planet's weather is covered by five geostationary weather satellites: the European Meteosat (0° longitude, Africa and Europe); GOES-EAST (75° west, Americas); GOES-WEST (135° west, Pacific); Japan's GMS (140° east – covering Australasia); and Russia's GOMS (76° east, Central Asia). All watch the atmosphere in the visible frequencies (as the human eye sees), the thermal infrared (to see temperature differences), and the VW (to see water vapour absorption differences).

WEIGHTLESSNESS

An object moving freely in a gravitational field, with no other forces acting on it, is in free fall. 'Weightlessness' is often used to describe the condition experienced by astronauts in free fall. Although they do not feel their weight, gravity is acting on them. It is sometimes said astronauts are weightless because they are beyond Earth's gravity. This is a fallacy. The gravity at the International Space Station is 88 per cent of that at Earth's surface. Astronauts are weightless because they are in free fall, not because there is no gravity in orbit.

WHIRLPOOL GALAXY

The Whirlpool Galaxy, M51, is a spiral that is interacting with a smaller companion galaxy NGC 5195, which brushed past it a few hundred million years ago. The Whirlpool is of historical interest for it was the first galaxy in which spiral structure was detected. At the time no-one appreciated its true nature as a separate system of stars far beyond our own Galaxy. Current estimates place the Whirlpool Galaxy at a distance of about 27 million light years.

))))➤ *Spiral Galaxies*

WHITE DWARFS

White dwarfs are the endpoint in evolution for the majority of stars, the core left behind after a star of low to moderate mass has shed its outer layers as a planetary nebula. Even though common, their dimness makes them difficult to spot. The first, a companion to Sirius, was not seen until 1862. Despite the name 'white' dwarfs they range in colour from blue to red, depending on the surface temperature. Over billions of years they cool and fade, from a starting point of more than 100,000°C (180,000°F) to around 4,000°C (7,200°F).

A typical white dwarf has a diameter only slightly greater than Earth's and a mass of 0.6 solar masses. The resulting densities are high, some billion kg/cubic metre (60 million lb/cubic ft); remarkably, a teaspoon of material from a white dwarf would weigh several tonnes.

ABOVE RIGHT: The Whirlpool galaxy, M51, was the first galaxy in which spiral structure was detected.

WIEN'S DISPLACEMENT LAW

Stars, planets and other astronomical bodies can be good approximations to black bodies. One of the characteristics of black-body radiation is that the wavelength of peak emission depends on the temperature of the body. The German physicist Wilhelm Wien (1864–1928) studied this relationship and, in 1893, came up with an expression which is now known as Wien's displacement law. It relates the wavelength of the peak of the spectrum to the temperature of the body:

$$\text{wavelength of peak emission } (\mu m) = 2900/T(K)$$

This allows astronomers to estimate the temperatures of celestial bodies from their spectra.

))))➤ *Spectra*

WIMPS

WIMPs (weakly interacting massive particles) are a possible candidate for dark matter. They are expected to be neutral particles with masses about 100 times that of the proton. If dark matter is present in our Galaxy then WIMPs should be all around us and detectable in laboratories on Earth. Several searches are underway, mostly using detectors set deep underground to avoid them being swamped by the effects of cosmic rays. To date no unambiguous indication of a WIMP has been seen, although an Italian-Chinese group has found more light flashes in summer than in winter. This would be expected since in summer Earth's velocity is in the same direction as the Sun's and so Earth sweeps faster through the Galaxy and through the postulated WIMP cloud.

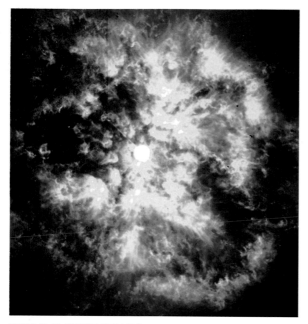

WOLF–RAYET STARS

High-mass stars leaving the main sequence suffer huge stellar winds with speeds up to 2,000 km/s (1,200 mi/s). These winds strips off their outer hydrogen layers at a rate of 10 million million tonnes per second. With the outer covering removed, the products of the nuclear burning in the star's interior come into view, giving rise to strong, broad emission lines in its spectrum, which originate in a dense expanding envelope.

These stars, often found at the centres of planetary nebulae, are known as Wolf–Rayet stars after their French discoverers, Charles Wolf (1827–1918) and Georges Rayet (1839–1906). Those showing prominent nitrogen lines are designated WN stars. Later in the star's evolution, when the helium produced in the CNO reactions is utilized to produce carbon (and the mass loss continues), the nitrogen lines disappear to be replaced by strong carbon and oxygen lines; these are classified as WC stars.

WORMHOLE

A hypothetical structure that allows different regions of space–time to be connected by tunnel-like shortcuts. A concept originally implied by solutions to equations arising in Einstein's general theory of relativity, modern cosmology suggests that space–time has, on very small scales, a foam-like structure pervaded by wormholes.

X-RAY ASTRONOMY

In the 1930s, physicists realized that the Earth's ionosphere must be heated by high-energy radiation from the Sun. Using a V-2 rocket in 1949 it was discovered that the Sun is a source of X-rays. Ten years later a Vanguard 3 was launched to investigate solar X-rays, determining that only prominences and the corona are hot enough to emit them. In 1962 a rocket was launched to search for X-rays created by solar radiation impacting on the Moon. Instead it found a powerful X-ray source in the constellation of Scorpius, now known as Scorpius X-1. Further discoveries followed from rockets and high-altitude balloons and, since the 1970s, surveys of the sky from orbiting satellites have revealed tens of thousands of cosmic X-ray sources. X-rays come from extremely hot gas (at 10^6–10^8 K), and the most important sources are interacting binary stars, supernova remnants, active galaxies and rich clusters of galaxies.

ABOVE LEFT: A Wolf-Rayet star, WR124 in Sagittarius, surrounded by a cloud of hot gas being ejected in a furious stellar wind.
ABOVE: The Chandra X-ray observatory, launched in 1999, is one of the most powerful instruments ever built for X-ray astronomy.

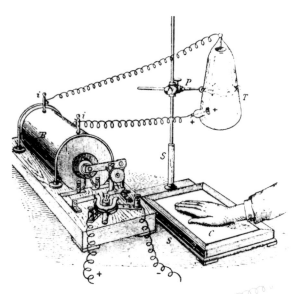

LEFT: The first X-ray machine, pictured here, was invented by Wilhelm Röntgen in 1895.

X-RAYS

X-rays were discovered by the German physicist Wilhelm Röntgen (1845–1923) in 1895. Coming soon after Hertz's discovery of radio waves it was expected that they too would prove to be electromagnetic waves, but they seemed at first to show none of the characteristics of light, such as reflection and refraction, that also characterized radio waves. It took until 1912 for physicists to discover that this was because their wavelength was extremely short, in the range 0.01–10 nm, many times shorter than light waves and comparable to the dimensions of atoms. X-rays are generated when high-speed electrons collide with a heavy metal target and give up their kinetic energy as electromagnetic radiation. Astrophysical sources of X-rays include plasmas with temperatures in the range of 10^6-10^8 K, and charged particles travelling at large fractions of the speed of light in magnetic fields.

YERKES OBSERVATORY

The Yerkes Observatory is near Wisconsin, USA. It was built in 1897 and takes its name from a Chicago millionaire, Charles Tyson Yerkes. He provided the money for the largest refracting telescope in the world, the Yerkes 1-m (40-in). Large lenses are difficult to make and support, and all the major telescopes following have been reflectors, which use mirrors instead.

YOUNG, JOHN (b. 1930)

American astronaut. One of nine astronauts chosen by NASA in October 1962, Young became the first of the group (which included Charles Conrad, Frank Borman and Neil Armstrong) to be assigned to a spaceflight, when he was named pilot of Gemini 3 in April 1964. He was assigned to flight crews almost continuously for the next nine years: in addition to flights on Gemini 3, Gemini 10, Apollo 10 and Apollo 16, he was backup pilot for Gemini 6, backup command module pilot for Apollo 7, and backup commander for Apollo 13 and Apollo 17.

)))➤ *Apollo Space Program, Gemini Space Program*

ZENITH

The point on the celestial sphere directly above an observer. The nadir is the opposite point, below the observer, 180° away and unseen beneath the Earth.

ZODIAC

An imaginary band around the celestial sphere, lying about 9° to each side of the ecliptic (the apparent annual path of the Sun), in which the Moon and planets (except, sometimes, Pluto) are found. In astrology the name is also given to the series of 12 constellations found in this band.

ZWICKY, FRITZ (1898–1974)

Swiss astrophysicist who first coined the word supernova in 1934 to describe a class of stellar outbursts different in scale and nature from the 'novae' known at that time. Zwicky suggested a link between supernovae and neutron stars, more than 30 years before the first neutron stars were discovered. In 1933 he was studying the Coma cluster of galaxies and found that the speeds of the individual galaxies were so high that they should have escaped long ago. He concluded that the amount of matter in the cluster was much higher than could be accounted for by the visible galaxies. Sometimes called 'missing mass' this matter is now usually called 'dark matter.'

PLANETS: PHYSICAL DATA

PLANET	AVERAGE DIAMETER[a] (EARTH = 1)	MASS (EARTH = 1)	VOLUME (EARTH = 1)	MEAN DENSITY (WATER = 1)
Mercury	0.383	0.055	0.056	5.43
Venus	0.950	0.815	0.857	5.24
Earth	1.000	1.000	1.000	5.52
Mars	0.532	0.107	0.151	3.93
Jupiter	10.973	317.83	1321.3	1.33
Saturn	9.140	95.16	763.6	0.69
Uranus	3.981	14.54	63.1	1.27
Neptune	3.865	17.15	57.7	1.64
Pluto	0.178	0.0021	0.0066	1.75

[a] At the 1-bar level in the atmosphere for Jupiter, Saturn, Uranus and Neptune.

PLANETS: ORBITAL DATA

PLANET	MEAN DISTANCE FROM SUN (AU)	ECCENTRICITY OF ORBIT	SIDEREAL PERIOD	MEAN SYNODIC PERIOD (DAYS)
Mercury	0.387	0.206	87.969 d	115.88
Venus	0.723	0.007	224.701 d	583.92
Earth	1.000	0.017	365.256 d	—
Mars	1.524	0.093	686.980 d	779.94
Jupiter	5.204	0.049	11.862 y	398.88
Saturn	9.582	0.057	29.457 y	378.09
Uranus	19.201	0.046	84.011 y	369.66
Neptune	30.047	0.011	164.79 y	367.49
Pluto	39.236	0.244	247.68 y	366.73

[a] R = retrograde. The rotation periods for Jupiter, Saturn, Uranus and Neptune are those of their magnetic fields.

OBLATENESS	SURFACE GRAVITY[a] (EARTH = 1)	ESCAPE VELOCITY (KM/S)	GEOMETRICAL ALBEDO
0	0.378	4.30	0.11
0	0.907	10.36	0.65
0.0034	1.000	11.19	0.37
0.0065	0.377	5.03	0.15
0.0649	2.364	59.5	0.52
0.0980	0.916	35.5	0.47
0.0229	0.889	21.3	0.51
0.0171	1.120	23.5	0.41
0	0.059	1.1	0.3

Source: National Space Science Data Center, NASA

INCLINATION OF ORBIT TO ECLIPTIC (DEGREES)	SIDEREAL PERIOD OF AXIAL ROTATION[a]	INCLINATION OF EQUATOR TO ORBIT (DEGREES)	NO. OF SATELLITES
7.00	58.646 d	0.01	0
3.39	243.019 d (R)	177.36	0
0.00	23.934 h	23.44	1
1.85	24.623 h	25.19	2
1.30	9.925 h	3.13	17
2.48	10.656 h	26.73	18
0.77	17.240 h (R)	97.77	21
1.77	16.110 h	28.32	8
17.16	6.387 d (R)	122.53	1

Source: National Space Science Data Center, NASA

THE BRIGHTEST STARS

STAR	POPULAR NAME	RA 2000.0 (H M)	DEC (° ')	APPARENT MAGNITUDE
α CMa	Sirius	06 45	-16 43	-1.44
a Car	Canopus	06 24	-52 42	-0.62
a Cen	Rigil Kentaurus	14 40	-60 50	-0.28c
a Boo	Arcturus	14 16	+19 11	-0.05v
a Lyr	Vega	18 37	+38 47	0.03v
a Aur	Capella	05 17	+46 00	0.08v
b Ori	Rigel	05 15	-08 12	0.18v
a CMi	Procyon	07 39	+05 14	0.40
a Eri	Achernar	01 38	-57 14	0.45v
a Ori	Betelgeuse	05 55	+07 24	0.45v
b Cen	Hadar	14 04	-60 22	0.61v
a Aql	Altair	19 51	+08 52	0.76v
a Cru	Acrux	12 27	-63 06	0.77c
a Tau	Aldebaran	04 36	+16 31	0.87
a Vir	Spica	13 25	-11 10	0.98v
a Sco	Antares	16 29	-26 26	1.06v
b Gem	Pollux	07 45	+28 02	1.16
a PsA	Fomalhaut	22 58	-29 37	1.17
b Cru	Becrux	12 48	-59 41	1.25v
a Cyg	Deneb	20 41	+45 17	1.25v
a Leo	Regulus	10 08	+11 58	1.36
e CMa	Adhara	06 59	-28 58	1.50
a Gem	Castor	07 35	+31 53	1.58c
g Cru	Gacrux	12 31	-57 07	1.59v
l Sco	Shaula	17 34	-37 06	1.62v
g Ori	Bellatrix	05 25	+06 21	1.64
b Tau	Alnath	05 26	+28 36	1.65
b Car	Miaplacidus	09 13	-69 43	1.67
e Ori	Alnilam	05 36	-01 12	1.69v
a Gru	Alnair	22 08	-46 58	1.73
z Ori	Alnitak	05 41	-01 57	1.74c
g²Vel		08 10	-47 20	1.75v
e UMa	Alioth	12 54	+55 58	1.76v
a Per	Mirphak	03 24	+49 52	1.79
e Sgr	Kaus Australis	18 24	-34 23	1.79
a UMa	Dubhe	11 04	+61 45	1.81c
d CMa		07 08	-26 24	1.83
h UMa	Alkaid	13 48	+49 19	1.85
e Car	Avior	08 23	-59 31	1.86v
q Sco		17 37	-43 00	1.86
b Aur	Menkalinan	06 00	+44 57	1.90v
a TrA	Atria	16 49	-69 02	1.91
g Gem	Alhena	06 38	+16 24	1.93
d Vel		08 45	-54 43	1.93
a Pav	Peacock	20 26	-56 44	1.94
a UMi	Polaris	02 32	+89 16	1.97v
b CMa	Mirzam	06 23	-17 57	1.98v
a Hya	Alphard	09 28	-08 40	1.99

c = Combined magnitude of double star; v = variable.

SPECTRAL TYPE	PARALLAX (")	DISTANCE (L.Y.)	ABSOLUTE MAGNITUDE
A1V	0.37921	8.60	1.45
F0Ib	0.01043	313	-5.53
G2V + K1V	0.74212	4.39	4.07c
K2IIIp	0.08885	36.7	-0.31
A0V	0.12892	25.3	0.58
G6III + G2III	0.07729	42.2	-0.48
B8Ia	0.00422	773	-6.69
F5IV–V	0.28593	11.4	2.68
B3V	0.02268	144	-2.77
M1Ia-M2Iab	0.00763	427	-5.14
B1III	0.00621	525	-5.42
A7V	0.19444	16.8	2.20
B0.5IV + B1V	0.01017	321	-4.19c
K5III	0.05009	65.1	-0.63
B1V	0.01244	262	-3.55
M1.5Iab	0.00540	604	-5.29
K0III	0.09674	33.7	1.09
A3V	0.13008	25.1	1.73
B0.5III	0.00925	353	-3.92
A2Ia	0.00101	3230	-8.73
B7V	0.04209	77.5	-0.52
B2II	0.00757	431	-4.10
A2V + A5V	0.06327	51.6	0.59c
M3.5III	0.03709	87.9	-0.56
B1.5IV	0.00464	703	-5.05
B2III	0.01342	243	-2.72
B7III	0.02489	131	-1.37
A1III	0.02934	111	-0.99
B0Ia	0.00243	1342	-6.38
B7V	0.03216	101	-0.73
O9.5 Ib + B0III	0.00399	817	-5.26c
WC8 + O9I	0.00388	841	-5.31
A0p	0.04030	80.9	-0.21
F5Ib	0.00551	592	-4.50
A0II	0.02255	145	-1.44
K0III + A8V	0.02638	124	-1.08c
F8Ia	0.00182	1792	-6.87
B3V	0.03239	101	-0.60
K3III + B2V	0.00516	632	-4.58
F1III	0.01199	272	-2.75
A1IV	0.03972	82.1	-0.10
K2IIb-IIIa	0.00785	415	-3.62
A1IV	0.03112	105	-0.60
A1V	0.04090	79.7	-0.01
B2.5V	0.01780	183	-1.81
F5-8Ib	0.00756	431	-3.64
B1II-III	0.00653	499	-3.95
K3II-III	0.01840	177	-1.69

Sources: The Hipparcos Catalogue and The Astronomical Almanac.

THE CONSTELLATIONS

NAME	GENITIVE	ABBREVIATION	AREA (SQUARE DEGREES)	ORDER OF SIZE
Andromeda	Andromedae	And	722	19
Antlia	Antliae	Ant	239	62
Apus	Apodis	Aps	206	67
Aquarius	Aquarii	Aqr	980	10
Aquila	Aquilae	Aql	652	22
Ara	Arae	Ara	237	63
Aries	Arietis	Ari	441	39
Auriga	Aurigae	Aur	657	21
Boötes	Boötis	Boo	907	13
Caelum	Caeli	Cae	125	81
Camelopardalis	Camelopardalis	Cam	757	18
Cancer	Cancri	Cnc	506	31
Canes Venatici	Canum Venaticorum	CVn	465	38
Canis Major	Canis Majoris	CMa	380	43
Canis Minor	Canis Minoris	CMi	183	71
Capricornus	Capricorni	Cap	414	40
Carina	Carinae	Car	494	34
Cassiopeia	Cassiopeiae	Cas	598	25
Centaurus	Centauri	Cen	1,060	9
Cepheus	Cephei	Cep	588	27
Cetus	Ceti	Cet	1,231	4
Chamaeleon	Chamaeleontis	Cha	132	79
Circinus	Circini	Cir	93	85
Columba	Columbae	Col	270	54
Coma Berenices	Comae Berenices	Com	386	42
Corona Australis	Coronae Australis	CrA	128	80
Corona Borealis	Coronae Borealis	CrB	179	73
Corvus	Corvi	Crv	184	70
Crater	Crateris	Crt	282	53
Crux	Crucis	Cru	68	88
Cygnus	Cygni	Cyg	804	16
Delphinus	Delphini	Del	189	69
Dorado	Doradus	Dor	179	72
Draco	Draconis	Dra	1,083	8
Equuleus	Equulei	Equ	72	87
Eridanus	Eridani	Eri	1,138	6
Fornax	Fornacis	For	398	41
Gemini	Geminorum	Gem	514	30
Grus	Gruis	Gru	366	45
Hercules	Herculis	Her	1,225	5
Horologium	Horologii	Hor	249	58
Hydra	Hydrae	Hya	1,303	1
Hydrus	Hydri	Hyi	243	61
Indus	Indi	Ind	294	49

NAME	GENITIVE	ABBREVIATION	AREA (SQUARE DEGREES)	ORDER OF SIZE
Lacerta	Lacertae	Lac	201	68
Leo	Leonis	Leo	947	12
Leo Minor	Leonis Minoris	LMi	232	64
Lepus	Leporis	Lep	290	51
Libra	Librae	Lib	538	29
Lupus	Lupi	Lup	334	46
Lynx	Lyncis	Lyn	545	28
Lyra	Lyrae	Lyr	286	52
Mensa	Mensae	Men	153	75
Microscopium	Microscopii	Mic	210	66
Monoceros	Monocerotis	Mon	482	35
Musca	Muscae	Mus	138	77
Norma	Normae	Nor	165	74
Octans	Octantis	Oct	291	50
Ophiuchus	Ophiuchi	Oph	948	11
Orion	Orionis	Ori	594	26
Pavo	Pavonis	Pav	378	44
Pegasus	Pegasi	Peg	1,121	7
Perseus	Persei	Per	615	24
Phoenix	Phoenicis	Phe	469	37
Pictor	Pictoris	Pic	247	59
Pisces	Piscium	Psc	889	14
Piscis Austrinus	Piscis Austrini	PsA	245	60
Puppis	Puppis	Pup	673	20
Pyxis	Pyxidis	Pyx	221	65
Reticulum	Reticuli	Ret	114	82
Sagitta	Sagittae	Sge	80	86
Sagittarius	Sagittarii	Sgr	867	15
Scorpius	Scorpii	Sco	497	33
Sculptor	Sculptoris	Scl	475	36
Scutum	Scuti	Sct	109	84
Serpens	Serpentis	Ser	637	23
Sextans	Sextantis	Sex	314	47
Taurus	Tauri	Tau	797	17
Telescopium	Telescopii	Tel	252	57
Triangulum	Trianguli	Tri	132	78
Triangulum Australe	Trianguli Australis	TrA	110	83
Tucana	Tucanae	Tuc	295	48
Ursa Major	Ursae Majoris	UMa	1280	3
Ursa Minor	Ursae Minoris	UMi	256	56
Vela	Velorum	Vel	500	32
Virgo	Virginis	Vir	1,294	2
Volans	Volantis	Vol	141	76
Vulpecula	Vulpeculae	Vul	268	55

THE NORTHERN & SOUTHERN HEMISPHERES

These two Index Charts provide a basic guide to the Northern and Southern hemispheres. The months around the rim of the northern hemisphere Index chart show when that part of the sky lies due south at around 10 p.m. – for example stars such as Leo will be well-displayed on evenings in March. In the case of the southern hemisphere Index chart, the dates show when that part of the sky lies due north at around 10 p.m.

NORTHERN HEMISPHERE

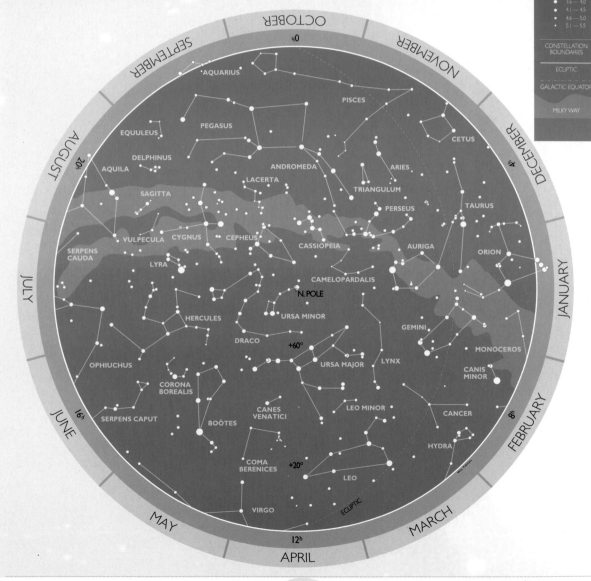

SOUTHERN HEMISPHERE

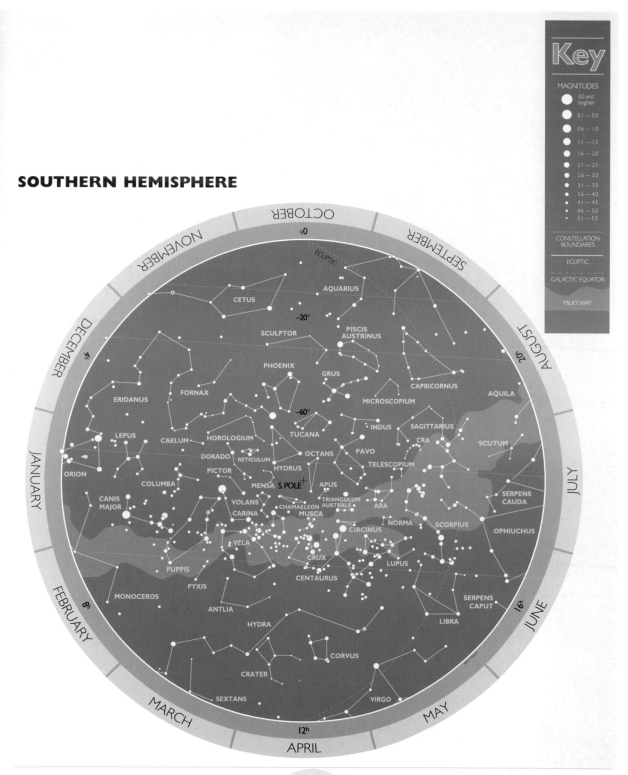

Key

MAGNITUDES

- 0.0 and brighter
- 0.1 — 0.5
- 0.6 — 1.0
- 1.1 — 1.5
- 1.6 — 2.0
- 2.1 — 2.5
- 2.6 — 3.0
- 3.1 — 3.5
- 3.6 — 4.0
- 4.1 — 4.5
- 4.6 — 5.0
- 5.1 — 5.5

CONSTELLATION BOUNDARIES

ECLIPTIC

GALACTIC EQUATOR

MILKY WAY

OCTOBER
NOVEMBER
SEPTEMBER
DECEMBER
AUGUST
JANUARY
JULY
FEBRUARY
JUNE
MARCH
MAY
APRIL

4^h
20^h
8^h
16^h
12^h

−20°
−60°

ECLIPTIC

CETUS
AQUARIUS
SCULPTOR
PISCIS AUSTRINUS
PHOENIX
GRUS
FORNAX
ERIDANUS
CAPRICORNUS
MICROSCOPIUM
AQUILA
LEPUS
CAELUM
HOROLOGIUM
TUCANA
INDUS
SAGITTARIUS
SCUTUM
DORADO
RETICULUM
OCTANS
PAVO
CRA
ORION
PICTOR
HYDRUS
TELESCOPIUM
SERPENS CAUDA
COLUMBA
MENSA
S. POLE
APUS
CANIS MAJOR
VOLANS
TRIANGULUM AUSTRALE
ARA
OPHIUCHUS
CARINA
CHAMAELEON
MUSCA
NORMA
VELA
CIRCINUS
SCORPIUS
CRUX
LUPUS
PUPPIS
CENTAURUS
PYXIS
MONOCEROS
SERPENS CAPUT
ANTLIA
LIBRA
HYDRA
CORVUS
CRATER
VIRGO
SEXTANS

THE LOCAL GROUP OF GALAXIES

GALAXY	RA 2000.0 (H M)	DEC (° ′)
M31 (NGC 224, Andromeda Galaxy)	00 43	+41 16
Milky Way		
M33 (NGC 598, Triangulum Galaxy)	01 34	+30 30
LMC	05 20	-69 27
SMC	00 53	-72 48
M32 (NGC 221)	00 43	+40 52
M110 (NGC 205)	00 40	+41 41
IC 10 (UGC 192)	00 20	+59 18
NGC 6822 (Barnard's Galaxy)	19 45	-14 48
NGC 185	00 39	+48 20
IC 1613	01 05	+02 08
NGC 147	00 33	+48 30
WLM (DDO 221)	00 02	-15 28
Sagittarius Dwarf	18 55	-30 29
Fornax Dwarf	02 40	-34 30
Pegasus Dwarf (DDO 216)	23 29	+14 45
Cassiopeia Dwarf (And VII)	23 27	+50 42
Sagittarius Dwarf Irregular (SagDIG)	19 30	-17 41
Leo I	10 08	+12 18
And I	00 46	+38 00
And II	01 16	+33 26
Leo A (DDO 69)	09 59	+30 45
Pegasus II (And VI)	23 52	+24 36
Aquarius Dwarf (DDO 210)	20 47	-12 51
Pisces Dwarf (LGS 3)	01 04	+21 54
And III	00 35	+36 31
Cetus Dwarf	00 26	-11 03
Leo II (DDO 93)	11 14	+22 10
Sculptor Dwarf	01 00	-33 43
Phoenix Dwarf	01 51	-44 27
Tucana Dwarf	22 42	-64 25
Sextans Dwarf	10 13	-01 37
Carina Dwarf	06 42	-50 58
And V	01 10	+47 38
Ursa Minor Dwarf (DDO 199)	15 09	+67 07
Draco Dwarf (DDO 208)	17 20	+57 55

* dIr = dwarf irregular, dSph = dwarf spheroidal.

TYPE*	ABSOLUTE MAGNITUDE	VISUAL MAGNITUDE	DISTANCE (MILLION L.Y.)
Sb I–II	-21.2	3.4	2.48
S(B)bc I–II	-20.9	–	–
Sc II–III	-18.9	5.7	2.58
Ir III–IV	-18.5	0.4	0.16
Ir IV/IV–V	-17.1	2.3	0.20
E2	-16.5	8.1	2.48
Sph	-16.4	8.1	2.48
Ir IV	-16.3	10.3	2.15
Ir IV–V	-16.0	9	1.63
Sph	-15.6	9.2	2.15
Ir V	-15.3	9.2	2.35
Sph	-15.1	9.5	2.15
Ir IV–V	-14.4	10.6	3.10
dSph	-13.8	–	0.10
dSph	-13.1	7.8	0.46
Ir V	-12.3	12.0	2.48
dSph	-12.0	12.9	2.25
Ir V	-12.0	15	3.85
dSph	-11.9	10.1	0.82
dSph	-11.8	13.2	2.64
dSph	-11.8	13	2.22
Ir V	-11.5	12.6	2.25
dSph	-11.3	13.3	2.54
Ir V	-10.9	14.1	3.10
dIr/dSph	-10.4	15	2.64
dSph	-10.2	13	2.48
dSph	-10.1	14.4	2.54
dSph	-10.1	11.5	0.68
dSph	-9.8	8.8	0.29
dIr/dSph	-9.8	–	1.30
dSph	-9.6	15.2	2.84
dSph	-9.5	10.3	0.29
dSph	-9.4	11	0.33
dSph	-9.1	15.9	2.64
dSph	-8.9	11	0.20
dSph	-8.6	11	0.26

Source: Adapted from Sidney van den Bergh, Publications of the Astronomical Society of the Pacific, April 2000.

HUMAN SPACEFLIGHT MISSIONS

The table below lists the important human spaceflight missions to have flown. All missions are included up to the end of 1975, and then only selected Space Shuttle and Soyuz missions are listed, marking further advances in mission complexity or other significant milestones of spaceflight.

SPACECRAFT	SPONSOR	CREW	LAUNCH DATE	DURATION	MISSION
Vostok 1	USSR	1	12-Apr-61	1h:48m	First manned spaceflight 1 orbit
Mercury-Redstone 3	USA	1	5-May-61	15m:22s	First American in space suborbital. Freedom 7
Mercury-Redstone 4	USA	1	21-Jul-61	15m:37s	Second suborbital flight. Liberty Bell 7
Vostok 2	USSR	1	6-Aug-61	1d:1h:18m	First flight longer than 24 hours; 17 orbits
Mercury-Atlas 6	USA	1	20-Feb-62	4h:55m	First American in orbit 3 orbits; telemetry falsely indicated heatshield unlatched. Friendship 7
Mercury-Atlas 7	USA	1	24-May-62	4h:56m	Initiated spaceflight experiments; manual retrofire error caused 400-km (250-mile) landing overshoot. Aurora 7
Vostok 3	USSR	1	11-Aug-62	3d:22h:22m	First twinned flight, with Vostok 4
Vostok 4	USSR	1	12-Aug-62	2d:22h:57m	First twinned flight. On first orbit came within 5 km (3 miles) of Vostok 3
Mercury-Atlas 8	USA	1	3-Oct-62	9h:13m	Developed techniques for long duration missions 6 orbits; closest splashdown to target to date 7 km (4.5 miles). Sigma 7
Mercury-Atlas 9	USA	1	15-May-63	1d:10h:20m	First US evaluation of effects of one day in space 22 orbits; performed manual re-entry after systems failure, landing 6.5 km (4 miles) from target. Faith 7
Vostok 5	USSR	1	14-Jun-63	4d:23h:6m	Second twinned flight, with Vostok 6
Vostok 6	USSR	1	16-Jun-63	2d:22h:50m	First woman in space; passed within 5 km (3 miles) of Vostok 5
Voskhod 1	USSR	3	12-Oct-64	1d:17m	Modified Vostok; first three-man crew in space; first without space suits
Voskhod 2	USSR	2	8-Mar-65	1d:2h:2m	Modified Vostok; first spacewalk 10 min via inflatable airlock
Gemini 3	USA	2	23-Mar-65	4h:53m	First American two-man crew; first piloted spacecraft to change its orbital path; first computer, allowing onboard calculation of manoeuvres
Gemini 4	USA	2	3-Jun-65	4d:1h:56m	First American spacewalk 21 min; first US 4-day flight; manual re-entry made after computer failure

SPACECRAFT	SPONSOR	CREW	LAUNCH DATE	DURATION	MISSION
Gemini 5	USA	2	21-Aug-65	7d:22h:56m	First use of fuel cells for electric power; evaluated guidance and navigation system
Gemini 7	USA	2	4-Dec-65	13d:18h:35m	Longest US flight for 8 years 206 orbits, record until Soyuz 9; rendezvous with Gemini 6
Gemini 6	USA	2	15-Dec-65	1d:1h:51m	First manned rendezvous, to within 6 feet of Gemini 7 as planned Agena was lost
Gemini 8	USA	2	16-Mar-66	10h:41m	First docking (with Agena) of one space vehicle with another; emergency re-entry after control malfunction; first Pacific landing
Gemini 9	USA	2	3-Jun-66	3d:21m	127-min EVA rendezvous but no docking with target; landed 0.8 km (0.5 miles) from recovery ship
Gemini 10	USA	2	18-Jul-66	2d:22h:47m	Docked with Agena 10 and used engine to attain record 763-km (474-mile) altitude; rendezvous with Agena 8; 39-min EVA by Collins
Gemini 11	USA	2	12-Sep-66	2d:23h:17m	Used Agena engine to attain record 1,369-km (850-mile) altitude; 163-min EVA by Gordon, connected Gemini and Agena by tether; first automatic computer-guided re-entry
Gemini 12	USA	2	11-Nov-66	3d:22h:34m	Final Gemini mission; Agena docking; record 5.5 hours of EVA by Aldrin, automatic computer-guided re-entry
Soyuz 1	USSR	1	23-Apr-67	1d:2h:48m	Cosmonaut killed in crash landing
Apollo 7	USA	3	11-Oct-68	10d:20h:9m	First piloted flight of Apollo spacecraft, command-service module only; first US 3-man flight; live TV footage of crew
Soyuz 3	USSR	1	26-Oct-68	3d:22h:51m	Rendezvous with unmanned Soyuz 2
Apollo 8	USA	3	21-Dec-68	6d:3h	First manned lunar orbit and piloted lunar return re-entry CSM only; first manned Saturn V; views of lunar surface televised to Earth
Soyuz 4	USSR	1	14-Jan-69	2d:23h:21m	First docking of two piloted spacecraft, with Soyuz 5
Soyuz 5	USSR	3	15-Jan-69	3d:54m	Docked with Soyuz 4; crew transfered by EVA to Soyuz 4
Apollo 9	USA	3	3-Mar-69	10d:1h:1m	First piloted flight of lunar module Earth orbit; 56-min EVA tested lunar suit
Apollo 10	USA	3	18-May-69	8d:3m	First lunar module orbit of Moon, descent to within 15,000 meters (50,000 feet) of Moon's surface; holds manned speed record, 11.0825 km/s (6.8863 mi/s) at atmosphere entry

SPACECRAFT	SPONSOR	CREW	LAUNCH DATE	DURATION	MISSION
Apollo 11	USA	3	16-Jul-69	8d:3h:18m	First lunar landing 20 Jul; 151-min lunar EVA; collected 22 kg (48.5 lb) of soil and rock samples; lunar stay time 21h:36m
Soyuz 6	USSR	2	11-Oct-69	4d:22h:42m	Rendezvous with Soyuz 7/8; first welding of metals in space
Soyuz 7	USSR	3	12-Oct-69	4d:22h:41m	Triple rendezvous with Soyuz 6/8; space station construction test; first time 3 spacecraft, 7 crew members orbited the Earth at once
Soyuz 8	USSR	2	13-Oct-69	4d:22h:51m	Triple rendezvous with Soyuz 6/7; part of space station construction test
Apollo 12	USA	3	14-Nov-69	10d:4h:36m	Second Moon landing; 2 lunar EVAs totalling 465 min; collected 33.9 kg (74.7 lb) of samples; lunar stay time 31h:31m
Apollo 13	USA	3	11-Apr-70	5d:22h:55m	Mission aborted following service module oxygen tank explosion; crew returned safely using lunar module; circumlunar return; holds manned altitude record, 400,187 km (248,665) miles above Earth's surface
Soyuz 9	USSR	2	1-Jun-70	17d:16h:59m	This flight marked the beginning of working in space under weightless conditions; endurance record for solo craft remains
Apollo 14	USA	3	31-Jan-71	9d:42m	Third Moon landing; 2 lunar EVAs totalling 563 min; collected 43.5 kg (96 lb) of lunar samples; lunar stay time 33h:31m
Salyut 1	USSR	0	19-Apr-71	175d	First space station; occupied by Soyuz 11 crew for 23 days; reentered 11-Oct-71
Soyuz 10	USSR	3	23-Apr-71	1d:23h:46m	Adjustment of an improved docking bay between the spacecraft and the orbiting Salyut space station, but no cosmonauts entered the orbiting station
Soyuz 11	USSR	3	16-Jun-71	23d:18h:22m	Docked and entered Salyut 1 space station; orbited in Salyut 1 for 23 days; crew died during re-entry from loss of pressurization
Apollo 15	USA	3	26-Jul-71	12d:7h:12m	Fourth Moon landing; first lunar rover use; first deep spacewalk; 3 lunar EVAs totalling 19h:8m; collected 77 kg (170 lb) of samples; lunar stay time 66h:54m; 38-min Worden EVA; subsatellite released
Apollo 16	USA	3	16-Apr-72	11d:1h:51m	Fifth Moon landing; 3 lunar EVAs totalling 20h:14m; collected 97 kg (213 lb) of lunar samples; lunar stay time 71:14; subsatellite released

SPACECRAFT	SPONSOR	CREW	LAUNCH DATE	DURATION	MISSION
Apollo 17	USA	3	7-Dec-72	12d:13h:51m	Sixth piloted lunar landing; 3 lunar EVAs totalling 22h:4m; collected 110 kg (243 lb) of samples; record lunar stay of 74:59; 66-min Evans EVA
Skylab 1	USA	0	14-May-73	2,249d	First US space station; occupied by Skylab 2, 3 & 4 crews; reentered 11-Jul-79
Skylab 2	USA	3	25-May-73	28d:50m	First American piloted orbiting space station; made long-flight tests, crew repaired damage caused during boost; 2 EVAs + SEVA
Skylab 3	USA	3	28-Jul-73	59d:11h:9m	Crew systems and operational tests, exceeded pre-mission plans for scientific activities; 3 EVAS totalling 13:44
Soyuz 12	USSR	2	27-Sep-73	1d:23h:16m	After Soyuz 11 accident, new life support equipment was tested
Skylab 4	USA	3	16-Nov-73	84d:1h:15m	Final Skylab mission; endurance record until Soyuz 29-Salyut 6; 4 EVAs, set then-record spacewalk of 7h:1m 52
Soyuz 19-ASTP	USSR	2	15-Jul-75	5d:22h:31m	First US/USSR joint flight; docked with Apollo 18 for 2 days; conducted experiments, shared meals, and held a joint news conference
Salyut 5	USSR	0	22-Jun-76	412d	4th space station; occupied by 2 crews for 65 days; reentered 8-Aug-77
Soyuz 21	USSR	2	6-Jul-76	49d:6h:23m	First Salyut 5 occupation 48 days; acid fumes forced return
Salyut 6	USSR	0	29-Sep-77	1763d	5th space station; occupied for 676 days by 5 long stay + 11 visiting crews; reentered 28-Jul-82
Soyuz 28	USSR	2	2-Mar-78	7d:22h:16m	First international crew USSR and Czechoslovakia, to Salyut 6
Soyuz 29	USSR	2	15-Jun-78	139d:14h:18m	First 100+ day flight, to Salyut 6; returned in Soyuz 31: Progress 2, 3 & 4 resupply the complex
Soyuz 30	USSR	2	27-Jun-78	7d:22h:3m	2nd international crew USSR and Poland, to Salyut 6
Soyuz 31	USSR	2	26-Aug-78	7d:20h:49m	3rd international crew USSR and East Germany, to Salyut 6; returned in Soyuz 29
Soyuz 32	USSR	2	25-Feb-79	175d:36m	Cosmonauts board Salyut 6; endurance record; returned in Soyuz 34: Progress 5, 6 and 7 resupply the orbiting complex
Soyuz 33	USSR	2	10-Apr-79	1d:23h:1m	4th international crew USSR and Bulgaria; failed to dock with Salyut 6 after engine failure

orbiting

SPACECRAFT	SPONSOR	CREW	LAUNCH DATE	DURATION	MISSION
Soyuz 35	USSR	2	19-Apr-80	184d:20h:11m	4th Salyut 6 long stay; endurance record; returned in Soyuz 37: Progress 8, 9 and 11 resupply the orbiting complex
Soyuz T2	USSR	2	5-Jun-80	3d:22h:19m	First manned spaceflight of the new spacecraft; manual docking with Salyut 6
STS-1, Columbia	USA	2	12-Apr-81	2d:6h:21m	First space shuttle flight; orbital test flight; some thermal tiles lost
STS-2, Columbia	USA	2	12-Nov-81	2d:6h:13m	First reuse of space shuttle; 2nd orbital test flight; test of Canadian robot arm RMS; 5-day mission halved by fuel cell fault
STS-6, Challenger	USA	4	4-Apr-83	5d:2h:14m	First Challenger flight; first shuttle EVA; Tracking & Data Relay Satellite TDRS
STS-7, Challenger	USA	5	18-Jun-83	6d:2h:24m	First US woman in space; first 5-person crew; 2 COMSATs, German platform SPAS-1
STS-9, Columbia	USA	6	28-Nov-83	10d:7h:47m	First German on US mission; first 6-person crew; first Spacelab Mission SL-1
41-B, Challenger	USA	5	3-Feb-84	7d:23h:16m	First untethered EVA & testing of MMU jetpack; first Kennedy Space Center landing; 2 COMSATs
Soyuz T10B	USSR	3	8-Feb-84	236d:22h:50m	First long-stay triple crew, to Salyut 7; 6 EVAs totalling 22h:56m; returned in Soyuz T11
41-D, Discovery	USA	6	30-Aug-84	6d:56m	First flight of Discovery; first commercial payload specialist; 3 communications satellites
51-A, Discovery	USA	4	8-Nov-84	7d:23h:45m	First satellite retrieval/return; 2 COMSATs
51-L, Challenger	USA	7	28-Jan-86	1m:13s	Exploded during liftoff, all were killed
Mir	USSR	0	20-Feb-86	—	New-generation space station with 6 docking ports; occupied by multiple crews
Soyuz T15	USSR	2	13-Mar-86	125d:1m	First Mir occupation; excursion to Salyut 7 5-May to 26-Jun; two Salyut EVAs totalling 8h:50m; -re-used descent module from T-10A abort
Soyuz TM2	USSR	2	5-Feb-87	326d:11h:18m	2nd Mir long stay; new endurance record; return in Soyuz TM-3
Soyuz TM4	USSR	3	21-Dec-87	365d:22h:39m	3rd Mir long stay occupation; new endurance record; 3 EVAs totalling 13h:40m; returned in
Soyuz TM6	USSR	3	29-Aug-88	240d:22h:36m	4th Mir long stay
STS-26, Discovery	USA	5	29-Sep-88	4d:1h	Redesigned shuttle makes first flight; Tracking/Data Relay Satellite TDRS-C
Soyuz TM7	USSR	3	26-Nov-88	151d:11h:9m	5th Mir long stay; returned in Soyuz TM6; Volkov/Krikalev in TM7
STS-30, Atlantis	USA	5	4-May-89	4d:56m	Magellan Venus orbiter launched on IUS stage, arrived Venus Aug 1990

SPACECRAFT	SPONSOR	CREW	LAUNCH DATE	DURATION	MISSION
STS-34, Atlantis	USA	5	18-Oct-89	4d:23h:39m	Galileo Jupiter orbiter launched on IUS stage, arrived Jupiter Dec 1995
STS-31, Discovery	USA	5	24-Apr-90	5d:1h:16m	Deployed Hubble Space Telescope HST; set Shuttle altitude record of 619 km (385 miles)
STS-41, Discovery	USA	5	6-Oct-90	4d:2h:10m	Ulysses solar probe launched on IUS stage
STS-47, Endeavour	USA	7	12-Sep-92	7d:22h:30m	50th shuttle mission; 1st black woman in space; 1st Japanese national; Lee & Davis 1st married couple to travel together in space; first Japanese Spacelab SL-J
STS-61, Endeavour new	USA	7	2-Dec-93	10d:19h:59m	First Hubble Space Telescope servicing mission; 5 EVAs for 4 crew totalling 35h:28m; Akers set US EVA duration record 29h:40m
STS-60, Discovery	USA	6	3-Feb-94	8d:7h:9m	First Russian on US shuttle; attempt to deploy the Wake Shield Facility a device to create vacuums in space failed; Spacehab 2
STS-71, Atlantis	USA	7	27-Jun-95	9d:19h:22m	First Mir docking/crew exchange, 100th US human spaceflight, Spacelab carried
STS-82, Discovery	USA	7	11-Feb-97	9d:23h:38m	2nd Hubble Space Telescope servicing mission; 5 EVAs for 4 crew totalling 33h:11m, replaced 10 instruments
STS-95, Discovery	USA	7	29-Oct-98	8d:21h:44m	SpaceHab-SM, SPARTAN-201; John Glenn reflight
STS-88, Endeavour	USA	6	4-Dec-98	11d:19h:18m	ISS assembly flight 2A, Unity Module
STS-96, Discovery	USA	7	27-May-99	9d:19h:13m	ISS assembly flight 2A.1; Starshine
STS-103, Discovery	USA	7	19-Dec-99	7d:23h:12m	3rd Hubble Space Telescope servicing mission; 3 EVAs for 4 crew totalling 24h:33m
Souyuz 2R	USSR	3	30-Oct-00	—	First crew on ISS – marks start of planned permanent human presence on the station
STS-92, Discovery	USA	7	05-Oct-00	—	100th Shuttle flight
STS-98 Atlantis,	USA	5	7-Feb-01	12d: 21h:20m	Destiny Laboratory Module delivered to the International Space Station
STS-108 Endeavour	USA	10	5- Dec-01	11d:19h:36m	Fourth crew to the International Space Station, third crew returned to Earth

WEB SITES

THE HISTORY OF ASTRONOMY/KEY PEOPLE

http://www.astro.uni.bonn.de/~pbrosche/hist_astr/ha_pers.html
One of the most exhaustive web sites of biographies on scientists who have shaped the history of astronomy.

http://www.bios.niv.edu/orion/history.html
A brief history of astronomy.

http://webhead.com/WWWWVL/Astronomy/astroweb/yp_history.html
Interactive atlas of world astronomy with detailed descriptions of the astronomy of cultures around the world.

http://www.gpc.peachnet.edu/~pgore/astronomy/astr10/ancient.htm
This web site explains basic types of ancient observatories.

http://es.rice.edu/ES/humsoc/Galileo
Hypertext source of information on the life and work of Galileo Galilei and the science of his time.

http://galileoandeinstein.physics.virginia.edu/lectures/tycho.htm
Scholarly lectures on the work of Tycho Brahe and his assistant, Johannes Kepler.

THE UNIVERSE

http://www.astro.ucla.edu/~wright/errors.html
A fun-filled web site outlining errors within some popular attacks on the Big Bang.

http://www.astro.ucla.edu/~wight/cosmology_faq.html
A good discussion forum for topics related to the Big Bang, the expansion of the Universe, models of the Universe, dark matter, the collapse of the Universe and much more.

http://www.image.gsfic.nasa.gov/poetry/ask/a11610.htm
Archive of NASA Image Space Science Question & Answers.

http://www.columbia.edu/cu/newrec/2416/tmpl/story.2html

Experiments with tiny particles that could reshape models of the Universe.

http://www.ssg.sr.unh.edu/406/Review/rev3.html
Geometrical models of the Universe.

http://www.acuniverse/freeserve.co.uk/history.htm
Brief summary of traditional theoretical models of the Universe.

http://www.time.com/time/time100/scientistprofile/hubble.html
Astronomers and thinking: a profile of Edwin Hubble.

http://antwrp.gsfc.nasa.gov/diamond_jubilee/d_1996/sandage_hubble.html
A profile of Edwin Hubble by Allan Sandage.

STARS AND GALAXIES

http://www.seds.org/messier/
Images and basic data for the Messier Catalogue of nebulae, showing many beautiful nearby galaxies.

http://www.astr.ua.edu/pairs2.html
The University of Alabama atlas of interacting galaxies.

http://www.astro.princeton.edu/~frei/galaxy_catalog.html
Catalogue of CCD images of a wide variety of galaxies obtained by Zsolt Frei and James Gunn. In addition to colour images of the galaxies, the raw data are available for quantitative analysis.

http://antwrp.gsfc.nasa.gov/apod/
Astronomy Picture of the Day. The archive of these pictures and explanatory texts.

http://antwrp.gsfc.nasa.gov/apod/lib/aptree.html
Contains an extensive section of items on galaxies.

http://cfpa.berkeley.edu/Bhfaq.html
A reader-friendly web site tutorial offering a fine non-technical overview of some of the most important properties of black holes.

THE SOLAR SYSTEM

http://www.sunblock99.org.uk
This is be the PPARC sponsored site; it was started for the 1999 eclipse but is being developed into a major educational site.

http://umbra.gsfc.nasa.gov/sdac.html
Contains lots of images and some movies from space and the ground; has a useful education link.

http://hesperia.gsfc.nasa.gov/sftheory/
Mainly about solar flares and related activity, but contains a useful dictionary of related terms.

http://www.mssl.ucl.ac.uk/www_solar/sunbasics/index.html
A nice easy introduction to the Sun with information on structure, dimensions, the solar cycle, coronal mass ejections, eclipses; also a short quiz.

http://www.lmsal.com/YPOP/
The Yohkoh movie theatre with a number of solar animations, recent pictures, and some education activities.

http://sunearth.gsfc.nasa.gov/eclipse/eclipse.html
A wealth of eclipse information for recent and upcoming eclipses.

http://seds.lpl.arizona.edu/nineplanets/nineplanets/nineplanets.html
The Nine Planets.

http://www.windows.umich.edu/
Windows to the Universe.

http://www.astronomy.com
Astronomy Magazine.

http://helix.nature.com/
Nature Helix.

http://www.jpl.nasa.gov/NASA/JPL

http://spacescience.com
Science at NASA.
http://exobio.ecsd.edu/Space_Sciences/Space Sciences Outreach.*

http://www.stsci.edu/
Space Telescope Science Institute.

http://sunearth.gsfc.nasa.gov/eclipse.html
NASA/Goddard Space Flight Center and Fred Espenak's Eclipse Home Page.

http://www.lowell.edu/
Lowell Observatory.

http://www.noaa.gov/
National Oceanic and Atmospheric Administration.

http://photojournal.jpl.nasa.gov/
Jet Propulsion Laboratory Photo Journal.

http://www.astronomy.com/
Astronomy magazine.

WATCHING THE SKY

http://www.skypub.com
Sky & Telescope magazine.

http://cdsweb.u-strasbg.fr/astroweb.html
Astronomy resources on the Internet.

http://cfa-www.harvard.edu/iau/cbat.html
Central Bureau for Astronomical Telegrams.

http://sohowww.nascom.nasa.gov
Solar and Heliospheric Observatory (SOHO).

http://www.bbso.njit.edu
Big Bear Solar Observatory.

http://setiathome.berkeley.edu
SET@home project.

http://www.lpl.arizona.edu/alpo/
Association of Lunar and Planetary Observers.

http://www.occultations.com
International Occultation Timing Association.

http://sunearth.gsfc.nasa.gov
Eclipses.

EXPLORATION OF STARS AND PLANETS

http://www.spaceport.com
General background to human spaceflight.

http://swampfox.fmarion.edu/web/planet/links.html
Links to the best astronomy sites.

http://www.jpl.nasa.gov/calendar/calendar.html#1099
Great calender of space events in the coming years.

http://pds.jpl.nasa.gov/planets/welcome.html
Comprehensive planet guide and missions.

http://pds.jpl.nasa.gov/
NASA's planetary data systems nodes – total planetary data.

http://bang.lanl.gov/solarsys/
Solar system pictures and historical stuff.

http://photojournal.wr.usgs.gov
General tour of the solar system.

http://photojournal.jpl.nasa.gov
A great picture library of solar system shots.

http://www.iki.rssi.ru/Welcome.html
The Russian Space Agency.

http://www.nasa.gov
The American Space Agency.

http://www.ccas.ru/~chernov/vsm/main.html
Russian Space Craft Museum – lots of rare pictures.

http://tele-satellit.com/tse/online/
Encyclopedia of unmanned artificial Earth satellites.

http://nssdc.gsfc.nasa.gov/planetary/chronology.html
Chronology of all missions.

http://solar.rtd.utk.edu:81/~mwade/spaceflt.html
Massive chronology of space flight.

http://leonardo.jpl.nasa.gov/msl/home.html
Mission and spacecraft library.

http://nmp.jpl.nasa.gov/
NASA's New Millennium Programme.
http://quest.arc.nasa.gov/pioneer10/
Pioneer 10 & 11 25th anniversary site.

http://mpfwww.jpl.nasa.gov
NASA's upcoming Mars Missions (including Pathfinder).

http://www.stsci.edu/pubinfo/latest.html
Hubble Space Telescope site.

http://www.jpl.nasa.gov/magellan/
Magellan mission to Venus.

http://www.jpl.nasa.gov/galileo/
Galileo mission to Jupiter and its moons.

http://ccf.arc.nasa.gov/galileo_probe
Galileo probe into Jupiter.

http://ulysses.jpl.nasa.gov/ULSHOME/ulshome.html
Ulysees Solar probe.

http://www.jpl.nasa.gov/mip/voyager.html
Voyager 1 & 2.

http://www.jpl.nasa.gov/cassini/
Cassini mission to Saturn and its moons.

http://www.estec.esa.nl/spdwww/huygens/
Huygen's mission to Titan.

http://stardust.jpl.nasa.gov/
Stardust mission to return a comet sample.

http://www.estec.esa.nl/rosetta/html/info0497.html
Rosetta mission to a comet.

http://hurlbut.jhuapl.edu/NEAR/
NEAR mission to an asteroid.

http://lunarprospector.arc.nasa.gov
Lunar Prospector.

FURTHER READING

THE HISTORY OF ASTRONOMY/KEY PEOPLE

Abbott, David (ed.), *Biographical Dictionary of Scientists: Astronomy*, Peter Bedrick, New York, 1984

Bertotti, B. et al, *Modern Cosmology in Retrospect*, Cambridge University Press, Cambridge, 1990

Bettex, Albert, *The Discovery of Nature*, Thames and Hudson, London, 1965

Chapman, Allan, *Dividing the Circle: The Development of Critical Angular Measurement in Astronomy 1500–1850*, New York and London, 1990

Duhem, Pierre and Roger Ariew (eds.), *Medieval Cosmology*, University of Chicago Press, Chicago, 1985

Gadalla, Moustafa, *Egyptian Cosmology*, Tehuti Research Foundation, London, 1997

Galilei, Galileo, *Siderius Nuncius* (1610), facsimile ed.

Hoskin, Michael (ed.), *Cambridge Illustrated History of Astronomy*, Cambridge University Press, Cambridge, 1997

Hoyle, Fred, *Astronomy*, Crescent Books, London, 1962

Kepler, Johannes, *Kepler's Dream*, University of California Press, Berkeley, 1965

Kepler, Johannes, *Epitome of Copernican Astronomy and Harmonies of the World* (Great Minds Series), Prometheus Books, New York, 1995

Leslie, John, (ed.), *Modern Cosmology & Philosophy*, Prometheus Books, New York, 1998

Liddle, Andrew, *An Introduction to Modern Cosmology*, John Wiley & Sons, New York, 1998

Newton, Isaac, Cohen, Bernard I. (trans.), *Mathematical Principles of Natural Philosophy*, Harvard University Press, Cambridge, Massachusetts, 1990

North, John, *Norton History of Astronomy and Cosmology*, Norton, New York, 1995

North, J. D., *The Measure of the Universe: A History of Modern Cosmology*, Dover Publications Inc., London, 1990

Walker, Christopher (ed.), *Astronomy before the Telescope*, British Museum Press, London, 1996

Westfall, Richard, *The Life of Isaac Newton*, Cambridge University Press, Cambridge, 1996

THE UNIVERSE

Al-Khalili, Jim, *Black Holes, Wormholes and Time Machines*, Institute of Physics Publishing, London, 1999

Allen, Harold, W. G., *Cosmic Perspective: Evolution and Reincarnation—The Demise of the Big Bang Theory*, Sunstar Publishing, Fairfield, Iowa, 1998

Bernstein, Jeremy, *Kinetic Theory in the Expanding Universe*, Cambridge University Press, Cambridge, 1988

Calder, Nigel, *Afterglow of Creation*, Arrow Books, London, 1993

Cornell, James, *Bubbles, Voids and Bumps in Time: The New Cosmology*, Cambridge University Press, Cambridge, 1989

Gribbin, John and Martin Rees, *The Stuff of the Universe*, Heinemann, London, 1990

Gribbin, John, *In Search of the Big Bang*, Penguin, London, 1998

Gribbin, John, *The Omega Point*, Heinemann, London, 1987

Gribbin, John, *The Birth of Time*, Yale University Press, Connecticut, 2000

Harrison, Edward, *Cosmology: The Science of the Universe* (2nd Edition), Cambridge University Press, Cambridge, 2000

Hawking, Stephen, *Brief History of Time: From the Big Bang to Black Holes*, Bantam, New York, 1998

Hawking, Stephen, *The Large-Scale Structure of Space-Time*, Cambridge University Press, Cambridge, 1973

Hogan, Craig, J., *Little Book of the Big Bang: A Cosmic Primer*, Springer-Verlag, New York, 1998

Hoyle, Fred, *Different Approaches to Cosmology: From a Static Universe Through the Big Bang Towards Reality*, Cambridge University Press, Cambridge, 2000

Layzer, David, *Constructing the Universe*, Scientific American Library, 1984

Liddle, Andrew, *An Introduction to Modern Cosmology*, John Wiley & Sons, New York, 1999

Moore, Patrick and Iain Nicolson, *Black Holes in Space*, Orbach and Chambers, 1974

Murray, Carl D. et al, *Solar System Dynamics*, Cambridge University Press, Cambridge, 2000

Nelson, P. G., *Big Bang, Small Voice: Reconciling Genesis and Modern Science*, Whittles Publishing, 1999

Silk, Joseph, *The Big Bang* (3rd edition), W. H. Freeman, 2001

Weedman, Daniel W., *Quasar Astronomy*, Cambridge University Press, Cambridge, 1986

STARS AND GALAXIES

Bertin, Giuseppe, *The Dynamics of Galaxies*, Cambridge University Press, Cambridge, 2000

Binney, James and Michael Merrifield, *Galactic Astronomy*, Princeton University Press, New Jersey, 1998

Challoner, Jack, *Equinox: Space*, Channel 4 Books, London, 2000

Danielson, Richard D. (ed.), *The Book of the Cosmos: Imagining the Universe from Heraclitus to hawking*, Perseus Books, 2000

Fanning, A. E., *Planets, Stars and Galaxies*, Dover Publications, London, 1986

Gaustad, John and Michael Zeilik, *Astronomy: The Comsic Perspective*, John Wiley & Sons, New York, 1990

Giacconi, R. and W. Tucker, *The X-Ray Universe*, Harvard University Press, Cambridge, Massachusetts, 1985

Lederman, Leon and David Schramm, *From Quarks to the Cosmos*, Scientific American Library, New York, 1989

Longhair, Malcolm S., *Our Evolving Universe*, Cambridge University Press, Cambridge, 1997

Luminet, Jean-Pierre, *Black Holes*, Cambridge University Press, Cambridge, 1993

Peacock, John A., *Cosmological Physics*, Cambridge University Press, Cambridge, 1999

Ridpath, Ian, *Collins Gem: Stars*, HarperCollins, London, 1999

Sparke, Linda S. and John S. Gallagher, *Galaxies in the Universe*, Cambridge University Press, Cambridge, 2000

Taylor, Roger, *Galaxies: Structures and Evolution*, Cambridge University Press, Cambridge, 1993

Taylor, Roger, *The Hidden Universe*, Ellis Horwood, 1991

Weedman, Daniel, *Quasar Astronomy*, Cambridge University Press, Cambridge, 1998

THE SOLAR SYSTEM

Ahrens, Donald C., *Meteorology Today: An Introduction to Weather, Climate, and the Environment*, Pacific Grove, California, 1999

Barnes-Svarney, Patricia, *Asteroid: Earth Destroyer or New Frontier?*, Plenum Publishing Corps, 1996

Calder, Nigel, *Comets: Speculation and Discovery*, Dover Publications, London, 1994

Davidson, Keay, *Carl Sagan: A Life*, John Wiley & Sons, New York, 1999

Grant, Edward (ed.), *Stars, Planets, & Orbs*, Cambridge University Press, New York, 1996

Hunt, Gary and Patrick Moore, *Atlas of Uranus*, Cambridge University Press, Cambridge, 1989

Levy, David, *Impact Jupiter: The Crash of Comet Shoemaker-Levy 9*, Plenum Publishing Corporation, 1995

Levy, David, *Shoemaker by Levy*, Princeton University Press, New Jersey, 2000

Ridpath, Ian and Wil Tirion, *Pocket Guide to Stars and Planets*, HarperCollins, London, 2001

Taylor, Peter O., *Observing the Sun*, Cambridge University Press, Cambridge, 1991

Vanin, Gabrieli, *Cosmic Phenomena: Comets, Meteor Showers, Eclipses*, Firefly Books, 1999

Weissman, Paul et al, *Encyclopedia of the Solar System*, Academic Press, 1998

Wilson, Robert, *Astronomy Through The Ages*, Taylor and Francis, London, 1997

Zeilek, Michael (ed.), *Astronomy: The Evolving Universe*, New York, 1999

WATCHING THE SKY

Audouze, Jean and Guy Israël (eds.), *The Cambridge Atlas of Astronomy*, Cambridge University Press, Cambridge, 1988

Covington, Michael, *Astrophotography for the Amateur*, Cambridge University Press, Cambridge, 1985

Garfinkle, Robert, *Star-Hopping: Your Visa to the Universe*, Cambridge University Press, Cambridge, 1994

Newton, Jack & Philip Teece, *The Cambridge Deep-Sky Album*, Cambridge University Press, Cambridge, 1984

Dickinson, Terence & Jack Newton, *Splendors of the Universe*, Paradise Kay Publications, Kingston, Ontario, 1997

Howard, N. E., *Standard Handbook for Telescope Making*, New York, 1984

Ridpath, Ian and Wil Tirion, *Monthly Sky Guide*, Cambridge University Press, Cambridge, 1996

Scagell, Robin, *Astronomy from Towns and Suburbs*, George Phillip, London, 1994

Scott-Houston, Walter and James O'Meara, *Deep Sky Wonders*, Sky Publishing Corporation, 1999

Sidgwick, John Benson, *The Amateur Astronomer's Handbook*, Dover Publications, New York, 1980

Stephenson, Bruce, et al, *The Universe Unveiled: Instruments and Images Through History*, Cambridge University Press, Cambridge, 2000

EXPLORATION OF STARS AND PLANETS

Aldrin, B. and M. McConnell, *Men From Earth*, Bantam, London, 1989

Allday, Jonathan, *Apollo in Perspective*, Institute of Physics Publishing, London, 1999

Baker, D., *Spaceflight and Rocketry, A Chronology*, Facts on File Inc, 1996

Bennett, Mary D. and David S. Percy, *Dark Moon*, Aulis Publishers, 1998

Cernan, E. and D. Davis, *The Last Man on the Moon: Astronaut Eugene Cernan and America's Race in Space*, St Martins Press, London, 1999

Freeman, Marsha (ed.), *Challenges of Human Space Exploration*, Springer-Verlag, New York, 2000

Gatland, K., *Space Technology, a Comprehensive History of Space Exploration*, Salamander, London, 1980

Godwin, Robert (ed.), *Apollo 13*, Apogee Books, 2000

Harland, David M., *Jupiter Odyssey, the Story of NASA's Galileo Mission*, Springer-Verlag, New York, 2000

Hurt, H., *For All Mankind*, Atlantic Monthly Press, 1988

Moore, Patrick, *The Guinness Book of Astronomy*, Fifth Edition, Guinness, London, 1995

Moore, Patrick, *Mission to the Planets: The Illustrated Story of the Exploration of the Solar System*, Cassell, New York and London, 1995

Newton, David E., *U.S. and Soviet Space Programs: A Comparison*, Franklin Watts, New York, 1988

Slayton, D. and M. Cassutt, *Deke! US Manned Space: From Mercury to the Shuttle*, Forge, 1994

Trux, John, *The Space Race*, New English Library, London, 1985

Wilhelms, D., *To A Rocky Moon, A Geologist's History of Lunar Exploration*, Arizona

Wunsch, Ssi Trautmann, *The Adventure of Sojourner: The Mission to Mars that Thrilled the World*, Mikaya Press, 1998

Zubrin, Robert and Richard Wagner, *The Case for Mars: The Plan to Settle the Red Planet and Why We Must*, Touchstone Books, 1997

SYMBOLS

c	Standard symbol for the speed of light
erg	Symbol used to denote units of energy
G	Standard symbol for the gravitational constant
H_0	Symbol for the constant in the Hubble expansion law
h	Standard symbol for the Planck constant
J	joule, unit of energy
K	kelvin, the unit of temperature in the absolute scale
log	Logarithm; a quantity representing the power to which a fixed number must be raised to produce a given number
m	Standard symbol for mass
N	newton, unit of force
nm	nanometer 10^{-9} m
N s	Newton second; used to indicate momentum
M_v	Standard symbol for absolute magnitude
m_v	Standard symbol for apparent visual magnitude
v	Standard symbol for velocity
z	Symbol commonly used to designate the Doppler shift ($z = \Delta\lambda/\lambda = v/c$ for velocities much less than the speed of light)

$'$	Symbol for arcminutes
$''$	Symbol for arcseconds
$\oplus$	Earth units; used to express bulk properties of planets or stars, e.g. $M_\oplus$ expresses Earth masses
$\odot$	Solar units; used to express bulk properties of planets or stars, e.g. $R_\odot$ expresses solar radii
α	The Greek letter alpha; sometimes used to designate an alpha particle
$\Delta\lambda$	The Greek letters delta lambda; used to designate a shift in wavelength, as in the Doppler effect
γ	The Greek letter gamma, sometimes used to designate a photon
λ	The Greek letter lambda, usually used to designate wavelength
ν	The Greek letter nu, the standard symbol for frequency; also used to designate a neutrino in nuclear reactions
π	The Greek letter pi, usually used to designate the parallax angle; also used for the ratio of the circumference of a circle to its diameter
σ	The Greek letter sigma, usually used to designate the Stefan-Boltzmann constant

The Greek Alphabet

Many bright stars are identified by a Greek letter along with the constellation that contains them. Generally they appear in decreasing order of brightness, with alpha (α) being the brightest.

α	Alpha
β	Beta
γ	Gamma
δ	Delta
ε	Epsilon
ζ	Zeta
η	Eta
θ	Theta
ι	Iota
κ	Kappa
λ	Lambda
μ	Mu
ν	Nu
ξ	Xi
o	Omicron
π	Pi
ρ	Rho
σ	Sigma
τ	Tau
υ	Upsilon
φ	Phi
χ	Chi
ψ	Psi
w	Omega

AUTHOR BIOGRAPHIES

Iain Nicolson *General Editor*

Iain Nicolson is a writer and lecturer in astronomy and space sciences, a Visiting Fellow of the University of Hertfordshire, and a Contributing Consultant to the magazine *Astronomy Now*. He lectures widely to societies and organisations and is a frequent contributor to the long-running BBC series, *The Sky at Night*.

Author of 20 books, he has contributed chapters and entries to a wide variety of texts and encyclopedias and has written hundreds of articles for magazines and journals. His most recent books include *Unfolding Our Universe* (Cambridge University Press, 2000) and *Stars and Supernovas* (BBC Books, 2001).

Until 1995, he was Principal Lecturer and Unit Leader in Astronomy at the University of Hertfordshire where he was responsible for undergraduate degree programmes in astronomy and astrophysics. A Fellow of the Royal Astronomical Society and a Member of the International Astronomical Union, he has also served as President of the Society for Popular Astronomy. In 1995 he received the Eric Zucker Award from the Federation of Astronomical Societies for his work in bringing Astronomy to the public.

Chris Cooper *The History of Astronomy, The Solar System*

Chris Cooper holds a degree in physics and has worked as a writer and editor in scientific publishing for 30 years. He has written many books on scientific subjects for young readers. He lives in Bedfordshire with his wife and two teenage children.

Pam Spence *Stars, Galaxies and The Universe*

Pam Spence has been interested in astronomy ever since she was small. She followed a degree in mathematics with an MSc in astronomy at the University of Sussex and worked on a research fellowship in solar physics at the Mullard Space Science Laboratory (UCL). She is a past President of the Federation of Astronomical Societies, has taught astronomy for the Open University and spent eight years editing a monthly national astronomy magazine. She is currently the Managing Editor of the *Encyclopedia of Astronomy and Astrophysics,* a post she combines with other astronomical commitments such as teaching a part-time course in astronomy at the University of Sussex. She has written three books and contributed to many more.

Carole Stott *Exploration of Stars and Planets*

Carole Stott is a full-time writer on astronomy and space, and was formerly a professional astronomer. She has authored more than 20 books for adults and children, including *New Astronomer, Space Exploration,* and *Fly the Space Shuttle*. She is a regular contributor to encyclopedias and science publications, and is a feature writer for the UK's best-selling magazine *Astronomy Now*. Before turning to full-time writing Carole was curator and then head of observatory at the Royal Observatory, Greenwich.

PICTURE CREDITS

AKG London: 64 (t), 149 (l), 172 (b)

Christies Images: 2001:19, 108 (t), 139, 145 (l)

Foundry Arts: 3, 5, 6, 7, 9, 11, 13 (b), 14, 16, 20, 22, 24 (b), 26 (l), 27, 33 (b), 34 (r), 36, 37 (t), 42, 43 (r), 43 (l), 48 (l), 53, 54 (t), 62, 63, 67 (l), 69 (b), 70, 71 (r), 72, 83 (t), 84 (t,b), 88 (b), 89, 90, 92 (t, b), 93, 100 (t), 101, 104 (t, b), 105 (t, b), 106 (t, b), 110, 111 (t), 112, 113, 114 (r), 115, 120 (b), 121, 123 (b), 124, 125, 127, 130 (t, b), 133, 134 (l), 135, 136, 137 (b), 141, 152, 153, 156 (l), 157, 159 (t, b), 160, 168 (t), 169, 170 (b), 172 (t), 176 (t), 177, 180, 182 (l, r), 184 (b), 185, 188 (r), 189 (b), 191 (t), 193 (b), 194, 195, 197, 198 (l, r)

Galaxy Pictures/Robin Scagell: 39 (l, r), 41 (b), 49, 52 (b), 60, 67 (r), 97 (b), 120 (t), 129 (t), 132, 142 (b), 167, 170 (t), 174, 175, 179 (l), 180 (r), 193 (t), Chris Livingstone 91 (l), Don Davis/NASA 51, Nigel Evans 114 (l), 122, Calvin J. Hamilton 48 (t), 111 (b), Eric Hutton 56, Philip Perkins 162 (b), Martin Ratcliffe 78 (r), 145 (r), ESA 87, Lowell Observatory 98 (b), NASA 44 (t), 86 (r), Dr Francisco Diego 40, Gordon Garradd 74 (t), 96, 162 (t), Michael Stecker 99 (t), 119, 126 (r), 137 (t), 150 (t), 168 (b), 191 (b), Howard Brown-Greaves 117, STSCI 75, John Dubinski, University of Toronto and San Diego Supercomputing Center 12 (t), Axel Mellinger 116, Pedro Re 155 (t)

Genesis Space Photo Library/Tim Furness: 35 (t), 44 (l), 61 (r), 71 (t), 102 (b), 103, 107, 118, 155 (b), 164, 196 (t), 196 (b)

Mary Evans Picture Library: 21 (t), 25, 37 (r), 41 (t), 50, 69 (t), 76, 77 (b), 80, 82, 91 (r), 94 (l), 108 (b), 134 (b), 149 (r)

Novosti Picture Library: 100 (b), 151 (l)

Science & Society Picture Library: 24 (t), 94 (r), 126 (l), 186 (t), NASA 192

Science Photo Library: 85, 166 (t)

Topham Picturepoint: 10, 12 (b), 15 (l), 21 (b), 28, 34 (l), 45, 47, 58, 65, 74 (b), 78 (l), 79, 81 (l), 86 (t), 98 (l), 109, 123 (t), 147, 151 (r), 173, 179 (r), 186 (b), 188 (l), 190 (t)

For further, comprehensive information on Stars, Planets and the physics of the universe please refer to the Collins Encyclopedia of the Universe, from which some of the material in this book has been derived.

INDEX